Reaching Forward

Also by Gary Henry

Diligently Seeking God

Reaching Forward

Daily Motivation to Move Ahead
More Steadily

Gary Henry

WordPoints
Nashville
www.wordpoints.com

Reaching Forward
Daily Motivation to Move Ahead More Steadily

www.wordpoints.com

First Edition. Copyright © 2009 by Gary Henry
All rights reserved. Printed in the United States of America
Library of Congress Control Number: 2008936374

ISBN-13: 978-0-9713710-1-9 – Print Edition
Revision 1.0.2

Cover design by Angela Underwood

WordPoints
106 Canton Court
Goodlettsville, TN 37072-2163

615-944-0694

Web: *www.wordpoints.com*
E-mail: *garyhenry@wordpoints.com*

Publisher's Cataloging-in-Publication Data
(Provided by Quality Books, Inc.)

Henry, Gary, 1950-
    Reaching forward : daily motivation to move ahead
more steadily / Gary Henry. -- 1st ed.
    p. cm.
    Includes index.
    LCCN 2008936374
    ISBN-13: 978-0-9713710-1-9
    ISBN-10: 0-9713710-1-6

    1. Spiritual life--Christianity--Prayers and
devotions. 2. Devotional calendars. 3. Meditations.
I. Title.

BV4811.H389 2009   242'.2
                              QBI08-200018

For Kyle & Katie Fisher

CONTENTS

JANUARY

FEBRUARY

MARCH

APRIL

MAY

JUNE

JULY

AUGUST

SEPTEMBER

OCTOBER

NOVEMBER

DECEMBER

PREFACE

THIS BOOK IS LONG OVERDUE, AND I APOLOGIZE FOR THAT. When *Diligently Seeking God* appeared, I thought it might take me two years or so to write the next book. But little did I know how *Diligently Seeking God* would change my life. Able to write only intermittently, it has taken me six years to put *Reaching Forward* in your hands, but here it is, finally. Thanks for not giving up on me.

There is a close connection between *Diligently Seeking God* and *Reaching Forward*. In the first book, we talked about deeply desiring a right relationship with God. In this book, we will talk about having a right attitude toward the future. Ideally, each of these leads to the other. If we're seeking God, we'll surely be interested in the future — and if we're interested in the future, we ought to seek God, because He is the only "future" worth reaching for.

As I said in the Preface to *Diligently Seeking God,* these kinds of things do not *by themselves* mean that we are in a right relationship with God and that we would go to heaven if we died right now. The gospel must be not only believed but *obeyed* before our sins are forgiven, and it takes more than merely "seeking" and "reaching" to do that. As I write, however, I never know who my readers are going to be, and that presents a problem. I want to give hope, but I never want to give *false* hope, especially to those who may think they've obeyed the gospel when in reality they haven't. So not knowing your circumstances, I believe I need to say: "Examine yourselves as to whether you are in the faith" (2 Corinthians 13:5).

I also need to clarify what I mean by the "future." When I talk about reaching forward, it is *heaven* that I am talking about. When we strive for earthly goals, those must always be tentative. In this book, however, we are talking about the only definite, untentative goal that we may have. All others must be held loosely, but heaven is the one goal we may hold with *a passionate grip that never lets go.*

But where do we go from here? Well, I plan to take a year off from writing and then begin a new book called *Obeying the Gospel*. This will be the greatest writing challenge I have ever set for myself, and I am quite eager to begin it. Already, I am reading and praying about this work, and I would appreciate your prayers too.

What I want to do in *Obeying the Gospel* is write 366 daily meditations on the steps that one takes to become a Christian. Some might think there is nothing left to say on this subject that has not been worn out. But there is, in fact, a good deal more to say. On the subject of baptism, for example, a person could spend a lifetime digging deeper into what the Scriptures teach on that topic.

So *Obeying the Gospel* will try to mine some of the treasures in God's word concerning our initial obedience to Christ. And in case you're wondering, it won't be just for those who have *not* obeyed the gospel. It will also be for those who *have* done so. I need to think more deeply about what I did when I became a Christian, and I hope that you'll enjoy thinking about those things with me.

But for now, I hope you'll think with me in this book about *Reaching Forward* — longing for the life that we can have in God when our work in this world is finished. These days, eternity is my passion, so much so that I have been accused of having a death wish. Maybe I do, but if I do, so did Paul. He was willing, as I am, to stay and work, but he left no doubt as to his longing when he said that to depart and be with Christ is *"far better"* (Philippians 1:23).

Within our generation, the other-worldly orientation of historic Christianity has shifted to a this-worldly emphasis, even in very conservative churches. Religion is no longer about heaven but about happiness right now. Yet Christianity was never meant to remove the groaning from life; it was meant to put it there! "For we know that if our earthly house, this tent, is destroyed, we have a building from God, a house not made with hands, eternal in the heavens. *For in this we groan, earnestly desiring to be clothed with our habitation which is from heaven"* (2 Corinthians 5:1,2).

Will you think about that with me?

If you will, let's get started.

G. P. H.

Reaching Forward

O Thou Beloved:
Love Eternal, my whole good,
happiness which has no bounds,
I desire to appropriate you
with the most vehement desire
and the most worthy reverence.
I desire to reserve nothing unto myself.

O Everlasting Light,
surpassing all created luminaries,
flash forth thy lightning from above,
piercing all the most inward parts of my heart.

Make clean, make glad,
make bright, and make alive my spirit,
with all the powers thereof,
that I may cleave to you in ecstasies of joy.

— Thomas à Kempis

January 1
ALPHA AND OMEGA

I am the Alpha and the Omega, the Beginning and the End.
I will give of the fountain of the water of life freely to him who thirsts.
He who overcomes shall inherit all things, and I will be his God
and he shall be My son. *Revelation 21:6,7*

GOD EXISTED BEFORE ALL THINGS, AND HE WILL EXIST AFTER ALL THINGS HAVE REACHED THEIR DESTINY. He is the Alpha and the Omega, the Beginning and the End. And since it is God who sent us out on our journey, it is God to whom we long to return. This longing is a part of our created nature. We may not choose to reach toward Him as we ought, but inwardly we have a persistent yearning to do so. We can no more change the fact that He is our Source than we can change the fact of our physical parentage. And what He is always asking us to do in this world is dispense with our denial and deal honestly with our heart's desire for Him.

First of all, God is the *reason* why we reach forward. We long for Him because He made us and put within our hearts a need for Him; we reach forward because He gave us a nature that tends in that direction. But second, God is also our *motive* for reaching forward. The mighty force that moves us is nothing less than this: it is *for His sake* that we want to be better than we are. Deep within our hearts, we want to love God *as He has loved us.* The third and most important point, however, is that God is the *goal* for which we reach. He alone is the answer to our questions, the fulfillment of our needs. And the sooner we're able to view God Himself as our goal, the better we'll be able to move forward with our lives.

To live in the world as it now is, is to be "away" from God. This is still His world, of course, and He is still very much present within it. But our sins have come between us and God. Like Adam and Eve, whose rebellion meant that they had to leave the Garden, all of us since then have had to live "east of Eden." What we are is not what we were meant to be. Yet while this truth is sobering, it need not be our final truth. A way has been made possible for us to overcome what we are. Tomorrow can be better than today, and there is a heaven beyond the best of all our tomorrows. But let us not be deceived or distracted: it is *God* who is both our Alpha and our Omega. Heaven is worth reaching for *only because He is there!*

From thee, great God, we spring, to thee we tend,
Path, motive, guide, original, and end.
SAMUEL JOHNSON

January 2
WHAT THE HIGHEST HOPE WILL DO

And everyone who has this hope in Him
purifies himself, just as He is pure. *1 John 3:3*

I T IS OUR HOPES THAT PRODUCE PROGRESS IN OUR LIVES. Both in our outward conduct and our inward character, we are moved to do better than we've done in the past by the hope that better things are waiting for us up ahead. From time to time, other incentives and motivations may have an influence upon us, yet none of these move us forward with anything like the strength of *hope*.

But there are many different kinds of hope, and some of these provide more power than others. Many of our hopes fall into the category of what may be called self-interest. Self-interest is not always a bad thing. Indeed, it can be very noble, as when we desire to inherit eternal life. But as powerful as some of our self-centered hopes may be, our real progress depends on something else. When what we hope for is that *God will be honored* (even when that honor seems to conflict with our own interests), that is when the door is opened to the kind of progress we most need to make in life.

When Paul was a prisoner in Rome, he naturally hoped that his life would be spared. But that was neither his highest hope nor his main concern: "For I know that this will turn out for my deliverance through your prayer and the supply of the Spirit of Jesus Christ, according to my earnest expectation and hope that in nothing I shall be ashamed, but with all boldness, as always, so now also Christ will be magnified in my body, whether by life or by death" (Philippians 1:19,20). What Paul hoped was that Christ would be "magnified" — whether by his life or by his death!

John wrote, "And everyone who has this hope in Him purifies himself, just as He is pure." Self-centered hopes are simply not powerful enough to "purify" us. In the long run, they will not keep us moving in God's direction and transform us into the glorious beings that we desire to become. If our progress is to reach its eternal perfection, our hopes must be centered on God's glory, not on our own preferences. Nothing else will do for us what has to be done. The hope that we may be a part of God's honor is the highest hope available to us. And if we wish to go anyplace other than where we've already been, we must lift our sights to this horizon.

All meaningful change starts with right aspiration.
KEITH YAMASHITA

January 3
ELEVATING OUR AIM, ENLARGING OUR DESIRES

But now they desire a better, that is, a heavenly country.
Therefore God is not ashamed to be called their God,
for He has prepared a city for them. Hebrews 11:16

SPIRITUALLY SPEAKING, ONE OF OUR MOST DANGEROUS TENDEN-CIES IS TO SETTLE FOR TOO LITTLE. When we've been disappointed by what life has shown us, we're tempted to lower our expectations. Yet a greater wisdom would often point us in the opposite direction. Our problem is not that we've desired too much, but that we've settled for too little. At least where God is concerned (and, in a certain sense, even where this world is concerned), we need to elevate our aim and enlarge our desires.

The problem of sin, in fact, comes down to the problem of abandoning the great desires that are our birthright from God. With regard to these desires, we have a spiritual adversary who whispers that he knows of "better" ways they can be satisfied, and we foolishly barter with him. But eventually we find that we've been cheated. What were promised to be superior satisfactions turn out to be pitifully inadequate pleasures. And in our flat, unfulfilled misery, we begin to complain about our desires, as if there was something unfair about our having been given them.

There are two tragedies here. One is that we allow ourselves to be defrauded of the life-giving joy that our Creator has in store for us. But the second is even more sorrowful: we give up longing for the joy of God and settle for a life of dreary disillusionment. Having robbed us of our heart's desire, our enemy "consoles" us with the lie that our hopes were too high to start with. "Nobody ever gets to have what he wants," he says. "You may as well get used to it." And somewhere in the nether regions there is a chorus of harsh, croaking laughter over the claiming of another victim.

Yet if the Scriptures teach anything, they teach that God is the God of joy (Nehemiah 8:10). What once could have been ours is not fully available in *this* world, broken as it is by our folly. But rather than sell out, we should seek the higher things *with renewed love*. And that is just what we'll do if, like our spiritual ancestors, we long in our hearts for "a better, that is, a heavenly country."

I pray for your desires that they may be great,
rather than for your satisfactions, which may be so hazardously little.
You are going forward toward something great.

CARL SANDBURG

THE NEXT STEP IS ALWAYS OUR MOST IMPORTANT

For I am the least of the apostles, who am not worthy to be called an apostle, because I persecuted the church of God. But by the grace of God I am what I am, and His grace toward me was not in vain. 1 Corinthians 15:9,10

LIKE PAUL, WE NEED TO FOCUS PRIMARILY ON OUR IMPROVEMENT RATHER THAN ON OUR DISAPPOINTMENTS. What has happened in the past is important, of course, but it is not nearly as important as what happens next. We may have taken many wrong steps, but none of these matter as much as the next step that we take.

When we've dug ourselves into a hole, it does not make good sense to continue digging the hole deeper. Yet that is what we often do. Disappointed and discouraged, we let ourselves be held captive by the thought that we can't change the past, and we continue to make the same mistakes (and maybe even worse ones). But it should help us to remember that *the next step is our most important.* Depending on what we do next, we will either help our situation or make it worse; we will either cut our losses or continue to increase them. And not only that, we'll make it either easier or harder to take the right steps later on. We're building today a momentum that'll either help us or hinder us tomorrow.

Despair is a vicious enemy, and we need to take the initiative against it. We can't afford to sit back and simply wish that we hadn't marred our past as we have. If our future is to be anything we can feel good about, we must get up and get busy. There is important work yet to be done, and the courage to take the next step is the key to progress. There comes a time when we have to have enough "true grit" to take the battle to the enemy, indignant about what he's already done in our lives and determined that the damage is going to *stop.* Here and now, we're making a clean break!

If we intend to seek God, it's necessary that we not only *think* but also *act* in His direction. Serving God faithfully means going ahead and doing the good that's possible in the present moment. The saved will be those who have *pressed ahead* — in faith, in hope, and in love. And doesn't victory finally come down to this simple thing: being dogged enough not to let ourselves be defeated by what we've done in the past? Even if, like the apostles, we've slept while we should have been on duty, our Lord would say to us what He said to them: "Rise, let us be going" (Mark 14:42).

Never let the sense of past failure defeat your next step.
OSWALD CHAMBERS

January 5
REACHING FORWARD

... but one thing I do, forgetting those things which are behind
and reaching forward to those things which are ahead, I press toward the goal
for the prize of the upward call of God in Christ Jesus. *Philippians 3:13,14*

MAKING A MORE COURAGEOUS CONNECTION BETWEEN TODAY AND TOMORROW IS NEITHER IMPOSSIBLE NOR IMPRACTICAL. Rather than stumble aimlessly toward the future in defeat, we can concentrate our minds on what God has made possible for us in His Son. And with our minds firmly fixed on God, we can reach forward with purpose and passion. Hope and courage and self-discipline can be the qualities that define us in the here and now.

Forgetting those things which are behind. There is a sense in which we need to "forget" the past. This does not mean that our memories are erased; it simply means that we *let go* of what has already happened. Many good things we may remember with gladness and many bad things we may remember with wisdom, but these memories must not confine us or keep us from our work.

Reaching forward to those things which are ahead. The things which are "ahead," of course, are spiritual things, things that have to do with God and with eternity. If these are to be ours, we must "reach forward." Exerting ourselves with regard to eternity must be our decision and our commitment. We will not *move* forward (at least in any significant sense) if we do not *reach* forward.

The apostle Paul was not a dabbler. God was more than merely one of his "interests." This *"one thing I do,"* he wrote. *"I press toward the goal for the prize of the upward call of God in Christ Jesus."* Here is the single-minded determination that separates the real seeker from the casual browser. Here is the consuming hunger and thirst that will find God or die. And here also is the courageous choice to look primarily toward the future rather than the past. What's in store for those who're willing to love God faithfully is beyond our ability to imagine just now. But since the beginning, everything that God has made known of Himself has made one thing increasingly clear: He is *worth* reaching for. In truth, He is the very best thing about tomorrow.

Make Him the Source, the Center, and the One who encompasses every
delight of your soul. Refuse to be satisfied any longer with your meager
accomplishments. Aspire to a higher, a nobler, and a fuller life.
Upward to heaven! Nearer to God!

CHARLES HADDON SPURGEON

DIFFERENT . . . AND BETTER

*Beloved, now we are children of God; and it has not yet
been revealed what we shall be, but we know that when He is revealed,
we shall be like Him, for we shall see Him as He is.* 1 John 3:2

To BE IN CHRIST IS TO BE MOVING TOWARD AN EXPERIENCE THAT MUST SURELY QUALIFY AS THE ULTIMATE EYE-OPENER. If we depart from this life in fellowship with Him, we will not have found ourselves on the other side for one instant before we realize two breathtaking things: (1) It is very *different* than we thought it would be, and (2) it is much *better* than we thought it would be.

In our present condition, we are not able to understand much more than the edges of God's reality. The limitations of our creaturely minds, compounded by the problems resulting from our sin, mean that our vessels are too small to hold more than a little understanding of God and His heavenly abode. God has revealed Himself to us wonderfully, of course, and what He has revealed is objectively true. Our limitation is not in the truth or accuracy of what we can know, but rather in the *extent* of that knowledge. And concerning heaven, God has said only that it will be "like" some of the more valuable things that we're acquainted with in this world.

As we reach forward to eternity, we should hold in our minds the most vivid concepts of God and heaven that the Scriptures will allow us to entertain. But as we hold these concepts in our minds, we need to hold them gently, or even tentatively. The truth is, great surprises are in store for God's faithful people, and even the most perceptive and wise should expect to have their imaginings *corrected* and *improved* by a greater reality when that time comes.

The God who created us for His glory is a God of such great goodness that no earthly visualization can take it in. But eventually, if we've yielded to His process of redemption, our eyes will be opened to the full extent of the majesty that we've wondered about for so long: ". . . it has not yet been revealed what we shall be, but we know that when He is revealed, we shall be like Him, for we shall see Him as He is." So while we are eager in our anticipation of heaven, let us also be humble, reverent, and open. Much about God remains to be seen. Little more than this do we really know: *heaven will be better than even our best guesses right now.*

Earth breaks up, time drops away,
In flows heaven, with its new day.

ROBERT BROWNING

January 7

IS IT GOD WE DESIRE,
OR A PARTICULAR PATH TO HIM?

Uphold my steps in Your paths,
That my footsteps may not slip.
Psalm 17:5

IF WE SEEK GOD SINCERELY, WE'LL BE WILLING TO GET TO HEAVEN BY ANY PATH THAT HE DEEMS BEST FOR US. But this willingness is not always easy. When the way home begins to look uncomfortably different from the path that we've pictured in our minds, the result may be resentment, if not outright rebellion. At times like these, we must learn to love God for His own sake and not insist on any particular set of conditions as we journey toward Him.

The Psalmist prayed, "Direct my steps by Your word, and let no iniquity have dominion over me" (Psalm 119:133). Such a prayer must be our own. And in our higher moments, we know that this is indeed what we desire: we want God to uphold our steps in *His* paths. We want His wisdom to supersede our own plans and preferences so that the greatest possible good is accomplished, not only for ourselves but for the world in which we live.

Certainly we must avoid any sort of *demanding* attitude toward God. If we have envisioned ourselves living and serving God within a particular set of circumstances, that may be well and good. But if life unfolds according to a different pattern, we must still maintain our reverence. Before we start acting as if our "rights" have been infringed, we need to do a reality check.

Long-term service to God requires flexibility, and most of us need to be more flexible in defining what our *possibilities* are. The good that God put us here to accomplish can be accomplished in more ways than we might think. We need to accept that there are numerous scenarios through which God could be glorified in our lives, and we must not be so wedded to one or two of these that we can't see the value in others. Is it not obvious from God's created world that He delights in variety? Let us not be so short-sighted or attached to "the way we always thought it would be" that we can't accept something else for the sake of His glory.

My goal is God himself, not joy nor peace,
Nor even blessing, but himself, my God;
'Tis his to lead me there, not mine, but his —
At any cost, dear Lord, by any road!

F. BROOK

TENACIOUS JOY

I will see you again and your heart will rejoice,
and your joy no one will take from you. *John 16:22*

JESUS SPOKE OF A JOY SO STRONG THAT THE WORLD WOULD NOT BE
ABLE TO TEAR IT FROM HIS DISCIPLES' HEARTS. Not even the worst
onslaughts of persecution could breach this bright fortress within
the souls of the faithful. To know this Friend — indeed, even to
seek Him — is to know a joy that makes even the weak strong.

And yet the joy that is available to us is not something we can
take for granted. Although it is strong, it is not impossible to lose.
Abraham Lincoln's famous saying that "Most folks are about as
happy as they make up their minds to be" is true from a spiritual,
as well as a worldly, standpoint. Discouragement is not something
that happens *to* us — it's something we *allow* to happen to us.

Whatever things may discourage us and deprive us of joy, we
need not wonder where these things come from. We have a spiritual adversary, Satan, who seeks our downfall, and to that end he
labors with malice and energy. His purpose is to undermine our
faith with doubt, replace our courage with confusion, and drag us
downward into despair. He is, to say the least, up to no good.

But we are taught to take a stubborn stand against the at-
tacks of our enemy: "Be sober, be vigilant; because your adversary
the devil walks about like a roaring lion, seeking whom he may
devour. *Resist him,* steadfast in the faith, knowing that the same
sufferings are experienced by your brotherhood in the world"
(1 Peter 5:8,9). We may be vulnerable, but we're not helpless. We're
free to choose the joy of truth over the sadness of deception.

The joy of seeking God is of such value that we ought to
guard it with our lives. This is something we should simply refuse
to give up. Real joy is worth more than anything we might exchange it for, it is a vital part of our defense against evil, and we
ought to hold it in our hearts with a tenacious grip. From day to
day, there is nothing the devil would despise any more than to see
us drink deep drafts of pure, joyous laughter. Those who are not
only joyful but *determined* in their joy are almost impossible for
him to defeat. Try as he may, there is little he can do with those
who've made up their minds to rejoice.

Refuse to be downcast. Refuse to be checked
in your upward climb. Love and laugh.

A. J. RUSSELL

January 9
TIME WASTED?

For this reason we also thank God without ceasing, because when
you received the word of God which you heard from us, you welcomed it
not as the word of men, but as it is in truth, the word of God, which also
effectively works in you who believe. *1 Thessalonians 2:13*

SOMETIMES WE RESIST CHANGES THAT WOULD BE BENEFICIAL.
Because changes often require an admission of past failure,
they make us uncomfortable. Called upon, for example, to change
a major conviction or principle, an older person may back away:
"To change, I'd have to admit that all these years I've been wrong,
and that would mean that most of my life has been wasted!"

Sometimes, we're embarrassed that it took us so long to *see*
what we should do. "If this was the right course of action, I would
have seen it sooner" sounds like a reasonable objection, but it may
be nothing more than the product of our stubborn pride.

At other times, we're embarrassed that it took us so long to
do what we should. Often, there is no way to improve our conduct
without drawing attention to the fact that our conduct *needed* to
be improved. But again, we would do well to beware of pride. If
we let pride keep us from moving forward, then we're being held
back by one of the most unhealthy influences in the world.

In most cases, however, our problem is simply that we find
it hard to break away from the "pull" of the past. If there is some
bad decision that we've been making for a long time, that decision
is now easy to make, despite its harmful consequences. Making
any other choice would require so much commitment and energy
that it seems more pleasant just to stay where we are. The drowsy
person finds it difficult to do anything but drift off to sleep.

Yet whatever our reasons for resisting change, we should rise
above them. The Thessalonians would have had as many reasons
as anyone for remaining "consistent" with their past. They, however, were willing to change for the better, and Paul praised them
for their courage: "When you received the word of God which you
heard from us, you *welcomed* it." When we, like these people, welcome into our lives the truth and its consequences, we may be sure
that the years that have led us to that point have not been wasted.
If God has been patient with us (and He surely has), let's make up
our minds that His patience will not have been in vain.

To live is to change, and to be perfect is to have changed often.
JOHN HENRY NEWMAN

January 10
MAKING A COMMITMENT TO CLOSENESS

"... then I will cause him to draw near, and he shall
approach Me; for who is this who pledged his heart
to approach Me?" says the LORD. *Jeremiah 30:21*

I T IS STRANGE THAT RELIGION IS SO OFTEN SEEN AS SOMETHING
FOR THE WEAK AND THE TIMID. Nothing could be further from
the truth. The business of rightly relating ourselves to God's
glory is not for the fainthearted, and the enjoyment of fellowship
with Him is not something that results from a whim or a mood.
Closeness to God comes from *commitment*, and we will not draw
near to Him unless that nearness is a strong and serious goal.

Many of us would say that we love God. If we actually do,
that's a good thing. But the truth about whether or not we love
Him is revealed by the depth of our *determination to be close to Him*.
So, how easily are we distracted from thinking about Him? How
much time do we spend actually working on our relationship with
Him? What price would we pay to keep from losing Him?

Not all who start out to seek God will enjoy Him in eternity.
Alluding to Israel's failure of faith in the wilderness, the Hebrew
writer said, "There remains therefore a rest for the people of God
... Let us therefore be diligent to enter that rest, lest anyone fall
according to the same example of disobedience" (Hebrews 4:9,11).

Are we willing, then, to make closeness to God the single requirement of our daily work? Are we willing to stake it *all* on this
one possibility: that the God who made us can be approached in
love? Are we willing to dedicate every day of our mortal pilgrimage to the learning of this love? If we are, then great goodness
awaits us. Drawing near to God would be impossible if God had
not opened the door in Jesus Christ, but even so, it takes a courageous commitment to draw near. "Who is this," God once asked,
"who *pledged his heart* to approach Me?" Unrivaled in the glory
of His love, this same God is our King, and in the end, none will
come near Him who have not *devoted* themselves to doing so.

What God in his sovereignty may yet do on a world scale
I do not claim to know, but what he will do for the plain man or woman
who seeks his face I believe I do know and can tell others. Let any man turn
to God in earnest, let him begin to exercise himself unto godliness, let him
seek to develop his powers of spiritual receptivity by trust and obedience
and humility, and the results will exceed anything he may have
hoped for in his leaner and weaker days.

A. W. TOZER

January 11
A KEY THAT OPENS MANY DOORS

Happy is the man who finds wisdom, and the man who gains
understanding; for her proceeds are better than the profits of silver,
and her gain than fine gold. Proverbs 3:13,14

IF WE'RE SERIOUS ABOUT IMPROVING OUR "QUALITY OF LIFE," WE
NEED TO WORK HARDER AT IMPROVING OUR THINKING. As we
reach forward to better things, both in this life and the one to
come, we need to spend less time on our circumstances and more
time on our wisdom. Better thinking is what our progress usually
depends on. It's a valuable key that opens a great many doors.

Removing falsehoods. Often, the thing that holds us back in
life is some wrong idea that is lodged in our minds. Wise people
work every day to remove as many falsehoods as they can from
their thinking. Like a New England farmer patiently removing the
rocks from his fields, we need to be getting rid of the untruths that
hinder our productiveness and our progress toward God.

Widening our perspective. Sometimes it's not an untruth that
hinders us but simply a failure to see *enough* of the truth. Many of
the most frustrating things in life are frustrating because we're so
bogged down in them we can't see what *else* is true. We should get
in the habit of "going to the balcony" and looking down on our
difficulties from a vantage point that offers a more complete view.

To God, our ill-informed efforts at self-improvement must
appear quite silly. We continue to hammer away at problems with
thoughts and attitudes that have proven over and over again to
be the wrong tools for the job. Wouldn't it be smart to get better
tools? "The significant problems we face cannot be solved at the
same level of thinking we were at when we created them" (Albert
Einstein). Without better thinking, we'll stay stuck in our ruts.

Ultimately, of course, the path to better thinking always takes
us into the Scriptures. Nothing can remove falsehoods and widen
our perspective more helpfully than God's own mind, and we are
at our problem-solving best when we're honestly searching the
Scriptures. In the long run, neither our thinking nor our doing will
get better if the Psalmist's prayer is not our own: "Open my eyes,
that I may see wondrous things from Your law" (Psalm 119:18).

Because there is no limit to how much you can improve
the quality of your thinking, there is no real limit to how much
you can improve your life.
BRIAN TRACY

January 12
THE ROAD THAT LEADS TO LIFE IS NOT EFFORTLESS

*Enter by the narrow gate; for wide is the gate and broad is the way
that leads to destruction, and there are many who go in by it.
Because narrow is the gate and difficult is the way which leads to life,
and there are few who find it. Matthew 7:13,14*

A S WE MAKE OUR WAY TOWARD BETTER THINGS, WE SHOULD
EXPECT TO MEET DIFFICULTY. "Narrow is the gate," Jesus said,
"and difficult is the way which leads to life." If our main interest
is in ease, we won't last long on this journey. Like most other good
things, fellowship with God requires some serious investment.
There is a price to be paid. There is an effort that must be exerted.

We should not be surprised at difficulty. The apostle Peter wrote,
"Beloved, do not think it strange concerning the fiery trial which
is to try you, as though some strange thing happened to you"
(1 Peter 4:12). As long as the devil is on the loose, we need not
expect the path to God to be unobstructed. And not only that, we
need not expect our bad habits to surrender without a fight. "All
things are difficult before they are easy" (Sir Thomas Fuller).

We should not be resentful of difficulty. As Paul and Barnabas returned from their first missionary journey, they revisited the congregations that had been established, "strengthening the souls of
the disciples, exhorting them to continue in the faith, and saying,
'We must through many tribulations enter the kingdom of God'"
(Acts 14:22). Resistance is a fact of life for all who would return to
God's rule. This fact should not make us resentful or bitter. By the
time we've finished our work, if not before, we'll see that hardships were not our foes but our friends. "In the difficult are the
friendly forces, the hands that work on us" (Rainer Maria Rilke).

We should not be defeated by difficulty. We may be *discouraged*,
but we need not be *defeated*. Being strong doesn't mean we never
stumble, and as far as our emotions are concerned, we won't always feel courageous. Yet there is one thing we can always do: *we
can refuse to give up.* When we fall, we can make the choice to get
back up. Heaven is a place for those too "stubborn" to settle for
the easier path, the one that Jesus said leads to destruction.

Does the road wind uphill all the way?
Yes, to the very end.
Will the journey take the whole long day?
From morn to night, my friend.

CHRISTINA GEORGINA ROSSETTI

January 13
WHAT'S AHEAD IS WORTH REACHING FOR!

For I consider that the sufferings of this
present time are not worthy to be compared
with the glory which shall be revealed in us. *Romans 8:18*

WHEN WE'RE DISCOURAGED AND WE'RE THINKING ABOUT TAKING THE EASY WAY OUT, IT'S IMPORTANT TO REMEMBER THE VALUE OF THE THINGS WE'RE REACHING FOR. Life with God is a treasure worth any price that ever has to be paid to receive it — and more important, the privilege of *simply being a person through whom God can glorify Himself* ought to mean more to us than anything else in the here or the hereafter. Whatever we're giving up, what we're getting is what we *want* to get most of all, isn't it?

When the price seems too painful to bear and we wish we could get back what we've given up, we need to recall how we evaluated things when we originally "counted the cost." Like the Olympic athlete who remembers every day his original decision (that the rewards of discipline and training are *worth* more than those of ease and indulgence, and that he *wants* the former more than he wants the latter), we must remember that "the sufferings of this present time are not worthy to be compared with the glory which shall be revealed in us." When the life of discipleship turns out to be hard, the wise Christian will say, "*Yes, but I'd still rather have the 'minuses' I have right now than the 'minuses' that would go with any other set of 'pluses'. The tradeoff is well worth it.*"

We should not let Satan deceive us as to the true value of things. When we barter with him, he has a way of making the things outside of God's will seem more valuable than they really are, and he carefully conceals the deadly downside of disobedience. He is, after all, the ultimate "con artist." Yet we are not helpless in our struggle against him. Faith — real trust in God's goodness — is the quality that can keep us in touch with reality. No matter what life looks like in the short term, and no matter what sacrifices are asked of us, we have good reason to believe that God is telling us the truth: *what's ahead is worth reaching for!* If we forget that, we're in danger of being seriously misled.

We master fear through faith — faith in the worthwhileness of life
and the trustworthiness of God; faith in the meaning of our pain and our
striving, and confidence that God will not cast us aside but will use each
one of us as a piece of priceless mosaic in the design of his universe.

JOSHUA LOTH LIEBMAN

STUPIDITY

How long will you slumber, O sluggard?
When will you arise from your sleep?
Proverbs 6:9

O UR ENGLISH WORD "STUPID" IS A WORD WORTH DOING SOME SERIOUS THINKING ABOUT. It comes from the Latin *stupere*, which meant "to be stunned." Usually we think of "stupidity" as extreme foolishness or a lack of intelligence, but in its most literal sense, "stupid" means dazed or stunned. The stupid person is in a "stupor," and what he needs is not to increase his intelligence but to wake up and pay attention. Stupidity is simply the state of being inactive and insensible when we ought to be alert.

Spiritually speaking, we need to shake off our stupidity, don't we? Too much of the time, we are lethargic and apathetic. Although there is work to do and dangers to watch out for, we doze off into such a state of insensibility that not even God can get our serious attention. Like Peter, James, and John, who fell asleep while Jesus was enduring His agony in Gethsemane (Matthew 26:36-46), we are drowsy. Our desire, it would seem, is for God to leave us alone and let us sleep just a little while longer.

Usually, it takes some huge, life-altering crisis to bring us to our senses. But the closer we get to the end of our lives in this world, the more most of us will wish that we'd waked up sooner. We don't really have to wait for tragedy to turn us upside down. If we make the choice, we can wake up on our own — and we can do so right now. We can shake ourselves into sobriety and determine that our minds will be wide awake from now on.

One good reason to wake up is so that we can be better stewards of the gifts God has given us. Our Father has endowed us with great capabilities, and these are to be used to further His purposes. We need to be more keenly *aware* of our abilities and our opportunities so that we can *use* these more fully. When we allow the devil to discourage us, we fall into a stupid, insensible daze — a sleepiness from which nothing comes that is truly worthwhile. There is so much more to the life of godliness than we've experienced and so much more to God Himself than we've ever known. Too long have we been stupid! Too long have we slept!

Compared to what we ought to be,
we are only half awake.

WILLIAM JAMES

DO WE FEAR TO GO WHERE GOD IS NOT?

*But Abraham said, "Son, remember that in your lifetime you received
your good things, and likewise Lazarus evil things; but now he is comforted
and you are tormented. And besides all this, between us and you there is a
great gulf fixed, so that those who want to pass from here to you cannot,
nor can those from there pass to us." Luke 16:25,26*

IF WE DEPART FROM THIS LIFE ALIENATED FROM GOD, WE WILL SPEND ETERNITY IN THAT CONDITION. Once our sojourn here is finished, there will be no more opportunity for reconciliation with our Creator: we will be forever banished from His presence.

Heaven and hell, of course, are not physical "places," but even so, Abraham said that there is a "great gulf fixed" between these realms. As much as those who are away from God might like to cross over and be where He is, even for a moment or two, that will not be possible. To end up in hell is to end up in a realm where there can never be any contact with God ever again.

Does the possibility of such a destiny impact our thinking with much power? Do we fear to go where God is not? We certainly ought to. Indeed, there is *something seriously wrong with our thinking* if we don't fear it. Like the foolhardy man whose courage is nothing more than ignorance of the real danger that he's in, if we don't fear the prospect of being separated from God, it's because we don't understand what that would be like.

We may think we've tasted being "without God in the world" (Ephesians 2:12). But in this world, even those who refuse God's redemption are still surrounded by touches of His grace. For now, the lost can still enjoy beautiful sunrises, friendly people, and civilizations based on moral principles, more or less. But in hell, there will be no trace of God whatsoever. All that will be left will be the soul-racking memory of the Love that we have lost forever.

Concerning heaven, the best thing about it is that God will be there. And concerning hell, the worst thing about it is that He *won't* be there. That ought to be what we fear, far more than the fire and brimstone. The bottom line is this: a right relationship with God is what we were created for, and if we lose Him, nothing can ever take His place. Without God Himself, hell would be hell even if we could keep every lesser blessing we've ever enjoyed.

If God should give my soul all he ever made or might make,
apart from himself, and giving it, he stayed away even by as much
as a hairbreadth, my soul would not be satisfied.

MEISTER ECKHART

January 16
CHOOSING OUR BASIC OUTLOOK

Therefore gird up the loins of your mind, be sober,
and rest your hope fully upon the grace that is to be brought
to you at the revelation of Jesus Christ. *1 Peter 1:13*

PAST, PRESENT, AND FUTURE. On most days, our thoughts move from one to the other many times. Indeed, one of the marvels of the human mind is that we're able not only to enjoy the present but also to remember the past and anticipate the future.

But concerning the past and the future, there is an important choice to be made: will our *primary* outlook in life be backward or will it be forward? As great as the gift of memory can be, the past should not be the *main* focus of our minds. Since life moves only in one direction, forward, it is wise to make that the chosen direction of our character. We need to have made up our minds that *hope* will be our basic, day-in-and-day-out orientation. And we need to be aware that that choice will often be difficult to make.

Paul wrote about forgetting the things which are behind and reaching forward to the things which are ahead. Sir William Osler echoed that sentiment when he gave this advice: "Shut out all of your past except that which will help you weather your tomorrows." What we've already experienced may have been painful or pleasant, but it must not be allowed to distract us from what's ahead. "Rest your hope *fully*," Peter said, "upon the grace that is to be brought to you at the revelation of Jesus Christ."

Abraham is the great biblical example of a forward-looking person. During the long years of his pilgrimage in Canaan, there would have been many moments when his mind drifted back to his home in Ur, and these memories would not have been altogether bad. Yet he chose the future as his basic outlook, the decisive direction of his character: "he waited for the city which has foundations, whose builder and maker is God" (Hebrews 11:10).

We ought to be warned by the story of Lot's wife that there are times when it is dangerous to look back (Genesis 19:23-26). And even when our memories are wholesome and helpful, it is wise to keep ourselves from being caught in the past. If even one day remains to us in this world, that means that there's good work yet to do — and the best is yet to come!

Look up and not down; look forward and not back;
look out and not in; and lend a hand.

EDWARD EVERETT HALE

January 17
WHERE SELF-DISCIPLINE COMES FROM

Therefore we also, since we are surrounded by so great a cloud
of witnesses, let us lay aside every weight, and the sin which so easily
ensnares us, and let us run with endurance the race that is set before us,
looking unto Jesus, the author and finisher of our faith, who for the joy that
was set before Him endured the cross, despising the shame, and has sat
down at the right hand of the throne of God. *Hebrews 12:1,2*

EVERY DAY THAT WE LIVE IN THIS WORLD, WE ARE TESTED. We are
faced with choices that test our character. Deep down inside,
what kind of people are we? When the *right thing* and the *easy
thing* are not the same, we must choose between them. Do we have
the character to do what we know is best, and to do that reliably
and consistently? Are we made of strong stuff or not?

Most of us could use a little more self-discipline and a little
more will power. We need the benefit of having trained our bodies
to carry out the dictates of our conscience. Paul said, "I discipline
my body and bring it into subjection" (1 Corinthians 9:27). But
how do we do that? Where does self-discipline come from?

*Self-discipline comes from having a hope that means enough to us
that we refuse to give it up.* We find the strength to say "No" only
when we have a powerful "Yes" burning within us. Like Jesus,
who "for the joy that was set before Him endured the cross," we
must endure our own crosses. The "joy set before us" is the key.

Actually, self-discipline is a form of *courage* — and courage is
always born of *hope*. When we can see the light that comes from
the lighthouse, fear of the darkness is lessened and we find the
strength to make for the harbor. So John wrote, "Beloved, now we
are children of God; and it has not yet been revealed what we shall
be, but we know that when He is revealed, we shall be like Him,
for we shall see Him as He is. And everyone who has this hope in
Him purifies himself, just as He is pure" (1 John 3:2,3).

If we are to grow strong in our character, therefore, and if
we are to acquire godly integrity in our conduct, we must focus
more on God. His glory must mean enough to us that the desire
for Him to be glorified is a powerful force constantly calling us to
higher ground. If God is to be glorified, there are some things that
we must give up, it's true. But the question is really one of *gaining*
things — *greater things that we should refuse to give up!*

Our Lord did not ask us to give up the things of earth,
but to exchange them for better things.

FULTON J. SHEEN

January 18
WHY DON'T WE TAKE GOD MORE SERIOUSLY?

Then He said to them, "Why do you sleep?
Rise and pray, lest you enter into temptation." *Luke 22:46*

IF WE'RE NOT AS WIDE-AWAKE AND EARNEST IN OUR EFFORTS TO-WARD GOD AS WE SHOULD BE, IT'S IMPORTANT TO ASK OURSELVES WHY THIS IS SO. There are many possibilities, obviously, but the following four reasons explain why most of us are so complacent. On an ordinary day, we don't take God more seriously because:

We don't think we need to. At the doctrinal level, perhaps we believe that our salvation is assured no matter what we do. As we see the Scriptures, diligence and devotion to God are non-issues; human effort is not necessary for spiritual maturity.

We don't think we have to. We may be bound by the tradition of "nominal" Christianity. Interested only in the bare minimum required by law, we dare anyone to prove that getting to heaven requires more than going to church . . . once in a while.

We're fearful and discouraged. Dragged down by past struggles, we're doubtful that it'll do any good to try again. We've broken so many commitments to God, we're afraid to make any more. Our spiritual growth is smothered under a blanket of pessimism.

We're lazy. Like the lukewarm Laodiceans (Revelation 3:15-18), we're negligent. What began as occasional outward acts of procrastination has become a settled attribute of our inward character. We don't see our negligence as a character trait, of course, but God does. He knows the dilapidated condition of our heart.

In all honesty, this last point is the crux of the matter for most of us. There comes a time when we have to ask ourselves what kind of people we are. We may have to admit that passion for God is just not a part of our *character* as it stands today — we've let ourselves get to the point where we *don't really care* about great causes. And if so, we're unfit for the human race. Malcolm Forbes put it bluntly: "People who never get carried away should be."

God is, of course, the greatest of all great causes. And if He is to get from us the attention He deserves, we must be unflinchingly honest about where we've been, where we really are, and where we truly want to go. It will take time and patience, but we can, if we choose, *acquire the character that it takes to take God seriously.*

No one keeps up his enthusiasm automatically. Enthusiasm must be
nourished with new actions, new aspirations, new efforts, new vision.
ANONYMOUS

January 19
THE IMPORTANCE OF GOALS TO GROW TOWARD

. . . that we should no longer be children . . . but, speaking the truth in love,
may grow up in all things into Him who is the head — Christ.
Ephesians 4:14,15

THERE'S NO DOUBT THAT WE NEED TO SET OUR HOPES ON HEAVEN, BUT WE ALSO NEED TO SET GOALS FOR OUR GROWTH IN THIS LIFE. Eternity with God is a worthy objective, to be sure, but that destiny is not an arbitrary reward handed out to some few who were "lucky" enough to be selected. Rather, it is the end of a road that has to be *traveled by conscious choice.* When the time comes, heaven will be a state of spiritual maturity for those — and *only* those — who *chose to grow* in that direction *while they lived in this world.*

As far as our character is concerned, there's a considerable gap between what we are now and what we need to be. With our present attitudes and values, we wouldn't enjoy living in a realm where God is the only pleasure, even if we were allowed to give it a try. Plainly, we need to grow in the quality of spiritual-mindedness. But growth in godly character does not take place by accident. Without setting deliberate goals, we simply "drift" — occasionally stumbling forward perhaps, but more often than not falling backward into further neglect and worldliness.

For one thing, our goals for spiritual growth need to be *higher.* We should aspire to greater growth in God than we've dared to dream about before. God is greater than our "modest" personal goals sometimes make Him out to be, and we should not underestimate the quality of character that He can help us — *yes, even us!* — to partake of (2 Peter 1:2-4). But also, our goals need to be more *specific.* It doesn't do much good to simply say, "I know I need to be a better person." Instead, we need to take an honest inventory of our personal traits on a regular basis and then make definite commitments, God being our Helper, to change our character.

Most importantly, however, we need to *study the character of Jesus Christ* and let Him define our concept of spiritual maturity. What we're aiming to do is "grow up in all things into Him who is the head." Doing that will often take us (as it did Him) in a different direction than the popular picture of "spiritual maturity."

Our first step in rediscovering an authentic Christian spirituality is
to gain a clear picture of a mature Christian. If we ignore this question,
spiritual growth will become an accidental occurrence.
GARY L. THOMAS

IT'S A SERIOUS SIN TO DISCOURAGE OTHERS

Let not those who wait for You, O Lord GOD of hosts,
be ashamed because of me; let not those who seek You
be confounded because of me, O God of Israel.
Psalm 69:6

A S WE REACH FORWARD TO GOD, WE ALL KNOW HOW FRUSTRAT-ING IT IS TO BE DISCOURAGED IN OUR EFFORTS. Knowing this, we ought to shrink from doing anything that would discourage someone else as they try to make progress. In the Lord's view of things, it is no slight offense to be a "stumbling block," particularly to those who've not yet acquired much strength of their own. Jesus said, "It is impossible that no offenses should come, but woe to him through whom they do come! It would be better for him if a millstone were hung around his neck, and he were thrown into the sea, than that he should offend one of these little ones" (Luke 17:1,2). The Lord considers it a serious sin to discourage others.

In another place, Jesus upbraided some of the religious scholars of His day: "Woe to you lawyers! For you have taken away the key of knowledge. You did not enter in yourselves, and those who were entering in you hindered" (Luke 11:52). As expert students of the Scriptures, these individuals might have been expected to be the first to recognize Jesus as the Messiah. When they refused to deal honestly with the evidence and enter the kingdom, their sin was a double transgression: "You did not enter in yourselves," Jesus said, "and those who were entering in you hindered."

But we, perhaps like these people, tend not to take responsibility. We're quick to take credit for any good influence we've had, but we're not so eager to accept blame when we've had a negative impact. If our associates have made bad choices, we would argue that those choices were their own responsibility; nothing we did "made" them act as they did. And that's true, obviously. But if others end up being lost for the sinful choices they made, we also may lose our souls for having made their choices more difficult.

"No man is so insignificant as to be sure his example can do no harm," wrote Edward Hyde. It's hard enough already for those around us to keep moving ahead. If, by our example, we make it even harder for them, we should expect God's displeasure. And not only that, we should expect to find our own lives less happy.

No deed that sets an evil example can bring joy to the doer.
JUVENAL

January 21
DON'T DESPISE THE DAILY GRIND!

And let us not grow weary while doing good,
for in due season we shall reap if we do not lose heart.
Galatians 6:9

OCCASIONALLY A DAY COMES ALONG WHEN A BIG EVENT INTRO-
DUCES SIGNIFICANT, AND OBVIOUS, CHANGE INTO OUR LIVES. If
the change is for the better, we go to bed and give thanks for the
growth we've experienced that day. Yet all of us know that life is
not made up of days like this. On most days, nothing very unusual
happens; we simply move through the ordinary routine of our
all-too-familiar schedule. And after weeks of nothing but the daily
grind, we tend to grow impatient, feeling that nothing is "happening" in our lives. But what should be our attitude toward the
ordinary? Do we simply have to endure the commonplace, hoping
that sooner or later another "big" day will come along?

Here's the answer: *we shouldn't despise the daily grind.* That is
where the real growth takes place. Our progress on average days
may not be as obvious as the progress we make on extraordinary
occasions, but the growth is real, and in a sense, it's more important. Healthy spiritual growth doesn't come in spurts; it comes
through "patient continuance in doing good" (Romans 2:7).

When we read the exciting account of the early days of the
church in Jerusalem, we're intrigued by the stories of martyrdom
and the proclamation of the gospel before kings and other great
audiences. But although these brethren did accomplish thrilling
things on certain days, no finer thing is said about them in the
Book of Acts than this simple statement: "And they continued
steadfastly in the apostles' doctrine and fellowship, in the breaking of bread, and in prayers" (Acts 2:42). *They continued steadfastly!*

We need to pay more attention to the simple doing of our ordinary "duty." Most people, even those of little character, can rise
to the occasion when they're in the spotlight. But the question is,
what will we do with *today* . . . when nothing will happen, when
no one will be looking, and when there'll be no particular reason
to do our best except a desire to keep on serving our King? It's
days like today that are the true test of our love for Him. If we're
not faithful in what is "least," what is "much" will not save us.

It is the daily strivings that count,
not the momentary heights.
A. J. RUSSELL

THE WAY WE ARE

... for you are still carnal. For where there are envy, strife, and divisions among you, are you not carnal and behaving like mere men?
1 Corinthians 3:3

WHEN, AS THOSE WHO PROFESS CHRIST, WE CONTINUE TO BEHAVE IN SPIRITUALLY IMMATURE WAYS, WE SHOULD NOT MAKE MATTERS WORSE BY MAKING EXCUSES. It does no good to minimize the seriousness of sinful decisions that we have made. I might like for my misdeeds to be seen as nothing more than personal quirks or foibles, but unworthy character and unacceptable conduct can't be excused by saying, "Well, that's just the way I am."

It may be true that some of my personal characteristics nudge me in the direction of sinful conduct. I may, for example, be more prone to anger than my next-door neighbor. But the most important issue is not my nature — it's my character. *Nature* is the package of tendencies that we were born with, but *character* is what we've done *with* that package, and that's what we'll be held accountable for at the judgment (2 Corinthians 5:10).

Most of us should go ahead and admit that we wouldn't be "the way we are" if we'd been working to improve our character as diligently as we should have been. Paul was not complimenting the Corinthians when he said, "You are still carnal." And in a similar vein, the writer of Hebrews said to his readers, "For though by this time you ought to be teachers, you need someone to teach you again the first principles of the oracles of God; and you have come to need milk and not solid food" (Hebrews 5:12).

In whatever spiritual condition we find ourselves, God surely understands. He understands, but He also expects better things of us. He knows how hard it is to go against our personal tendencies, and He's eager to help. But He requires that we make an honest effort. As our Great Physician, He will take a more active approach than simply to give sympathy and say, "Well, I guess that's just the way you are." He gave His *life* to get us *over* the way we are.

Our spiritual enemy is an awesome foe, but we can do more than roll over and play the victim. "Resist the devil," James wrote, "and he will flee from you" (James 4:7). *Forward* is the direction we need to move, but we won't *move* forward if we don't *reach* forward. Let's do it without delay. No more excuses.

"That's just the way I am" is a confession of sloth, not humility.
GARY L. THOMAS

IF WE DON'T FORGIVE, WE'RE PARALYZED

And Joseph said to his brothers, "Please come near to me." So they came near. Then he said: "I am Joseph your brother, whom you sold into Egypt. But now, do not therefore be grieved or angry with yourselves because you sold me here; for God sent me before you to preserve life." *Genesis 45:4,5*

AS IMPORTANT AS IT IS TO MAKE FORWARD PROGRESS, WE OFTEN PUT OURSELVES IN A POSITION WHERE IT'S IMPOSSIBLE TO DO SO. We paralyze ourselves by failing to forgive. Having done little to rid our hearts of resentment, we find that our minds do little but replay the past. Energy that should be spent building a better future is wasted debating our case and demanding apologies.

But consider Joseph. His brothers had sold him into slavery, an act that was not only unjust but treacherously so. He might have spent the rest of his life looking for a chance to settle the score for this grievance, but instead he was eager to extend forgiveness as soon as possible. What can we learn from him?

To forgive others, we don't have to wait until they seek our forgiveness. When Joseph forgave his brothers, they had done little to show that their sorrow was of a godly sort, and they certainly had not asked for his forgiveness. Yet Joseph saw the wisdom of extending his forgiveness unilaterally and unconditionally.

To forgive others, we don't have to wait until they have received God's forgiveness. Our forgiveness and God's forgiveness are two different things. To open the path to progress in our own lives, we may need to go ahead and forgive someone as Joseph did. God's forgiveness, however, has some conditions attached to it, and two of these are godly sorrow and repentance (2 Corinthians 7:8-10). It may be a long time after we have forgiven someone before they seek God's forgiveness and receive it on His terms. During this time, we can release the part of the debt that is owed to us. We can simply turn the matter over to God, to be dealt with in His time (1 Peter 4:19). He can be counted on to do what is perfectly right.

Granted, there are times when it's wise to await the other person's repentance before God (Matthew 18:15-17; Luke 15:11-32), but even in these instances we can still let go of ill will and focus on reaching forward. When it comes to crooked things, it's a lot easier to straighten out those in the future than those in the past.

It is the act of forgiveness that opens up the only possible way
to think creatively about the future at all.

DESMOND WILSON

January 24
THE DANGER OF LOOKING BACK

> But Jesus said to him, "No one, having put his hand to the plow,
> and looking back, is fit for the kingdom of God." *Luke 9:62*

IT IS BY THE GRACE OF GOD THAT WE HAVE COME AS FAR AS WE HAVE IN THE JOURNEY OF LIFE. We are not apostles and we may not have been guilty of murdering Christians as Paul was, but we can still identify with his sentiment: "I am the least of the apostles, who am not worthy to be called an apostle, because I persecuted the church of God. But by the grace of God I am what I am . . ." (1 Corinthians 15:9,10). Thanks to God's patience with us, we've been given the time we needed to learn and to grow and to improve. Some things, we're now glad to say, are in the past.

We need to exercise a degree of caution in the way we think about our past. We wouldn't have done the things we used to do if they hadn't been attractive to us, and we need not think that they couldn't become attractive *again* if we gave them the opportunity. We may have grown stronger, but we're not yet invincible.

It would be impossible to forget completely the sins of our past. In fact, it wouldn't be good to forget them; we need the memory of those things to keep us humble. But if we can't keep certain memories from coming back occasionally, we can at least refuse to "entertain" them hospitably. We may have to look back for practical reasons now and then, but we dare not look back *longingly*.

When we break with our sins, God commands us to do so cleanly and decisively. It's a strong thing that Jesus says when He teaches that if we "look back" after putting our hands to the plow, we are "not fit for the kingdom of God." We do not properly honor Him as our Lord if our choice to follow Him is not wholehearted. The commitment to say "Yes" to Him must be accompanied by an emphatic "No" to the sins that have previously separated us from Him. That definite "No" is a necessary part of *repentance*.

It's a dangerous thing to replay the still-enjoyable aspects of the memory of sin. Like Lot and his family who were told to leave Sodom and not look back, we need, in the case of some things, *to leave them alone for the rest of our lives*. We can't afford to have any fine print in our contract with God. By His grace, we've been able to close certain doors. Reopening them is . . . well, *unthinkable*.

To forsake sin is to leave it without
any thought of returning to it.
WILLIAM GURNALL

CHANGE: OUR UNWELCOME BENEFACTOR

*Most assuredly, I say to you, unless a grain of wheat falls into the ground
and dies, it remains alone; but if it dies, it produces much grain.
He who loves his life will lose it, and he who hates his life in this world
will keep it for eternal life. John 12:24,25*

A N HONEST LOOK AT OUR LIVES WOULD INDICATE THAT WE HAVE
BENEFITED FROM CHANGE. Many, perhaps most, of the best
things in our individual characters are creative adaptations to
changes we were forced to accept earlier in our lives. The loss of a
job and the resultant move to another city, for example, required
adjustments in our attitude that we would not have made otherwise. And ever since, we've benefited from that attitude alteration.

Yet we resist change. Because of the uncertainty of the future
and the possibility that change may entail pain and personal loss,
we not only resist it, we fear it. If change is our benefactor, it is an
unwelcome one. It's somewhat like surgery: whatever good it may
do for us, we don't like it and we don't look forward to it.

Inside our "comfort zone," there is much ease — much ease,
but little *growth*. Sometimes ease is what we need, of course, but if
all we ever had was ease, we would not grow. As good as growth
is, however, we would rarely give up our ease in order to grow.
Most of the time, we have to be goaded in the direction of growth
by changes that are forced upon us from the outside.

From the Christian's standpoint, change and its attendant
"trials" can be seen to produce *endurance* and *a deeper faith*. "My
brethren," James wrote, "count it all joy when you fall into various
trials, knowing that the testing of your faith produces patience"
(James 1:2,3). Abraham is the great example of how this works.
If it had been up to him, he probably wouldn't have chosen to
leave his home in Ur. But having endured that unexpected change
faithfully, he knew more about trusting God than he could have
learned in a hundred years back home (Hebrews 11:8-16).

Reaching forward requires a willingness to embrace change.
It is silly to say that we want to get better and stay comfortable at
the same time; we can't stay put and still move forward. And since
change will come to us all, our choice is simply a choice of *attitude:*
will we resist change and make ourselves miserable, or will we accept it with gratitude for the good things that it makes possible?

Change is the nursery of music, joy, life, and eternity.
JOHN DONNE

LED BY LIGHT TO HIS DWELLING

Oh, send out Your light and Your truth! Let them lead me;
Let them bring me to Your holy hill and to Your tabernacle.
Then I will go to the altar of God, to God my exceeding joy;
And on the harp I will praise You, O God, my God.
Psalm 43:3,4

GOD IS A GOD OF LIGHT AND TRUTH AND EXQUISITE BEAUTY.
Anyone who has a taste for these things will be drawn to
Him, and the more powerfully we love these things, the more God
will mean to us. If we wish to be strongly motivated in our devotion to God, then we must intensify our love for the qualities that
He possesses. There is no use trying to keep on serving God if the
virtues that characterize Him are not things that appeal to us.

Psychologists tell us that many of us are "loss averse," meaning we experience more pain from our losses than we do pleasure
from our gains. Thus the fear of negative consequences is, for
many of us, a more powerful motivator than the desire for positive
consequences. When it comes to our spiritual motivation, we *don't*
want to go to hell more than we *do* want to go to heaven.

Perhaps this is true. I remember the World Series one year.
After the final out in the hard-fought final game, the television
camera showed the heartbroken scene in the losing dugout: some
players had their faces buried in their hands, others had tears
streaming down their cheeks. The announcer let the scene speak
for itself for a moment and then, himself a former major league
player, said, "Losing hurts more than winning feels good."

It need not be this way, however. We need not spend our lives
simply moving *away* from things. There are wondrously great
things to move *toward,* and we need only cultivate our taste for
them to be powerfully drawn by their attraction. In a sense, this
is the very challenge of the Christian life, to learn a new, deeper
set of loves. In another sense, however, these loves don't need to
be "learned." They're already there as a result of our creation in
God's image. We just need to be more honest and openly acknowledge the things that move us most deeply. The darkness is to be
avoided, yes. But even more than that, the light is to be loved. The
Lord is to be worshiped "in the beauty of holiness" (Psalm 29:2).

The human soul hungers for beauty — to experience beauty,
and to create beauty — just as powerfully as our bodies hunger for food.
Our souls wither when they are beauty-deprived.

THOMAS KINKADE

January 27

CHILD-LIKE WONDER

Assuredly, I say to you, unless you are converted
and become as little children, you will by no means
enter the kingdom of heaven. *Matthew 18:3*

IT IS EASY FOR A CHILD TO LOVE THE THINGS THAT GOD HAS MADE
AND TO BE DRAWN BY THESE THINGS TO LOVE GOD HIMSELF.
Innocent and free, a child responds very naturally to goodness and
beauty; he or she takes genuine delight in the multifaceted myster-
ies of creation. A cloud . . . a tree . . . a squirrel. There is nothing
that is not of interest, nothing that does not make the heart throb
with wonder and longing for something (or Someone) beyond.

A time comes, however, if the child lives long enough, when
these things begin to lose their interest. And the reason? Sin has
entered the heart, throwing everything into disarray. There is now
delusion and falsehood. Values have been turned upside down.
Cynicism has set in. The child, now no longer a child, is busy,
not enjoying the creation, but trying to own it and manipulate it
to selfish advantage. Now, if he ever notices a cloud, a tree, or a
squirrel, he goes to one of two extremes: either he (1) disregards
them completely or (2) worships them rather than their Creator.

All of this is profoundly sad. Yet it would be far sadder if it
were not for the gospel of Jesus Christ, through which it is possible to be forgiven and to recover the child-like wonder and honest humility with which we used to respond to God's goodness.
The child that we used to be is not gone forever but simply buried
under layers of adult pride and busyness. We should be encouraged to know that there are choices we're capable of making that
will open our hearts back up to the powerful pull of truth and joy.

We need to make these choices and go back to our younger
hearts. "Unless you are converted and become as little children,
you will by no means enter the kingdom of heaven," Jesus said. In
the kingdom, there are many new things to be learned. But before
we can learn them, there is a good deal of grown-up "stuff" that
needs to be unlearned, especially our desire for counterfeit pleasures rather than the real ones that God has provided.

I was a little stranger who was surrounded by innumerable joys when
I arrived here . . . I knew nothing of sickness or death. In the absence
of these I was entertained like an angel with the works of God.
Heaven and earth sang my Creator's praise.

THOMAS TRAHERNE

January 28
GRADUAL GROWTH

... till we all come to the unity of the faith and of the knowledge
of the Son of God, to a perfect man, to the measure of
the stature of the fullness of Christ. *Ephesians 4:13*

W E ARE AN IMPATIENT PEOPLE, AND WHEN THINGS NEED TO
BE FIXED, WE PREFER THEM TO BE FIXED QUICKLY. If there are
problems, we demand instant solutions, and we have little toler-
ance for delay in obtaining the results we seek. In our culture, the
concept that some plan might take a *lifetime* to be accomplished is
unthinkable. Long before that, we would have concluded that the
plan wasn't working — we would have changed plans.

Spiritual growth, of course, does take time, and we need to be
more *patient* than we often are, both with other people and with
ourselves. But I suggest that what we really need is to be more
humble. We must put our pride in its place and be willing, perhaps
for quite a long time, to be novices or beginners. Between us and
God, there is a long road to be traveled. All who've gone before
have had to make the journey. Should we be exempt? If we're expecting God to provide us a shortcut, who do we think we are?

But we also need *courage*. Our Lord's own journey took Him
through painful territory, and He endured all of it patiently, humbly, and courageously. So the Hebrew writer says, "Consider Him
who endured such hostility from sinners against Himself, lest you
become weary and discouraged in your souls. You have not yet
resisted to bloodshed, striving against sin" (Hebrews 12:3,4).

At the present time, none of us is anything more than a work
in progress. Our characters are unfinished and not yet ready for
direct communion with God. But we're *on the way* to that goal, if
indeed we've obeyed the gospel of Christ and are remaining true
to the confession of our faith. Each day God's hammer and chisel
are at work on us, chipping away at the sin that has hardened
around our hearts. Since we're still alive and able to talk about
it, one thing ought to be obvious: *God has not given up on us!* And
neither should we. Eventually, God's methods, however ineffective they may seem right now, will be seen to have been the best.
Meanwhile, let's trust the process and give it time — nothing less
than a *lifetime* — to work. It may be slow, but it's very, very sure.

... knowing God and developing faith is a gradual process.
There are no shortcuts to maturity. It takes time to be holy.
ERWIN W. LUTZER

BOTH ACTIVE AND CONTEMPLATIVE

> . . . the report went around concerning Him all the more;
> and great multitudes came together to hear, and to be healed
> by Him of their infirmities. So He Himself often withdrew
> into the wilderness and prayed. *Luke 5:15,16*

COMPARING THE CHRISTIAN LIFE TO A MELODY, THERE ARE TWO KEYS THE MELODY CAN BE PLAYED IN: ACTIVE AND CONTEMPLA-TIVE. Some Christians tend in the direction of active service while others tend toward quiet devotion. Neither is inherently wrong; there is a need for both. We should be cautious before criticizing someone for not doing discipleship exactly as we do it.

In the life of Jesus and His apostles, we see some times of activity and other times of quietness. "Then the apostles gathered to Jesus and told Him all things, both what they had done and what they had taught. And He said to them, 'Come aside by yourselves to a deserted place and rest a while.' For there were many coming and going, and they did not even have time to eat" (Mark 6:30,31). Just so, the life of the individual Christian will move through different periods, some more active and some more contemplative.

But what about the body of Christ? Is there not room in the kingdom for individuals whose overall lives tend more in one direction than the other? The answer should be an obvious *Yes!* The body needs all, and we all need each other. As Paul warned, "The eye cannot say to the hand, 'I have no need of you'; nor again the head to the feet, 'I have no need of you'" (1 Corinthians 12:21).

If I'm a more active Christian and you're more contemplative, I need your example to remind me to take time for spiritual refreshment. And if I'm more contemplative and you're more active, I need your example to remind me that Christianity is about more than just "my God and I." Together we're stronger than we would be without the influence of the other, and we should be careful not to criticize or minimize the other. Neither of us has a personality or style of service that is inherently superior to others. And arguing over who's putting the emphasis where it's most needed is little more than a waste of time. None of us, all by ourselves, will get the emphasis right; it's *together* that the Lord's work gets done.

> There are two kinds of Christian living. One is a life of activity. The other is
> the contemplative life. These two lives are united. It is impossible to live the
> one without having some of the other.
>
> ANONYMOUS, *THE CLOUD OF UNKNOWING*

COURAGEOUS REASON

... who through faith subdued kingdoms, worked righteousness, obtained promises, stopped the mouths of lions, quenched the violence of fire, escaped the edge of the sword, out of weakness were made strong, became valiant in battle, turned to flight the armies of the aliens. *Hebrews 11:33,34*

FAITH IS APT TO GET US INTO TROUBLE. Unlike mere "belief," real faith leaves the comforts of home and gets out there where the real fight is taking place between good and evil. It is willing to take risks in the course of serving the Lord's will. Based on what God has done in the observable realm of history, we reason that He is telling us the truth about the unseen realm, and we are willing to follow that reasoning out onto the battlefield of life.

The key element in the kind of faith that takes risks is *trust*. We are willing to put any number of things in jeopardy in the short run because we have confidence that, in the long run, the Lord will not let us down. "For this reason I also suffer these things," Paul wrote; "nevertheless I am not ashamed, for I know whom I have believed and am persuaded that He is able to keep what I have committed to Him until that Day" (2 Timothy 1:12).

A well-reasoned faith will impart not only courage but also determination and persistence. In Luke 5:17-26, there is the story of some people who brought to the Lord a paralyzed man for Him to heal. There was such a crowd, they could not get to the Lord. Undeterred, however, "they went up on the housetop and let him down with his bed through the tiling into the midst before Jesus" (v.19). Jesus was pleased with the persistence of their effort, and He knew it to be the result of faith: "When He saw their faith, He said to him, 'Man, your sins are forgiven you'" (v.20).

The courage that comes from genuine faith is far different from the cowardice that tags along behind superficial faith. In John 12:42, we read that "even among the rulers many believed in Him, but because of the Pharisees they did not confess Him, lest they should be put out of the synagogue." If this kind of faith could save, even the demons would be in heaven: "You believe that there is one God. You do well. Even the demons believe — and tremble! But do you want to know, O foolish man, that faith without works is dead?" (James 2:19,20). So the question is not "What do you believe?" but "What are you willing to do about it?"

Faith is reason grown courageous.

SHERWOOD EDDY

January 31
COURAGEOUS DESIRE

Then He turned to the woman and said to Simon, "Do you see this woman? I entered your house; you gave Me no water for My feet, but she has washed My feet with her tears and wiped them with the hair of her head. You gave Me no kiss, but this woman has not ceased to kiss My feet since the time I came in. You did not anoint My head with oil, but this woman has anointed My feet with fragrant oil. Therefore I say to you, her sins, which are many, are forgiven, for she loved much. But to whom little is forgiven, the same loves little." Then He said to her, "Your sins are forgiven." *Luke 7:44-48*

IF THERE'S ONE THING THAT IS OBVIOUS ABOUT LOVE, IT'S THAT LOVE WANTS TO SHOW ITSELF. Love (that is, *real* love) is active. Like a healthy toddler, it can't sit still for very long. It always wants to be doing something, preferably to act out its desires.

Like faith, love is not only active, it is willing to take significant risks. The woman in Luke 7, whose love led her to anoint the Lord's feet with expensive oil, risked several things to show her love. For one thing, she accepted the risk of *real loss*. The ointment was costly, but wanting to show her love, she was willing to make a sacrifice (suffer an actual, couldn't-afford-it loss) to do so. But second, she accepted the risk of *the disapproval of others*. To show her love for the Lord, she pushed past the "respectable" crowd and did something that incurred criticism from those, like Simon, who loved the Lord with nothing more than an official love.

Today, we need to be careful, but we also need to be brave. Love doesn't give us the right to do anything we please in showing our love for the Lord. We know nothing about what pleases Him except what He has revealed to us in His word, and we dare not disregard the Scriptures in deciding how to show our love. But that said, it's important for us to be courageous in the desires of our love. All the scriptural correctness in the world will not accomplish anything if it is not carried out in active love.

"The loving are the daring" (Bayard Taylor). Our lives and our relationship with God would be richer if we loved Him more deeply, dreamed of showing our love more extravagantly, and then demonstrated our faith more boldly and bravely. It's time we got over our fears: our fear of being hurt and our fear that others will think we're crazy. What if the woman in Luke 7 had stifled her desire and done the "sensible" thing? Well, the world — and certainly the Lord's cause — would have been much the poorer.

Have the courage of your desire.
GEORGE GISSING

February 1
LOVE AND . . . HAPPINESS?

> I will very gladly spend and be spent for your souls.
> *2 Corinthians 12:15*

THE SATISFYING THING ABOUT LOVE IS NOT THAT WE GET HAP-PINESS BUT THAT WE GIVE IT. We may be glad when those we love return our love in ways that make us happy, but that doesn't always happen. When it doesn't, we need to remember that real love doesn't *require* being returned. When it is unrequited, love may grieve, but it can still survive and even thrive, as it did in the case of Paul. He longed to be loved by his friends in Corinth, but his love didn't *depend* on that happiness. He would love them even if it meant giving and giving and giving until there was nothing more to give. "I will very gladly spend and be spent for your souls," he said, knowing full well that the feeling was not mutual.

Our modern concept of love is so self-centered that the idea of love without happiness seems ridiculous. Why would a person love anyone or anything if it didn't bring him happiness? This, for example, is why marriage is such a transitory, vulnerable thing in our culture. Most spouses now live under something like the following threat from their partners: "If you ever fail to bring me the happiness I think I deserve, then I will be released from any obligation to keep the vows that have guaranteed my love for you."

And we don't do much better when it comes to God, do we? We think of God solely in terms of how much happiness we get in return for loving Him, and if at any time He fails to see the subject of happiness in the same way we do, we feel free to sidestep our commitments to Him. If God ever stands between us and anything we think is necessary for us to be happy, we just go around Him.

Yet there is a higher path we could follow. It's an old-fashioned path, admittedly. It's the way of *joy*. Joy, unlike happiness, does not depend on whether what "happens" to us is pleasing. It's not at the mercy of circumstances. Instead, it's grounded in deep, unchangeable truth. And the love that flows from *a joyful commitment to truth* will gladly give itself and keep on giving. All it needs is the privilege of singing some part (just *any* part) in the great chorus that glorifies God. All it wants is that Christ "will be magnified in my body, *whether by life or by death*" (Philippians 1:20).

> With love one can live even without happiness.
> FEODOR DOSTOEVSKY

ON BEING A "CHEERFUL GIVER"

So let each one give as he purposes in his heart, not grudgingly
or of necessity; for God loves a cheerful giver.
2 Corinthians 9:7

WHAT DOES IT TAKE TO GET YOU TO DO THE RIGHT THING? Do
you coast along neglectfully disregarding certain priorities
until a crisis makes action imperative? Does life have to hold a gun
to your head before you get busy and do what's right?

Most of us would have to say that we're guilty of habitual
neglect when it comes to putting first things first. We don't act
until the threat of some unpleasantness forces us to act. But if
so, doesn't that mean that we've become, at least in one sense,
"grudging" givers? If it's only under constraint or necessity that
we finally step up to our responsibilities, is that the kind of free
and "cheerful" giving that our great and loving God deserves?

The people of Israel in the Old Testament certainly illustrate
the fact that human beings have a tendency to forget God when
things are going well. Over and over again the cycle repeated
itself: (1) Enjoying the Lord's blessings, they would lapse into ingratitude and unfaithfulness. (2) God would threaten punishment,
or actually bring it to pass, and Israel would repent. (3) God's
blessings would return, and it would only be a matter of time before another period of ingratitude and unfaithfulness began.

Take an honest look at the pattern of your own life. Do you
consistently give of yourself to God "cheerfully" — that is, without having to be made to? During times of ease and comfort, do
you continue to pour yourself out to God in prayerful reverence
and loving thankfulness? Do you delight in the worship of God, or
do you only do it to avoid the consequences of not doing it?

Fortunately, God loves us and is patient with us. For the time
being, He will continue to goad us, if necessary. But He's looking
for us to grow beyond the need for goads and threats and negative
incentives. He desires the free, cheerful love of a grateful people.

There are three kinds of giving: grudge giving, duty giving, and
thanksgiving. Grudge giving says, "I hate to," duty giving says, "I ought to,"
thanksgiving says, "I want to." The first comes from constraint, the second
from a sense of obligation, the third from a full heart. Nothing much is
conveyed in grudge giving since "the gift without the giver is bare."
Something more happens in duty giving, but there is no song in it.
Thanksgiving is an open gate into the love of God.

ROBERT N. RODENMAYER

February 3
DEVOTION DURING DIFFICULTY

And being in agony, He prayed more earnestly. Then His sweat
became like great drops of blood falling down to the ground.
Luke 22:44

DEVOTION TO GOD DURING TIMES OF DIFFICULTY PRESENTS SOME
SPECIAL CHALLENGES. There is, of course, a sense in which
it's easier to seek God when we're beset with problems. (Indeed,
times of crisis are the *only* times that some people seek Him.) But
in another sense, it's harder to love God with any warmth of affection when our circumstances are such that He seems far away.
What should we do about our devotional life when we're passing
through some ordeal of suffering or emotional barrenness?

*As much as possible, we should hold on to our regular daily times
of devotion.* Doing this is not easy, as we all know, but it's important to *try*. Difficulty, especially tragedy, almost always involves
a disruption of our regular daily schedule. But if, for example,
we normally devote ourselves to a few moments of prayer at the
beginning of each day, it's important to try to maintain that habit
even on the hard days. When crisis makes an appearance in our
lives, if we can hold on to any semblance of our usual devotional
discipline, it helps us to meet our challenges in a stronger way.

We should not forget to be grateful. Simply because we, at a
given moment, may be experiencing something of the bitterness of
life, that does not mean that God is not still on His throne, ruling
with benevolence and grace. Even on our darkest day, there is still
much more to be thankful for than there is to regret. During painful times, it's especially important to try to maintain our perspective and recognize that our pain is not the *whole* truth about life
in the world (or even our *own* life in the world). We need to give
thanks to God every day, and not just on the pleasant days.

We should persevere. The fact of the matter is, God is never far
away from us. Not really. It's just that we *feel* like that at certain
times. At those times, we must make up our minds to maintain
our faith and obedience, knowing that seasons of spiritual dryness
and desolation are only temporary. In time, the feelings that we
want to have about God will return. Meanwhile, God is still God!
Even when our feelings waver, our love for Him must not.

Love is . . . devoted and thankful to God, trusting and hoping in him even
when not enjoying his sweetness; for none can live in love without suffering.
THOMAS À KEMPIS

February 4
PEACE AND TRUTH

These things I have spoken to you, that in Me you may have peace.
In the world you will have tribulation; but be of good cheer,
I have overcome the world. *John 16:33*

JESUS SAID, "YOU SHALL KNOW THE TRUTH, AND THE TRUTH SHALL
MAKE YOU FREE" (JOHN 8:32). Cloudy vision and confused notions about what is real are at the root of the problem of sin, and
Jesus came to clear up our vision and reacquaint us with the truth.
To the extent that we let Him adjust our understanding, we will
gain a greater measure of freedom and also many other things that
freedom makes possible, such as peace and confidence.

On the eve of His crucifixion, Jesus spoke with His disciples
about both truth and peace. First He said, "I am the way, the truth,
and the life" (John 14:6), and later He said, "Peace I leave with
you, My peace I give to you; not as the world gives do I give to
you. Let not your heart be troubled, neither let it be afraid" (v.27).
These two statements are inseparable. It was only because He was
the true way to God that Jesus could promise peace, and we need
to understand that peace can't be enjoyed on any basis but that of
truth: in other words, *of God's version of reality.* If we reject the truth
about God and our responsibilities to Him, then our hopes will be
blighted by fear, no matter what soothing lies we tell ourselves.

But if truth banishes fear, it doesn't do so automatically.
For truth to give us peace, we must value it enough to pursue it
diligently. We must dig for it, appreciate its worth, and apply its
principles to our decisions twenty-four hours a day, seven days a
week. It is a potent force, but not even truth can liberate those who
are lazy and lack the desire to learn (Proverbs 17:16).

Out of all the truths that can give us peace, the greatest are
those that concern God Himself, and the greatest of these is that
He is the sovereign Ruler of His creation. Whatever forces oppose
His benevolent will right now will be brought back under His rule
or else banished from His presence on Judgment Day. When we
are grounded in this truth about God, we can be guarded by the
promise that those who're rightly related to Him through Christ
will share in His victory. "In the world you will have tribulation,"
Jesus said, "but be of good cheer, I have overcome the world."

Unceasing peace is the result of truth.
Stress and grief are the products of falsehood.
GUIGO I

February 5
WHAT DO WE HOPE TO GAIN?

> . . . he who plows should plow in hope, and he who
> threshes in hope should be partaker of his hope.
> *1 Corinthians 9:10*

WHAT'S IN IT FOR US? That is what most people want to know when the subject of "religion" comes up. And then we go to two extremes. Either (1) we turn religion into nothing more than a spiritual scheme for our own health, wealth, and happiness, or (2) we reject the worship of God completely with the cynical comment heard in Malachi's day: "It is useless to serve God; what profit is it that we have kept His ordinance?" (Malachi 3:14). The thought does not occur to us that it may be profitable — and even joyful! — to serve God whether it "pays" us to do so or not.

The subject of *hope* is certainly a scriptural subject. Like its companions *faith* and *love*, hope involves an attraction to unseen realities that are desirable. The Christian is moved by hope to make adjustments that would not be made otherwise. But notice carefully the texts that speak of hope. The hope that leads to a pure life is *the hope of our being like Christ* (1 John 3:2,3), not the hope of our lifestyle being more trouble-free. And the hope of the gospel is *"Christ in you, the hope of glory"* (Colossians 1:27).

Naturally, there must be some benefit to serving God, or we would not do it. But we will be more powerfully motivated when that benefit has to do more with God and less with ourselves. When we are moved by a deep, thrilling desire for His glory, at whatever cost that glory must be gained, then we'll make real progress in life. We won't think in terms of personal benefit, but only of rightful service, and what we hope to gain will be the soul-satisfying knowledge that *we are rightly related to His glory*, He by His grace having made it possible for us to please Him again.

It all comes down to the joy of *giving* as opposed to the joy of *getting*. Jesus taught that the former is greater than the latter: "It is more blessed to give than to receive" (Acts 20:35). With respect to God, there are many things to be "received" by us, and these are not insignificant motivators to the devout life. But none of these come close to the joy of giving glory to God: the sheer joy of taking our rightful place in the symphony of His creation.

A person will turn away from the world and engage in serious prayer
because there is a strong desire for the things of God.
PSEUDO-MACARIUS

February 6

WOULD WE REFUSE THE GREAT INVITATION?

A certain man gave a great supper and invited many, and sent his servant
at supper time to say to those who were invited, "Come, for all things are
now ready." But they all with one accord began to make excuses.
Luke 14:16-18

WE ARE NEVER MORE FOOLISH THAN WHEN WE SAY NO TO GOD. We act as if God were trying to force us into an unnatural, undesirable way of life, when in reality He is inviting us to experience something very, very good. He is not trying to hurt us but rather to help us. When we say no to Him, we are refusing to accept the love He longs to give us. That is, in fact, what sin always is: a foolish unwillingness to let ourselves be loved by our God.

We would not ever turn down what God has for us, of course, if we were not deceived. When we choose to do something other than God's will, we've been led to believe that we're acting in our best interests. But we should not be under any delusion as to where that lie comes from. To the Corinthians, Paul wrote, "I fear, lest somehow, as the serpent deceived Eve by his craftiness, so your minds may be corrupted from the simplicity that is in Christ" (2 Corinthians 11:3). Our adversary, the devil, has had long experience in making absurd foolishness seem like great wisdom.

But we should not let ourselves be fooled so easily. The biblical injunction "Do not be deceived" (Galatians 6:7) is a command. It implies that we can make the choice to keep our eyes open, and that is what we should always insist on doing. We know far too much about God to believe that He would invite us to anything other than the greatest of banquets, and when Satan suggests otherwise, we should have enough sense to simply say, "Shut up!"

God is inviting us to enjoy everything that is truly good about life. Jesus said, "I have come that they may have life, and that they may have it more abundantly" (John 10:10). What we should understand is not only that God offers us *life* but that He puts His offer in the form of an *invitation*. "The Spirit and the bride say, 'Come!' . . . Whoever desires, let him take the water of life freely" (Revelation 22:17). Who in his right mind would turn this down? When we "make excuses," aren't we making a tragic mistake?

Who would prefer to be poor? Who would choose to be sick?
What hungry person could possibly walk away from a banquet table?
O Lord, help me to respond warmly to your gracious invitation.

BERNARD BANGLEY

February 7
ARE WE WILLING TO BE WEAK?

And He said to me, "My grace is sufficient for you, for My strength
is made perfect in weakness." Therefore most gladly I will rather boast
in my infirmities, that the power of Christ may rest upon me.
2 Corinthians 12:9

OFTEN WE HAVE NO CHOICE BUT TO TOLERATE WEAKNESS FOR A
WHILE, BUT WE'RE NOT CONTENT TO REMAIN WEAK FOR VERY
LONG. If we have deficiencies or inadequacies, we want them
removed as quickly as possible. We don't like being weak. And
we adopt an almost demanding attitude about the matter: *God had
better get rid of our neediness!* In our lexicon, "dependency" is the
ultimate bad word, and "self-confidence" is the ultimate good one.
If serving Him leaves us still weak and needy, what good is God?

Spiritually speaking, however, the attitude we call "self-confidence" can be a dangerous thing. What feels like strength may
be little more than pride. If we're not careful, we can fall into the
error of thinking that we're getting by on our own. As long as the
good times roll, we can deceive ourselves into thinking that we
need no help. Yet without God, we would perish in an instant, and
it's sinful to forget that fact. Not only is it sinful, it's ridiculous. If
we ever suppose that we can get by without God's help, then we
are simply, and quite seriously, out of touch with reality.

It's true, of course, that by self-confidence we often mean little
more than optimism, and optimism is certainly preferable to pessimism. But even here, our optimism needs to be grounded in what
God can do, not what we can do. There is no doubt whatsoever as
to the eventual outcome of the war between good and evil, and we
need to confront our daily problems in the confidence that God's
victory over His enemy is certain. The war has already been won.

Paul had to learn that God's strength "is made perfect in
weakness," and we need to learn it too. Although it sounds contradictory, an admission of our weakness is the only way to be
strong. Not only that, it's the only way to make progress. We can't
really be useful to the Lord until our pride has been broken, perhaps by some lifelong "thorn in the flesh," and we've been helped
to understand that God's grace is all we ever really have to have.

Christ is never strong in us until we are weak. As our strength diminishes,
the strength of Christ grows in us. When we are entirely emptied
of our own strength, then we are full of Christ's strength.
As much as we retain of our own we lack of Christ's.

WILLIAM TYNDALE

February 8
Broken Wings

Therefore I take pleasure in infirmities, in reproaches,
in needs, in persecutions, in distresses, for Christ's sake.
For when I am weak, then I am strong.
2 Corinthians 12:10

ONE OF THE MOST DIFFICULT KINDS OF WEAKNESS TO ENDURE IS PHYSICAL DISABILITY. Even for the person of extraordinary spiritual strength, it is hard to keep a positive focus on God when the body is not able to function normally or is racked with pain. We understand, at least in theory, that spiritual concerns are more important than physical ones, but the fact is, our bodies are the instruments through which our spirits must do most of their work. When the instrument is broken, it isn't easy to maintain joy and give thanks. What, then, should be our attitude toward physical impairments or diseases, especially those of a serious nature?

We should "go to the balcony" and look at each day from a larger *perspective.* If today is difficult, for whatever reason, the thing we must always do is see today against the backdrop of eternity. Today's truth may be hard to bear, but it's never the whole truth.

We should give thanks, if not for the pain, at least for the progress *it produces in our character.* There is no more challenging text in the New Testament than James 1:2,3, which says, "My brethren, count it all joy when you fall into various trials, knowing that the testing of your faith produces patience." The testing is not pleasant, and none of us should be so naive as to suggest that the physical sufferer should just smile and be happy. Yet if suffering bathes our hearts in humility and reminds us to lean on God, it has done us a significant favor. "Therefore I take pleasure in infirmities," Paul could say, ". . . for when I am weak, then I am strong."

We should understand that our troubles are not unique. Paul also wrote, "No temptation has overtaken you except such as is common to man" (1 Corinthians 10:13). We may not personally know anyone who has had to endure what we're enduring, but what about the millions who've lived since the world began? Whatever our affliction, others *have* coped with it — and some have coped with worse. Truth to tell, every person we've ever met is hurting in some way. Some become bitter, while others become better.

I thank God for my handicaps; for, through them,
I have found myself, my work, and my God.
HELEN KELLER

IN THIS WE GROAN

For we know that if our earthly house, this tent, is destroyed,
we have a building from God, a house not made with hands, eternal
in the heavens. For in this we groan, earnestly desiring to be clothed
with our habitation which is from heaven . . .
2 Corinthians 5:1,2

CREATED FOR FELLOWSHIP WITH GOD BUT LIVING IN A WORLD THAT IS BROKEN BY SIN, WE FREQUENTLY FIND OURSELVES CRYING OUT FOR RELIEF. We earnestly desire, as Paul put it, "to be clothed with our habitation which is from heaven." And most of us have observed that "groaning" is not too strong a word for what we do when the troubles of this world press down on us.

We need to be reminded that groaning is not wrong. Rather than the act of a weak person, it's often that of a strong person whose eyes are open to what's gone wrong in the world. Wouldn't Jesus be the most notable example of how a strong person can sorrow? As He approached the tomb of His friend Lazarus, He "wept" (John 11:35). Then the account says that He arrived at the tomb "groaning in Himself" (v.38). We need to dispense with the idea that spiritually mature people never hurt and never cry.

Not only is groaning not inconsistent with godliness, here is another thing, amazing but true: *groaning is not inconsistent with joy!* The most joyous of God's people are those who deeply, and even sorrowfully, cry out for His redemption. Indeed, it's often the bitterness of groaning that makes our hope so sweet. The godly life fits the definition of "bittersweet," and it's quite appropriately compared to childbirth, an ordeal full of groaning, surely, but not without the joy that comes from hope: "The whole creation groans and labors with birth pangs together until now" (Romans 8:22).

The Psalmist sang that "weeping may endure for a night, but joy comes in the morning" (Psalm 30:5). "In this we groan," said Paul, speaking of our fleshly bodies. But if we're faithful in our walk with God, our groaning is helping us get to our goal more fervently. *Groaning* and *earnestly desiring* are simply two sides of the same coin. The gospel, after all, is good news, but only to those who've sorrowed over their separation from God. Having obeyed the good news, they're now *yearning* for a final homecoming with Him, *reaching forward* to that day with every ache of their hearts.

Life is a bridge of groans across a stream of tears.
PHILIP JAMES BAILEY

February 10
STRENGTH FROM BROKENNESS

And the Lord said, "Simon, Simon! Indeed, Satan has asked for you, that he
may sift you as wheat. But I have prayed for you, that your faith should not
fail; and when you have returned to Me, strengthen your brethren."
Luke 22:31,32

HAVING SUFFERED THE PAIN OF SORROW (AND MAYBE HAVING
STUMBLED IN OUR FAITH), WE ARE STRONGER FOR HAVING HAD
THAT EXPERIENCE — IF WE RESPOND TO IT IN THE RIGHT WAY. Like a
broken bone that is stronger at the spot where it was mended, we
can gain strength from our brokenness, if we make that choice.

Our chosen response to suffering is what makes the difference, of course. And choosing correctly is not easy. There are two
opposite dangers that must be avoided. On the one hand, we must
stay away from *self-pity,* but on the other, we must steer clear of
self-righteousness. When we've been broken by some experience in
life, we tend to veer back and forth between these extremes. With
practice, however, we can learn to respond to heartbreaks with a
balance of reverence, gratitude, and humility — and when we do,
we find that hardships help us more than they hurt us.

In what sense, though, can we say that broken people are
"stronger"? Well, for one thing, those who've had their hearts
broken are often wiser and less vulnerable to certain temptations.
After Peter had denied the Lord three times and recovered, he
would have been more vigilant in that particular area for the rest
of his life. But not only that, faith, hope, and love are often more
"real" to those who've been tried by fire. Job, for example, was a
man of considerable faith before his ordeal, but after it was over,
he found that his faith was a finer thing by far (Job 42:5,6).

Not everybody has to be broken by sorrow in order to learn
spiritual strength; some are wise enough to learn from others' ordeals (Proverb 21:11; 22:3). Yet there can be no question that those
who are the strongest spiritually are often those whose hearts have
been torn apart and then mended. Life in this world is hard, we
must be frank to say. It is ugly, and it is dangerous. We're never
more than a step away from sorrow or shame, and the weight of
the world may not be something we can bear without breaking.
Being broken, however, need not be the end of the story.

The world breaks everyone and afterwards
many are strong at the broken places.
ERNEST HEMINGWAY

February 11
A HEART WILL FIND ITS HOME

. . . eternal life to those who by patient continuance in doing good seek for
glory, honor, and immortality; but to those who are self-seeking and do not
obey the truth, but obey unrighteousness — indignation and wrath,
tribulation and anguish, on every soul of man who does evil, of the Jew first
and also of the Greek; but glory, honor, and peace to everyone who works
what is good, to the Jew first and also to the Greek. *Romans 2:7-10*

IN OUR HEART OF HEARTS, EACH OF US "SEEKS" SOMETHING. The
evidence of our daily words and deeds may suggest that we're
actually seeking something different than what we *say* is most
important to us (Romans 6:16), but the fact remains, we each seek
something. By our nature, we are seeking creatures. We're always
moving, always "growing" in some direction or another.

Every kind of seeking that we may engage in has its own set
of consequences. Ungodliness, for example, cannot lead anywhere
except away from God. If a person travels that path and refuses to
change, there is only destination he can arrive at. Similarly, godliness has an inevitable destination, albeit a very different one.

Depending on what we seek, we will each arrive at a "goal"
that is the ultimate outcome of our seeking. The Scriptures speak
of the "end" of our choices in this world. In one place, for example, Paul asks those who had become Christians, "What fruit did
you have then in the things of which you are now ashamed? For
the *end* of those things is death. But now having been set free from
sin, and having become slaves of God, you have your fruit to holiness, and the *end*, everlasting life" (Romans 6:21,22).

So there is a sense in which our hearts *will* find their way to
the "home" that they have sought. It is senseless to suppose that a
person can spend his lifetime seeking the things of this world and
then in eternity find himself enjoying the things of God. No, the
worldly heart will find its way to a very different home than the
heart set on God. It will reap what it has sown (Galatians 6:7,8).

But our destiny is not determined by fate or divine decree. If
we have to admit that our hearts have not been seeking God, we
can decide to start doing so. We can learn to love God with all our
hearts, and when we do so, we'll begin moving toward the home
that will someday be found by all who have truly loved Him.

> Every love has its own force; and it cannot lie idle in the soul
> of the lover. Love must draw the soul on. Do you, then, wish
> to know the character of a love? See where it leads.
>
> AUGUSTINE OF HIPPO

February 12
PRAYING FOR LIGHT

So he, trembling and astonished, said, "Lord, what do You want me
to do?" Then the Lord said to him, "Arise and go into the city,
and you will be told what you must do." *Acts 9:6*

WHEN SAUL OF TARSUS REALIZED THE IDENTITY OF THE ONE
WHO HAD APPEARED TO HIM ON THE DAMASCUS ROAD, HE
ASKED THE RIGHT QUESTION: "LORD, WHAT DO YOU WANT ME TO
DO?" The awareness that he was in the presence of God was
followed by a recognition that his life was seriously out of line
with God's will. At that moment, he knew little of what would be
involved in serving God, but he did understand that he needed
to move in the direction of honest obedience. This man had a
reverent, receptive heart, and he was ready to make whatever
adjustments were needed to begin doing what God wanted. His
question was simply, "Lord, what do you want me to do?"

Like Paul, we need to see that Christianity is an active en-
deavor, not merely an intellectual interest. Judging by our life-
styles, many of us apparently believe that being a Christian is
nothing more than being "aware" of God's power to save us. But,
in fact, Christianity is a walk, a changed way of life, a new manner
of living. "Do you despise the riches of His goodness, forbearance,
and longsuffering," Paul would later write, "not knowing that the
goodness of God leads you to repentance?" (Romans 2:4).

So when we pray, what kind of help do we ask for? What kind
of "light" do we seek? If we come to Christ with anything less
than a desire to obey Him, we may get the same abrupt "welcome" that John the Baptist gave to some of his hearers: "Brood of
vipers! Who warned you to flee from the wrath to come? Therefore
bear fruits worthy of repentance" (Matthew 3:7,8).

*The light that we should ask for is light to illuminate the road we're
going to travel!* If our interest in Christ is just an intellectual interest
or if we have no real intention of traveling the road shown to us,
then no light will be given to guide us. Guidance is only for those
who're going somewhere! So if we're *reaching* forward, we should
pray for light — but our intention must be to *move* forward.

O for a closer walk with God,
A calm and heavenly frame,
A light to shine upon the road
That leads me to the Lamb!

WILLIAM COWPER

GOD IS NOT NEUTRAL TOWARD OUR NEEDS

> Now may the God of peace . . . make you complete in every good work
> to do His will, working in you what is well pleasing in His sight, through
> Jesus Christ, to whom be glory forever and ever. Amen. *Hebrews 13:20,21*

THERE IS NOTHING "OBJECTIVE" ABOUT GOD'S ATTITUDE TOWARD
US. We are creatures brought into being by His love, and when
a way for us to be redeemed could only be purchased by the life of
His Son, He did not stop short of making that sacrifice. The question of our well-being is one in which He has a vested interest,
to say the very least. He is for us. He is on our side. He is passionately biased in our favor. There is nothing good for us in this
whole wide world that He is not eager and able to provide.

There is a sense in which God is eager to do good for every
person He has created, even those who show no respect to Him.
Jesus said that "He makes his sun rise on the evil and on the good,
and sends rain on the just and on the unjust" (Matthew 5:45).

Then, there is a sense in which He cares for those who have
obeyed the gospel of His Son and who have remained faithful to
Him. It is to obedient Christians that Peter wrote, "Let those who
suffer according to the will of God commit their souls to Him in
doing good, as to a faithful Creator" (1 Peter 4:19). "Humble yourselves under the mighty hand of God," he continued, ". . . casting
all your care upon Him, for He cares for you" (1 Peter 5:6,7).

But there is a third point that must be made. *Even when it is
God's faithful saints who are under consideration, the needs that He is
most eager to supply are those relating to His rule.* When Paul made
his familiar statement in Philippians 4:13, "I can do all things
through Christ who strengthens me," he was not speaking of goals
like making a million dollars or winning an Olympic gold medal.
He was simply stating his confidence that Christ wouldn't let him
go without anything he needed to do His, that is, Christ's, work.

Whatever God expects us to do *to accomplish His purposes,* He
will help us do! And help in doing *those* things is what we ought
to desire, far more than we desire His help with lesser concerns. In
anything related to the gospel of Christ, we needn't worry about
coming up short. He will "make [us] complete in every good work
to do His will, working in [us] what is well pleasing in His sight."

> God eagerly awaits the chance to bless
> the person whose heart is turned toward Him.
>
> ANONYMOUS

February 14
THE HIGHEST USE OF THE HUMAN MIND

. . . I meditate on all Your works;
I muse on the work of Your hands.
I spread out my hands to You;
My soul longs for You like a thirsty land.
Psalm 143:5,6

JUST AS THERE IS NO HIGHER OBJECT OF OUR THINKING THAN GOD, THERE IS NO HIGHER USE OF OUR MINDS THAN TO THINK ABOUT HIM REVERENTLY. If we think of our minds as "instruments" that God entrusted to us, the most noble and powerful use to which those instruments can be put is to use them meditating on Him in a way that properly reflects His glory. Most of us do meditate on God from time to time, but we can do better about it than we do. In regard to the use of our minds, most of us make two mistakes.

First, we don't think about God enough. Yes, we think about Him while offering thanks before meals, while doing our daily Bible reading, and while attending church services. But few of us have cultivated the habit of meditating on Him as we go about the round of our daily activities. And perhaps fewer of us have ever retreated from our regular activities for times (perhaps a day or two) of extended prayer and concentration on God Himself.

But second, we don't think about God reverently enough. Even when we do think about God, too frequently we think only of what we need God to do for us, rather than meditate on Him for His own sake. Our thoughts about God are too self-centered and selfishly motivated. We must learn to think about God in such a way that our ideas are characterized by words like these: awe, wonder, worshipfulness, penitence, humility, gratitude, and love.

One consequence of our failure to think often and reverently about God is that our *actions* toward Him tend to be weak and ineffectual. We are not as powerfully motivated as we would be if our thoughts dwelled on Him more worshipfully and for greater lengths of time. There's no use denying that our actions spring from our thinking — and if our thinking were to be filled with the adoration of God, just imagine what the result would be! Our deeds would be drawn toward Him with a force that all the evil armies of hell would be helpless to stop.

Without doubt, the mightiest thought the mind can entertain
is the thought of God, and the weightiest word in any
language is its word for God.

A. W. TOZER

DESIRING THE PROCESS

My brethren, count it all joy when you fall into various trials,
knowing that the testing of your faith produces patience. But let
patience have its perfect work, that you may be perfect
and complete, lacking nothing. *James 1:2-4*

THERE ARE CERTAIN PEOPLE WHO, RATHER THAN WORKING TO ACHIEVE GOALS, SPEND MOST OF THEIR TIME LOOKING FOR SHORTCUTS. Unwilling to accept the *process* that leads to a result, these folks are always angling for some advantage that will eliminate the journey and get them to the end of the rainbow right now.

Some students, for example, would like to know their stuff without studying. Some athletes would like to win the trophy without training their bodies. Some businesspeople would like to get rich without investing their money. Some farmers would like to reap the harvest without working the field. Some soldiers would like to win the war without fighting the battle.

And some Christians, let's face it, would like to be spiritually mature without going through the process of spiritual growth.

In reality, however, those who would be mature in God's eyes must pass through some difficult stages. We're a long way from where we need to be, and the destination can't be reached without crossing the distance. It's foolish (and dangerous) to try.

But here is the point: we should not only *tolerate* the process of growth, we should *embrace* it willingly, gratefully, and even joyfully. The process of spiritual growth involves no small amount of pain. But James says that we are to *"count it all joy when you fall into various trials, knowing that the testing of your faith produces patience."* The pain is not pleasant, but it *produces* something that is very pleasant, and for that reason we should embrace the process with joy. It is not too much to say that we should *desire* the process. We desire it because we desire what it leads to, and we are grateful for the manner in which God has deemed it best for us to get there.

It is sad to see a person who does nothing more than "put up with" today while he frantically looks for some shortcut to tomorrow. How foolish. Today is how we get to tomorrow! And if today is difficult, as it often will be in this world, we ought to do more than tolerate it. We ought to taste it deeply and give thanks for it.

Everyone wants peace, but very few
care for the things that produce it.

THOMAS À KEMPIS

February 16
NO OTHER ENTRANCE

... strengthening the souls of the disciples, exhorting them
to continue in the faith, and saying, "We must through many
tribulations enter the kingdom of God." *Acts 14:22*

IT IS ONLY TO BE EXPECTED THAT WE WILL MEET RESISTANCE IN OUR PROGRESS TOWARD GOD. Satan will surely try to defeat us with problems and pains, and God knows that it's better to allow these difficulties than to prevent them. "We must through many tribulations enter the kingdom of God," said Paul and Barnabas as they encouraged certain new converts to remain steadfast.

In the *Homilies* of Pseudo-Macarius, there is this observation: "We read in the Bible about some people who pleased God. They are considered God's friends and favorites. We miss one important detail. They suffered for God. . . . We applaud them and wish we could be honored in a similar way, but we ignore the cost."

Not only do we ignore the cost, some of us avoid difficulty so often that a pain-free life almost appears to be our main priority. But come to think of it, why should we want to be exempt from hardships that so many of our brethren have suffered? How fair would it be for us to be granted the special consideration of an easier path to God? Do we not remember that old hymn *Am I a Soldier of the Cross?* The second stanza should prick our conscience: "Must I be carried to the skies on flowr'y beds of ease, while others fought to win the prize and sailed through bloody seas?"

The matter really comes down to a simple question: do we really want our hearts to be adjusted to God's holiness or not? If we do, there is a price to be paid and a discipline to be submitted to. Jesus' glory was on the other side of His suffering, and so it must be with us (Mark 8:34). Paul wrote that he was glad to have made sacrifices in order to know Jesus Christ: "that I may know Him and the power of His resurrection, and the fellowship of His sufferings, being conformed to His death, if, by any means, I may attain to the resurrection from the dead" (Philippians 3:10,11). The crown of Christ is for those who, with Him, have borne His cross.

We must through many tribulations enter the kingdom. There is no other entrance.

Character cannot be developed in ease and quiet. Only through
experience of trial and suffering can the soul be strengthened,
vision cleared, ambition inspired, and success achieved.

HELEN KELLER

February 17

HARD TIMES

For the LORD your God is bringing you into a good land, a land of brooks
of water, of fountains and springs, that flow out of valleys and hills . . . a land
in which you will eat bread without scarcity, in which you will lack nothing.
. . . When you have eaten and are full . . . beware that you do not forget
the LORD your God. *Deuteronomy 8:7-11*

POVERTY IS NOT AN EASY EXPERIENCE, BUT IF WE STOP TO THINK
ABOUT IT, IT'S OBVIOUS THAT WEALTH HAS ITS DIFFICULTIES TOO.
When we speak of "hard times," we need to be careful. For all the
hardship we face when we suffer a shortage of life's necessities,
we face an even greater challenge when we suffer a surplus.

The challenge of prosperity is greater because it challenges us
at the level of our character. Poverty's hardship is mostly physical
or outward, but affluence presents a host of harder problems that
are spiritual in nature. Granted, there are some spiritual issues that
must be dealt with when we're poor, but most people who've been
poor would report that they found their inward characters growing in positive ways during that experience. By contrast, most
people would have to say that their characters tend to weaken
when life is completely comfortable. Indeed, it's all we can do to
keep from *dying* in the suffocating atmosphere of affluence.

Paul made an interesting statement in Philippians 4:11,12: "I
have learned in whatever state I am, to be content: I know how
to be abased, and I know how to abound. Everywhere and in all
things I have learned both to be full and to be hungry, both to
abound and to suffer need." It takes some "know how" to be full
and to abound without losing our souls! When we're wealthy, our
spiritual survival is anything but automatic. In fact, according to
Jesus, the odds are quite against it: "And again I say to you, it is
easier for a camel to go through the eye of a needle than for a rich
man to enter the kingdom of God" (Matthew 19:24).

These truths have sobering implications for those of us who
live in one of the wealthy nations, particularly the United States
of America. We face some spiritual hardships that our brethren
in poorer cultures don't have to deal with, and frankly, we're not
handling our abundance conspicuously well. We're "full," but in
all too many cases, we're letting our spirits starve to death.

If adversity hath killed his thousands,
prosperity hath killed his ten thousands.

ROBERT BURTON

February 18
TEMPTED TO SWITCH GOALS

Again, the devil took Him up on an exceedingly high mountain, and
showed Him all the kingdoms of the world and their glory. And he said to
Him, "All these things I will give You if You will fall down and worship me."
Then Jesus said to him, "Away with you, Satan! For it is written, 'You shall
worship the LORD your God, and Him only you shall serve.'"
Matthew 4:8-10

OUR ADVERSARY, THE DEVIL, IS A MASTER OF DECEIT. He has
found some very creative ways to persuade us to move
toward him rather than toward God. He knows that what we
want is joy, and he shrewdly tempts us to seek it on his terms. His
argument runs something like this: "I'm not asking you to desire
anything different; I'm just showing you a better way to get what
you desire." But that is a lie. He knows it, and we know it too, as
soon as we take the bait. The path he offers is not simply a better
path to the same destination; it's a different destination altogether.
The devil is asking us, in the most ultimate sense, to switch goals.

How many people would do what the devil suggests if they
knew what he was up to? If we knew that death, not joy, would
be the result of going his way, we wouldn't go there, would we?
But many of us do know what the devil is up to. Why do we let
ourselves be seduced into changing the direction of our lives?

For most of us, the answer is not hard to find. When we
switch goals, we think of ourselves as doing it only *temporarily!*
After we've indulged ourselves, we'll get back on the path to God.
And we naively suppose that since God will see our sin as nothing
more than an insignificant "lapse," nothing very radical or traumatic will be required of us in the way of repentance. But what we
fail to see is how *insulting* to God's love our sin is. When we turn
away from a God who has loved us to follow His Archenemy, we
take our place in the ranks of those who're in *rebellion* against God.

We need to see sin for what it is: a worshiping of the wrong
god. Sin — any sin — is a denial of God. Samuel summed it up
starkly when he said to Saul, "Rebellion is as the sin of witchcraft,
and stubbornness is as iniquity and idolatry" (1 Samuel 15:23).
Not many of us would want to be known as idolaters, but that's
what it comes down to when, at the devil's suggestion, we exchange God, our hearts' true desire, for anything else at all.

The whole effort — the object — of temptation is to induce us
to substitute something else for God. To obscure God.

R. H. STEWART

February 19

NO DELIGHT

But you have not so learned Christ, if indeed you have heard Him
and have been taught by Him, as the truth is in Jesus: that you put off,
concerning your former conduct, the old man which grows corrupt
according to the deceitful lusts . . .
Ephesians 4:20-22

A S LONG AS WE DELIGHT IN EVIL, WE WON'T HAVE MUCH SUCCESS
REMOVING IT FROM OUR LIVES. In any contest between the head
and the heart, the heart will almost always win. Our loves, whatever they may be, are powerful things. They direct our actions
almost irresistibly. For that reason, we must constantly work on
our desires and diminish those that lead us away from God.

In dealing with our desires, there is one thing it helps to understand: most of the time, it is not our desires themselves that are
wrong, but rather our willingness to fulfill them in unlawful ways.
The Scriptures teach that temptation comes to us in three basic
ways: "the lust of the flesh, the lust of the eyes, and the pride of
life" (1 John 2:16). With each of these, the devil is simply trying to
exploit some natural desire that God has given us.

For example, when Eve was tempted to eat the forbidden fruit
in the Garden of Eden, she saw "that the tree was good for food,
that it was pleasant to the eyes, and a tree desirable to make one
wise" (Genesis 3:6). It was not wrong, in itself, for her to be physically hungry or to desire the possession of something beautiful or
even to have the satisfaction of being wise and personally significant. The problem lay in the devil's suggestion that she should *go
outside the boundaries of God's will* to satisfy these desires. When she
turned away from God's provision for each of these and tried to
fulfill them in a "better" way, she sinned — and she died.

So how do we get rid of our sinful desires? We do so, first,
by recognizing the murderous lie behind the devil's offer. Then,
remembering that our desires have been given to us by God, *we
must hold on to our love for Him.* However pleasurable an unlawful
act might be, the thought of gaining that pleasure in a way that
grieves God ought to be so repugnant that the deed seems repul-
sive. With Joseph, we must learn to say sincerely, "How then can I
do this great wickedness, and sin against God?" (Genesis 39:9).

As long as I delight in any evil, as long as sensuality is more gratifying than
purity, indiscretion than moderation, flattery than correction, how can I even
aspire to friendship which springs from an esteem for virtue?

AELRED OF RIEVAULX

February 20
NEW DELIGHT

. . . and be renewed in the spirit of your mind, and that you
put on the new man which was created according to God,
in true righteousness and holiness.
Ephesians 4:23,24

IF IT'S IMPORTANT TO HATE SIN, IT'S EVEN MORE IMPORTANT TO LOVE RIGHTEOUSNESS. The love of God involves not only being repulsed by the idea of disobedience; it means being *attracted* by the opposite idea: the idea of obedience. Living within our Father's love must come to be, among other things, *delightful.*

In Ephesians 4, Paul discussed the two sides of godliness. Whereas we used to take delight in disobedience, "you have not so learned Christ, if indeed you have heard Him and have been taught by Him, as the truth is in Jesus" (vv.20,21). So we must "put off, concerning [our] former conduct, the old man" (v.22). But that is only half the battle. On the positive and more important side, we must "be renewed in the spirit of [our] mind" (v.23). We must make the choice to "put on the new man" (v.24).

If we've been satisfying our desires in unlawful ways for a long time, it will not be easy to learn a new set of delights. It can be done, though, and making the *commitment* to do so is the first step. If we want to be people who take deep delight in pleasing God, we must get past our *what ifs,* our *maybes,* and our *yes buts* and make an actual commitment to be renewed in our thinking.

The good that awaits us is so much more joyful than the counterfeit pleasures we've been accustomed to, our main regret will be that we didn't delight in God sooner. We'll scold ourselves for having been so foolish for so long. What were we thinking?

Counterfeits can be quite convincing, it's true. The things we used to enjoy were really enjoyable, or we wouldn't have spent so much time with them. But whatever pleasures may have come from satisfying ourselves unlawfully, the lawful satisfaction of those same desires is so much deeper and more genuine that the comparison defies description. The "new delight" we can have in God is the real thing. It's what we were made for. It's everything we've dreamed of and then some. And the main thing about it is that it centers on God Himself. He, finally, is all we really desire.

Show unto me, O Lord, your mercy, and delight my heart in it.
Let me find you, whom so longingly I seek.

JEROME

February 21

HE CAN REBUILD A RUINED HEART

He has sent Me to heal the brokenhearted, to proclaim liberty
to the captives, and the opening of the prison to those who are bound;
. . . to give them beauty for ashes, the oil of joy for mourning, the garment
of praise for the spirit of heaviness; that they may be called trees of
righteousness, the planting of the LORD, that He may be glorified.
Isaiah 61:1-3

AS FAR AS GOD IS CONCERNED, NONE OF US IS A HOPELESS CASE.
If our hearts have been ruined by sin, He can rebuild them.
And not only *can* He give us "beauty for ashes" and "the oil of joy
for mourning," but He *desires* to do so. Yet we should not be naive.
God's help is not unconditional, and it can't be enjoyed without
commitment on our part. A renovated heart doesn't come from:

Wishful thinking. Whatever has gone wrong in our lives, it is
possible to recover from our mistakes, but more is required than
simple dreaming. An actual "conversion," or turning, must take
place. The apostle Peter said, "Repent therefore and be converted,
that your sins may be blotted out, so that times of refreshing may
come from the presence of the Lord" (Acts 3:19). In the Scriptures,
there are no "times of refreshing" without radical repentance.

Faith only. In the New Testament, we find a clear pattern with
regard to conversion. Beginning with Pentecost (Acts 2:37-39) and
continuing through each subsequent account of conversion (Acts
8:35-39; 16:14,15; etc.), those who had heard the gospel and were
convicted of their sinfulness were told to be baptized in order to
receive the remission of their sins. Paul, for example, was told by
Ananias, "And now why are you waiting? Arise and be baptized,
and wash away your sins, calling on the name of the Lord" (Acts
22:16). If we want God to reconstruct our broken-down hearts, we
must be on the inside of a forgiven relationship with Him, and in
the New Testament, baptism was always the door through which
that relationship had to be entered (Romans 6:3,4; Galatians 3:27).

Let us not miss the point, however. When we turn to God,
faithfully obeying the gospel, what we're seeking salvation from is
the wreckage of our own hearts. And the wonder of the gospel is that
God can do this. He can rebuild a heart that we have wrecked.

O Lord, the house of my soul is narrow; enlarge it that you may enter in.
It is ruined, O repair it! It displeases your sight; I confess it, I know. But who
shall cleanse it, or to whom shall I cry but unto you? Cleanse me from my
secret faults, O Lord, and spare your servant from strange sin.

AUGUSTINE OF HIPPO

February 22

LEARNING TO BE GLAD WHEN GOD IS GLAD

Love . . . is glad when truth is glad.
1 Corinthians 13:6 Barclay

HERE'S A SUGGESTION: MAKE GOD'S HAPPINESS THE MAIN GOAL OF YOUR LIFE. That's a somewhat strange suggestion, obviously. The main goal of most people is to make *themselves* happy, and the idea that we ought to be more concerned about God's pleasure than our own would strike some folks as odd.

But Paul said that love is "glad when truth is glad," and truth is glad when what happens is that through which God can show forth His glory most greatly. Truth rejoices when God's purposes are fulfilled. It finds pleasure in the same things that He does. It looks at everything from His perspective and is never happier than when He has been pleased (2 Thessalonians 1:11,12).

To what extent are we a people committed to truth? Is our love for God such that we are "glad when truth is glad"? It's easy to say "yes" with our lips, but what does the evidence of our way of life in the real world suggest? When the requirements of truth involve the sacrifice of our own happiness, what then? Is God's gladness a higher priority than our own pleasure? This is a question that most of us will find it uncomfortable to answer honestly.

If we want to grow in this area, we need to begin taking a larger perspective on the issue of happiness. In eternity, the *only* people who will be happy are those who are able to rejoice in the gladness of God. In this life, we may travel a path that goes somewhere different than God is going and, for the time being, delude ourselves into thinking that we're happy. But that is only because God's eternal purposes have not yet reached their final fulfillment. When that time comes, His victory will be complete and absolute. If by then we haven't learned to rejoice in the truth of His goodness, we will be sent away from Him forever. The only ones who'll *remain* with Him will be those who can honestly *rejoice* with Him. But after eternity has begun, it will be too late to begin acquiring a taste for the things that make God glad. Now is the time to do that. Now is the time to modify our likes and our dislikes — so that what we like most of all is to rejoice at the joy of our Father.

Does everything in my life fill His heart with gladness, or do I constantly complain because things don't seem to be going my way? A person who has forgotten what God treasures will not be filled with joy.

OSWALD CHAMBERS

February 23
THINK TWICE BEFORE YOU PRAY FOR JUSTICE

He has not dealt with us according to our sins,
Nor punished us according to our iniquities.
Psalm 103:10

SOMETIMES WE FEEL THAT LIFE HAS NOT REPAID US FOR THE EFFORT WE'VE PUT FORTH. We know that we've made some mistakes, but even so, we feel that there's an unfair difference between what we've given and what we've gotten in return. And so we cry to God for justice. We appeal to Him to set the record straight — and to make up for the blessings that life has withheld from us.

Well, it certainly is true that in specific instances we may have been wronged and that justice has not yet been done. In such cases, the instruction of the Scriptures is clear: "Therefore let those who suffer according to the will of God commit their souls to Him in doing good, as to a faithful Creator" (1 Peter 4:19). When real injustice has been committed, it is right to make a heartfelt plea for vindication: "How long, O Lord, . . . until You judge and avenge our blood on those who dwell on the earth?" (Revelation 6:9-11).

But before we pray for God's justice, most of us need to think twice. However wrongfully we may have been treated in particular situations, if *all* the evidence bearing on our case were to be brought into the courtroom, it would be seen that, on the whole, the injustices we've *suffered* don't add up to the injustices we've *committed*. We may have been mistreated here and there, but all things considered, if we've been shortchanged, it's in the area of punishment rather than that of blessing! David had grievous enemies against whom he had legitimate complaints, but David also knew that the larger truth was this: God "has not dealt with us according to our sins, nor punished us according to our iniquities."

God is a God not only of justice, but also of patience. Most of us would say we're glad that He's been patient with us personally, punishing us less than we deserve. But if God chooses to be patient with those who've wronged us, punishing them less than they deserve, shouldn't we be grateful for that too? And besides, in some cases we may not even have been wronged. As the Lord sees things, our "enemies" may have a better case than we do.

Could it be that you deserve the unpleasantness you are now experiencing?
Did you bring it on yourself? If you are in any way to blame
then you should patiently endure the pain.
LAWRENCE SCUPOLI

February 24
MAMMON IS OUR MAJOR OBSTACLE

You cannot serve God and mammon.
Matthew 6:24

THOSE WHO ARE SERIOUSLY REACHING FORWARD IN LIFE WILL
RUN INTO NO BIGGER OBSTACLE THAN "MAMMON." Money and
material possessions, while not wrong in themselves, tend to draw
our hearts and our hopes away from God, and their temptation is
so powerful that none of us can say we've mastered the difficulty.
This is a problem that no human being can afford to ignore.

The problem of mammon affects every individual. When
Jesus said, "You cannot serve God and mammon," He was speaking to an audience that probably included more poor people than
rich. The difficult decision whom to serve, whether God or mammon, is universal. It's the fundamental choice that every person
must make who lives in the world, whether rich or poor.

Mammon has to do with *this* world. And all we have to do
to "worship" it is to make it our top priority or our main interest.
Some of what's in the world is manmade, of course, and manmade
things that are evil should be avoided completely. But even if
we're only talking about the good things God has made, we have
to make a choice whether to worship the *creation* or the *Creator*.
When we worship God, He gives us many gifts to enjoy (and then
let go of) as we make our way to heaven, but if we have such a
fixation on God's gifts that *He, the Giver*, gets only what's left over
of our love, then we've become worshipers of mammon.

The most foolish thing we can do is *assume* that we've got
it all under control. We are never in more danger that when we underestimate the power that mammon has to attract *our own hearts*.
The fact is, it has a seductive, powerful pull on virtually every
human being. And if we say we've got our this-worldly desires
under control, almost any objective party could probably look at
the way we spend our time and see that we don't. When it comes
to spiritual priorities versus worldly ones, many of us are attempting a juggling act that we're not nearly skilled enough to pull off.

Materialistic concerns and one-sided values are never sufficient to fill the
heart and mind of a human person. A life reduced to the sole dimension of
possessions, of consumer goods, of temporal concerns will never let you
discover and enjoy the full richness of your humanity. It is only in God — in
Jesus, God made man — that you will fully understand what you are.

JOHN PAUL II

LOVE TRANSFORMS SUFFERING

*Beloved, do not think it strange concerning the fiery trial which is
to try you, as though some strange thing happened to you; but rejoice
to the extent that you partake of Christ's sufferings, that when His glory is
revealed, you may also be glad with exceeding joy. 1 Peter 4:12,13*

CONCERNING SUFFERING IN THIS LIFE, THE QUESTION IS NOT WHETHER WE'LL SUFFER BUT SIMPLY HOW WE'LL DEAL WITH IT. All of us will encounter hardships and heartaches during the days of our pilgrimage. Some of these pains we'll bring upon ourselves; others will be unprovoked and undeserved. In every case, however, there is one crucial thing that lies within our control: *love*.

When we're called upon to endure any kind of unpleasantness, our frame of mind is a matter of choice on our part. Why not, then, see our suffering through the eyes of love? If we have no honorable choice but to suffer, we can at least choose to suffer lovingly. From the list of possible reasons why we would submit to pain, we can select love and let that be our motive.

It's important to recognize that *without* love, suffering has relatively little value, at least from the standpoint of the Christian. Paul went so far as to say, "Though I give my body to be burned, but have not love, it profits me nothing" (1 Corinthians 13:3). What a tragedy it would be to have drunk the bitter dregs of disappointment and defeat in this life, perhaps even being persecuted as a Christian, and then to find out that, because we had no love, our suffering was nothing more than . . . suffering.

With love, though, suffering is *transformed*. It's not that the suffering goes away. It's simply that when motivated by love, an ordeal becomes an ordeal with a high meaning and a glorious goal. It's hard to imagine how Jesus could have gotten through Gethsemane without this perspective: "Greater love has no one than this, than to lay down one's life for his friends" (John 15:13).

So "rejoice to the extent that you partake of Christ's sufferings." When you suffer, make sure you do it with a heart of love. Appreciate the privilege of suffering *with* Christ. Whatever you must endure, endure it not with bitterness or self-righteousness but with humility and reverence. Think of patience as a gift that you can give to your Father, a token of real, deep-down gratitude.

*Love makes the whole difference
between an execution and a martyrdom.*
EVELYN UNDERHILL

February 26
LOVE LETS US BE FREE

... pursue righteousness, faith, love, peace
with those who call on the Lord out of a pure heart.
2 Timothy 2:22

LOVE LIBERATES US FROM THE MAIN THING WE NEED TO BE LIBER-ATED FROM: ABSORPTION WITH OURSELVES. Sin turns us entirely inward; it twists our thinking into a selfish shape. And if we've been sinning long enough that it's become a habit, our thinking (i.e., our values, motives, desires, and goals) has probably come under the control of one basic consideration: *what we want*. Even when we do good deeds for others, we may do them because, basically, such acts of kindness help us to feel about ourselves the way we want to feel. Sin captures us in a very selfish cage.

One of the grand effects of the gospel of Christ is that it frees us from this preoccupation with ourselves. Paul said that the goal or object of Christian teaching is love: "The purpose of the commandment is love from a pure heart, from a good conscience, and from sincere faith" (1 Timothy 1:5). This kind of love is the very antithesis of selfishness. It lifts us out of the bog of self-centered thinking and sets us free to enjoy a new and better focus. It gets us out of ourselves and into a connection with all those things external to ourselves that we were meant to be related to.

Love is clearly vital to our connection to *other human beings*, especially our fellow Christians. Without the self-sacrificial love produced by the gospel, we wouldn't be able to love others, at least with the highest kind of love (John 13:34,35). But what a difference the gospel makes! "Since you have purified your souls in obeying the truth through the Spirit in sincere love of the brethren, love one another fervently with a pure heart" (1 Peter 1:22).

But more importantly, love is vital to our connection to *God*. Sin is the root of the problem, certainly, and until that barrier is removed by the gospel, we can't have any fellowship with God. But even with our past sins forgiven, there can be no fellowship if we remain self-centered. So if we're Christians, we need to let our hearts be transformed — *opened up* — by love. "Let all those who seek You rejoice and be glad in You; and let those who love Your salvation say continually, 'Let God be magnified!'" (Psalm 70:4).

O pure and sacred love! It frees us
from personal vanity. It is cleansing.
BERNARD OF CLAIRVAUX

WILDERNESS

Immediately the Spirit drove Him into the wilderness.
And He was there in the wilderness forty days, tempted by Satan,
and was with the wild beasts; and the angels ministered to Him.
Mark 1:12,13

STRANGE AS IT SEEMS, SOME THINGS GROW BEST IN BARREN PLACES. Faith and spiritual maturity are two such things. These qualities can flourish in a "wilderness" of difficulty. Just when it seems they can't survive, they do survive and even grown stronger.

Yet faith and spiritual maturity don't *automatically* grow in the midst of difficulty. They only do so when we make right choices in regard to our attitude. When tribulations test us and we're driven out into the desert to wrestle with the devil, it's critically important that we discipline our minds. The wilderness is no place for the weak-minded or the careless. Much depends on how we train ourselves to think, and the greater the difficulty, the greater the consequences that come from the attitude that we adopt.

Knowing Jesus as we do from the New Testament, what would have been His attitude toward His wilderness experience? First, He would not have been *naive* about it. He knew too much about the enemy to be flippant about the matter of temptation. Second, He would not have *complained* about being tested. His attitude would not have been one of resistance or resentment. And third, He would not have *bragged* about His ordeal. Successful though He was in dealing with difficulty, He would not have been smug about it, nor would He have thought condescendingly about others who had not suffered as much as He had. Concerning the wilderness, Jesus' thinking would have been realistic, courageous, and respectful of others, whether they had suffered much or little.

During Jesus' days in the wilderness, He was helped by the Father: "angels ministered to Him." Like Jesus, we can be sure of God's help during the times when we're tested. We need to maintain an attitude toward difficulty similar to that of Jesus, but if we will think as He thought, we'll be helped as He was helped, if not with angels then with whatever other help God knows we need. Having been helped, then, we'll have a spirit more sturdy, more healthy, and more deeply devoted to the God in whom we trust.

The lives that are getting stronger
are lives in the desert, deep-rooted in God.
OSWALD CHAMBERS

February 28
SEEING OUR HURTS AS HOMESICKNESS

For we who are in this tent groan, being burdened, not because we
want to be unclothed, but further clothed, that mortality may be swallowed
up by life. . . . So we are always confident, knowing that while we are at
home in the body we are absent from the Lord.
2 Corinthians 5:4,6

WHEN OUR HEARTS ARE HURTING, WE OFTEN FAIL TO SEE WHERE THE HURT IS REALLY COMING FROM. Specific injuries, losses, and disappointments do hurt by themselves, obviously, but most of the time the void that we think would be filled if we could have back the thing we've lost is much deeper than we think. We may think we "need" the earthly thing that we've lost, but in all likelihood the pain we feel having lost that thing is simply a reminder of a deeper, and more important, void: *the loss of direct friendship with God.* The joy of seeing our God's face is what we need most. In this life, we long for that joy with a pain that can rightly be called "homesickness." And until, in Christ, we're reunited with our Father, every hurt we experience in this world will just be a reminder of how empty our hearts are until they're filled with God.

Paul said that "while we are at home in the body we are absent from the Lord." That doesn't mean we can't have fellowship with God in this life. We can, and that fellowship involves true joy. But as long as we live in this world, broken as it is by sin and sorrow, the fellowship we can have is little more than a foretaste or down payment on the direct, face-to-face communion we'll be able to have with God in heaven (Revelation 22:4,5). Deep down, that's what we long for. And that's why our hearts hurt right now.

So how does it help us to recognize this truth? It certainly doesn't make our hurts disappear. What it does do, however, is restore our perspective on what has gone wrong. And it reminds us that God is working toward a *lasting* solution to our *real* problem. Rather than patch our wounds with a superficial bandage, He gave His Son to atone for our sins. And that opens the door to hope — hope that our hearts will be filled up when we reach *home.*

So it is that men sigh on, not knowing what the soul wants, but only
that it needs something. Our yearnings are homesickness for heaven. Our
sighings are sighings for God, just as children cry themselves to sleep away
from home and sob in their slumber, not knowing that they sob for their
parents. The soul's inarticulate moanings are the affections, yearning for the
Infinite, and having no one to tell them what it is that ails them.

HENRY WARD BEECHER

FIGHTING THE GOOD FIGHT

Fight the good fight of faith, lay hold on eternal life,
to which you were also called and have confessed the good
confession in the presence of many witnesses.
1 Timothy 6:12

THOSE WHO WISH TO "LAY HOLD ON ETERNAL LIFE" MUST "FIGHT THE GOOD FIGHT OF FAITH." There is no path to heaven that doesn't lead through territory occupied by the devil. If we're to reach our desired destination, we're going to have to fight. Indeed, it sometimes seems that we have to fight every step of the way.

We should be careful in our conclusions, though. Just because we're experiencing conflict, that does not by itself guarantee that we're on the right path. There is such a thing as carnal combat, and those who engage in it often don't have the honesty to see that their agenda is their own rather than God's. But even so, there is no denying that warfare is inevitable if we're serious about seeking God. To *reach forward*, we have to *struggle with sin*.

Are we cowardly? If we're too timid to fight for what's right, we won't make it to heaven. In Revelation 21:8, the list of those who will be lost eternally is headed by the "cowardly." If we take the course of least resistance, we'll end up somewhere other than the realm where God is. It takes courage to seek Him truthfully.

Are we careless? Considering the intensity and intelligence of our adversary, we ought not to be naive. We're being nothing more than silly if we think we can serve God faithfully and never experience any difficulty. Peter said, "*Gird up the loins of your mind,* be sober, and rest your hope fully upon the grace that is to be brought to you at the revelation of Jesus Christ" (1 Peter 1:13).

Unfortunately, we often think of the "good fight of faith" as a war against other people who (we presume) are not as committed to God's truth as we are. As often as not, however, the thing that must be fought is not an outward foe but some inward temptation. The good fight of faith is, first and foremost, a *personal struggle* against what the devil is trying to do to *us*. We need, then, to "resist him" (1 Peter 5:9). We need to fight for our lives with commitment and courage. We need, with real indignation, to draw the line and refuse to yield a single inch to our adversary.

Jesus invited us, not to a picnic, but to a pilgrimage;
not to a frolic, but to a fight.

BILLY GRAHAM

THE PURSUIT OF GOD . . . OR MERE POLEMICS?

> If anyone teaches otherwise and does not consent to wholesome
> words, even the words of our Lord Jesus Christ, and to the doctrine
> which accords with godliness, he is proud, knowing nothing, but is
> obsessed with disputes and arguments over words, from which come
> envy, strife, reviling, evil suspicions, useless wranglings of men of
> corrupt minds and destitute of the truth, who suppose that godliness
> is a means of gain. From such withdraw yourself. *1 Timothy 6:3-5*

IN THE GODLY PERSON'S LIFE, A CERTAIN AMOUNT OF CONFLICT
IS UNAVOIDABLE, YET IF WE FIND IT "THRILLING," WE PROBABLY
NEED TO TAKE AN HONEST INVENTORY OF OURSELVES. If we enjoy
engaging an opponent (as many do, quite frankly), we may find
ourselves substituting combat for the building of character. At
least some of the time, we may have to admit that we're pursuing
mere polemics rather than God Himself. Living in a society where
competition in all its myriad forms is almost a national obsession,
we need to watch out. When we find ourselves in conflict with another person over some spiritual matter, what are our real motives
for waging war? What is it that we're really seeking? And if we act
insulted when anyone questions our management of controversy,
we probably need to be cautioned more than the average person.

Warning No. 1. We should minimize controversies that are
merely verbal in nature. Not every conflict is equally significant,
and those that are simply arguments over the proper definition of
words are among the least significant. Paul warned against those
who are "obsessed with disputes and arguments over words."
We need to have the good sense and the honesty to admit when a
disagreement is more semantic than it is substantive.

Warning No. 2. We should take care not to confuse victims of
the enemy with the enemy himself. Even when controversy is necessary, it helps to remember that our human opponent is, at worst,
a victim of the enemy (2 Timothy 2:24-26). The real enemy is the
devil, and that's where our fury needs to be focused.

In the end, our religion must be more than words. The Lord
would surely say to us the same thing Paul said to the Corinthians,
"I will come to you shortly, . . . and I will know, not the words of
those who are puffed up, but the power" (1 Corinthians 4:19).

> Truth lies in character. Christ did not simply speak the truth;
> he was Truth — truth through and through,
> for truth is a thing not of words but of life and being.
>
> FREDERICK WILLIAM ROBERTSON

March 2
JOURNEY'S END

Then they cry out to the LORD in their trouble, and He brings them out of
their distresses. He calms the storm, so that its waves are still. Then they are
glad because they are quiet; so He guides them to their desired haven.
Psalm 107:28-30

THOSE WHO TAKE THE TIME TO VISUALIZE THEIR GOAL ARE NOT
MERE DREAMERS; THEY ARE THE REAL DOERS. It's not a waste of
time for us to contemplate where we're going. In fact, if we don't
make that a part of our daily devotional discipline, it's not likely
that we'll get to our destination. If we desire it, we must think
about it. We must think about it frequently and fondly.

Thinking vividly about our goal keeps it from slipping down
on our list of priorities. If we don't stop throughout the day to
remember and remind ourselves what we want most, the time will
come when something else takes the place of heaven in our hearts.
There are simply too many distractions around us. It's dangerous
to let a day go by without refreshing our focus on eternity.

None of us has the wisdom to get to our destination without
guidance, and although you may not have thought about it much,
there's a link between goal-meditation and guidance. The more
vividly we envision our goal, the more open we will be to God's
instructions about how to get there. For one thing, meditating on
where we're going helps us see the great gap between where we
are and where we want to be. It humbles us and helps us see the
superiority of His plan for getting us across the distance.

Fervently contemplating the end of our journey also has a
steadying influence on us. With spiritual goals, it is the same as
with earthly goals: the people who can endure the most hardship
are those who keep their goal most clearly in mind. So losing our
focus is a dangerous thing. It robs us of our perseverance.

But concerning our goal, the thing, above all, that must be
kept clear is that our goal is God. He Himself is the end of our
journey. Being conformed to His character is what we desire, and
being able, when the time comes, to see His face is what we long
for. It does not matter, at least not much, whether our passage is
comfortable. What matters is that we are making progress and
that our progress is toward God. In the end, those who are pure in
heart will see God. "He guides them to their desired haven."

The clearer your target, the better you will weather emotional storms.
THOMAS À KEMPIS

March 3

THE FREEDOM OF A RIGHT FOCUS

Then one of them, a lawyer, asked Him a question, testing Him, and saying,
"Teacher, which is the great commandment in the law?" Jesus said to him,
"'You shall love the LORD your God with all your heart, with all your soul,
and with all your mind.' This is the first and great commandment. And the
second is like it: 'You shall love your neighbor as yourself.' On these two
commandments hang all the Law and the Prophets." *Matthew 22:35-40*

WE ARE FREE TO CHOOSE OUR THOUGHTS, BUT WE ARE NOT FREE TO CHOOSE THE CONSEQUENCES OF THOSE THOUGHTS. For example, suppose that in a certain situation we're faced with the choice of whether to think generous thoughts or selfish thoughts. We're free to go either way, but having chosen, we need not think that we can get the results that would have come from the other choice. Ideas have always have consequences, sooner or later, and we need to see the importance of governing our thinking so as to get the consequences we desire . . . and avoid all the others.

In today's text, Jesus said that the most important commandment is to love God and the second most important, to love our neighbor. At the very least, this teaching gives us the key to constructive thinking. If we make the love of God and our neighbor the primary points around which our minds revolve, good results must surely follow. If, as the Scriptures teach, we reap what we sow (Galatians 6:7,8), there is no better sowing than to focus our love on these two objects. When we do this, the law of cause and effect will work to our benefit rather than our detriment.

But look at the price we pay when we *don't* have our hearts focused rightly: (1) Our *energy* is dissipated. (2) Our *love* is distracted. (3) Our *joy* is diluted. When we fritter ourselves away in the pursuit of worldly values, we set in motion a train of very undesirable consequences. By letting our minds take the course of least resistance, we forfeit the very best that life has to offer.

There is an important sense in which we are held captive by the thoughts we choose to think. To be liberated from enslavement to sinful thoughts, then, we must let ourselves be captivated by higher values: the love of God and His creatures. For us, freedom does not mean having no master; it means having a wise and loving Master. To bind ourselves to Him — *with committed love* — is to be set free from the consequences of every lesser love.

If thou intend not nor seek nothing else but the pleasing of God
and the profit of thy neighbor thou shalt have inward liberty.

THOMAS À KEMPIS

March 4
SEEKING GOD WITH GRATITUDE

And one of them, when he saw that he was healed, returned, and with a loud
voice glorified God, and fell down on his face at His feet, giving Him thanks.
And he was a Samaritan. So Jesus answered and said, "Were there not ten
cleansed? But where are the nine? Were there not any found who
returned to give glory to God except this foreigner?" *Luke 17:15-18*

IT IS BETTER TO SEEK GOD WITH GRATITUDE THAN WITH DESPERATE
DEMANDS. However much we seek Him when we're in need of
help that He can give us, we need to continue to seek Him after
the help has been given. Like the lone Samaritan who returned to
give thanks for having been cleansed of his leprosy, we need to
feel as deep a longing to show our appreciation to the Lord as we
felt a longing for His help in the first place. We are a selfish people
indeed if the only time we have any use for God is when we're
unable to get what we want on our own. It must be in times of
comfort, no less than times of crisis, that we seek our Father's face.

It's important to remember that we're never really able to get
what we want "on our own." Even when life is going well and we
seem to be motoring along without much help, that is never actually the case. Without God's help each instant, we would perish.
There is not a single moment when we're not completely depen-
dent on His support, and only a fool would distinguish between
times when we need God and times when we don't. The truth is,
we need Him — no, we *require* Him — at all times (Acts 17:28).

If we are to make steady progress toward God, it will help
us to work on the *consistency* with which we seek Him. Having
learned a little of His greatness, we need to seek His glory day
in and day out. God is our King, period. That fact is not altered
by the fluctuations in our circumstances or our feelings, and the
amount of attention we pay to Him ought not to depend on these
things, either. If we seek Him *for His sake,* that reason will be present twenty-four hours of every day, whether we feel needy or not.
For most of us, this consistency takes some learning, but we can
do it. Paul said, "Everywhere and in all things *I have learned* both
to be full and to be hungry, both to abound and to suffer need"
(Philippians 4:12). It's not easy, but like him, we can learn how to
abound without forgetting God or failing to give thanks.

You pray in your distress and in your need; would that you might also
pray in the fullness of your joy and in your days of abundance.

KAHLIL GIBRAN

March 5
THE TROUBLES OF A TEMPORARY HOME

For we know that the whole creation groans and labors
with birth pangs together until now. Romans 8:22

WHEN BAD DAYS COME, WE NEED TO PAY ATTENTION TO THE RE-
MINDER THAT WE'RE BEING GIVEN. Good days are reminders
too, of course; they remind us that God created the world. But bad
days should remind us that the present world, tragically broken
by our own sinfulness, is a dangerous place to settle down.

If our hearts are set on God, we are on our way to a place that
can truly be called home. A "rest" awaits us, if we're among the
"people of God" (Hebrews 4:9). But we haven't yet reached our
rest, and until we do, we are sojourners — temporary residents in
a country not our own, strangers in a strange land.

But we tend to forget, don't we? We forget that we're aliens,
and we fall into the habit of thinking like permanent citizens
who're quite at home here and have no desire to leave.

Because that's a dangerous tendency, God sees to it that the
fields of our thinking get plowed up from time to time. In the lives
of some, it may be a "thorn in the flesh." For others, it may the
tragic loss of something they thought they couldn't bear to lose. It
may be the unending difficulty of some unpleasantness that won't
go away. It may be temptation. It may be failure. It may be sickness or the specter of death. But God loves His faithful people too
much to let them forget the home He has prepared for them.

What do we do with these reminders, as painful as they often
are? At the very least, we should be grateful for them. But also, we
should bear them with humility, dignity, and courage. And above
all, we should not fail to let them have their intended effect on us.
If God is reminding us, we should let ourselves be reminded and
not waste the care that He's bestowing upon us.

Moses spoke powerfully when he recalled Israel's hardships:
"[God] humbled you, allowed you to hunger, and fed you with
manna which you did not know nor did your fathers know, that
He might make you know that man shall not live by bread alone;
but man lives by every word that proceeds from the mouth of the
LORD" (Deuteronomy 8:3). Some things we dare not forget, and
from time to time, these things God will "make us know."

Happy is the trouble that loosens our grip of earth.
CHARLES HADDON SPURGEON

March 6

NO TIME FOR NEGLIGENCE

Be sober, be vigilant; because your adversary the devil walks about
like a roaring lion, seeking whom he may devour. *1 Peter 5:8*

WATCHFULNESS IS AN ATTITUDE WE CAN HARDLY DO WITHOUT. God happens to have a great adversary, and if we take God's side, that means we have the same adversary that God does. In his arrogant rebellion against God, Satan is bent on the destruction of every personal being God ever made. To the battle-field of the human heart, the devil brings weapons of considerable craftiness, and our spiritual survival will be extremely unlikely, if not impossible, if we don't wake up and watch out. "Be sober, be vigilant," is what Peter said, and he wasn't wasting words.

Yet negligence is a widespread problem, and not only among those who are foolish and indifferent. All too often, those who've been around long enough to know better still show little concern. Consider two "occasions" when we may let our guard down:

Spiritual maturity. Curiously enough, the more mature we be-come in the Lord, the less we sometimes see the need for a humble and cautious mentality. Secretly, we may even pride ourselves on our ability to handle certain temptations — temptations that we wouldn't advise the less mature to expose themselves to. But don't we see the difference between courage and foolhardiness?

Old age. As we get closer to heaven, it's natural that we cease to be actively concerned about certain dangers. We begin to face life, as Mark Twain said, "with the serene confidence of a gambler with an ace up his sleeve." Yet we still need to be careful. Daniel was ninety years old or more when he had his lion's den experi-ence (Daniel 6:1-23). And Abraham was at least a hundred and ten before the Lord decided it was time for the most excruciating test of his faith (Genesis 22:1-19). At their age, who would have thought such struggles would still have to be endured? Is our enemy so blinded by his hatred that he refuses to give up?

As for God, His victory is absolutely certain. The decisive battle was painfully fought at the Cross and decisively won in the Resurrection. But as for us, *we've not yet made our final choice.* "Be faithful until death" (Revelation 2:10) is not a command that can be put on autopilot, and right now is no time for negligence.

You must watch, pray, and fight. Expect your last battle to be the most
difficult, for the enemy's fiercest charge is reserved for the end of the day.
CHARLES HADDON SPURGEON

March 7
ESTABLISHED HEARTS

You also be patient. Establish your hearts, for the
coming of the Lord is at hand. *James 5:8*

ON THE EVE OF HIS CRUCIFIXION, JESUS SAID TO HIS DISCIPLES,
"LET NOT YOUR HEART BE TROUBLED; YOU BELIEVE IN GOD, BE-
LIEVE ALSO IN ME" (JOHN 14:1). No doubt He would say the same
thing to us. If His followers needed to hold on and keep hope
alive back then, it's no less important for us to keep a steady head
during the difficulties of the present day. Whatever comes to pass
in this frustrating world, we must not let it throw us into doubt or
despair. The King is coming back to set things straight, and it may
be sooner rather than later. "Be patient," James wrote. "Establish
your hearts, for the coming of the Lord is at hand."

We are taught in the gospel to be a people of hope, and the
hope we can have is much more than wishful thinking or blind
optimism. It's an optimism based on solid, historical evidence that
God can be counted on to keep His word. After Jesus was buried,
His tomb was found empty, just as He had promised it would
be. That empty tomb has never had any adequate explanation —
except that Jesus was actually raised from the dead. And if the
Resurrection is true, then He's everything He claimed to be: our
God, our Savior, and our Lord. If the Resurrection is true, there is
hope! "In the world you will have tribulation," He once said, "but
be of good cheer, I have overcome the world" (John 16:33).

Wisdom, then, is a bittersweet thing. Solomon said, "In much
wisdom is much grief" (Ecclesiastes 1:18). The more we know of
the world, the sadder it is to contemplate the tragedy of our sin
and its consequences. But the brokenness of the world, as sad as it
is, is not the whole story. Jesus has defeated our enemy and taken
the sting out of his worst weapon. If we've obeyed the gospel
faithfully, then "our citizenship is in heaven, from which we also
eagerly wait for the Savior, the Lord Jesus Christ" (Philippians 3:20).

God hasn't finished redeeming us yet, but there's no doubt
that He will. Our responsibility is to wait — and to do so with
delight rather than dreariness. However many things there are to
endure, there are even more to enjoy. Among these, there is the
strong love of a Savior who said, "Let not your heart be troubled."

All human wisdom is summed up
in two words — wait and hope.
ALEXANDER DUMAS

DAYS WELL SPENT

See then that you walk circumspectly, not as fools but as wise,
redeeming the time, because the days are evil.
Ephesians 5:15,16

WE HAVE ONLY A LIMITED NUMBER OF DAYS TO LIVE IN THIS WORLD, AND IT'S IMPORTANT TO HAVE THE CONFIDENCE THAT WE'VE SPENT THEM WELL. We need to be able to go to bed each night knowing that we've used the resources of that day to the best of our personal abilities and have "redeemed" the time.

This doesn't mean that every single day must be spent in full-throttle, no-time-for-leisure "work." The best use of some days is to rest. In the Law of Moses, it should be noted, God *required* the people of Israel to rest one day out of every seven. And though the Sabbath law does not apply directly to us today, the point should not be missed: God understands our need for rest and replenishment, and the *correct* use of many days is to engage in those very things. "Days well spent" does not mean "all work and no play."

On any given day, however, whatever should be done with *that* day — whether work, play, or some combination of the two — that is what we should do. As the days come and go, we need to have the good feeling that we're using life as God wants us to use it, rather than wasting it doing things that were never meant to be done or things that were meant for someone else to do.

For fallible creatures like us, living the godly life comes down to the business of making regular *improvement*. Reaching forward means doing a little better with each day than was done with the day before. If we take a moment or two at the end of the day to reflect on what we've done (and it's wise to make that a habit), it's a wonderful feeling to know that, with that day, we've taken a step forward in our stewardship of life — we've brought another thing or two under the benevolence of God's will and made ourselves a bit more completely the vessels of God's glory. In an age obsessed with "self-esteem," we should understand that healthy self-respect can only come from hearing God say to us at day's end, "Well done, good and faithful servant" (Matthew 25:21).

Begin well and go on to better. Do everything for the glory of God
and the benefit of others. Consider time lost if you do not use it
to at least think of the glory of God and seek for a way to do
something for someone else's advantage.

JOHN BRADFORD

HINTS OF GLORY

All Your works shall praise You, O LORD,
And Your saints shall bless You.
Psalm 145:10

E VERY INSTANCE OF BEAUTY IN THE NATURAL WORLD IS A HINT
THAT POINTS TOWARD THE GLORY OF GOD HIMSELF. Whatever
God has made bears some resemblance to its Maker. Like the artist
whose every brush stroke says something about the artist himself,
God has left evidence of Himself in the things that He has made
(Acts 14:17). The tokens of God's glory in this world are beckoning
us to another world, one with a far greater glory.

We, however, won't "get the point" of these hints of glory if
we don't stop to think about them. If we're so busy with the details of our self-centered concerns that we never notice the works
of God, it should be no surprise that we have difficulty maintaining our faith. With everything that He has created, God is inviting
us to meditate on Him, the Creator. When we don't "stop to smell
the roses," it's not only enjoyment that we miss, it's also worship!

But perhaps we do notice the hints of God's glory around us,
we just don't experience them very deeply. If so, we'd do ourselves a favor by learning to savor these things and relish them.
When I was a boy, I could derive extraordinary pleasure from a
Hershey chocolate bar. I wouldn't just eat it, I would *contemplate* it
as I ate! With each small rectangle, I would taste it just as long as I
could, actually thinking about how good it tasted. Wouldn't it be
wise to enjoy God's works with this kind of lingering thoughtful-
ness? We need not just to taste them but to *relish* them.

If we long to know God, we'll be eager to enjoy each evidence
of Him in the world, and these hints of glory will send us into the
Scriptures to learn of His character. But think about this: all that
we can learn of God now is only a small portion of what is waiting
to be learned in eternity, when the faithful will surely say to God
what the Queen of Sheba said to Solomon, "It was a true report
which I heard in my own land about your words and your wisdom. . . . and indeed the half was not told me. Your wisdom and
prosperity exceed the fame of which I heard" (1 Kings 10:6,7).

Place all your delight in Him. Say, "O my God,
You are the universal source of all good things! The perfections
of Your creation are but a faint shadow of Your glory."
LAWRENCE SCUPOLI

March 10
GOD'S WORKS: SEEN AND UNSEEN

"Which is easier, to say to the paralytic, 'Your sins are forgiven you,'
or to say, 'Arise, take up your bed and walk'? But that you may know
that the Son of Man has power on earth to forgive sins" — He said to the
paralytic, "I say to you, arise, take up your bed, and go to your house."
Mark 2:9-11

MOST OF US TEND TO HOLD OUR TRUST IN RESERVE UNTIL WE'VE CHECKED THINGS OUT FOR OURSELVES. When told about something that's hard to believe, we disbelieve it until we have seen it "with our own eyes." We've been taught not to be naive or gullible, and we know that a certain amount of skepticism is healthy.

Yet this tendency, if carried too far, can get us into trouble. While it's good to do our own thinking and double-check before we put our trust in something, it's not good to close our minds with a rigid I-won't-believe-it-until-I-see-it-myself attitude. In regard to God, many of the most important things that we need to believe lie in the realm of spiritual reality. It is not possible (at least not yet) for us to personally verify the truth of these things with our own senses, and it's a foolish person indeed whose spiritual knowledge is limited to what he himself has seen.

When God asks us to accept unseen realities, however, He does not ask us to do so without any reason or support. If there is something in the spiritual realm that we need to accept His word for, He never asks for that acceptance without having offered a sufficient guarantee in the physical realm that His word is dependable. Jesus, for example, asked His hearers to believe that He could forgive the sins of the paralyzed man in Mark 2:1-12, a spiritual claim that they certainly could not verify with their own senses. Yet He backed up that claim by physically healing the man. In effect, He was saying, "Believe that I can do the impossible in the spiritual realm, which you can't see, based on My having done the impossible in the physical realm, which you *can* see."

Everything that God has ever done in the physical world, from the first moment of creation until now, shouts to us powerfully concerning the kind of God that He is: almighty, wise, good, and, above all, *trustworthy*. If in the Scriptures He asks us to take His word for certain things, it's only after He has *proven* Himself to be perfectly truthful — time and time and time again.

All I have seen teaches me to trust the Creator for all I have not seen.
RALPH WALDO EMERSON

March 11
INSATIABLE

He who loves silver will not be satisfied with silver;
Nor he who loves abundance, with increase.
This also is vanity. *Ecclesiastes 5:10*

MOST PEOPLE RECOGNIZE AT LEAST SOMETHING OF THE UNIQUE-NESS OF HUMAN NATURE. We are *personal* beings. Among all the many forms of life on our planet, even the higher forms of animal life, we are distinct. We can have relationships with other beings, especially those of our own kind, that are richer and deeper than the relationships any other creatures are capable of. For better or worse, we are "people," and we have needs that can only be filled by other beings with a similar nature. A human being who spends his life dealing always with "things" and never with other persons is almost always going to find life flat and unfulfilling.

Yet we are more than personal beings: we are also *spiritual* beings. There is a need within us for something beyond what even the other personal beings in this world can provide. That need, of course, is for the God who created us, the God who transcends the limits of the physical universe in which we live. Having been created by Him, we need Him. This need is not optional. It is not something we decide to have or not to have. It comes as a part of our creation in the image of God Himself (Genesis 1:27).

We can no more eradicate our spiritual nature than we can eradicate our personal nature. We can't do away with our need for God without destroying ourselves. We can, however, *ignore* that need and waste our lives attempting to slake our thirst with other satisfactions. In the long run, it doesn't work, but many of us spend our lives doing it anyway, and a sad emptiness is the result.

We need to pay more attention to the spiritual yearnings that tug at us. That nagging feeling that there must be "something more" to life than what we've experienced is an important clue to the meaning of life. There is a great deal more to life than the physical fulfillments — even the *personal* fulfillments — that are available to us now. Eternity is in our hearts (Ecclesiastes 3:11), and without God our desires will always be . . . insatiable.

Nothing less than God can fill our soul. Its capacity is designed
for God alone. If we try to fill it with earthly things, we will never
be satisfied. Lovers of God will be at peace when they are filled
with God through desire and meditation.

RICHARD ROLLE

March 12
WE NEED MORE THAN BETTER MOODS

You therefore, beloved, since you know this beforehand, beware lest you
also fall from your own steadfastness, being led away with the error of the
wicked; but grow in the grace and knowledge of our Lord and Savior
Jesus Christ. To Him be the glory both now and forever. Amen.
2 Peter 3:17,18

ALTHOUGH WE'D OFTEN LIKE TO FEEL BETTER EMOTIONALLY, THAT IS NOT THE THING THAT WE NEED MOST. What we need, much more than any "inspirational" uplift, is to make *actual progress in the quality of our character*. The spiritual life is not primarily about *feeling* better. It's about *change* for the better. It's about growth. It's about *real, objective movement toward God*. Regardless of the fluctuation of our feelings, being a Christian means growing "in the grace and knowledge of our Lord and Savior Jesus Christ."

Reevaluation. The daily question we need to ask ourselves is not "How am I feeling?" but "Where am I in relation to God?" Paul wrote, "Examine yourselves as to whether you are in the faith" (2 Corinthians 13:5). Answering that question honestly may not give us a cozy fireside feeling, but it will open the door to something we need more than better moods: genuine growth.

Repentance. Honest reevaluation of ourselves won't help us, of course, unless we have the courage and the will to make the changes that our self-inventory has pointed out a need for. And when changes need to be made, we don't need a speaker or writer who'll make us feel wonderful, just as we are. We need a friend who'll provoke us to repent and move forward in our character.

Renewal of Commitment. The chances are good that many of us already know about areas in which we need to improve, based on past examinations of ourselves and decisions to do better. Falling backwards is a habit that we all have. So the third thing we need, more than better moods, is to get a fresh grip on our commitments every day. Significant spiritual progress comes from the frequent remembering — and remaking — of our promises to God.

So do you feel better after reading this? Maybe you do, and maybe you don't. But today, you can decide to seek God faithfully whether your feelings are flowing in that direction or not.

That man is perfect in faith who can come to God in the utter dearth of his
feelings and his desires, without a glow or an aspiration, with the weight of
low thoughts, failures, neglects, and wandering forgetfulness, and say to
him, "Thou art my refuge because thou art my home."

GEORGE MACDONALD

March 13
BEARING WHAT WE NEED TO HEAR

I still have many things to say to you,
but you cannot bear them now.
John 16:12

LEARNING WHAT WE NEED TO KNOW IS A GRADUAL PROCESS. At the present time, none of us can say that we've received all of the truth that the Lord has to impart. That is why serious study of the Scriptures should be a part of our daily activity. Each day, we need to be adding a little to our storehouse of knowledge.

But coming to a full understanding of God's will involves more than study. Many things that we come across in our study will not "sink in" because we're not yet ready to hear them. Perhaps we've not experienced the things in life that would allow us to see the real significance of what the Lord is saying. Perhaps we don't have the desire for obedience that would let us recognize the truth of particular passages. Or perhaps our study habits are not mature enough for us to penetrate the meaning of certain texts. There may be many reasons, but the bottom line is that we don't always "hear" what God's word is saying to us.

To His apostles, Jesus said, "I still have many things to say to you, but you cannot bear them now." These things would be made available to them later on, when they were more ready to receive them. This illustrates the fact that God is patient with those who are trying to learn. If we honestly want to do His will, He will see that we have the time and opportunity to learn. He will not ask us to understand more than we're able to receive at the present time.

But therein lies the problem. Often, it is not our lack of *ability* but our lack of *willingness* to hear. As the Jewish proverb puts it, "The truth is not always what we want to hear." And even when the problem is a lack of ability, that lack of ability may be the result of *neglect* on our part. If we've not made growth in obedience a priority, it should come as no surprise that our understanding is immature and undeveloped. And if this is the case, we need to repent. We need to set ourselves the goal of greater obedience.

Lord, give me the strength to bear the full impact of the truth as it applies to me. Help me, for the sake of Your glory, to be willing to hear whatever I need to hear. Speak, Lord, for your servant hears.

We are the vessels, the containers, so that the first work
after the new birth is to cultivate the habit of receptivity.

NORMAN GRUBB

March 14
YOUR WRECKAGE CAN BE REPAIRED!

. . . Christ Jesus came into the world to save sinners, of whom I am chief.
However, for this reason I obtained mercy, that in me first Jesus Christ
might show all longsuffering, as a pattern to those who are going
to believe on Him for everlasting life. *1 Timothy 1:15,16*

UNDER THE INFLUENCE OF THE GOSPEL OF CHRIST, SAUL OF
TARSUS BECAME A RADICALLY DIFFERENT MAN. The change
was not superficial or temporary; it was deep and lasting. And
later, writing now as Paul the apostle, he could offer himself as
an example to prove just how sinful a person can be and still be
saved by the gospel: "I obtained mercy, that in me first Jesus Christ
might show all longsuffering, as a pattern to those who are going
to believe on Him for everlasting life." If the prosecutor's charge is
that a truly wicked person can never change, Paul is "Exhibit A" to
the contrary. He is a courage-giving "pattern" to anyone who has
ever worried that they might be a hopeless case or a lost cause.

Most people, if they're honest, know what it's like to struggle
with deeply ingrained character flaws. As we struggle to remove
these flaws, we become frustrated. In time, we may come to doubt
that real change is even possible. Sometimes we start thinking that
way because we've been influenced by *determinism,* which says
that at birth we are already "determined"; whatever we "are,"
that's what we'll always "be." At other times, we may be plagued
with a *victim mentality.* We see ourselves as the victims of circumstances and influences that are more than we can handle.

My suspicion, however, is that most of the time our problem
is just plain *discouragement.* The devil fights against us with a war
of attrition; he keeps coming back, coming back, and coming back,
trying to wear us down. After a while, our cause looks like it's lost.

But the great hope of the gospel is that, while life lasts, none
of us is a lost cause. Our defeats need not be final. Our failures
need not be fatal. Real change for the better is always possible.

Whoever you are, my friend, believe this: *your wreckage can
be repaired.* If God can turn a fire-breathing, murderous Pharisee
into the great apostle of grace, he can surely help you get pointed
in the right direction. Your fate is not fixed, and you're not just a
victim. You are a living person capable of great growth.

When you feel that all is lost, sometimes
the greatest gain is ready to be yours.
THOMAS À KEMPIS

March 15
NO NEED TO KNOW THE TERRITORY

*And see, now I go bound in the spirit to Jerusalem, not knowing
the things that will happen to me there. Acts 20:22*

IN SECULAR AFFAIRS, WE USUALLY WANT TO KNOW WHAT'S GOING
TO HAPPEN. Much of our planning is based on prediction: how
can we be prepared if we don't know what events we'll have to
deal with? And so we expend a lot of energy trying to forecast the
future. A successful and safe "journey," we think, depends on having a map of the exact territory we'll be passing through. And not
only do we try to forecast the future, we try to control it. As much
as possible, we want to pick our itinerary for ourselves.

In spiritual affairs, however, we have to learn a different kind
of security. As Andrew Dhuse said, "God's will is not an itinerary
but an attitude." We aren't told what the future holds. The journey
may take us along any number of different routes, none of which
we can predict or be prepared for. So no map is given to us, only a
Compass, and we're to be content to be guided by God.

In the course of doing the Lord's work, Paul needed to go to
Jerusalem, where there might be danger. But Paul could live with
uncertainty. With his heart fixed on God, he didn't need to know
what was going to happen: "I go bound in the spirit to Jerusalem,
not knowing the things that will happen to me there."

Abraham is another example of how this works. Comfortable
in Ur, Abraham was called upon to let go of the familiar, predictable path he'd gotten used to. "Get out of your country," God said,
"from your family and from your father's house, to a land that I
will show you" (Genesis 12:1). And Abraham trusted God enough
to let Him decide what territory would have to be traversed. "He
went out, not knowing where he was going" (Hebrews 11:8).

Today, most of us have some definite ideas about the kind
of life we want. We have one or two scenarios in our minds that
describe the paths we'd prefer to take between here and heaven.
But we need to be careful. We must not hold on to those scenarios
so tightly that we can't let go of them. And we must not be too de-
pendent on knowing in advance what kind of lives we're going to
end up with. The truth is, we don't *need* to know the territory. We
don't need a map. We only need a Compass that we can count on.

> Abraham did not know the way,
> but he knew the Guide.
> LEE ROBERSON

March 16
DESPERATE DAYS

For we do not want you to be ignorant, brethren, of our trouble
which came to us in Asia: that we were burdened beyond measure,
above strength, so that we despaired even of life.
2 Corinthians 1:8

DAYS COME NOW AND THEN WHEN WE CAN SEE SO LITTLE HOPE THAT GIVING UP THE STRUGGLE SEEMS TO BE THE ONLY THING WE CAN DO. There are times when the burdens are not just heavy, they are "beyond measure, above strength," as Paul said. His ordeal in Asia was so severe, he said that he "despaired even of life." And while our own troubles may not be so dangerous that our physical lives are threatened, most of us do know what it means to despair. We know what it's like to be in such darkness that our hearts harbor little hope that we'll ever see the light again.

On such desperate days, we need, first of all, to be honest. If the truth is that we're struggling to hang on to hope, we need to acknowledge our hopelessness — to ourselves, to God, and perhaps to some trusted friend who can encourage us. There's no need to pretend that we're stronger or braver than we really are.

But having been honest, we need also to be "stubborn." We need to have enough holy hardheadedness about us that we simply refuse to let the devil defeat us. There may be many things we can't do, but we can choose to keep going a little while longer, even though there seems to be little point in doing so. If we're going to go down, we at least can go down swinging.

We never display a finer faith than when we keep on going, against all odds. When the obstacles seem insurmountable but we continue to reach forward — and *upward* — that's when we show ourselves most clearly to be creatures made in God's image. Faith, trust, and hope are qualities that only personal beings can have, and that's what we are: *personal* beings. Not helpless victims, but persons with the wondrous and undeniable power of *choice*.

So on desperate days, let's do the one thing that frustrates the enemy of our souls the most: let's keep going. He (and only he) would like to see us give up, but we can say no to that option. When we're hurting and the hurt seems nearly unbearable, we can take at least one more step. Our God is worth that much and more.

We all need faith for desperate days. . . . Desperate days
are the stepping-stones on the paths of light.
S. CHADWICK

DEEP JOY

Yes, we had the sentence of death in ourselves, that we should not trust in
ourselves but in God who raises the dead, who delivered us from so great a
death, and does deliver us; in whom we trust that He will still deliver us,
you also helping together in prayer for us, that thanks may be given by many
persons on our behalf for the gift granted to us through many.
2 Corinthians 1:9-11

GREAT DISCOURAGEMENT, AND EVEN DESPAIR, CAN BE THE SOIL
IN WHICH DEEP JOY GROWS. If we survive our desperate days
(and survive is what we should always choose to do), we can find
ourselves afterward having a more responsive heart. Suffering can
teach us how to rejoice in a way that is more genuine and true.

Not all joys are created equal. Some are richer and deeper
than others. We need the lighter kind, of course, the many casual
joys of ordinary living that we should never take for granted. But
we also need the more meaningful joys, those that resonate within
us at deeper levels. And the deepest joys of this kind are those that
we've "discovered" in the midst of despair. These joys have, in a
manner of speaking, been bought at a higher price, and they are
exceedingly valuable. We all know how much these deeper joys
mean to us, yet we often forget that they couldn't be ours if the
price of pain and hardship had not been paid.

Hardships give God an opportunity to show us His grace, and
the display of God's grace gives us an opportunity to pour out our
gratitude to Him. Not only that, when God blesses us, that gives
others an occasion for thanksgiving too. So Paul, for example,
could say that he was glad for his own deliverance from death
because it gave his brethren reason to rejoice: "that thanks may be
given by many persons on our behalf for the gift granted to us."

So we should learn to give thanks for the difficulties that
make possible a greater joy. The point is not that we should go
looking for pain and suffering, but rather that when these things
happen to appear in our lives, we should respond to them rightly.
A right response would include, among other things, the attitudes
of *acceptance* and *thankfulness*. We can be thankful not for the pain
but for its result: a heart more joyously fixed on God. Slowly but
surely, God is conforming us to His character. Sometimes with
pleasure and sometimes with pain, He is teaching us what love is.

If joy is not rooted in the soil of suffering, it is shallow.

C. F. D. MOULE

IN A BROKEN WORLD, WE YEARN FOR UNITY

For it pleased the Father that in [Christ] all the fullness should dwell, and by
Him to reconcile all things to Himself, by Him, whether things on earth or
things in heaven, having made peace through the blood of His cross.
Colossians 1:19,20

ONE OF THE THINGS THAT ALMOST EVERY PERSON LONGS FOR IS
UNITY. We use words like *togetherness, harmony,* and *wholeness*
as positive words that describe something we wish there was more
of in our lives. Wouldn't we dearly love to have more peace within
ourselves, with our neighbors, and, most of all, with our God? Yes,
we would, and we even like to imagine a physical world where
the forces of nature weren't at war, a peaceable kingdom where
things weren't torn apart by tornadoes and typhoons.

Yet if unity is what we desire, there is precious little of it to
be found in the world that now is. Here, the norm is enmity, not
unity. We don't have to look any further than the newspaper — or
in the mirror — to know that many, many things have gone awry.

The promise of the gospel, of course, is that God is working
toward a great reconciliation of all things in Jesus Christ. In Him
all the "fullness" dwells, and in Him God has solved the problem
of sin, which is the root cause of every kind of brokenness, both inside us and in the outside world. "Having made peace through the
blood of His cross," God is now moving the history of this world
to a triumphant conclusion. The time is coming when everything
will be put back together, and all who are willing to live in the harmony of His wisdom will enjoy the peacefulness of that wisdom
forever. When that day dawns, there will be no more brokenness,
no more being "at odds" with anyone or anything. Every trace
of rebellion and disruption will have been justly banished from
God's presence, never to trouble the peace of His kingdom again.

But the time for that has not yet come, though our prayer is
that it soon will: "O Lord, come!" (1 Corinthians 16:22). For now,
we are called to live with a certain "tension" in our hearts: the
tension that comes from deeply longing for something that's not
available in this world. This tension, this longing, is not meant to
discourage us; it's meant to teach us what we need.

Our spiritual thirst keeps us yearning for the unity of all things
and for communion with the divine. But we seek in vain
for perfection within creation.

PAUL CIHOLAS

March 19
WHAT'S OUR PROBLEM?

*For what profit is it to a man if he gains
the whole world, and loses his own soul?*
Matthew 16:26

DIFFICULTIES ARE NOT HARD TO FIND. The average person's life presents a thorny thicket of problems that have to be dealt with. Indeed, on some days it seems that we do little more than run from one problem to the next. We can hardly get one fire put out before another breaks out somewhere else.

But out of all the things that need fixing, which one needs fixing the most? Which issue in life is the main issue? One measure of our spiritual maturity (and even our earthly maturity) is the way in which we prioritize our problems. The immature give most of their attention to problems that are of no more than secondary importance, while the more mature see the things that matter most and give their primary attention to those things. So if the way we spend our time and the problems we choose to work on are any indication, how mature can we say that we are, really and truly?

Anyone who has read the New Testament will know that it takes a definite position on the question of what's important and what's not. Jesus put it in the form of a question: "For what profit is it to a man if he gains the whole world, and loses his soul?" *Our main problem is our broken relationship with God.* As long as that problem goes unfixed, we are pathetic and profitless creatures, even if we're able to fix every other problem in the world.

Millions of people would say *Amen!* to the importance of God — but these same people spend most of their time working on issues other than their relationship to Him. Our schedule books simply don't support our claim that spiritual concerns are No. 1 in our lives. We rush through our days, accomplishing little more than the rearrangement of deck chairs on a ship that is sinking.

The daily challenge that confronts us is not only to *see* what most needs to be worked on, but to *keep* that concern in the cross hairs of our attention. In the end, it will be evident that most of the "urgent" matters that tried to claim our attention were simply inconsequential. Before it's too late, we need to stop our frantic fixing of things "out there" and start working on things "in here."

It is not a world out of joint that makes our problem
but the shipwrecked soul in it.
P. T. FORSYTH

March 20
SEEKING THE LIGHT OF GOD

And this is the condemnation, that the light has come
into the world, and men loved darkness rather than light,
because their deeds were evil. For everyone practicing evil hates
the light and does not come to the light, lest his deeds should
be exposed. But he who does the truth comes to the light,
that his deeds may be clearly seen, that they
have been done in God. *John 3:19-21*

GOD'S TRUTH IS ALWAYS REPRESENTED IN THE SCRIPTURES AS "LIGHT." In contrast to the darkness, in which we may not "see" clearly and may mistake one thing for another, the light shows everything for what it really is. When God speaks, we are presented with the *facts:* about Him, about His offer of forgiveness for our sins, and about what He would have us to do. As Oswald Chambers said, "Light is God's point of view."

But we don't always want to hear God's point of view, particularly when it reveals the need for serious adjustments to be made in our character and conduct. "The light has come into the world, and men loved darkness rather than light, because their deeds were evil." Darkness hides much that light would uncover.

So we never make a more important decision than when we decide what our attitude will be toward the light of God. Will we actively seek it and then gratefully welcome it? Or will we run from it and resent the pain that it causes to our conscience?

It may indeed be painful, at least at first, to "come to the light." If we've been in the darkness for a long time, we've probably gotten used to a certain kind of comfort, the false comfort that comes not from things being well with us but from our failing to see how seriously off course we've been. Darkness has allowed us to live with a false sense of security, perhaps for a very long time.

But light changes all of that. In the light, we see our situation as it is. We see the truth about the gaping chasm between where we are and where God wants us to be. We see the ugly fact of our irresponsibility, our ingratitude, our rebellion. We see our sin.

Our destiny, then, hangs upon our decision about the light. Either we'll accept the momentary pain of repentance, or we'll suffer the eternal pain of regret. Jesus said that it is the *truth* that will make us free (John 8:32). Is that what we seek or not?

I am not judged by the light I have,
but by the light I have refused to accept.
OSWALD CHAMBERS

A LOVE WORTH DYING FOR

For I am already being poured out as a drink offering,
and the time of my departure is at hand.
2 Timothy 4:6

LIFE IS ONE OF OUR MOST PRECIOUS POSSESSIONS, BUT IT SHOULD NEVER BECOME AN IDOL TO US. Life is good, but it is not God. There are things more valuable than life, and one of these is *honor.*

When Daniel's three friends, Shadrach, Meshach, and Abed-Nego, were commanded to worship the image that King Nebuchadnezzar had set up or be thrown into the fires of a great furnace, they chose to die, if need be, rather than back out of their promises to God. They said, "Our God whom we serve is able to deliver us from the burning fiery furnace, and He will deliver us from your hand, O king. But if not, let it be known to you, O king, that we do not serve your gods, nor will we worship the gold image which you have set up" (Daniel 3:17,18). Their vows to God weren't negotiable, and their love for Him was worth dying for.

I once had a friend who told me that he'd entered into a serious business contract that had ended up causing him great emotional pain. Keeping the contract had become so difficult that he felt he simply could not continue to do what was right. "If I don't break this contract, I am literally going to die," he said. But even if that were true (and it probably wasn't), wouldn't death with honor be preferable to life with dishonor? In God's scale of values, a great blessing is pronounced on the person of integrity who "swears to his own hurt and does not change" (Psalm 15:4).

Many of us are plagued by the lack of any worth-dying-for love in our lives. As far as God is concerned, we have no commitments to Him that are not negotiable. He gets our reverence only up to the point where He stands between us and the "life" we think we deserve, at which point we're often willing to deny Him.

But there's a great irony here: if we give up our honor to hold on to life, the result is not more life but a losing of all that life was ever meant to be! Jesus said, "He who loves his life will lose it, and he who hates his life in this world will keep it for eternal life" (John 12:25). We do ourselves a huge favor, and more important, we show the greatest honor to God, when we *loosen our grip on life.*

Pray that your loneliness may spur you into finding
something to live for, great enough to die for.
DAG HAMMARSKJÖLD

March 22
POVERTY AND WEALTH

> So when Jesus heard these things, He said to him, "You still lack
> one thing. Sell all that you have and distribute to the poor, and you
> will have treasure in heaven; and come, follow Me." But when he
> heard this, he became very sorrowful, for he was very rich.
> *Luke 18:22,23*

WE DO WELL TO REMEMBER THE DIFFERENCE BETWEEN TEMPORAL WEALTH AND SPIRITUAL WEALTH. It is possible to have one without the other. Consider that there are four categories or conditions of "prosperity" in which we may find ourselves:

(1) *Poor, both temporally and spiritually.* The person who has no treasures of any kind, either in this world or in heaven, is destitute in the worst possible way. This person is poor inside and out.

(2) *Rich, both temporally and spiritually.* This sometimes happens, as in the case of Abraham (Genesis 13:2), but it is exceedingly rare. Few of us are exceptions to the general rule that "it is easier for a camel to go through the eye of a needle than for a rich man to enter the kingdom of God" (Matthew 19:24). The tendency of earthly treasures to steal time and attention that ought to go to God is a tendency stronger than most people can resist.

(3) *Poor temporally, but rich spiritually.* To the church in Smyrna, Jesus said He knew of their poverty. Nevertheless, He said, "You are rich" (Revelation 2:9). We may lack the wealth that the world enjoys now, but if we've obeyed the gospel and are faithful to our Lord, then we're the possessors of a wealth that time can't touch, an "inheritance incorruptible and undefiled and that does not fade away, reserved in heaven for you" (1 Peter 1:4).

(4) *Rich temporally, but poor spiritually.* Unfortunately, this is how many of us who live in the affluent nations of the world would have to be classified. We've prospered financially, and yet our souls are starving. We have money, but money is all we have. We don't see how poor we really are, like the Laodiceans whom the Lord rebuked: "You say, 'I am rich, have become wealthy, and have need of nothing' — and do not know that you are wretched, miserable, poor, blind, and naked" (Revelation 3:17).

If the Lord were to tell us to get rid of what we have, what would we do? Would we, like the rich young ruler, refuse to become poor that we might gain the thing that is wealth indeed?

He is poor who has nothing but money.
ANONYMOUS

SINS OF IGNORANCE, SINS OF WEAKNESS

For we all stumble in many things.
James 3:2

EVEN WHEN WE'RE SINCERELY COMMITTED TO GOD, THERE ARE TIMES WHEN WE FAIL TO DO HIS WILL. We "stumble," as James said, or in Paul's words, we are "caught" or "overtaken" by sin (Galatians 6:1). We try to be perfect, but we fall short.

Ignorance. We don't know enough of the truth to act truthfully all of the time. There are blind spots in our vision and gaps in our understanding; none can deny it. So Paul, for example, prayed for the Colossians: "that you may be filled with the knowledge of His will . . . that you may walk worthy of the Lord, fully pleasing Him, being fruitful in every good work" (Colossians 1:9,10).

Weakness. Peter, James, and John knew better than to go to sleep while the Lord was praying in Gethsemane, yet they did so. Without excusing their error, Jesus was sympathetic: "The spirit indeed is willing, but the flesh is weak" (Matthew 26:41).

There is a third possibility, of course, and that is *rebellion.* If we know what we should do and we deliberately refuse to do it, the reason is not so much weakness as it is defiance. To do this is to do something described in the Scriptures as being extremely serious (Hebrews 10:26,27). We dare not reject God so boldly.

Yet even when our sins are inadvertent, in most cases we still have some personal responsibility. It often happens that we're more ignorant and weak than we *ought* to be, given the time and opportunity God has granted us to grow (Hebrews 5:12). The person who pleads with the Lord, "But I didn't know better," may hear Him say, "You *would* have known better if you'd had the desire to learn. You didn't grow because you didn't *want* to grow!"

All things considered, we need to adopt David's attitude toward sin: "Who can understand his errors? Cleanse me from secret faults. Keep back Your servant also from presumptuous sins; . . . Let the words of my mouth and the meditation of my heart be acceptable in Your sight, O LORD, my strength and my Redeemer" (Psalm 19:12-14). There is no sin that isn't dangerous, and the sooner we *learn* better and *do* better, the better we'll honor God.

There are two causes of sin. Either we don't know what
we ought to do or we refuse to do what we know we should.
The first cause is ignorance. The second is weakness.

AUGUSTINE OF HIPPO

March 24
BENEFIT OF THE DOUBT

*For with what judgment you judge, you will be judged;
and with the measure you use, it will be measured
back to you. Matthew 7:2*

IT WOULD BE A BETTER WORLD IF EACH OF US WOULD BE AS PATIENT WITH OTHER PEOPLE AS WE ARE WITH OURSELVES. When it comes to mistakes that we have made, we tend to be very "understanding," but we aren't always so lenient toward the mistakes made by those around us. But Jesus Christ calls upon us to grow in this area of our thinking, and there are several ways we can do this:

When others have erred, we can place the best possible interpretation on the evidence. Very few things happen in this world that aren't capable of more than one explanation. Rather than jump to the worst possible interpretation, we need to do for others what we always hope they'll do for us: believe the best until the facts force a more negative conclusion, which is then accepted reluctantly.

We can give others time to improve. Every single one of us is a work in progress. At present, we continue to make mistakes that we hope we'll not make quite so often in the future. Consequently, we hope that others will extend grace to us and allow us the time we need to make the adjustments we're trying to make. Wouldn't it be wise to give them the same consideration?

We can see others more from the viewpoint of their potential and less from that of their present performance. When Jesus spoke to the adulterous woman who had been brought to Him, He did not condone her sin. In fact, He commanded her to repent: "Go and sin no more" (John 8:11). In saying that, however, He showed more compassion than her accusers had shown. In His view, she was more than a person who had sinned — she was a person with potential, one who could *overcome* the bad choices she had made!

It ought to be sobering for us to remember that a day of accounting awaits us all, a day when we'll be judged by God. At that time, we'll want God to show every possible leniency to us. But Jesus warned, "With what judgment you judge, you will be judged; and with the measure you use, it will be measured back to you." And James said, "Judgment is without mercy to the one who has shown no mercy" (James 2:13). So we need to ask: what kind of accounting by God are we setting ourselves up for?

If you put up with yourself, why not put up with everyone else.
GUIGO I

THE RIGHT KIND OF FEAR BEGETS COURAGE

And do not fear those who kill the body
but cannot kill the soul. But rather fear Him who is able
to destroy both soul and body in hell. *Matthew 10:28*

SOMETIMES OUR COURAGE FAILS US NOT BECAUSE WE LACK BOLD-NESS BUT BECAUSE WE LACK THE RIGHT KIND OF FEAR. We mistakenly think that the key to greater courage would be greater self-confidence, and so we fire up our "Can Do!" attitude. After a while, our attitude gets dangerously close to pride. In our mad scramble for greater "strength," we forget the meaning of reverence. We no longer tremble before our Creator. We lose our fear of God. And at that point, lesser fears begin to dominate our lives.

Contrary to what many people think, fear is not always a bad thing. If we could find a way to banish every form of fear from our hearts, we would find ourselves weaker as a result, not stronger. The thing that's wrong with us most of the time is not that we're afraid, but that we have too little fear for the things we *should* be afraid of. Fear is not the problem; it's what we choose to fear.

To be specific, there is too much fear in our relationship with other people because there is too little fear in our relationship with God. "Do not fear those who kill the body but cannot kill the soul," Jesus commanded. "But rather fear Him who is able to destroy both soul and body in hell." This is not a command that many of us take seriously, and consequently, we spend our lives fearing what other people can do to us. A healthy measure of godly fear, however, would free us from this "humanly" fear.

Godly fear involves a remarkable irony. When we learn to relate to God with real reverence, we become more *humble,* but at the same time, we become more *bold.* As we grow in the recognition of our *weakness* versus God, we grow in the recognition of our *strength* versus the devil (2 Corinthians 12:9). Indeed, the devil can do very little to intimidate those who genuinely fear God. As strong as the devil may seem at times, he is a coward at heart. There are those whom he actually fears, and he is most afraid of those who're not afraid of him. So we're told, "Submit to God. Resist the devil, and he will flee from you" (James 4:7).

Haven't we wasted too much of life already in unnecessary fear? Now's the time to learn where real strength comes from.

Where the fear of the Lord guards the door, the enemy cannot enter.
FRANCIS OF ASSISI

March 26
DON'T MISTAKE THE MEANS FOR THE END

*... always learning and never able
to come to the knowledge of the truth.*
2 Timothy 3:7

W E CAN'T GROW STRONG WITHOUT USING THE MEANS GOD HAS
PROVIDED TO THAT END, BUT WE MUSTN'T FORGET WHAT THE
END IS. The "trees" are sometimes so interesting, we lose sight of
the "forest." We can become so caught up in the activities of spiritual growth that we begin enjoying them alone, just for their own
sake. As strange as it may seem, we can lose touch with God while
busying ourselves with the deeds of the devotional life.

Everyone is familiar with the concept of the "professional student," the individual who enjoys college life so much that he just
keeps going to school indefinitely, never moving on to the life that
college was supposed to prepare him for. There is a similar phe-
nomenon in the religious life. Sometimes we see people who are
"always learning and never able to come to the knowledge of the
truth." But before we criticize them, we need to ask to what extent
we ourselves have "moved on." After all our spiritual activity, do
we really have a more concentrated focus on God Himself?

One of the hardest things in life to learn is *balance.* But here
is an area where balance is truly needed. The devil would like to
see us become obsessed with religion and forget about God, so
we must acquire the ability to engage in — and even enjoy — the
things that lead us to God without making idols of these things.
All of these activities, as pleasant as they are, are a means to a
great End. We must constantly bring our minds back to that End.

This is hard for all of us, but it's especially hard when we're
just starting out in the Christian life. Compared to the emptiness
of the world, life in Christ offers so many things to enjoy: worship,
study, prayer, relationships, and many more. The challenge is to
keep moving toward God Himself and not get sidetracked by these
preliminary enjoyments, no matter how pleasant and essential
they are. These can't be neglected (spiritual "experts," take note),
but neither can they be allowed to become the main attraction.

Beginners in the faith often develop a kind of spiritual avarice. They can't get
enough of God. They can't attend enough services to satisfy them. They join
study groups. They read book after book. They spend much time on these
things rather than getting down to the basics of living a spiritual life.

JOHN OF THE CROSS

THE DANGERS OF HAVING BEEN HERE LONGER

*Better a poor and wise youth than an old and foolish king
who will be admonished no more. Ecclesiastes 4:13*

JUST AS THERE ARE SPECIAL CHALLENGES FOR THOSE WHO ARE
YOUNG IN THE FAITH, THERE ARE ALSO SOME FOR THE OLDER. One
of these is the pride that comes from comparing ourselves to those
who are our juniors, spiritually speaking. "May God help us to
avoid thoughts such as these: *But I have been here the longest. I have
worked harder. Someone else is being favored"* (Teresa of Avila).

Pride is especially dangerous because of its subtlety. It can
take many different forms, some of which are extremely hard
to see when we are the ones who are guilty. If we think only of
blatant egotism and arrogance, we may judge ourselves to be free
of pride, but we need to think twice. It may be that some of the
attitudes we classify as "spiritual maturity" are actually forms of
pride, nicely disguised as the virtues of strength and wisdom.

For example, it's hard for experienced Christians to keep
satisfaction with their experience from sliding off into the swamp
of *smugness.* Perhaps we would never say so, and perhaps we're
clever enough to keep others from knowing we think this way, but
inwardly we may feel a warm, condescending glow of ever-so-
subtle superiority when we think how little others have suffered.
"When they've been around as long as we have, they'll see things
differently," we sigh, congratulating ourselves for being older.

If you think you're not troubled by this particular malady, ask
yourself this question: how willing am I to be *corrected* by someone
with far less experience than I? The patronizing, "mature" smile
with which you listen to criticism from your juniors is probably
a sign of pride, and you may need to listen to Solomon: "Better
a poor and wise youth than an old and foolish king who will be
admonished no more." Hasn't pride closed many an older ear?

Whether we're young or old in the faith, it's a good idea to
minimize the amount of time we spend making comparisons. It
really doesn't matter whether we are ahead of or behind someone
else in life's experience. We won't have been in heaven for five
seconds before we realize how absolutely silly such comparisons
are. The only gap that matters is the gap between us and God!

Beware of thinking about your seniority.

TERESA OF ÁVILA

ON LOVING OUR ENEMIES

For if you love those who love you, what reward have you?
Do not even the tax collectors do the same? And if you greet
your brethren only, what do you do more than others?
Do not even the tax collectors do so? *Matthew 5:46,47*

LOVING THOSE WHO HAVE HARMED US IS ONE OF THE SIMPLEST THINGS JESUS EVER COMMANDED, AND ONE OF THE HARDEST. It's simple because it's very basic and goes right to the heart of what's important in life. Yet it's hard because it goes so strongly against the grain of the worldly thinking to which we're accustomed.

It should be noted that our ideas are often quite naive concerning the meaning and practice of loving our enemies. Whatever it does mean, loving our enemies *doesn't* mean we enjoy being in their presence or have a warm, fuzzy feeling when we think about them. It doesn't mean that we practice the same social relationship with them that we'd be able to practice if they repented of their wrongs. And it doesn't mean that we never cry out to God for justice to be done. David, for example, loved his enemies with a remarkable love, as evidenced by his treatment of Saul, his worst enemy (2 Samuel 1:17-27). It was not inconsistent, however, for David to pray, "Revive me, O LORD, for Your name's sake! For Your righteousness' sake bring my soul out of trouble. In Your mercy cut off my enemies, and destroy all those who afflict my soul; for I am Your servant" (Psalm 143:11,12).

The key is that David had learned to see his enemies in the same light that God did, with both love and a respect for justice. If our enemies refuse to repent of their wrongs, we should not only accept God's justice but long for it to be done (Revelation 6:10). At the same time, we should be willing to make significant sacrifices, as God did, to make their return from sin possible. God did more than talk about loving His enemies; He went so far as to sacrifice His Son's life for them. What treasure would we sacrifice — truly *sacrifice* — to promote the salvation of our enemies?

Worldly relationships are built on mutual goodwill, but God has set His people a much higher goal. If we're among His people, *we must act with love and justice even when these aren't reciprocated.*

It is a small thing to wish well and do well to one who has done you no evil.
It is far greater — a magnificent goodness — to love your enemy,
and to wish and do well to one who is trying to harm you.

AUGUSTINE OF HIPPO

RESPECT FOR THE NAME OF GOD

And you shall not swear by My name falsely,
nor shall you profane the name of your God;
I am the LORD. *Leviticus 19:12*

ONE EVIDENCE OF HOW LITTLE REGARD WE HAVE FOR GOD IS THE FLIPPANT WAY IN WHICH WE SOMETIMES USE HIS NAME. It is possible, no doubt, to be scrupulous in the use of God's name and still not have any reverence for Him in our hearts. But in today's meditation, we want to focus on the inside-out problem: the problem of the person who has no inward respect for God and that lack of respect shows up in the person's outward speech. There are basically three ways we may disrespect God and His name:

Swearing. To swear is to invoke God as the guarantee that we're going to do as we say. For instance, the person who says, "This is what I'm going to do, by God" is swearing. But Jesus taught that our statements ought not to require any oath to back them up. "Let your 'Yes' be 'Yes,' and your 'No,' 'No.' For whatever is more than these is from the evil one" (Matthew 5:37).

Profanity. Profane speech is that which makes common or crude use of words that should be held as sacred and used only with great reverence. It's not uncommon anymore to hear the words "God" and "Jesus Christ" thrown around so casually one wonders if the speakers even realize whose names they are using.

Cursing. When a person curses, he calls down God's wrath upon someone, verbally wishing them harm. "Damn you" is shorthand for "I hope God will damn your soul to hell." Even thinking this about someone is serious, but speaking it out loud — using God's name to vent our anger on others — is a monstrous evil. It is no light matter to wish the loss of someone's soul.

Why are these things so serious? Might we not consider them harmless foibles, less dangerous than sins that actually hurt other people? Well, the problem has to do with the heart. Crude words, and certainly irreverent ones, are almost always symptomatic of a heart that is turned away from God. So Jesus said, "By your words you will be justified, and by your words you will be condemned" (Matthew 12:37). So the next time you feel like "cussing," check your heart. Where is your spiritual father, above or below? Does your speech show that you're a humble worshiper of God?

To curse is to pray to the devil.
GERMAN PROVERB

NOT CONTENT WITH TRUE CONTENTMENT?

*But now after you have known God, or rather are known by God,
how is it that you turn again to the weak and beggarly elements,
to which you desire again to be in bondage?*
Galatians 4:9

IT'S A FOOLISH THING TO DO, BUT WE SOMETIMES TURN AWAY FROM GOD TO SATISFY OURSELVES WITH THINGS THAT ARE FAR LESS SATISFYING. To the amazement of all who love us, we trade the better for the worse, going down the scale of values rather than up. Paul, for example, expressed surprise that his Galatian brethren were turning away from the gospel to things that, by comparison, were nothing more than "weak and beggarly elements." What sense does it make to do this, he said, "after you have known God?"

Any time we turn back to worldly satisfactions after having known godly contentment, we go backwards from freedom to bondage. There is no allurement the devil has ever offered anyone that does not result in some kind of enslavement. He always promises greater freedom, but what he always delivers is slavery. "Do you desire again to be in bondage?" Paul asked the Galatians.

It's hard to imagine how "frustrating" our faithless decisions must be to our Heavenly Father. Having offered us, at the price of His Son's blood, the only thing that deserves the name "contentment," He sees us act like we're still looking for something more fulfilling. Unwilling to strip us of our free will and force us to remain at His side, He waits, in love, for us to make good, wise decisions. Too often, we do nothing in return but break His heart.

Rejecting what we've come to know of God's will is so foolish, none of us would ever do it if we weren't deceived. But therein lies the power of sin. The devil is shrewd enough to make slavery seem, for the moment, like it's better than what we have.

It would help us if we paid more attention to the grace God has shown us. We need to be more *consciously grateful* to Him, meditating on the deep, genuine peace that can be found only within the boundaries of the gospel. Do these boundaries limit us? Yes, they do, but let's not lose touch with reality: *what God is "holding back" from us is death!* If we forget that fact, we're apt to find ourselves dissatisfied with what He has graciously provided.

If we are not nourished by the Bread from heaven,
we will satiate ourselves with crumbs from the world.
ERWIN W. LUTZER

March 31
GOD, THE PERFECTLY FAITHFUL

Therefore let those who suffer according to the will
of God commit their souls to Him in doing good,
as to a faithful Creator. *1 Peter 4:19*

IF OUR HEARTS HAVE NOT COME TO REST IN GOD, WE WILL SEARCH IN VAIN FOR ANY OTHER PLACE THAT IS SAFE. Our Creator is the only personal being who can be counted on unreservedly. We may commit ourselves to Him without fear, there being no possibility that He will ever betray us or fail to keep His commitments.

From our vantage point, there may *seem* to be times when God has forsaken us, although that is never actually the case. A child, thinking that a monster is hiding in the dark corner of his bedroom, may fear that his parents have forsaken him, when in reality they're standing just outside the door. Just so, there may be times when our immediate circumstances cause us to doubt God's faithfulness, but if we could see everything that is going on, our doubts would disappear. We shouldn't let either our short-term vision or our feelings call God's faithfulness into question.

We tend, perhaps also because of short-term vision and feelings, to try to find a perfect source of trust in other human beings. When we do this, we set ourselves up for disappointment. No one except God can be counted on perfectly, and the ways in which we find this out are often heartbreaking. David, who was more than once betrayed by a close friend, knew the sadness of this experience: "For it is not an enemy who reproaches me; then I could bear it. Nor is it one who hates me who has exalted himself against me; then I could hide from him. But it was you, a man my equal, my companion and my acquaintance" (Psalm 55:12,13).

We should not become cynical or bitter about our fellow human beings in this regard. Indeed, we must keep our hearts open to trustful relationships. It's more than worth the risk. But we shouldn't expect of others what God alone is able to deliver. Only God can be a *perfect* source of confidence, and it's sinful on our part to try to make anyone else fill the role that He alone was meant to fill. He is infallibly trustworthy. We may "commit [our] souls to Him in doing good, as to a faithful Creator."

People change and fail. You cannot depend on them.
Those that are for you today may be against you tomorrow. They are
as variable as the wind. But Christ is eternally faithful.

THOMAS À KEMPIS

DETERMINED NOT TO MISS OUT

Therefore, since a promise remains of entering His rest,
let us fear lest any of you seem to have come short of it.
Hebrews 4:1

REACHING THE GOAL OF HEAVEN REQUIRES A HEALTHY MEASURE OF OLD-FASHIONED DETERMINATION. When we're choosing what kind of inner character we're going to have, we must choose to have traits like single-mindedness and stick-to-itiveness. We must be tenacious. When it comes down to it, we must be so determined not to miss out on heaven that we *refuse to be deterred.*

Our assurance of heaven should rest primarily on our confidence in God. There is no doubt as to His faithfulness. But since heaven is only for those who choose to receive it from Him on His terms, there is the question of who will make that choice and who will not. Satan is in the business of persuading as many people as possible to accept his offer rather than God's, and even after we make our choice to go God's direction, Satan continues to discourage us, in the hope that we'll change our mind. Unfortunately, many do change their minds, and the Hebrew writer was right to warn his readers: "Therefore, since a promise remains of entering His rest, let us fear lest any of you seem to have come short of it."

Not only do we have an adversary who's intent on discouraging us, the world we live in presents its own share of discouragement. Our environment is a sad one, seriously damaged by sin; there is no shortage of circumstances that tend to dishearten us and dash our hopes. This world is a far cry from what it would have been had sin not entered the picture, and it's a far cry from what we'll enjoy later, when God has fully restored our created nature and removed the effects of our sin. Are we willing to wait for what's ahead? There's more than a little truth to the old Latin maxim: "Endure, and save yourself for happier times" (Virgil).

Only those will enjoy heaven who have enough character to be patient, and patience comes down to what the old-timers used to call "grit." But mark it well: grit is not something some people are born with and others are not. It's a matter of choice on the part of every person. Furthermore, it's not a choice that can be made once and then forgotten. While the world still stands, each new day will ask us for another decision. *Are we determined to see God?*

He that can't endure the bad will not live to see the good.
JEWISH PROVERB

INVINCIBLE FAITH

For I know that my Redeemer lives,
And He shall stand at last on the earth.
Job 19:25

FAITH IN JESUS CHRIST, IF IT IS GENUINE, IS ONE OF THE STRONGEST FORCES KNOWN TO THE HUMAN RACE. In fact, it's possible to possess a faith that is, for all practical purposes, *invincible.*

Invincible faith, however, is not merely the intellectual acceptance of the fact that Jesus is the Son of God. No, the power to withstand great hardship comes from believing that, as the Son of God, Jesus Christ is one day going to gain complete victory over every form of evil and injustice. *The person who truly believes that will not be defeated by anything that happens in the meantime.*

Toward the end of Revelation, we have this description of one of John's visions: "Now I saw heaven opened, and behold, a white horse. And He who sat on him was called Faithful and True, and in righteousness He judges and makes war. His eyes were like a flame of fire, and on His head were many crowns. He had a name written that no one knew except Himself. He was clothed with a robe dipped in blood, and His name is called the Word of God. And the armies in heaven, clothed in fine linen, white and clean, followed Him on white horses. Now out of His mouth goes a sharp sword, that with it He should strike the nations. And He Himself will rule them with a rod of iron. He Himself treads the winepress of the fierceness and wrath of Almighty God. And He has on His robe and on His thigh a name written: KING OF KINGS AND LORD OF LORDS" (Revelation 19:11-16).

Invincible faith comes not from finding a way to be unconquerable ourselves, but from disciplining our minds to believe in the unconquerability of our King. It is impossible that He will be defeated, and this truth is well attested by everything that has ever been known about Him. When, in the face of temporary opposition, we choose to believe that the ultimate victory will be His, then we adopt a faith that the devil can do little to vanquish. And it is to us that Jesus Christ says, "To him who overcomes I will grant to sit with Me on My throne, as I also overcame and sat down with My Father on His throne" (Revelation 3:21).

Perseverance is our supreme effort of refusing
to believe that our hero is going to be conquered.
OSWALD CHAMBERS

April 3
CALM ENOUGH TO CONSIDER

He who has knowledge spares his words,
And a man of understanding is of a calm spirit.
Proverbs 17:27

IT IS DANGEROUS TO LET OUR MINDS BECOME SO AGITATED THAT WE CAN'T CONSIDER OUR ACTIONS CAREFULLY. Our adversary, the devil, specializes in confusion. He loves to prey upon minds that are torn and upset by multiple worries, and he often has his greatest success in tempting us when we're so beset by cares that we act on impulse, failing to consider the consequences of our actions.

Solomon observed that "a man of understanding is of a calm spirit." But how can we have a "calm spirit" when many stressful things come at us at once, all of which have to be considered? There surely can be no question that this is one of life's most difficult challenges, and there are no easy answers. Like most difficult things, however, cultivating a calm mind is a matter of *training*.

Our brains may have a more complicated connection to our spirits than the other parts of the body, but the brain (i.e., the physiological mind) is still a part of the body, and as such, it has to be trained to serve, rather than hinder, the spirit. Naturally unruly and seemingly with a will of its own, the mind has to be put in its place, disciplined, and taught to *help* us get to heaven.

Training our minds to be calm is like every other kind of training in that it has to be done in small steps. It's a matter of incremental growth over time. What we do is put ourselves on a deliberate regimen of training, and we "exercise" each and every day. We find some little thing we can do today to help calm our minds, and that victory encourages us to do the same tomorrow.

At the very least, we need to consciously *value* a calm spirit. We need to pursue it, and when we find ourselves without it, we need to be wise enough to see the danger we're in and make godly efforts to recover our calmness as soon as possible. If we can't always be calm, we can certainly grow in that direction. Today, like every day, there is some step you can take that will lead to a mind that's more peaceful — and more *careful*. What is that step?

A calm mind is a great asset in this life. Without it your devotional life
will not bear much fruit. If your heart is troubled, you are vulnerable
to the enemy of the soul. When you are agitated, you are not able
to make good decisions. You will stumble into snares.

LAWRENCE SCUPOLI

April 4
HUMBLE ENOUGH TO WORSHIP

The Pharisee stood and prayed thus with himself, "God, I thank You that I
am not like other men — extortioners, unjust, adulterers, or even as this tax
collector. I fast twice a week; I give tithes of all that I possess."
Luke 18:11,12

JUST AS AGITATION GETS IN THE WAY OF CAREFULNESS, PRIDE GETS
IN THE WAY OF WORSHIP. Nothing in the spiritual life is more
important than awe and utter respect before God, and so if pride
hinders us from being reverent, it's a deadly danger to our souls.

What is pride, really? It can be thought of in two directions:
toward God and toward other people. Toward God, pride is a
sense of *independence,* and toward other people, it's a sense of
superiority. In both cases, pride is *a sinful sense of self-satisfaction.*
Pride sees itself as doing a pretty good job of standing on its own
two feet before God; it believes it has the inside track as far as God
is concerned, so that God will make special allowance for any
mistakes that might be made. And in regard to other people, pride
pats itself on the back (secretly, of course, and always with admirable "humility") that it sees things from a more mature vantage
point than some others, especially its rivals and its enemies.

If this is what pride is, then, it should be obvious that it's a
great hindrance to worship. Indeed, one way of looking at pride
is to see it as the *opposite* of worship. The spirit of worship is the
spirit of selfless wonder at the majesty of God — the *smallness* of
self in God's presence. And for sinful beings like us, it's also the
spirit of brokenness and repentance. Our hearts may be proud, or
they may be worshipful, but they can't be both. And if they're not
worshipful, then we're lost. It doesn't matter how many hardships
we think we've overcome. Without real reverence, we're lost.

There is no living person who does not need to be constantly
vigilant concerning pride. It's the source of all other sin, and it can
creep into our hearts in so many disguises that, too often, it gets in
the door and seizes the throne room of our hearts before we know
what's happened. More often than not, it gets past our defenses
wearing a cloak of humility. "And the devil did grin, for his dar-
ling sin / Is pride that apes humility" (Samuel Taylor Coleridge).

Beware of a proud and haughty spirit. This sins puts a great barrier
between an individual and God. You will have a hard time being aware
of God as long as you are filled with pride. If it gets angels cast out of
heaven, it will certainly keep your heart out of heaven.

RICHARD BAXTER

April 5
PRESCHOOL

Now no chastening seems to be joyful for the present, but painful;
nevertheless, afterwards it yields the peaceable fruit of righteousness
to those who have been trained by it. *Hebrews 12:11*

IT IS SOMETIMES THROUGH HARDSHIP THAT GOD GETS OUR ATTEN-
TION AND PREPARES US TO LEARN FROM HIM. Not everyone has
to experience hardship in order to become receptive to God, but
many of us do. Many of us have to be "trained" by God's chastening. And while this is not "joyful for the present," it later "yields
the peaceable fruit of righteousness," as the Hebrew writer said.

Often it is our *attitudes* that need adjusting before God's word
can have much influence on us. If we're accustomed to thinking
in worldly terms, we're simply not open to God's perspective. We
have to learn the hard way that we've not been taking enough of
reality into consideration. Our minds have to be pried open by trials and tribulations, and sometimes we're not receptive even then.

One of our most hindering attitudes is the insistence that we
already know what we need to know. We're not teachable because
we see no *need* to be taught. Rather than be taught, we'd rather be
the ones doing the teaching, and we expend the biggest portion of
our energy trying to get the world around us to adjust itself to our
thinking. We have no time to listen, as busy as we are.

And so, through the Psalmist, God says to us: "Be still, and
know that I am God" (Psalm 46:10). We won't have the proper
reverence for God until we've gotten "still," and stillness in God's
school may not be something we willingly accept. We may have to
be *forced* to be still by the "preschool" of pain and suffering!

But if we have trouble being "still" enough to hear God, we
also have trouble being "quiet." Rather than shutting our mouths
and listening, we talk and talk and talk: informing God what we'd
like to have done, explaining to Him the uniqueness of our situation, and sometimes even calling into question His management
of the universe. Is it any wonder we can't hear the truth? Is it any
wonder God has to confine us to a corner and clamp His loving
hand over our mouths, until we stop squirming and . . . listen?

When God gets us alone through suffering, heartbreak, temptation,
disappointment, sickness, or by thwarted desires, a broken friendship, or a
new friendship — when He gets us absolutely alone, and we are totally
speechless, unable to ask even one question, then He begins to teach us.

OSWALD CHAMBERS

April 6
GRATEFUL FOR THE WORK GOD GIVES US

If the whole body were an eye, where would be the hearing? If the whole
were hearing, where would be the smelling? But now God has set the
members, each one of them, in the body just as He pleased.
1 Corinthians 12:17,18

THE KINGDOM OF CHRIST IS A REALM WHERE DEFINITE WORK
IS DONE. To be a Christian is more than an honorary status
conferred upon us; it is a manner of living, a way of life. If we
have the idea that "being" a Christian involves no more than the
passive enjoyment of being saved, we have a thing or two to learn
about the New Testament. There, Christians worked and served,
actively and energetically. The body of Christ *does* things!

But just as the body of Christ has work to do, it's also true
that the individual members of the body each have a unique part
to play in that work. If we're Christians, we don't simply have a
generic contribution to make; we have a particular work to engage
in that is uniquely our own. Each of us is a one-of-a-kind package
of strengths and abilities, and we're going to have to answer for
whether those gifts were used in ways that were well suited to us.

Most of us are aware that the church is compared in the
New Testament to the human body, a unified organism made up
of many different parts, all of which contribute uniquely to the
body's activity. Almost humorously, Paul asks, "If the whole body
were an eye, where would be the hearing? If the whole were hearing, where would be the smelling?" The body simply could not
function without having *different* parts that do *different* things.

We know this, and yet what do we do? We identify certain
types of Christian service as more important, and we spend our
lives fretting over who has which ability. In a word, this is *sinful.*

In the Lord, we need to take three steps: (1) We need to
prayerfully *discover* what it is the Lord wants us personally to be
doing with the abilities we have (or can acquire). (2) We need to
get comfortable in our own skin and *accept* the role that is ours to
play, regardless of where it ranks on any worldly scale of values.
(3) We need to *rejoice* in our role and be grateful for the work God
gives us. After all, God has set us in the body "just as He pleased."

The Lord knows us as we really are. He gives each of us work to do.
He understands what is most appropriate for us, what will be helpful
to him, and what will be good for others.
TERESA OF ÁVILA

April 7

SICK OR SINFUL?

For since the creation of the world His invisible attributes are clearly seen,
being understood by the things that are made, even His eternal power and
Godhead, so that they are without excuse, because, although they knew God,
they did not glorify Him as God, nor were thankful, but became futile in
their thoughts, and their foolish hearts were darkened. *Romans 1:20,21*

WE WON'T MAKE MUCH HEADWAY OVERCOMING SIN UNTIL WE ADMIT OUR PERSONAL SINFULNESS. Yet it's the modern trend to downplay the individual sinner's responsibility for his wrong-doing. Phyllis McGinley said it well: "People are no longer sinful. They are only immature or underprivileged or frightened or, more particularly, sick." There is currently a reluctance even to use the word "sin." We prefer words like "disorder" or "dysfunction," as if our evil deeds were simply something that happened *to* us.

Yet Paul wrote that when it comes to sin, we are "without excuse." Any sin that any of us has ever committed has been a fail-ure to show, first, *honor* to God and, second, *gratitude* to Him. And these are *very serious failures — failures for which we are fully respon-sible.* If we ultimately stand before God having done these things, it will be perfectly just of Him to banish us from His presence forever. Our only hope is the gospel of Christ, which is a plan of forgiveness based on grace. Yet the grace is extended only to those who have enough love for the truth to acknowledge the damage they've done, without any attempt to soften the situation.

The gospel is certainly good news. It's nothing less than the best news humanity has ever heard. But the news of God's for-giveness can only be good for us individually and personally if we first accept the full extent of the bad news. And the bad news is that we are selfish rebels against God who deserve not the least bit of "understanding" on His, or anyone else's, part. If we fail to swallow this bitter medicine, there'll be no *godly* sorrow in our hearts, and we'll be no closer to God's forgiveness than the re-spectable, excuse-making folks who came to hear John the Baptist preach. They had no sense of having done anything very seriously wrong, but the welcome they received from God's messenger was blunt: "Brood of vipers! Who warned you to flee from the wrath to come? *Therefore bear fruits worthy of repentance*" (Matthew 3:7,8).

And ofttimes excusing of a fault
Doth make the fault the worse by the excuse.

WILLIAM SHAKESPEARE

BEING "HUMAN" REQUIRES NO APOLOGY

For You have made him a little lower than the angels,
And You have crowned him with glory and honor.
Psalm 8:5

DAVID MARVELED AT THE MAJESTY OF GOD'S CREATION AND WAS AMAZED THAT GOD GAVE HUMAN BEINGS SUCH A GLORIOUS AND HONORABLE PLACE IN THAT CREATION. "You have made him to have dominion over the works of Your hands," David sang to God. "You have put all things under his feet, all sheep and oxen — even the beasts of the field, the birds of the air, and the fish of the sea that pass through the paths of the seas" (Psalm 8:6-8). Humanity is the crowning jewel of the physical cosmos, all the rest of which was made mostly to be a habitat or home for humankind.

We sometimes excuse our mistakes by saying that we're "only" human, as if human beings were such limited creatures that nothing more than mistakes could be expected of them. The truth, however, is just the opposite. If we have anything to apologize for, it's for being *less* than human! Our trouble is not our humanity; it's that we're content to think and act as mere beasts, rather the noble creatures we truly are, made in the image of God.

Jesus of Nazareth was the most fully human being who has ever lived. What we see in Him is a living example of what God had in mind when He designed the human race. He shows us our true dignity in God's plan — and also the absurdity of the devil's plan to give us a "higher" place than God has let us have.

The challenge that is set before us, then, is not to be "only" human, but to be *fully* human. It's not a burden but a privilege to be such creatures as we are. We should accept the honor that God has bestowed upon us. Our God-given endowments are wonderful; we should be grateful for them and use them to the praise of His glory. Sin has surely marred God's making of us, but He has made a way, in His Son, for our created dignity to be restored. So rather than complain or make excuses about our "nature," we should be reaching for our destiny. In every word and deed, we should be showing what a glorious thing it is to be human.

O Lord God, we pray that we may be inspired to nobleness of life
in the least of things. May we dignify all our daily life. May we set such
a sacredness upon every part of our life that nothing shall be trivial,
nothing unimportant, and nothing dull, in the daily round.

HENRY WARD BEECHER

April 9

PUTTING PAIN INTO PERSPECTIVE

In this you greatly rejoice, though now for a little while, if need be, you have
been grieved by various trials, that the genuineness of your faith, being
much more precious than gold that perishes, though it is tested by fire, may
be found to praise, honor, and glory at the revelation of Jesus Christ.
1 Peter 1:6,7

PAINFUL CIRCUMSTANCES, LIKE MOST THINGS IN LIFE, CAN BE
LOOKED AT IN MORE THAN ONE WAY. As Christians, we ought
to want to look at everything, including something as unpleasant as pain, in a *truthful* way. In short, we ought to want to view
it as God Himself does, and usually this means looking at it from
a wider perspective. When we're hurting, we need to see more of
the reality of the situation than the mere fact that we're hurting.

One thing we need to understand clearly is that anyone who
lives in this world, a world ruined by sins committed before we
got here, is going to hurt. The experience of pain is a fact of life, an
unavoidable difficulty. No one knows this more than Jesus Christ,
who suffered greatly despite never having made a single bad decision as to His own manner of living. If right living protected a person from pain, Jesus would never have known pain, but not only
did He know it, He knew it deeply. He was "despised and rejected
by men, a Man of sorrows and acquainted with grief" (Isaiah 53:3).

Yet if pain is necessary, much of the anguish that often goes
with it is not. And again, Jesus is our example. He drank deeply of
the cup of torment, but even in the moments of His greatest agony,
it's hard for us to imagine Him experiencing any of the negative
emotions that normally make pain so horrible for us. For example,
much of our suffering comes from anger, resentment, and self-pity.
But Jesus refused to respond to pain in any of these ways, and consequently His pain was much purer. Peter, therefore, referring to
Christ's attitude toward pain, said to his fellow Christians, "Arm
yourselves with also the same mind" (1 Peter 4:1).

We may find it hard to do, but it's possible even to *rejoice* in
the midst of pain. "In this you greatly rejoice," said Peter, "though
now for a little while, if need be, you have been grieved by various trials, that the genuineness of your faith . . . may be found to
praise, honor, and glory at the revelation of Jesus Christ." The difference is in perspective: *seeing pain against the backdrop of salvation.*

Pain is inevitable. Suffering is optional.
ANONYMOUS

April 10
EVERYTHING BURNS AWAY BUT THE BEAUTY

*For our citizenship is in heaven, from which we also eagerly wait
for the Savior, the Lord Jesus Christ, who will transform our lowly body
that it may be conformed to His glorious body, according to the working
by which He is able even to subdue all things to Himself.*
Philippians 3:20,21

IF WE MAKE RIGHT CHOICES IN OUR ATTITUDE TOWARD IT, PAIN CAN HAVE A "REFINING" EFFECT ON US. We can be better people, with purer hearts, as a result of having experienced difficulty and overcome it. Indeed, pain can leave us with character qualities so beautiful they are fit to be taken into eternity with us.

None of us can rightly deny that our characters *need* some refining. If we compare ourselves to other sinful people, it may appear that the shape we're in is not all that bad. But that's the wrong comparison. *The standard of comparison is Jesus Christ.* A character like His is what we'd have right now if we'd never sinned, and that's what God is wanting us to have in eternity.

Pain is a part of the process of renovation and renewal that we need to undergo. Given the seriousness of our malady — by our sinful choices, we have declared stubborn rebellion against the God of heaven — we shouldn't wonder that radical surgery is needed to fix the problem. Cutting away the cancer that has invaded our souls can't be done without our feeling some pain.

But God's work of character renovation won't need to go on always. If we've been cooperative while the renovation was being done, there'll come a time when we're ready — ready to inhabit a realm where there is no more rebellion against God and no more irresponsibility. We're not there yet, but the time is surely coming.

So we need to remember the passing nature of pain. It's an ugly reality, yes, but even now it's not all of reality, and when compared to the reality that's *ahead,* waiting for those who've sought God faithfully, pain can be clearly seen as a temporary problem. At present, it happens that we're still in the temporary part of God's scheme of redemption. But the eternal part is coming, and that's where our hearts and minds need to be fixed: "For our citizenship is in heaven, from which we also eagerly wait for the Savior, the Lord Jesus Christ, who will transform our lowly body that it may be conformed to His glorious body."

The beauty remains; the pain passes.
AUGUSTE RENOIR

April 11
WHEN OUR QUESTIONS ARE NOT ANSWERED

The secret things belong to the LORD our God, but those things
which are revealed belong to us and to our children forever,
that we may do all the words of this law.
Deuteronomy 29:29

NOT EVERY QUESTION WE MIGHT ASK OR WISH AN ANSWER TO IS
GOING TO BE ANSWERED. It is presumptuous to think that God
must grant information on every question we might think to ask,
and we need to be very cautious about issuing subpoenas to the
Ruler of the Universe. In particular, questions about *why things
are as they are* and questions about *what is going to happen* are often
queries that, from His perspective, we'd be better off not knowing about. We may think we need to know and may even become
demanding in our prayers, but the questions are still met with
silence. About many things, God's word says simply . . . nothing.

Do you remember the freedom with which you asked questions as a child, and the firmness with which your parents often
had to say that certain questions were not ones they felt it wise to
answer? The eagerness with which children ask questions is not
a fault. Indeed, it is refreshing, and God must surely look with
paternal love on this aspect of our childishness. But we must be
careful not to push past childish inquisitiveness into the realm of
irreverent insistence and demandingness. *We must be willing for
Him to correct our notions of what is important for us to know.*

Moses said to Israel, "The secret things belong to the LORD
our God, but those things which are revealed belong to us and to
our children forever, that we may do all the words of this law." It
takes *trust* to accept God's decision about the "secret things," and
it also takes *courage*, for it's often frightening to be left without information that we think is essential to our survival. Yet if we trust
Him, we will do this. When we don't have all the information we
want, we must be content to have Him. He is all we *have* to have.

What God says is important. But what He does *not* say is
also important, and if we respect His statements, we should also
respect His silences. In fact, it's probably true that our foolish
fascination with certain unanswered questions is the result of our
failure to be nourished by the truths that have been revealed. *If
we'll digest it, what God has already said will more than meet our needs.*

He who hath heard the Word of God can bear his silences.
IGNATIUS OF LOYOLA

April 12

BEREFT

. . . having no hope and without God in the world.
Ephesians 2:12

IF WE REFUSE TO HAVE A RIGHTFUL CONNECTION TO GOD, WE DOOM OURSELVES TO THE WORST KIND OF LONELINESS IN THE WORLD. Without God to be our companion, we are bereft: left alone and without something we desperately need. Never are we more to be pitied than when we are "without God in the world."

Being alone is a thing we all fear to some extent. Yet the kinds of loneliness we fear the most are not those that we *should* fear the most. We think we're in desperate straits when we're bereaved of some earthly relationship we thought we had to have to be happy, but we hardly feel a twinge of loneliness when we're bereft of God. We live rebellious, unrepentant lives such that God can have nothing to do with us, and yet as long as we have a few earthly relationships, we don't worry too much about loneliness. We're alone in the worst way, but we don't feel it, much less fear it.

Jesus, who knew all the lesser kinds of loneliness that we can know, also knew the greatest. On our behalf, He tasted the ultimate form of bereavement: separation from God. On the cross, He cried, "My God, My God, why have You forsaken Me?" (Mark 15:34). At that hour, Jesus was experiencing not merely the loneliness of one or two people alienated from God, but the full sorrow of every sin committed by every human being who had ever lived or ever would. He knows full well what being *bereft* means, and He would have us look at this matter more realistically.

Today, when we cut ourselves off from God by our sinful denials of Him, rarely do we let ourselves recognize how bereft we are. As long as this world stands, it is possible to occupy ourselves with other activities — and convince ourselves that we're not all that lonely. Yet without God, we are bereaved of the thing our hearts need most deeply, and we are hastening toward a day of awful confrontation with the truth. To have no hope and be without God in the world is a nightmare of loneliness to any honest person. But honest or not, to be without Him in the *next* world will be worse — worse than any earthly nightmare can know.

No one is so much alone in the universe as a denier of God.
With an orphaned heart, which has lost the greatest of fathers, he stands
mourning by the immeasurable corpse of the universe.
JOHANN PAUL FRIEDRICH RICHTER

April 13

JOYFUL LONGING

. . . Jesus Christ, whom having not seen you love. Though now you do not
see Him, yet believing, you rejoice with joy inexpressible and full of glory,
receiving the end of your faith — the salvation of your souls.
1 Peter 1:7-9

IT IS POSSIBLE TO BE CONTENTED AND UNFULFILLED AT THE SAME
TIME. Even though our deepest longings won't be completely
satisfied until our Lord returns, we can still live in the present with
a sense of satisfaction at God's goodness. And looking at it from
the other direction, even though we experience the peace that
passes understanding right now, we can live with a joyous expectancy that the best is yet to come. Contentment and desire need
not be contradictory. We can long for God with a joy that's just as
deep as our longing. Indeed, our longing can be a part of our joy.

Peter wrote that we can "rejoice with joy inexpressible and
full of glory," since we are "receiving the end of [our] faith — the
salvation of [our] souls." It's important to notice that this inexpressible joy can be ours even though the end of our faith, the final
salvation of our souls, has not yet been received. Our joy is the joy
of *hope.* It's the joy of those who're confident that they're on the
path that leads to their Father. We're grateful to be going home!

And yet our joy can be more than the joy of hope: we can
learn to enjoy the *process* that is leading to our salvation. We are
indeed on a path, and we haven't yet reached the end of it. But the
path itself is full of pleasant things, things that have been created
by God for us to enjoy along the way. Surely it would be wrong to
have our hearts so set on heaven that we failed to appreciate the
goodness of the journey by which God plans to get us there.

The Christian really does have the best of both worlds. So
when we say godliness is profitable for all things, for "the life that
now is" and for "that which is to come" (1 Timothy 4:8), we ought
to be espousing more than a theory; we ought to be stating our
own experience. We need to be people who reach forward eagerly,
but also those who reach forward *gratefully.* We need to long for
God fervently, but to long for Him with a joy that is *real right now.*

We are not to make the ideas of contentment and aspiration quarrel, for God
made them fast friends. A man may aspire and yet be quite content until it is
time to rise; and both flying and resting are but parts of one contentment.
The very fruit of the gospel is aspiration. It is to the heart what spring is to
the earth, making every root, and bud, and bough desire to be more.

HENRY WARD BEECHER

April 14
THE POSITIVE CHOICE IS POSSIBLE!

For this commandment which I command you today is not too mysterious
for you, nor is it far off. It is not in heaven, that you should say, "Who will
ascend into heaven for us and bring it to us, that we may hear it and do it?"
Nor is it beyond the sea, that you should say, "Who will go over the sea for
us and bring it to us, that we may hear it and do it?" But the word is very
near you, in your mouth and in your heart, that you may do it.
Deuteronomy 30:11-14

IF WE'RE STILL ALIVE, THEN IT'S WITHIN OUR POWER TO MAKE
WHATEVER CHOICE GOD WOULD WANT US TO MAKE. No matter
how many wrong choices we've made in the past, we have the
freedom to make the right choice now. Outwardly, it may take
time to reverse the damage that our past choices have wrought,
but inwardly, we can at this very moment begin being the person
that we know God wants us to be. The positive choice is possible!

Sometimes we feel that we've done so badly for so long that
there is no hope for us. But this sinking sense of hopelessness
comes from hell, not from heaven. It's only our enemy who wants
us to give up. Our Father wants us to live. He wants us to take the
simple, honest step that it's always possible to take: *the one immediately before us.* If we choose to take that step, there is nothing the
devil can do to stop us, although he'd surely like to do so.

But it does us little good to have the power of choice if we
don't use it. We shouldn't waste the marvelous dignity and honor
that God conferred on us when He gave us our freedom of will.
His grace toward us should not be "in vain" (1 Corinthians 15:10).

One encouraging thing to keep in mind is that each positive
choice creates strength. If we choose in the present moment to do
what is right, we'll find the next moment much easier to deal with.
Every good decision leads to another. We'll be helped by a favorable momentum that makes our forward progress less difficult.

Whatever our choices may be, God is not neutral about them.
Having gone to great lengths to save us, He wants us to choose
life. If we fail to choose it, He'll have to let justice be carried out, of
course. But that will break His heart. "'For why should you die, O
Israel? For I have no pleasure in the death of one who dies,' says
the Lord GOD. 'Therefore turn and live!'" (Ezekiel 18:31,32). Today,
we can turn. This very instant, we can say yes to life.

At any moment in life we have the option to choose
an attitude of gratitude, a posture of grace, a commitment to joy.
TIM HANSEL

April 15

NO COMFORTABLE CROSS

... knowing this, that our old man was crucified
with Him, that the body of sin might be done away with,
that we should no longer be slaves of sin.
Romans 6:6

PRIOR TO OUR CONVERSION, MOST OF US UNDERSTOOD, AT LEAST ON SOME BASIC LEVEL, THAT WE MUST "DIE WITH CHRIST." But unless we're among the few who've truly counted the cost of discipleship, we probably underestimated the pain that would be involved in having our "old man . . . crucified with Him." As we begin to discover how painful it is for our old habits to be put to death, we may back away from the process. We didn't expect that any part of being a Christian would be so painful. We're surprised by the unpleasantness of it all. Perhaps we even resent or resist it.

Yet there is no such thing as a comfortable crucifixion. The word "excruciate" is simply a variation of the word "crucify," and so in a quite literal sense, death by *crucifixion* is always *excruciating*. If our Lord chose the concept of crucifixion to describe the removal of sin from our lives, then we ought not to expect that process to be entirely pleasant. Deeply rooted habits can't be easily denied or conveniently removed. Their destruction requires nothing less than the dying of the person that we used to be.

But if we saw where sin takes people, we'd be willing to make any sacrifice to be free of it. Jesus said that if we couldn't keep our right eye or our right hand and still stay away from sin, then we'd be better off plucking out our eye or cutting off our hand (Matthew 5:29,30), however painful those removals might be.

If the crown that awaits us requires that we first go to the cross and die, then the crown is worth every bit of the cross. Paul said that "if we died with Christ, we believe that we shall also live with Him" (Romans 6:8). It would be worth dying a thousand times if that meant we could live with Christ. But let's not be silly. Our cross can't be any more painless than His. It's going to hurt.

If we are wise, we will do what Jesus said: endure the cross
and despise its shame for the joy that is set before us. To do this is to submit
the whole pattern of our life to be destroyed and built again in the power of
an endless life. And we shall find that it is more than poetry, more than sweet
hymnody and elevated feeling. The cross will cut into our lives where it
hurts worst, sparing neither us nor our carefully cultivated reputation.
It will defeat us and bring our selfish life to an end.

A. W. TOZER

April 16

CHECKMATE

They shall drive you from men, your dwelling shall be with
the beasts of the field, and they shall make you eat grass like oxen.
They shall wet you with the dew of heaven, and seven times shall pass
over you, till you know that the Most High rules in the kingdom
of men, and gives it to whomever He chooses. *Daniel 4:25*

SOMETIMES WHEN WE THINK WE'RE REACHING FORWARD TOWARD
GOD, THE DIRECTION IN WHICH WE'RE ACTUALLY REACHING IS
AWAY FROM HIM. Although we may not have the honesty to admit
it to ourselves, we're fighting against God. Our plans are opposed
to His purposes. And when that happens, we're fortunate when
God steps in and blocks our progress. In fact, God is never more
gracious than when He defeats our worldly ambitions and shuts us
up to the consequences of our actions. When He puts us in checkmate, hemming us in, He is showing a great love for us indeed.

We need to understand that as long as God is still blocking
our path and defeating us, that's a good sign. It's a sign that He's
still trying to win us back to His way. Much worse would be the
next stage in the process: the stage in which God gives us up and
abandons us to the futility and frustration of our own way.

Nothing worse could be imagined than to be abandoned by
God, and yet the Scriptures teach that that is exactly what He will
do if we insist on not getting the point when He blocks our path.
Concerning those who adamantly refused to "retain God in their
knowledge," Paul wrote that "God gave them over to a debased
mind, to do those things which are not fitting" (Romans 1:28).
J. B. Phillips's paraphrase of this statement is vivid: God "allowed
them to become the slaves of their degenerate minds."

So when we find ourselves checkmated by God, we ought
to be thankful. By all rights, He should have given up on us long
ago, but in His grace He has not yet done so. We ought to respond
rightly, in both word and deed, to the fact that God has blocked
our path. When He has shut us up and left us nowhere to go, we
should react with *repentance* and *obedience*. Rather than resentment,
a greater *reverence* should be our chosen response. It is, after all,
not a disgrace to be put in checkmate by God. What would be a
disgrace would be to suffer and suffer and suffer — and be too big
a fool to learn the lesson that He's trying to teach us.

Every story of conversion is the story of a blessed defeat.
C. S. LEWIS

April 17
BEING LOST TAKES PERSISTENCE TOO

But you are not willing to come to Me that you may have life.
John 5:40

IN THE END, THOSE WHO WILL BE LOST WILL BE THOSE WHO HAVE INSISTED ON BEING LOST. God has gone to great lengths to provide for our redemption from sin, and He waits for a long time for us to turn around and come back to Him. He pleads with us, imploring us to accept the reconciliation that He has made possible (2 Corinthians 5:20). If we end up refusing to let Him save us, it will be despite everything He could do to win our hearts. The truth is, it takes a lot of "persistence" to keep saying no to God.

C. S. Lewis once observed that the unbeliever is always in danger of having his faith overthrown. As long as he lives in this world, the unbeliever is surrounded by the tokens of God's grace and many other powerful evidences of His reality. And so an atheistic parent who wanted his children to follow in his footsteps would always need to be worried about the "corrupting" influences they would be encountering every day. Given the many ways that God tries to get our attention, it would take an extraordinarily *determined* child to resist all of that and stay an unbeliever.

But sometimes, determined is exactly what we are in the matter of disobedience. Isaiah spoke with more than a little irony when he condemned those who were "mighty" and "valiant" in the pursuit of dissipation: "Woe to men mighty at drinking wine, woe to men valiant for mixing intoxicating drink" (Isaiah 5:22).

In the Book of Proverbs, one of the leading characteristics of the fool is that he *insists* on doing evil, despite many opportunities to change his mind. "A prudent man foresees evil and hides himself, but the simple pass on and are punished" (Proverbs 22:3). Sadly, it's the fool's "steadfastness" that keeps him in trouble.

God's plea is for us to turn around and come back in His direction. If we'll do that, we'll live, but if we won't, then we'll die (Ezekiel 18:27,28). So in a sense, there's only one sin that will kill us, and that's the sin we refuse to repent of and seek God's forgiveness for. If we end up being lost eternally, it won't be because we made mistakes — it'll be because we *persisted* in our mistakes.

No man is condemned for anything he has done: he is condemned
for continuing to do wrong. He is condemned for not coming out
of the darkness, for not coming to the light.
GEORGE MACDONALD

CONSEQUENCES CAN'T BE AVOIDED FOREVER

What fruit did you have then in the things of which you are
now ashamed? For the end of those things is death. But now having
been set free from sin, and having become slaves of God, you have your
fruit to holiness, and the end, everlasting life. *Romans 6:21,22*

EVERY PATH LEADS SOMEWHERE. Every action in which we engage — indeed, every thought that we think — takes us one
step further down a road that leads to some destination.

Speaking of the godless way the Christians in Rome had lived
before their conversion to Christ, Paul asked, "What fruit did you
have then in the things of which you are now ashamed?" All of
our actions, both the godly and the ungodly, bear some kind of
"fruit." In the case of ungodliness, the fruit is deadly. "The end of
those things," Paul wrote, "is death." Death is not just the arbitrary punishment of God for evildoing; it's the inevitable *result*
or *consequence* of it. Death is simply *the end of that road.* If a person
travels that way and refuses to change, death is the only place he
can get to. It's where that road leads, no matter who the traveler is.

Choices always entail consequences. Since we have free wills,
we can make our choices freely, but having made our choices, we
can't then choose our consequences. The consequences are unalter-
ably attached to the choices, and we can't have the former without the latter. We may, it's true, avoid the consequences for some
period of time — but we can't do so forever. Some day, there will
be a payday, and when it comes, we need not be surprised.

It's an immutable principle that "whatever a man sows,
that he will also reap" (Galatians 6:7). To believe otherwise is to
deceive ourselves and mock God. But it's not just in eternity that
we'll reap as we've sown; the harvest begins before we die. There
can't be any question that the consequences of our actions begin
to come down on us well before the Judgment Day. Paul spoke
of those who, while still living, were "receiving in themselves the
penalty of their error which was due" (Romans 1:27).

Are you and I ready to eat the fruit of our ways? We might as
well be, because the "banquet" is surely being prepared for us and
we'll have no choice but to eat it when it's set before us. We can
run, but we can't hide. The law of cause and effect is no respecter
of persons, and it'll catch up with every last one of us eventually.

Everybody, sooner or later, sits down to a banquet of consequences.
ROBERT LOUIS STEVENSON

April 19
DOES YOUR LIFE LOOK DESPERATE?

This I say, therefore, and testify in the Lord, that you should no longer
walk as the rest of the Gentiles walk, in the futility of their mind, having their
understanding darkened, being alienated from the life of God, because of the
ignorance that is in them, because of the hardening of their heart . . .
Ephesians 4:17,18

FOR ALL PRACTICAL PURPOSES, MOST PEOPLE LIVE AS IF THERE
WERE NO GOD. One doesn't have to be a newspaper reporter
to have noticed that there is a vast amount of desperation in the
world. In one form or another, fear and hopelessness have grown
so common that we've almost gotten used to them. Whatever we
might say we believe, our lives in the real world, outwardly at
least, often look like those of people who have little hope.

If there were no such thing as God, of course, all of this would
make sense. If there was nothing beyond the confines of this world
worth reaching forward to, desperation would be an understand-
able (if still unfortunate) response to the condition the world is in.

But many of us believe there is a God. We believe there are
things worth reaching for in eternity, if we choose to do so, and
even in this life, we believe there are principles and values that
can make a difference for good in our thinking. How is it that we,
of all people, live like individuals whose backs are to the wall? If
people can't tell any difference between us and our non-Christian
neighbors in the way we handle the discouragements of life, what
kind of commentary is that on our convictions? And what kind of
reflection does that cast upon the One whom we confess as Lord?

If, through the gospel of Christ, we've been forgiven of our
sins and reconciled to God, then we're no longer among those who
have "no hope and [are] without God is the world" (Ephesians
2:12). Whatever may be our sorrow, we should not "sorrow as others who have no hope" (1 Thessalonians 4:13). As Christians, we
may still be many things, but *desperate* should not be one of them.

We don't think what's right and do what's right just for the
sake of appearance, of course. But even so, if those who know us
would say that we seem to be just as desperate as anyone else in
the world, that ought to give us pause to think. If people can't *see*
any difference, then *is* there any difference? If we don't *seem* to be
reaching forward, then *are* we reaching forward? Are we really?

The mass of men lead lives of quiet desperation.
HENRY DAVID THOREAU

April 20

ON BEING GLAD THAT GOD IS GOOD

Then Moses rose early in the morning and went up Mount Sinai . . .
Now the LORD descended in the cloud and stood with him there,
and proclaimed the name of the LORD. And the LORD passed before him
and proclaimed, "The LORD, the LORD God, merciful and gracious,
longsuffering, and abounding in goodness and truth . . ."
Exodus 34:4-6

MOSES WAS GIVEN A GLIMPSE OF GOD THAT NO OTHER HUMAN BEING HAS EVER BEEN GIVEN. Exodus 33:11 says that "the LORD spoke to Moses face to face, as a man speaks to his friend." After Moses' death, it was said that "there has not arisen in Israel a prophet like Moses, whom the Lord knew face to face" (Deuteronomy 34:10). But it's helpful to remember *what* God revealed to Moses. It was not just that God was *real* but that He was also *good:* "The LORD, the LORD God, merciful and gracious, longsuffering, and abounding in goodness and truth."

In Hebrews 11:6, we are told that to come to God we must believe two things about Him: that He *is* (existence) and that He is a *rewarder of those who diligently seek Him* (benevolence). If the first takes faith, the second does as well. In a world where short-term appearances can call God's goodness into question, we need to hang on to the indisputable evidence that God has given of His good will toward us — nowhere more clearly than at the Cross.

We ought not to take the goodness of God for granted. God might have existed and been something very different than the God that He is. But as it turns out, He is a God who is benevolently inclined toward us, and He has *revealed* Himself to be that kind of God. We can't know God perfectly or completely, but what we can know of Him, we can know truly. We don't have to speculate about it; we can know for sure that our God is good.

Knowing that God is "merciful and gracious, longsuffering, and abounding in goodness and truth" should make us want to reach out to Him. He is a God for whom we can yearn with admiration and love. We dare not forget that He is also a God of justice, who will banish us from His presence forever if we refuse to lay down our rebellion against Him. But oh, how nourishing it is to know that His inclination and His fervent desire are to save us.

While the name of God is secret and His essential nature
incomprehensible, He in condescending love has by revelation
declared certain things to be true of Himself.

A. W. TOZER

April 21
WHEN MEANING MAKES A THING IMPORTANT

> . . . and Joshua said to them: "Cross over before the ark of the Lord your
> God into the midst of the Jordan, and each one of you take up a stone on his
> shoulder, according to the number of the tribes of the children of Israel, that
> this may be a sign among you when your children ask in time to come,
> saying, 'What do these stones mean to you?'" *Joshua 4:5,6*

IS THERE A RING ON YOUR FINGER THAT HAS A MEANING OUT OF ALL PROPORTION TO THE SIZE OF THE RING ITSELF? Perhaps there is. And we treasure many other things that have more importance than their physical size would indicate: photographs, mementos, keepsakes, and such. An antique sofa and an album of baby pictures might both be irreplaceable, but if the house were burning down, most of us (the mothers among us, at least) would grab the baby pictures to save, and not just because they're easier to carry!

Take time to find out what things mean. Years later, there might not have been many people in Israel who knew what that pile of rocks on the west bank of the Jordan meant. But those who took the time to find out would have been rewarded with a bit of knowledge that was both interesting and beneficial. These days, most of us stay so busy with our own trivia, we rarely stop to ask the meaning of even the most important things around us. But we're the losers when we fail to ask, "What does that mean?"

Take time to appreciate what things mean. In regard to God, there are a number of events, observances, and even physical objects (what about your own Bible?) that have deep meaning attached to them. Do we appreciate these? Do we count them among our treasures? We need to take precautions against ever becoming so jaded that the meaningful things in life seem stale or dull.

Teach your children what things mean. We do our children a disservice when we allow them to reach maturity without having been taught what the truly important things in life mean. Meanings have to be handed down, and so it's the privilege and responsibility of each generation to see that its young people know what those who've gone before have found meaningful.

Few things are inherently valuable; it's what they *mean* to somebody that makes them so. So meanings are very important, and we'd be better off if we spent more time thinking about them.

> The least of things with a meaning is worth more
> in life than the greatest of things without it.
> CARL JUNG

April 22
SOMETHING MORE THAN OURSELVES

*And the LORD God said, "It is not good that man should
be alone; I will make him a helper comparable to him."*
Genesis 2:18

WE ARE NOT SELF-SUFFICIENT CREATURES. We need contact with other beings who have a nature that corresponds to ours. And not just contact, we need the many benefits encompassed by the word "relationship." We've been constituted such that our needs can't be completely fulfilled within our own identities. We need something more than ourselves, something outside of ourselves. "It is not good," God said, "that man should be alone."

It is true that we *vary* in the amount of human contact and relationship that we have to have to be happy. Some of us can get by with a minimum of those things, while others would find it hard to be happy without a bit more. In a pinch, of course, all of us could survive alone on a deserted island if we had to do it, but even so, the *norm* for human beings is that we need one another.

But if that's important to realize, it's even more important to realize that we need relationship with *our Creator*. We need something *above* ourselves! And that relationship is one that we really can't do without. We may delude ourselves into thinking that we're getting along without Him, for a while, but the fact is, we'd do less damage to ourselves trying to do without oxygen than trying to do without God. Try as we may, we can't *not* need Him!

Whether it's relationship to other human beings or relationship to God, "loneliness" is the word that describes the absence of those relationships. And while you may think there are plenty of problems worse than loneliness, let me tell you that the emptiness of spirit denoted by this word is a terrible thing: it's terrible not because it's painful but because it's the root of so many other problems that plague us. Having been created by God with needs that can only be filled in relationship with others, when those needs are not filled, many harmful things begin to happen.

So what's the point? It's simply that we ought to *cherish* the idea of rich relationship, both with God and with others who've been created in His image. We ought to work on *building* good relationships in every way that we can. And finally, the *maintenance* of our relationships ought to be one of our *most pressing priorities*.

Loneliness is the first thing that God's eye nam'd not good.
JOHN MILTON

April 23
PROFESSED BELIEFS VS. PRACTICAL BELIEFS

They profess to know God, but in works they deny Him.
Titus 1:16

W HAT WE REALLY BELIEVE ABOUT GOD IS OFTEN SOMETHING
OTHER THAN WHAT WE PROFESS TO BELIEVE. We may say we
believe He exists, for example, but if our actions are inconsistent with that belief, time after time, it would be fair to question
whether we really believe what we say. Even in the affairs of this
life, our real "master" is the one whom we actually "serve," and
when it comes to God, Paul asked the obvious question: "Do you
not know that to whom you present yourselves slaves to obey, you
are that one's slaves whom you obey, whether of sin leading to
death, or of obedience leading to righteousness?" (Romans 6:16).

But please don't misunderstand. I'm not saying that we deliberately lie about our faith, claiming to believe one thing when
we know that our real belief is something else. I'm simply sug-
gesting that our words usually reflect what we know is *right* to
believe, what we *want* to believe, and so forth, while our actions
may indicate that — *for all practical purposes* — our *real* beliefs run
in another direction. We don't always have the thing Paul said we
should be aiming for: a "faith unfeigned" (1 Timothy 1:5 KJV).

If there is a discrepancy between what we profess and what
we practice, how should we go about removing it? We could, of
course, get rid of the gap by lowering our profession to the level of
our practice, but that would amount to giving up and selling out
to the devil. But there are better things that we can do, surely.

First, we can be more honest about the gap between our profession and our practice. We can pray more frankly and openly to
God about that. Second, we can elevate our practice to the level of
our profession, always seeking God's help in doing so. He wants
us to obey what we say we believe, and He will help us to do so if
we let Him. But third, we can accept the fact that we are going to
be judged on the basis of our practice, not our profession. In the
end, it's our *deeds* that God will judge (2 Corinthians 5:10) — not
what we said we believed, not what we wanted to believe, and not
what we were planning to believe someday. Whether we admit it
or not, it's a fact: *what we actually do is what we really believe.*

Can a faith that does nothing be called sincere?
JEAN RACINE

IN THE MIDST OF IT ALL

For the earnest expectation of the creation
eagerly waits for the revealing of the sons of God.
Romans 8:19

THERE IS A SENSE IN WHICH WE NEED TO GET MORE COMFORTABLE
WITH THE IDEA OF *IMPERFECTION*. The perfection of this world
having been broken by sin, God long ago set in motion a plan that
will culminate in the creation of a new heavens and earth, not
physical but spiritual, for all those who've accepted His pardon.
The major portions of the plan are already complete, but the final
end has not been reached, and so while time on earth remains, we
must be content to live in the midst of a movement *toward* perfection. As long as we live, nothing that we'll have the opportunity
to deal with will ever be anything other than incomplete. And the
sooner we get comfortable with that idea, the better off we'll be.

To be sure, there is another sense in which we ought *not* to get
comfortable with imperfection. Complacency is a dangerous trait,
and we dare not let ourselves become *satisfied* with the incomplete-
ness of this world. We can't afford to lower our standards.

But I believe we'll reach forward more fervently if we go
ahead and *accept* the fact that in this life we will never be anything
more than incomplete. Recognizing that, for the time being, we're
not going to see anything more than God's work "in progress," we
are then free to dream and yearn and long for the time when His
plan will reach its climax, and we can finally go home. Accepting
the as-yet unfinished nature of God's purposes keeps us from
demanding more of this life than it's capable of delivering.

In Romans 8:22,23, Paul wrote of our "groaning" in this world:
"For we know that the whole creation groans and labors with birth
pangs together until now. Not only that, but we also who have the
firstfruits of the Spirit, even we ourselves groan within ourselves,
eagerly waiting for the adoption, the redemption of our body."
So the Christian who groans should hardly be surprised . . . but
neither should he be discouraged! "Beloved, now we are children
of God; and it has not yet been revealed what we shall be, but we
know that when He is revealed, we shall be like Him, for we shall
see Him as He is" (1 John 3:2).

We must learn how to live as incomplete beings in an unfinished
universe. We see God's process from the middle, not the end.

PAUL CIHOLAS

April 25
PATIENCE WHILE WE MAKE PROGRESS

Now to Him who is able to keep you from stumbling,
And to present you faultless
Before the presence of His glory with exceeding joy,
To God our Savior, who alone is wise,
Be glory and majesty,
Dominion and power,
Both now and forever. Amen.
Jude 24,25

As LONG AS WE REMAIN IN THIS WORLD, IMPERFECTIONS WILL BE A FACT OF LIFE. If we've obeyed the gospel and become Christians, we're somewhere along a path that leads to perfect holiness. Some have been Christians longer and are a bit further down the path than others, but none of us, not even the most mature, can say that we're without sin (1 John 1:8-10). We're all works in progress. So since it's God's plan for our sanctification to be accomplished gradually through a *process*, we need to be patient with God (and with ourselves) while the process is underway.

Although we make mistakes and lapse into old habits, God is able, as Jude wrote, to keep us from falling away from Him completely. He can strengthen us and present us "faultless before the presence of His glory with exceeding joy." We should discipline our thinking and hold on to the confidence that God knows what He's doing and is perfectly capable of removing the remainder of sin from our lives. Meanwhile, we must not expect perfection before the time for that perfection arrives (1 John 3:2,3).

This is no argument for complacency or careless indulgence in sin. "How shall we who died to sin live any longer in it?" (Romans 6:2). We're simply saying that as we reach forward to God's holiness, we must not demand a perfection of ourselves that is impossible at this point. We must accept the fact that we're on a *journey*.

The important thing right now, then, is not perfection but progress. No less than absolute perfection should be our *goal*, but as we work toward that goal, we'll make more progress if we concentrate on taking the steps that are immediately before us. Those are always steps that we're capable of taking, and we should be both *thankful* to take them and *content* to take them.

The rising of devotion in an ordinary soul is like the dawning
of a new day. Darkness is not driven away immediately. Light comes
in small increments, moment by moment.
FRANCIS DE SALES

April 26
GOD SEES BEHIND OUR PERSONALITIES

Your sin will find you out.
Numbers 32:23

NOW AND THEN WE ALL MAKE A SERIOUS MISTAKE: WE SACRIFICE OUR PRINCIPLES IN ORDER TO GAIN SHORT-TERM "SUCCESS." We take short cuts. We go for quick fixes. We try to get by using nothing but the smoke-and-mirrors techniques of personality and persuasive speech. Rather than do the hard, time-consuming work of building godly character and doing what is eternally *right*, we succumb to the tempting appeal of things that have a more visible payoff in the short term. But while it's possible to utilize personality rather than principle (for a while, at least), we ought to be more attracted to the benefits and joys of *long-term reality.*

Don't we understand that the deficiencies and drawbacks of our short cuts will come back to haunt us? Our sins will surely find us out. No matter what we're doing, if we leave the Lord and His principles out of our calculations, our project will fail sooner or later. "Unless the LORD builds the house, they labor in vain who build it; unless the LORD guards the city, the watchman stays awake in vain" (Psalm 127:1). God can't be safely ignored.

Some people, it's true, are amazingly clever at getting what they want in the short term, with seemingly little attention paid to the principles of long-term reality. And for those who're not as naturally adept at these things, our bookstores are filled with volumes on self-help, psychology, and communication skills. Getting what we want is reduced to the relatively simple matter of networking, making the right moves, communicating effectively, and of course, dressing for success. We are a deeply superficial people.

But in the absence of genuine godliness and deep-down integrity, none of the successes gained by these techniques will stand the test of time. God sees behind our personalities, and if we only knew it, most other people do too. Eventually the Law of the Farm will prevail. We will reap as we have sown. We may wish there were, but there is no short cut to any harvest worth having.

In most one-shot or short-lived human interactions, you can use
the Personality Ethic to get by and to make favorable impressions
through charm and skill and pretending to be interested in other people's
hobbies. But eventually, if there isn't deep integrity and fundamental
character strength, the challenges of life will cause true motives to surface
and human relationship failure will replace short-term success.

STEPHEN R. COVEY

April 27
THE SET OF OUR SAILS

And Elijah came to all the people, and said, "How long will
you falter between two opinions? If the LORD is God, follow Him;
but if Baal, follow him." But the people answered him not a word.
1 Kings 18:21

WHEN IT COMES TO GOD, WE WON'T MAKE MUCH PROGRESS
IF WE "FALTER BETWEEN TWO OPINIONS." There is a certain
amount of difficulty that has to be overcome in the course of our
journey toward God, and that difficulty won't be overcome if we
haven't made up our minds and committed ourselves to making
the journey. The roadside will be littered with the bleached bones
of those who wavered — those who weren't sure what their opinion was as to the importance of God and weren't sure whether
devoting themselves to Him was something they wanted to do.

Less important excursions in life often don't require any
definite goal or decisiveness on our part. For me, one of life's great
joys is the joy of walking, and there are some times when I set out
on a walk without any notion of where I want to go. It's enjoyable
just to walk. The destination might change during the walk, and
side trips can easily be taken. On such a walk, a little haphazard-
ness doesn't hurt; it may even enhance the pleasure of the trek.

But haphazard progress won't get us to heaven. We won't reach
God by casually strolling through life admiring the scenery. God
is the God of those who "diligently seeking Him" (Hebrews 11:6),
and that implies the necessity of *conscious decision.* If God is our
goal, we won't *move* toward Him if we don't *reach* for Him.

In the end, there'll only be two groups of people. The dividing
line won't be between the fortunate and the unfortunate, or between those who had it easy and those who had it hard; it will be
between those who decided to go to heaven and those who didn't.
When "every wind of doctrine" (Ephesians 4:14) is gusting every
which way, it's the set of our sails that'll get us home.

One ship drives east and another west,
with the self-same winds that blow;
'tis the set of the sails and not the gales
that determines where they go.
Like the winds of the sea are the ways
of fate, as we voyage along through life;
'tis the set of a soul that decides its goal
— and not the calm or the strife.

ELLA WHEELER WILCOX

April 28
SEEKING, SEARCHING, STRIVING

If you seek her as silver,
And search for her as for hidden treasures;
Then you will understand the fear of the LORD,
And find the knowledge of God.
Proverbs 2:4,5

W E'RE NOTHING BUT FOOLISH IF WE THINK WE CAN OBTAIN THE
SILVER AND GOLD OF GOD'S GOODNESS WITHOUT ANY HARD
WORK. As for wisdom, Solomon said that she will be found by
those who "seek her as silver" and "search for her as for hidden
treasure." No less can be said for God Himself. He must be sought
with a certain amount of doggedness and discipline. Those who
expect to "understand the fear of the LORD, and find the knowledge of God" should be prepared to do some mountain climbing.

To say this is not to teach "works righteousness." Whatever
conditions God may have set for a right relationship with Him, the
meeting of those conditions on our part in no way earns the gift
that is given. Our salvation is by the goodness of God's grace. But
at the same time, God's grace is not for the lazy, and He has constructed the reality of this world such that He won't be found by
those who're not willing to seek Him. So think of it this way: hard
work on our part is not *sufficient* to find God, but it is *necessary.*

Unfortunately, the worldly often work harder at their projects
than the godly work at theirs. And sometimes, they even show
greater good sense and cleverness. Jesus said that "the sons of this
world are more shrewd in their generation than the sons of light"
(Luke 16:8). In his comments on this text, William Barclay said, "If
only the Christian was as eager and ingenious in his attempt to
attain goodness as the man of the world is in his attempt to attain
money and comfort, he would be a much better man."

Yet it's not just the lazy who fail to exert effort; it's also the
desperate. Faced by daunting difficulties, we just give up and fail
to make the effort. And, of course, Satan, our enemy, loves to have
it so. He takes perverse delight in the fear that keeps us from taking even one step in God's direction. But he need not have the last
word. We can determine that, God being our helper, we will summon the courage, the self-respect, and the energy to . . . *act!*

Surrendering to despair is man's favorite pastime. God offers
a better plan, but it takes effort to grab it and faith to claim it.
CHARLES R. SWINDOLL

REACHING FOR THE WRONG THINGS

Then Samuel said to the people, "Do not fear. You have done all this
wickedness; yet do not turn aside from following the LORD, but serve the
LORD with all your heart. And do not turn aside; for then you would go after
empty things which cannot profit or deliver, for they are nothing."
1 Samuel 12:20,21

LIKE THE PEOPLE OF SAMUEL'S DAY, WE NEED TO BE WARNED
AGAINST GOING AFTER "EMPTY THINGS WHICH CANNOT PROFIT
OR DELIVER." Empty things are those that are fruitless and ineffective. They promise great thirst-quenching fulfillments but deliver
nothing but dryness and dust in the end. And empty things are all
that we can seek if we "turn aside from following the LORD."

God Himself is what we were created to seek. When we reach
forward to Him, we're doing the most natural thing in the world.
"Eternity" has been planted in our hearts (Ecclesiastes 3:11), and
that being true, we can't really *not* need God. But if God is what
we need, we must be careful to give our hearts what they need *and
nothing less than that.* Empty things will leave our hearts empty!

But as we determine to reach for the right things, it is sometimes hard to be honest about what we're really reaching for. We
tell ourselves that it's God we're reaching for when in reality it's
often certain blessings *from* God that we're primarily interested in.
It's not God Himself that we seek but only a certain path to God.
And if our particular path to God turns out to be different from
what we had in mind, we sometimes falter in our faithfulness. But
we need to be like Job, just as willing to trust God when it doesn't
"pay" as when it does. It must be *God* that we want, period.

It's a fact that we are a "reaching people." By our very nature,
we strain forward, eager to get in touch with *something* that can
fill our needs. Foolishly, however, we often reach for the wrong
things, things that can't satisfy us in the long run. And this is
no small problem; it's a matter of life and death. If in our need
we grasp the wrong thing, we doom ourselves to death. So the
question is not really whether we'll "reach forward" or not; we
will satisfy our desires in one way or another. The only question
is whether our "satisfactions" will kill us or not. It pays a very
thirsty man to be very careful what he allows himself to drink.

Thirst must be quenched! If our desires are not met by God,
we will quickly find something else to alleviate our thirst.

ERWIN W. LUTZER

April 30
BUT WHAT IF . . . ?

For as the rain comes down, and the snow from heaven, and do not return there, but water the earth, and make it bring forth and bud, that it may give seed to the sower and bread to the eater, so shall My word be that goes forth from My mouth; it shall not return to Me void, but it shall accomplish what I please, and it shall prosper in the thing for which I sent it.
Isaiah 55:10,11

THE VERY ESSENCE OF FAITH IS TO "TRUST AND OBEY." If a certain course of action seems wise to us and looks like it might lead to satisfactory results, it doesn't take much faith to follow that course. But when we can't see how a particular thing is going to turn out, or if we have a hunch that it might turn out disastrously, it takes faith to trust the person who formulated the plan and simply carry out the instructions that have been given to us.

We can only imagine what faith it took for Abraham to "trust and obey" when God said to leave his home in Ur (not to mention the things that God later commanded him to do). But faith was indeed the key. "By faith Abraham obeyed when he was called to go out to the place which he would receive as an inheritance. And he went out, *not knowing where he was going*" (Hebrews 11:8).

Today, many of us try to be people of faith, but our faith often fails us. What God says can seem so contrary to common sense that we balk at obeying Him. So when someone points out to us, "This is what God says," we tend to respond, "But what if . . . ?"

Even in worldly affairs, however, we shouldn't always decide our course of action pragmatically, based on what we think will "work." Our definition of what will "work" is often flawed, and in any case, we can't see far enough ahead to know what the outcome of any decision will be. So we need to base our decisions *on proven principles rather than predictions of particular outcomes!*

In spiritual matters, we can take it for granted that God's way will always work, that is, it will always accomplish the purpose that He had in mind, whether that purpose is clear to us or not: "[My word] shall not return to Me void, but it shall accomplish what I please, and it shall prosper in the thing for which I sent it." So the question is not what will happen, but what our principles should be. And that's just what God has given us in the Scriptures: a treasure chest of valid, time-tested, true-north *principles.*

If one can be certain that his principles are right, he need not worry about the consequences.
ROBERT ELLIOTT SPEER

May 1
AIMLESS CONDUCT

*. . . knowing that you were not redeemed with corruptible things,
like silver or gold, from your aimless conduct received by tradition
from your fathers. 1 Peter 1:18*

D ECIDING TO "REACH FORWARD" REQUIRES A GOOD BIT MORE
THAN JUST GETTING BUSY. Our actions have to be motivated
by a love for God, and they have to be within the limits of His will
and His purposes. Having been redeemed from the "aimless conduct" in which we used to engage, we must now devote ourselves
to deeds that are purposeful and fruitful with regard to God.

One of the main things that distinguishes the Christian's life
is that it is *going somewhere that really matters.* If there were no God,
nothing that happens would have any meaning. From birth to
death, our lives would be no more than the "busyness" of spin-
ning our wheels. But God does exist, and what that means is that
history is not just history — it is His-story. The plot is moving
toward a climax that will redound to His eternal glory, and if we
allow ourselves to be reconciled to Him through His Son, then
every deed we do can help move the plot toward its great end.

We need to live, work, and serve in the confidence that what
we do in the Lord is eternally worthwhile *whether we can see that
right now or not.* Paul wrote, "Therefore, my beloved brethren, be
steadfast, immovable, always abounding in the work of the Lord,
knowing that your labor is not in vain in the Lord" (1 Cor. 15:58).
Your labor is not in vain in the Lord. What glorious, life-changing
words! What a difference they ought to make for us on days when
we can't see that it does any good to try to do what's right.

But we need to take the time to "take stock" of the way we're
living our lives. If we've become Christians, then we have the *opportunity* to be busy about the most important things in the world
— but really, are those the things that we're busy about most of
the time? Is our day-to-day activity connected to our principles in
a harmonious way? Are we walking our talk? Is it really God that
we're reaching forward to, or must we admit that we're preoccupied with lesser things? These questions aren't just important; they
ought to be *urgent* as well. If we're not busy about the Father's
business, then our conduct is not going anywhere — it's aimless.

It is not enough to be busy; so are the ants.
The question is: what are we busy about?

HENRY DAVID THOREAU

May 2
NOSTALGIA: HANDLE WITH CARE

Do not say, "Why were the former days better than these?"
For you do not inquire wisely concerning this.
Ecclesiastes 7:10

IT'S HARD TO REACH *FORWARD* AND *BACKWARD* AT THE SAME TIME. Yet I fear that's the very thing we often try to do. We say we're reaching forward, but the pull of nostalgia can tug at our hearts so strongly that we catch ourselves trying to make the world like it *used* to be rather than the way it *ought* to be, as if "used to be" and "ought to be" were exactly synonymous. The net effect of our exertions in life is often more backward than forward.

Nostalgia is a wonderful thing, and not many folks love it any more than I do. But nostalgia must be handled with care. If we don't watch out, it can hinder us in our journey toward God. So here are a few tips on enjoying the past in a helpful, healthful way.

(1) Whatever good may have been done previously, today is the only day any new activity can be done. We can enjoy the past, and we can certainly learn from it. But yesterday's work is already done, and that work won't suffice for today. Thinking about the past (or anything else, for that matter) can't be a substitute for today's *action*.

(2) We must learn to be grateful for the past without worshiping it. Having the right attitude toward past, present, and future is a matter of *balance*. If there are good things about the days gone by, we must love those things neither too little nor too much. Maintaining that balance requires making frequent adjustments.

(3) Even if the past was better than the present in some ways, it is fruitless to wonder why. None of us — not even the philosophers — have enough information to answer the question, "Why is the world changing as it is?" The farmer must stick to seed-sowing and not worry too much why the weather's not what it used to be.

When we get to wondering "Why were the former days better than these?" we need to understand that *the past wasn't really as wonderful as we remember it.* After all, our memories are quite selective, remembering a few pleasant things and forgetting others that weren't so pleasant. So while the good old days may do our hearts good to ponder, they don't serve very well as a goal for the future.

Through the centuries the people have dreamed
of a Golden Age and longed for its return, unconscious that
they dream of a day that has never been.

GUY E. SHIPLER

May 3
THE TREE OF LIFE

He who has an ear, let him hear what the Spirit says to the churches.
To him who overcomes I will give to eat from the tree of life, which is
in the midst of the Paradise of God. *Revelation 2:7*

IN A SENSE, THE THING WE'RE LOOKING FOR IN THIS WORLD IS THE
THING THAT WAS LOST IN EDEN. And what God has in store for us
beyond this world is described in terms that hark back to the original Garden: "To him who overcomes I will give to eat from the tree
of life, which is in the midst of the Paradise of God."

Beneath our longing for many other things, it is really "life"
that we long for. And though we cling to biological life as if it were
our most prized possession, what we really desire is something
more: we long to be alive *spiritually*. Jesus Christ claimed to be the
Giver of life on that level. "I have come that they may have life,
and that they may have it more abundantly" (John 10:10).

When Adam and Eve sinned, desiring to know all that God
knew, even if they had to disobey Him to get that knowledge,
they were expelled from Eden and their access to the Tree of Life
was cut off (Genesis 3:22-24). As the long years of their mortality
wound down, they surely must have regretted their decision many
times. And we, their heirs, should be warned: our own quest for
knowledge is a poor substitute for the life that we have lost. Lord
Byron's lines were never more true than today: "Sorrow is knowledge: they who know the most / Must mourn the deepest o'er the
fatal truth, / The Tree of Knowledge is not that of Life."

Yet through the gospel of Jesus Christ, we can have all that the
word "life" was ever meant to convey. And the amazing thing is,
the life that is available to us right now in Christ is, at its very best,
only a foretaste of the fuller life that awaits us. That life is what
we're reaching for, straining toward it with every ounce of our
strength. And the confident, powerful hope of *that* life releases us
from the fear of letting go of *this* life — for to the faithful Christian,
physical death has become the mere door to real life, that which is
life *indeed*. "Inasmuch then as the children have partaken of flesh
and blood, He Himself likewise shared in the same, that through
death He might destroy him who had the power of death, that
is, the devil, and *release those who through fear of death were all their
lifetime subject to bondage*" (Hebrews 2:14,15).

He who lives to live forever, never fears dying.
WILLIAM PENN

REACH FOR HOLINESS BEFORE HAPPINESS

Pursue peace with all people, and holiness,
without which no one will see the Lord.
Hebrews 12:14

HOLINESS IS A HIGHER PRIORITY THAN HAPPINESS. It should rank higher in our scale of values than happiness, and maintaining its presence in our lives should be a matter of more pressing concern. The pursuit of holiness should be what we're known for.

To say that anything is more important than happiness sounds absurd to our modern ears, of course. The very idea flies in the face of popular philosophy. Even when it comes to *religious* philosophy, most people nowadays take it as their basic premise that God "wants us to be happy." We even use that benchmark to decide what God's will is in the first place. Faced with various interpretations of scriptural teaching, we choose the one that we think would make us the happiest. And if someone challenges the correctness of our decision, our reply is often predictable: "Well, I just can't believe that God wouldn't want me to be happy."

But while the "pursuit of happiness" may be a social and political priority, it does not rank at the top of any scriptural list of criteria by which our conduct is to be decided. Although long-term joy, properly defined, was His objective (Hebrews 12:1,2), Jesus often chose the difficult over the easy, and the painful over the pleasant: "Not My will, but Yours, be done" (Luke 22:42).

None of this is meant to imply that happiness is unimportant. It certainly is important, to some extent. But to whatever extent happiness matters, the way to achieve it is not to make it the main objective in life, as many people do. Happiness comes mostly to those who are willing to be unhappy, if need be, while they work on goals of greater significance. God, our Creator, is a better manager of our happiness than we are, and in the long run, we'll be happier if we seek Him first and let Him decide how much happiness we can handle without forgetting Him. If we had to, we could survive the loss of any amount of happiness, but no one can survive the absence of holiness. So that's the thing most worth pursuing . . . and if we don't do that, then death will be our doom.

No man should desire to be happy who is not at the same time holy.
He should spend his efforts in seeking to know and do the will of God,
leaving to Christ the matter of how happy he shall be.

A. W. TOZER

May 5
DO IT BECAUSE YOU DON'T WANT TO

But I discipline my body and bring it into subjection, lest, when I have
preached to others, I myself should become disqualified.
1 Corinthians 9:27

IT'S HEALTHY TO DO SOMETHING EVERY DAY THAT WE REALLY DON'T
WANT TO DO — JUST FOR THE EXERCISE. There is a great benefit in
practicing the art of self-discipline, that is, engaging in it regularly
just for the sake of building our mental muscles.

When Paul said that he "disciplined" his body and brought
it into "subjection," he spoke of something that requires a bit of
unpleasantness from time to time. By its very nature, training
requires us to get out of our comfort zone. If we never call upon
our "muscles" to do anything more than what they want to do,
then we never gain the ability to do anything more than that. It's
just that simple. And so we ought to look for opportunities to do
things that we don't want to do. It's one good way that we grow.

Have you ever watched someone "exercising"? Many of the
bodily movements by which strength and agility are developed
would be ridiculous if we did them for any reason other than
training or exercise. Take sit-ups, for example. There is only one
reason to do sit-ups: *to make your abdominal muscles do things they
don't want to do.* No one would ever do it for any other reason except . . . training . . . practice . . . exercise . . . discipline. When you
do sit-ups, you're demonstrating that you grasp one of life's great
principles: *there is value in doing things that don't want to be done.*

Nothing is more valuable than to have our faculties — mental
and spiritual, as well as physical — trained and ready to respond
to important needs. But having faculties that will respond to important needs is not something that happens overnight or without
any effort. When the big tests of life come along, we won't be
ready for them if we haven't been training for them before then.
So today, if there's some unpleasant little duty that could easily be
procrastinated, do it just because you don't want to. Take that little
opportunity to put the flesh in its place. Teach your body to take
orders from your spirit. Someday, you'll be mighty glad you did.

Keep the faculty of effort alive in you by a little gratuitous exercise every day.
Be systematically ascetic or heroic in little unnecessary points. Do every day
or two something for no other reason than that you would rather not do it, so
that when the hour of dire need draws nigh, it may find you not unnerved
and untrained to stand the test.

WILLIAM JAMES

May 6
THAT WOULD BE PROGRESS

He who would love life and see good days, let him refrain his tongue from evil, and his lips from speaking deceit. Let him turn away from evil and do good; let him seek peace and pursue it.
1 Peter 3:10,11

MAKING BIG PROGRESS IN LIFE IS JOYFUL, BUT MAKING LITTLE PROGRESS MAY BE MORE IMPORTANT IN THE LONG RUN. Giant strides, however pleasant they may be on rare occasions, don't get the world's work done. That is done by little steps, taken daily.

Aesop's fable, "The Tortoise and the Hare," is a powerful commentary on life, isn't it? In that story, the hare ran in spurts, making great progress once in a while, but the race was won by the tortoise, who wasn't capable of doing anything very big; but he kept at it, steadily taking whatever steps he could take, with the result that he outperformed his more flashy competitor.

In a similar way, real progress in life doesn't usually require doing big things that make headlines in the newspaper. It consists of doing little things regularly, like those suggested by Peter: being careful about our language, turning away from evil deeds, pursuing peace, and so forth. Those are steps *all* of us can take.

Little steps can often be more important than their size alone would indicate. Just as the Lord judges things by the level of *sacrifice* they require (Mark 12:41-44), I believe He also judges them by the amount of *courage* that is needed (Mark 15:43). When it takes courage to take even a small step, that courage transforms the step into one that looms quite large, at least in the Lord's eyes.

Today, we may not be capable of doing *all* that needs to be done in our relationship with God. Nevertheless, there is some small step that we *could* take, and if we'd just take it, that would be progress. If we did this seemingly insignificant thing, that would represent forward movement — and the devil would be defeated by just that much. As our adversary, he doesn't want us to take *any* step, and when we summon the courage and love for God to *do the small thing that is within our reach*, the devil is discouraged! So whatever else may happen today, let's do some small thing out of love for God. If we did even that much, *that would be progress*. And making progress is what this hard life is all about.

Courage doesn't always roar. Sometimes courage is the quiet voice
at the end of the day saying, "I'll try again tomorrow."
MARYANNE RADMACHER

ON LAZINESS AND LEAKY HOUSES

Because of laziness the building decays,
And through idleness of hands the house leaks.
Ecclesiastes 10:18

IF THE GOAL IS GODLY CHARACTER, THAT GOAL WILL NOT BE REACHED BY ACCIDENT OR BY INACTIVITY. The fact that salvation is by grace means many things, but *it doesn't mean that the lazy will be saved*. To Timothy, Paul wrote, "Be diligent to present yourself approved to God" (2 Timothy 2:15). It's only those who love God enough to seek Him *energetically* who one day will receive the benefit of having sought Him. The lazy are going to be lost!

Physically speaking, a building "decays" when it's owners don't maintain it, and "through idleness of hands the house leaks." Do-nothingism never leads to anything but a dilapidated state of affairs. Left to themselves, physical things deteriorate.

In the spiritual realm, the consequences of laziness are even more serious. A house leaking because its roof has not been maintained is nothing compared to a human soul that has been neglected. When effort is not expended to grow toward God, the corruption and decay that result in the human heart are shocking.

So the disciplines that lead to godliness take *work*. This work does not earn or merit our salvation, it's true. But it's also true that without work we will certainly *forfeit* our salvation (Hebrews 6:11,12). Heaven is for the interested, the energetic, and the industrious. And we need not say that we're industrious toward God if our actual daily habits don't show that. Whether it's serving others in the name of Christ or the more private activities of Bible study, prayer, and meditation, we can't claim to be working hard on the "house" of our godliness if, at the end of the day, our timelog doesn't show that we've spent much time doing these things. Under normal circumstances, a lack of activity indicates a degree of laziness. And laziness leads to leaky houses, always.

> I discover an arrant laziness in my soul. For when I am to read a chapter in the Bible, before I begin I look where it ends. And if it ends not on the same side, I cannot keep my hands from turning over the leaf, to measure the length on the other side; if it swells to many verses, I begin to grudge. Surely my heart is not rightly affected. Were I truly hungry after heavenly food, I would not complain of meat. Scourge, Lord, this laziness of my soul; make the reading of your Word, not a penance, but a pleasure to me; so I may esteem that chapter in your Word the best which is the longest.

SIR THOMAS FULLER

May 8
JUST A FEW MORE DAYS

So Jacob served seven years for Rachel, and they
seemed only a few days to him because of the love he had for her.
Genesis 29:20

ATTITUDES LIKE LOVE AND HOPE CAN SHORTEN WHAT OTHER-
WISE MIGHT SEEM LIKE A LONG TIME. Although time passes
at exactly the same rate every day, the passage of time can feel
shorter if our hearts are filled with the anticipation of something
very good. So for the joy of being married to Rachel, Jacob gladly
endured his servitude to Laban for seven years: ". . . they seemed
only a few days to him because of the love he had for her."

As we live and wait for the Lord's return, the passage of time
will seem much shorter if we live out our sojourn in *hope*. It may,
in fact, be many days until we see Him, but if our heart is where
it needs to be, it will only seem to be a few days. As the familiar
old hymn put it, "Just a few more days to be filled with praise, /
And to tell the old, old story; / Then, when twilight falls, and my
Savior calls, / I shall go to Him in glory" (Charles H. Gabriel).

Jesus promised to come back and take His faithful people to
heaven (John 14:1-3; Acts 1:9-11). He did not tell His disciples then,
and the Bible does not tell us now, that His return is imminent (1
Thessalonians 5:1,2). But listen: the Bible *does* teach that we are to
live *as if Christ's return were imminent* . . . because it very well may
be! There is no day, then or now, when the Lord is not "at hand"
(Philippians 4:5), and we are taught to live every single day of our
lives in the expectation of seeing Him return. *It could be today!*

Peter wrote that we are to "look for" and "hasten" the coming of the day of the Lord (2 Peter 3:12). That means that we are to
think of it lovingly and hopefully, just as Jacob would have "has-
tened" the coming of the day when he could marry Rachel.

But if hope shortens the time of our waiting for the Lord, it
also turns it into a time of *joy*. We are not merely to endure the
days of our waiting but to go so far as to *enjoy* them. It was to
a church that had as many hardships as anybody else that Paul
wrote, "Rejoice in the Lord always. Again I will say, rejoice! . . .
The Lord is at hand" (Philippians 4:4,5). This is the Lord "whom
having not seen you love. Though now you do not see Him, yet
believing, *you rejoice with joy inexpressible*" (1 Peter 1:8).

He that lives in hope dances without a fiddle.
ANONYMOUS

May 9
METAMORPHOSIS

For if we have been united together in the likeness of His death,
certainly we also shall be in the likeness of His resurrection.
Romans 6:5

TO BE A CHRISTIAN IS TO BE A PERSON UNDERGOING A GREAT CHANGE. What we are today is not what we will have become tomorrow — and each day after that, until our lives are done. We are creatures in the act of "becoming." As Paul wrote, "We all, with unveiled face, beholding as in a mirror the glory of the Lord, are being transformed into the same image from glory to glory, just as by the Spirit of the Lord" (2 Corinthians 3:18). We have already died to our old selves, but what we shall be "in the likeness of His resurrection" is not yet fully known. Only time will tell.

In nature, we're familiar with the metamorphosis by which, for instance, a caterpillar becomes a butterfly. The astonishing thing about this process is the *radical difference* between the caterpillar and the butterfly. Who could have predicted such a change?

But metamorphosis in the spiritual realm is very different than that in the physical realm in that it involves the freedom of the will of those who are being transformed. A caterpillar doesn't have any say in what kind of butterfly he'll turn out to be, but we do have a say in what we become. In fact, it's by our choice that we determine whether we will be transformed into glorious beings (partaking of the divine nature) or horrible monsters (partaking of nothing but the corruption that comes from death and decay).

Life in God is what has aptly been called the Great Adventure. No small part of this adventure is the joy of seeing ourselves unfold and develop into fully mature persons. What right-thinking person can fail to be excited about being transformed in this way?

When what we "are" frustrates us, we shouldn't give up on ourselves. One day, we will be glorious creatures, but we're not there yet. And even in this life, few of us have yet matured into the persons that others will remember us as being after we're gone. The most that can be said is that we're *becoming* the persons we were created to be. But that is saying quite a lot! In God, both the destination and the journey are things to be thankful for. Let's not fail to appreciate the awesome *process* that we're in the middle of.

People become who they are.
Even Beethoven had to become Beethoven.
RANDY NEWMAN

May 10
HEARTS THAT DON'T TURN BACK

All this has come upon us; but we have not forgotten You,
nor have we dealt falsely with Your covenant. Our heart has not
turned back, nor have our steps departed from Your way.
Psalm 44:17,18

HOLDING TRUE TO OUR COMMITMENT TO GOD IS EASIER AT SOME TIMES THAN AT OTHERS. On some days, the wind is at our back, helping us to go in the right direction, but on other days, the wind blows fiercely in our face, making it awfully tempting to turn back. But we can't keep our commitment to God just when it's easy. In fact, when remaining faithful is hard, that's when it's *especially* important to stay the course. We may be afflicted, persecuted, or even chastened with hardship by God Himself, but come what may, we must be people whose hearts don't turn back.

To live is to be moving. On any day, we're always going to be "going" one direction or another. It's important, then, to keep from going backward. We may not be making as much forward progress as we'd like, and at times it may seem that we're standing still. But at least we can determine not to go backward.

All of us, of course, are *tempted* to turn back. There is not a one of us who hasn't (at least secretly) given some thought to throwing our faith away and just living like the world. Jesus may have thought about it on other occasions as well, but in Gethsemane, He certainly thought about turning back. In His prayer, He confessed to *wanting* to turn back . . . but He made the choice to go forward. And like our Lord, we need to go forward toward God with a passion and a determination that *simply will not be denied!*

When a decision has to be made whether to follow God or turn back, it's important not to let that decision be made by our feelings alone. As good and valuable as our feelings may be (they were given to us by God), they are, by themselves, no true test of what God wants us to do. And mark it well: *our feelings are no test of whether God is "near" us or not.* At all times, God is certainly with us, supporting us and helping us to do what is right, whether it feels that way or not. And so, in darkness, doubt, and difficulty, we need to hang on to our faith and simply *refuse* to turn back.

In times of dryness and desolation we must be patient and wait with resignation the return of consolation, putting our trust in the goodness of God. We must animate ourselves by the thought . . . that we have not necessarily lost his grace because we have lost the taste and feeling of it.

IGNATIUS OF LOYOLA

May 11
THE RACE IS NOT TO THE SWIFT

I returned and saw under the sun that —
The race is not to the swift,
Nor the battle to the strong,
Nor bread to the wise,
Nor riches to men of understanding,
Nor favor to men of skill;
But time and chance happen to them all.
Ecclesiastes 9:11

IT WOULD BE AN INTERESTING EXERCISE TO TRY TO PREDICT WHO WILL AND WHO WILL NOT MAKE IT TO HEAVEN. Of the people you know, for example, who are the ones who will see God's face in His eternal kingdom? Whatever criteria you used to make such a forecast, there's a good chance that many of your predictions wouldn't come true. It's an obvious fact in this world: we are often *surprised* at how people's spiritual lives turn out. Some whom we think are bound to remain faithful to the Lord turn out to be little more than disappointments, while others we had little hope for end up being the most faithful. *The race is not to the swift!*

The reason predictions of any kind are hard is that life is full of *unexpected turns of events.* As far as people's spiritual lives are concerned, God is able to bring into play factors that we could never have foreseen but which totally change the outcome. He never overrides anyone's freedom of will, but He certainly does intervene providentially in ways that produce surprising results.

But if the race is not to the swift nor the battle to the strong, what does that mean? What should be our attitude about that fact?

First, we need to put away our "crystal balls." Especially when we're trying to influence someone who seems to be a "hopeless case," we need to allow that things may turn out better than we think they will. We should just go ahead and do whatever's right today, and let the future turn out to be whatever it will.

But second, we need to quit thinking that everything depends on us. We need to leave more room in our calculations for *God* to do what *He* can do. Any time God is involved, "it ain't over till it's over," and many more good things may turn up than we, or anyone else, could have produced or predicted. The race may look like it's lost, but still be won — despite our lack of swiftness.

The disillusionment with our own abilities is, perhaps, one
of the most important things that can ever happen to us.
TIM HANSEL

WILL OUR DESIRES BE FULFILLED OR FRUSTRATED?

The fear of the wicked will come upon him,
And the desire of the righteous will be granted. . . .
The hope of the righteous will be gladness,
But the expectation of the wicked will perish.
Proverbs 10:24,28

THERE IS A SENSE IN WHICH IT IS ONLY THE RIGHTEOUS WHO WILL "GET WHAT THEY WANT." Eventually, those who have circumvented God's will to obtain their desires find that the satisfaction of their desires did not bring them fulfillment but only frustration.

The deceitfulness of sin is that it takes desires that God gave us and persuades us to *fulfill those desires in illegitimate ways*. Take sexual desire, for example. God gave us that desire and provided for its genuine fulfillment. When we, however, try to fulfill that desire in ways that God has forbidden, not only do we sin but we fail to get the thing we thought we were after. It may be momentarily pleasurable, but no amount of sexual immorality will ever be as gratifying in the long run as committed love within the marriage relationship. But that's simply one example. The same thing can be said of *any* desire. Fulfill it in God-appointed ways and you'll get what you want. Fulfill it in forbidden ways and you'll eventually find yourself frustrated. "The hope of the righteous will be gladness, but the expectation of the wicked will perish."

It's arrogant to presume that we can take whatever we want, however we wish to get it, and then enjoy it as much as we want. We may, in fact, take whatever we want, but God has it within His power to *withhold from us the enjoyment of what we've taken*. In Ecclesiastes, we're taught that the person who acquires "riches and wealth" may consider himself blessed only if God has also "given him the power to eat of it" (Ecclesiastes 5:19; 6:2). So "getting what we want" may turn out to be harder than we thought.

I believe two things are needful: (1) We need to be *grateful* for the hopes and aspirations and desires that God has planted within our hearts, and (2) we need to be willing for those desires to be fulfilled *on His terms*. God wants nothing but the best for us. To seek anything other than His will for our lives is to put our feet on a path that leads to nothing but disappointment in the end.

Man finds it hard to get what he wants because
he does not want the best; God finds it hard to give because
he would give the best and man will not take it.

GEORGE MACDONALD

May 13
DO OUR ACTIONS SHOW APPRECIATION?

But Hezekiah did not repay according to the favor shown him,
for his heart was lifted up; therefore wrath was looming over him
and over Judah and Jerusalem. *2 Chronicles 32:25*

WHEN HEZEKIAH ERRED BY SHOWING ALL HIS TREASURES TO THE ENVOYS FROM BABYLON, HIS ERROR WAS ALL THE WORSE BECAUSE IT SHOWED A LACK OF APPRECIATION FOR GOD'S GRACE. Hezekiah had been sick and about to die, but he prayed that God would spare his life, and God did exactly that. And so after that, when in his pride "his heart was lifted up" and he acted foolishly toward the Babylonian representatives (2 Kings 20:12-19), Hezekiah demonstrated a lack of gratitude for the mercy that God had extended to him. As the text says, he "did not repay according to the favor shown him." And that's a serious mistake.

When we're thinking as we should, there is no greater motivation to do what's right than the awareness that God, or even someone else, has treated us better than we deserve. Knowing that we've been shown mercy humbles us and moves us to do better.

But we don't always think as we should, do we? And when grace is shown to us and we take it for granted, receiving it thoughtlessly and unappreciatively, there is no greater sin. One of the saddest stories in the New Testament is the one in Luke 17:11-19, where the Lord healed ten men of their leprosy. When only one, a Samaritan, came back to thank the Lord, He said, "Were there not ten cleansed? But where are the nine? Were there not any found who returned to give glory to God except this foreigner?"

Do we do any better than the unthankful nine? We wouldn't remain alive today if it weren't for God's grace. We've been forgiven of sins that we didn't deserve to have forgiven. God has been patient and longsuffering with us, far past the point when justice would have blasted us out of existence. But do we "repay according to the favor shown [us]"? Too many times, we do not.

Jesus said, "If you love Me, keep My commandments" (John 14:15). Basically, we say "thank you" to God for His grace and favor by *obeying His will*. And in particular, we show gratitude for God's grace by extending grace to others. "For judgment is without mercy to the one who has shown no mercy" (James 2:13).

Gratitude is born in hearts that
take time to count up past mercies.
CHARLES EDWARD JEFFERSON

May 14
ONLY TRUTH SHOWS THE WAY TO GOD

Oh, send out Your light and Your truth!
Let them lead me;
Let them bring me to Your holy hill
And to Your tabernacle.
Psalm 43:3

I N AN AGE WHEN IT'S POPULAR FOR PEOPLE TO MAKE UP THEIR OWN SPIRITUALITY, IT'S IMPORTANT TO REMEMBER THE VITAL ROLE OF TRUTH. If God is an objective reality, then neither He Himself nor the path by which He may be approached are matters of subjective opinion. We are not at liberty (1) to set the terms of our own salvation or (2) to define anything as "worship" that tickles our fancy.

Yet this is the day of "feel good" religion. When it comes to God's character, we envision Him in any way that is congenial to us, and when it comes to religious practice, we reject anything that does not stroke our self-image. Yet *truth* is what we need, at all costs. Imagine yourself on the deck of the *Titanic* as it began to sink. It might have made you feel better to be told the ship wasn't sinking and that everything was fine. But wouldn't the *truth* have been more valuable? As hard as it might have been to deal with reality, doing that would have been the only way to survive.

Spiritually, we are where we are right now because of "darkness." The distorted versions of reality that our adversary has presented us with have darkened our understanding to such an extent that we're incapable of finding our way back to God. The answer to David's question, "Who can understand his errors? (Psalm 19:12), is *no one* — unless that person allows the light of God's truth to dispel the darkness and reveal the way back home. Our prayer ought to be the same as William Cowper's hymn: "O for a closer walk with God, / A calm and heavenly frame, / A light to shine upon the road / That leads me to the Lamb!"

It's a wonderful truth that God can be known, and an even more wonderful truth that we can be redeemed from our sins and brought back to Him. But our redemption won't be accomplished if we're not willing to know God *as He truly is,* and it's primarily in the language of *the Scriptures* that He reveals Himself as He truly is. The only question is: what will we *do* with this information?

The sacred page is not meant to be the end, but only
the means toward the end, which is knowing God himself.

A. W. TOZER

May 15

HARVEST OF JOY

Those who sow in tears
Shall reap in joy.
He who continually goes forth weeping,
Bearing seed for sowing,
Shall doubtless come again with rejoicing,
Bringing his sheaves with him.
Psalm 126:5,6

INTO EVERY LIFE SOME RAIN MUST FALL, AND EACH OF US HAS "SOWN" HIS SHARE OF TEARS. But God has made it possible that those who "sow in tears shall reap in joy." We might wish the harvest time were already here, but that time is not yet. For all we know, it *may* be very near, and in fact, we are taught to live each day in the *expectation* of Christ's return. But for now anyway, the harvest is still future. Rather than speculate or worry about the reasons for God's delay of the harvest, we should enter willingly into these days of sowing, even if it is tears that must be sown. In the words of John Greenleaf Whittier's poem, "Thine is the seed time: God alone / Beholds the end of what is sown; / Beyond our vision weak and dim / The harvest time is hid with him."

It takes faith, of course, to hold on to the confidence that the sowing of tears will be followed by a reaping in joy. On many days, it certainly doesn't seem like things are going to work out that way. But we must choose to have the attitude of Paul: "I know whom I have believed and am persuaded that He is able to keep what I have committed to Him until that Day" (2 Timothy 1:12).

If we're "reaching forward to those things which are ahead" (Philippians 3:13), that means we're "looking for and hastening the coming of the day of God" (2 Peter 3:12). For a while yet, *this* is the world where our work must be done and where, yes, our tears must be sown. But this world is not all there is. If we've obeyed the gospel of Christ and are living our lives in Him, then we're moving toward a realm where our tears will give way to utter joy. "And God will wipe away every tear from their eyes; there shall be no more death, nor sorrow, nor crying. There shall be no more pain, for the former things have passed away" (Revelation 21:4).

Beyond this vale of tears
There is a life above
Unmeasured by the flight of years
And all that life is love.

JAMES MONTGOMERY

May 16
SEEKING FOR . . RECOGNITION?

*Take heed that you do not do your charitable deeds
before men, to be seen by them. Otherwise you have
no reward from your Father in heaven.*
Matthew 6:1

NOTHING TESTS OUR CHARACTER ANY MORE THAN HAVING TO CHOOSE BETWEEN MOTIVES. When there is a good deed to be done, for example, our character is tested: will we do it simply to glorify God or will we do it "to be seen by men"? That is a hard choice — much harder than most of us are willing to admit.

Praise itself is not evil, of course, but there's no denying that it has the potential to hurt us. Indeed, it's a rare person who can receive more than a moderate amount of recognition and not have his or her attitude marred by it. That doesn't stop us from wanting it, however. As Norman Vincent Peale once said, "Most of us would rather be ruined by praise than saved by criticism."

As for our motives, it's hard to be honest as to what they really are. The desire to be noticed and recognized as having done something good can be so subtle that it can be our real motive at times when we would say that it isn't. In a given situation, it's difficult to see when the thing that we really want is to be praised.

Perhaps it is stating it too strongly to say that we want "to be seen by men." But what about that word "recognized"? A little appreciative attention is an intoxicating thing. Once we've experienced it, even as children, it's easy for that to become the payoff that we seek (be truthful now!) in every transaction thereafter.

The needs of self, including the need to be appreciated, are not unimportant, of course. But God has set up reality such that *self's needs are satisfied most fully when we put our priorities elsewhere.* Jesus said, "But seek first the kingdom of God and His righteousness, and *all these things shall be added to you*" (Matthew 6:33).

So let's be very honest. *Why* do we do what we do for God? Do we serve Him as faithfully in private as in public? If no one ever noticed or thanked us, would we be content simply to know that God had been glorified? And if so, would we then avoid the opposite sin: being privately smug, knowing that we are "big" enough to do what's right even though nobody appreciates us?

*I cannot say "Thine is the glory" if I am
seeking my own glory first.*
ANONYMOUS

May 17
INEVITABLE RETURN

Then the dust will return to the earth as it was,
And the spirit will return to God who gave it.
Ecclesiastes 12:7

THERE IS NO AVOIDING THE APPOINTMENT THAT EACH OF US HAS TO BE JUDGED BY THE GOD WHO MADE US. When our lives have finally run out, we will die. And when that happens, "the dust will return to the earth as it was, and the spirit will return to God who gave it." Having been created by God, our spirits will return to Him. We will give account of ourselves. It is inevitable.

We are creatures, or created beings. If we simply "happened" to exist as a result of merely physical processes, then at some point we would cease to exist. But we didn't just happen to exist; we were *created*, and it is to our Creator that we will return. Where we are going has more than a little to do with where we came from!

We are accountable to our Creator. To be personal beings is a truly awe-inspiring fact. It means that we bear *responsibility for our actions.* Freedom of the will is a marvelous gift, and the use of it is something that we shall have to answer for at the end of our lives. "For we must all appear before the judgment seat of Christ, that each one may receive the things done in the body, according to what he has done, whether good or bad" (2 Corinthians 5:10).

By far the most important question in life is whether, having returned to God, we will be allowed to *remain* with Him. If we leave this life in a right relationship with God, we will hear Him say, "Enter into the joy of your lord" (Matthew 25:21). But if not, we will hear, "I never knew you; depart from Me" (Matthew 7:23).

Yet the anticipation of our return to God need not be fearful — it ought to be joyful. That prospect can't be joyful if we spend the years of our sojourn here in selfish indulgence, disregarding the things of God, and in fact, it can't be joyful if we simply live carelessly. But there is no reason why all of us can't make the same deliberate choices that Paul did and be able to say what he said: "The time of my departure is at hand. I have fought the good fight, I have finished the race, I have kept the faith. Finally, there is laid up for me the crown of righteousness, which the Lord, the righteous Judge, will give to me on that Day, and not to me only but also to all who have loved His appearing" (2 Timothy 4:6-8).

All days travel toward death, the last one reaches it.
MICHEL DE MONTAIGNE

WHEN WE'RE MOVED BY LOVE

For love is as strong as death, . . .
Its flames are flames of fire,
A most vehement flame.
Many waters cannot quench love,
Nor can the floods drown it.
Song of Solomon 8:6,7

IF IT'S FORWARD THAT WE WANT TO MOVE, LOVE IS THE MOST POW-ERFUL THING TO PROPEL US IN THAT DIRECTION. As a motivator, love really has no equal. It's "as strong as death." It burns with a flame that "many waters cannot quench." If someone you know is trying to do something and love is the reason why, you'd be wise to get out of the way. The thing is very likely going to happen.

Wouldn't we reach forward more fervently in life if our love for God were more affectionate? If the word "passion" accurately described our love for God, could anything hold us back? For too long, most of us have loved God too little and with too little fire.

The love that we so desperately need in our relationship to God is a thing that we can choose to have. We are commanded to love the Lord our God with all our heart, all our soul, and all our mind (Matthew 22:37), and that is a command we are capable of obeying. We can choose to think rightly about God, and then we can feed our minds on the truths that He has revealed about Himself in the Scriptures. When we do that with the genuine intent to be what He created us to be, we will find ourselves loving Him, adoring Him, and longing to be with Him now and forever.

It is no mere happenstance that God ordained the Lord's Supper for His people. Of all the things that can feed our love, none is more powerful than meditating, with other Christians, on the staggering, unfathomable love shown at the cross of Christ.

The world, the flesh, and the devil must be *fought*. But the simple fact is, we fight a losing battle if love is left out of the mix. If we don't have the help of our *hearts* in serving God, it's not likely that we'll hold out to the end. So, my friend, it is imperative that your activities be motivated by love, first for God and second for your neighbor. If that's the case (and God certainly knows whether it is or not), then discouragement will not defeat you. Other motives may falter, but "many waters cannot quench love."

Love can hope where reason would despair.
LORD GEORGE LYTTELTON

May 19
IN OUR HEARTS, DO WE TURN BACK TO EGYPT?

This is he who was in the congregation in the wilderness with
the Angel who spoke to him on Mount Sinai, and with our fathers, the one
who received the living oracles to give to us, whom our fathers would not
obey, but rejected. And in their hearts they turned back to Egypt . . .
Acts 7:38,39

IF WE'RE HONEST, WE'LL ADMIT THAT WE SOMETIMES LOOK BACK AND LONG FOR THE WORLD THAT WE'VE BEEN DELIVERED FROM. Just as the people of Israel foolishly thought, once they were in the wilderness, that their lives had been better back in Egypt, so we may think that the difficulties of doing what's right are too hard and that we had it better back when we simply lived for the moment. It's a fact that gaining freedom from slavery involves a good deal of danger and discomfort, whether the slavery is physical or spiritual. And we may think that although being a slave had its disadvantages, they were at least tolerable in comparison to the more grievous hardships of freedom. And so our old "comfort zone" calls us. It's tempting to give up the struggle and go back.

On one occasion, when Jesus was impressing on His disciples the need for decisive action, He said, "Remember Lot's wife" (Luke 17:32). In the act of escaping the destruction of Sodom, Lot's wife perished, not for going back but for simply looking back.

On another occasion, Jesus said, "No one, having put his hand to the plow, and looking back, is fit for the kingdom of God" (Luke 9:62). We show ourselves unthankful and unworthy of the grace that has been granted to us if we look back from our work in the Lord and think that we had it better before the work began.

Does this mean we should never even *think* about our pre-Christian past? No, but it does mean that we should reject that past decisively and never give the thought of going back a chance to get a grip on our minds. To the extent that thinking about the past helps motivate us to serve God more faithfully, then we should think about it. Paul, for example, seemed to work harder as an evangelist when he thought about his past (1 Corinthians 15:9,10). But if thinking about "Egypt" tempts us to go back there, even if it's just in our hearts, then we must determine not to do it. After all, it is not backward but *forward* that we are reaching.

Shut out all of your past except that which
will help you weather your tomorrows.
SIR WILLIAM OSLER

May 20
LET US RUN THE RACE

Therefore we also, since we are surrounded by so great a cloud of witnesses, let us lay aside every weight, and the sin which so easily ensnares us, and let us run with endurance the race that is set before us. *Hebrews 12:1*

BETWEEN NOW AND THE TIME OF OUR DEPARTURE FROM THIS LIFE, THERE IS A "RACE" THAT HAS TO BE RUN. And frankly, the image of a race is mainly an image of pain. Anyone who has ever run a footrace of any distance knows that before the end finally comes, every muscle in the runner's body cries out for relief. And the longer the race, the more tempting it is to simply . . . quit running.

A great cloud of witnesses. When we run as God's people, we are doing something that many, many others have done before us. And the writer of Hebrews describes those who've gone before as a "great cloud of witnesses," a stadium full of supportive spectators cheering us onward with the hearty cry, "You can do it!"

Lay aside every weight. In addition to supporters, we also happen to have a spiritual adversary whose purpose it is to defeat us. We must not let him have his way. The "sin which so easily ensnares us" must be laid aside. It's a very simple matter. Either we decide to lay our sins aside, or they will be the undoing of us.

Run with endurance. We are not in a sprint but a marathon. For all we know, it may be many years before the time comes for us to rest. But remember the "cloud of witnesses"? One of those witnesses is Paul, who wrote toward the end of his life, "I have finished the race" (2 Timothy 4:7). He did it, and we can do it too.

But there's no chance we'll do what Paul did if we're not motivated by what motivated him: *the glorious prospect of being with Christ forever.* He said that he had sacrificed every worldly thing that ever mattered to him: "that I may gain Christ and be found in Him . . . that I may know Him and the power of His resurrection, and the fellowship of His sufferings, being conformed to His death, if, by any means, I may attain to the resurrection from the dead" (Philippians 3:8-11). Any goal less powerful than this will fail to keep us going. We must fix our hearts upon our Lord and determine that we are going to run the race, come whatever may. There can be no question or equivocation about it. So let us not merely study or think about running the race. *Let us run the race.*

To believe in heaven is not to run
away from life; it is to run toward it.
JOSEPH D. BLINCO

May 21
THE LONGSUFFERING OF THE LORD IS SALVATION

. . . and consider that the longsuffering of our Lord is salvation.
2 Peter 3:15

PETER WROTE THAT WE OUGHT TO LOOK FORWARD TO OUR LORD'S RETURN, AND IF HIS RETURN IS DELAYED, LOOK UPON THAT DELAY AS THE VERY THING THAT MAKES OUR SALVATION POSSIBLE. There is no way around the fact that our salvation depends on the Lord's longsuffering. If He were as impatient as we are, our opportunity for improvement would have run out long ago. If we end up being saved, we will owe that salvation to the Lord's willingness to wait.

Opportunity for repentance. The Lord's delay in returning is not license to enjoy our sins for a while longer; it's an extended opportunity to get those things out of our character. Paul asked the pertinent question when he said, "Do you despise the riches of His goodness, forbearance, and longsuffering, not knowing that the goodness of God leads you to repentance?" (Romans 2:4).

Opportunity for spiritual growth. In terms of our spiritual maturity, none of us is where we need to be. We need more time to grow, and that is just what the Lord is giving us with His longsuffering. While He waits, we must use every day as a day of growth.

Opportunity for evangelism. Not only does the Lord's longsuffering mean salvation for us, it can mean salvation for those around us too. The more time we have before the end, the more time we have to get His message out to others. Every day the world still stands is a day that must be used evangelistically.

When Paul wrote to the church in Corinth, he used an expression that ought to suggest the most horrifying thing imaginable. He said, "We then, as workers together with Him also plead with you not to *receive the grace of God in vain*" (2 Corinthians 6:1). Do we *receive the grace of God in vain?* To do that would be to *waste* the patience and longsuffering that God has shown us, ending up being lost despite the fact that God waited and waited and waited. If God has not yet come to judge the world that does not mean that He is indifferent to evil; it means that He is still holding the door of salvation open. His longsuffering is nothing less than our salvation. We are the world's greatest fools if we don't see that.

> Hell is God's justice;
> heaven is his love;
> earth, his longsuffering.
>
> ANONYMOUS

FAR ABOVE US

"For My thoughts are not your thoughts,
Nor are your ways My ways," says the LORD.
"For as the heavens are higher than the earth,
So are My ways higher than your ways,
And My thoughts than your thoughts."
Isaiah 55:8,9

AS WE REACH TOWARD GOD, WE NEED TO UNDERSTAND THAT WE ARE REACHING *UPWARD*. In every conceivable way, God is *above* us. His ways and His thoughts are as far above ours "as the heavens are higher than the earth." Obviously, our wisdom and power are less than His, but what's more important, our "authority" is less than His. He is the Creator; we are His creatures. He is the King; we are His subjects. He is far above us in every way.

Hierarchy. It may not be in fashion nowadays, but the notion of "hierarchy" is a valid concept. Everywhere we look, from the physical cosmos to the animal kingdom, reality is ordered in hierarchies and structured in ranks. And somewhere deep inside, we understand that this is necessary and beneficial. It's time we admitted that there is nothing inherently demeaning about occupying a lower rank than someone else in the larger scale of life.

Humility. Accepting the fact that God is above us and we are under His rule, we need to have the humility to *welcome* His perspective, His thoughts, and His will for our lives. In our real-life decisions, we need to *yield* to the high wisdom that He alone has.

Happiness. There are great benefits that flow from having the right attitude toward all that is around us, and it's no exaggeration to say that the greatest happiness of all is that of taking our proper place in the vast scheme of God's creation, gladly under His rule.

If the truth be told, we *need* something superior to us to yearn for and to reach toward. Though we often suppose that independence, autonomy, and equality are the things we need, what we really need is some One *higher* than we — One in whose supremacy and sovereignty we may rest. Even in this life, security comes from having good rulers and good laws, and certainly in the life to come, what we long for is the perfect, benevolent rule of a King who is, as Paul wrote, eternal, immortal, and all-wise. To Him "be honor and glory forever and ever. Amen" (1 Timothy 1:17).

Man, whether he likes it or not, is a being
forced by his nature to seek some higher authority.

JOSÉ ORTEGA Y GASSET

May 23
FULL MOUTHS, EMPTY SOULS

All the labor of man is for his mouth,
And yet the soul is not satisfied.
Ecclesiastes 6:7

WHAT IS MOST IMPORTANT TO MOST PEOPLE IS THE SATISFACTION OF THEIR WORLDLY DESIRES. Even if they acknowledge that there are some spiritual realities over and beyond the concerns of this world, most people spend most of their time trying to satisfy the latter rather than the former. Basically, as the writer of Ecclesiastes observed, "the labor of man is for his mouth." And maybe we wouldn't put it so strongly, but when Paul described some by saying that their "god is their belly" (Philippians 3:19), he might easily have been commenting on our own culture.

And yet, for all our effort, we end up being distinctly *unsatisfied*. No matter what we manage to enjoy, the question still seems to be: *Is that all there is?* So frankly, what should be our attitude?

First, we need to admit the transitory nature of all temporal pleasures and possessions. Yes, it's right to enjoy what God has created in this world, but we shouldn't expect more from this enjoyment than it was intended to deliver. We may "hold" these things, as long as we're willing to let go of them at any moment.

Second, we need to spend less time pursuing these things and more time seeking God. With our words we may say that God is our most pressing priority, but if our schedule books show that on most days we spend very little time on that pursuit, who are we fooling? Where our heart is, there our "To Do" list will be also.

Ultimately, we can't "get" anything more out of our existence than what we "want." And so we need to be careful what we want. Eventually, all of our alternatives come down to two choices: (1) We can live for no higher fulfillment than our worldly desires, and having gotten them, find ourselves still empty inside, or (2) we can hunger and thirst for righteousness and find ourselves "filled" where it counts the most (Matthew 5:6). To the Samaritan woman at the well, Jesus said, "Whoever drinks of this water will thirst again, but whoever drinks of the water that I shall give him will never thirst. But the water that I shall give him will become in him a fountain of water springing up into everlasting life" (John 4:13,14). It's worth asking whether we really believe that or not.

Naught but God can satisfy the soul.
PHILIP JAMES BAILEY

May 24
NEEDFUL TO KNOW

LORD, make me to know my end,
And what is the measure of my days,
That I may know how frail I am.
Psalm 39:4

AT THEIR LONGEST, OUR LIVES IN THIS WORLD ARE QUITE BRIEF. With astonishing swiftness, we enjoy our youth, reach our maturity . . . and then suddenly find ourselves facing the end. Sooner or later, we all come to appreciate what Job meant when he said, "My days are swifter than a weaver's shuttle" (Job 7:6).

It is undeniably true that our earthly lives go by quickly, and we need to know that it's true. We may not *want* to know it, but we *need* to know it. The more frankly we face that fact, the more reverently we'll live our lives while they last. So David was a wise man when he prayed, "LORD, make me to know my end, and what is the measure of my days, that I may know how frail I am."

Look at what happens when we don't face life's brevity:

(1) We spend the first half of life prodigally. Prodigal actions are wasteful, that is, they spend limited resources as if they were unlimited. Isn't that the way we "spend" our days prior to middle age? Thinking the "supply" is unlimited, we're not very careful.

(2) We live without regard for God. Failing to face the brevity of life, we also fail to take God into account in our actions. If we even believe there will be a day of judgment, we assume it's so far in the future that it has little bearing on our day-to-day conduct.

(3) We live with little perspective, which causes us to err in our decisions. Many of our most important decisions are made on the basis of assumptions about "how much time we've got left," and faulty assumptions in that area can seriously skew our judgment. Taking our lease on life for granted, we make shortsighted choices.

So we need to live life with death in mind. Our minds should be governed by neither a morbid fascination with death nor a gloomy fatalism, but simply a healthy understanding that *we have only a few days in which to get our work done.* When the time came for Jesus to die, He had accomplished His life's work in the time that was granted to Him, and He could say, "It is finished" (John 19:30). Is there any chance that you and I can say the same?

Here's death, twitching my ear:
"Live," says he, "for I am coming."

VIRGIL

May 25
WE'RE HINDERED IF WE TRY TO SEE AHEAD

By faith Abraham obeyed when he was called to go
out to the place which he would receive as an inheritance.
And he went out, not knowing where he was going.
Hebrews 11:8

UNFORTUNATELY, OUR DESIRE TO KNOW THE FUTURE OFTEN TURNS INTO A DEMANDING ATTITUDE TOWARD GOD. We demand to know what is going to happen. We insist on seeing what's ahead. We put the Lord on notice that if we're going to follow Him, He had better tell us the territory the road is going to take us through.

Yet when God told Abraham to leave his home in Ur, Abraham had enough faith to obey God without being told where the journey would take him. "He went out, *not knowing where he was going.*" We need to work on having that kind of trust in God.

More than most of us realize, we are *hindered* by our attitude toward the future. For one thing, worry about what's going to happen tends to paralyze us; it keeps us from taking steps in any useful direction. But also, trying to see ahead frustrates our faith and keeps it from growing. It's in the actual *exercise* of faith that faith grows, and the only way faith can be exercised is to take steps that are based on trust in God rather than our own wisdom and foreknowledge. If we insist on walking by sight rather than by faith, we ought not to be surprised that our faith remains small.

One thing is certain: God knows what He is doing and He can be counted on to take care of us no matter where He asks us to go. In Abraham's case, Canaan was no doubt very different than anything he could have imagined back in Ur, but the result of sojourning there was also much better than anything he could have enjoyed elsewhere. Abraham "waited for the city which has foundations, whose builder and maker is God" (Hebrews 11:10). As long as he was going toward God, it didn't matter what happened to him in the meantime. It ought not to matter much to us, either.

Most of us go through life praying a little, planning a little, jockeying for position, hoping but never being quite certain of anything, and always secretly afraid that we will miss the way. This is a tragic waste of truth and never gives rest to the heart. There is a better way. It is to repudiate our own wisdom and take instead the infinite wisdom of God. Our insistence upon seeing ahead is a real hindrance to our spiritual progress. God has charged himself with full responsibility for our eternal happiness and stands ready to take over the management of our lives the moment we turn to him.

A. W. TOZER

May 26
THE MOST FUTILE FIGHT IN THE WORLD

O children of Israel, do not fight against
the LORD God of your fathers, for you shall not prosper!
2 Chronicles 13:12

IF THERE IS ANYTHING CERTAIN IN THIS WORLD, IT IS THAT GOD'S PURPOSES WILL BE FULFILLED IN THE END. Whenever we work at cross purposes with God, our failure is not a matter of *if* — it's only a matter of *when*. Awesome foe that the devil is, not even he and his angels can thwart the things that God is doing to reconcile the world to Himself. Sooner or later, all that has ever been done in despite of God will amount to no more than a few off-color threads, which God wisely wove into the great tapestry of His scheme of redemption. It's a simple fact: "There is no wisdom or understanding or counsel against the LORD" (Proverbs 21:30).

Disobedience. It should be obvious that we can't get away with defying God's law, and yet judging from our actions, we seem to think that's possible. For a time, we may think we've found a way to beat the law of cause and effect, but when the crop comes in, as it surely will, it will be clear that we've reaped what we've sown.

Desires. The great lie that the tempter tells us is that if we fulfill our God-given desires outside the limits of the Creator's will, the result will be better than what He was willing for us to enjoy. It is a lie, however. There is no shortcut to any place worth going to. Outside God's will there is no better life; there is only death

As the saying goes, we can't really break God's law; we can only break ourselves against it. But we shouldn't resent that fact; we should be grateful for it. Anytime our actions are antithetical to God's purposes, the sooner we find out about that, the better off we'll be. When God frustrates our plans and vetoes our projects, He is not merely saying, "No, you can't go that way." He's also saying, "Look over here. Here's a better way." Our prayer should be that He will bring to nothing, as soon as possible, any course of action on our part that is inconsistent with His plan for this world. And we ought never to be more grateful than when He has defeated the foolish little kingdoms that we set up in defiance of His.

God speaks to us unceasingly through the events of our life,
through the firmness with which he negates our petty human ordering of it,
through the regularity with which he disappoints our plans and our attempts
to escape, through his endless defeat of all our calculations by which we
hoped to become able to do without him.
LOUIS EVELY

The end of a thing is better than its beginning.
Ecclesiastes 7:8

IT'S A BLESSING THAT WE DON'T KNOW THE EXACT DATE OF OUR
DEATH, BUT SOMETIMES WE CAN KNOW THAT WE'RE APPROACHING
THE END, AND WE OUGHT TO APPROACH THE END WITH A CERTAIN
EAGERNESS. After all, we can't have our cake and eat it too. We
can't reach toward God and still cling to this life at the same time.
As our "departure" (2 Timothy 4:6) draws near, we ought to tingle
with the excitement of a child anticipating summer vacation!

(1) *The closer we are to the end, the more we have to be thankful for.*
Life in this world can be hard, none can deny. But even at its hardest, there are always things to enjoy: snow in the winter, flowers
in the spring, a friend's smile, a grandmother's hug. The longer
we live, the more these things tend to accumulate — and to give
pleasure. When we're old, we've had more time to be blessed.

(2) *The closer we are to the end, the more we can put things into
perspective.* It takes time for some things to make sense, and when
we're young, we haven't lived long enough to look at events from
anything but a very short perspective. Toward the end, however,
we can judge the value of things much more easily, because we
can see them within a larger context. Age widens the "lens" of life.

(3) *The closer we are to the end, the closer we are to being with God
in heaven.* Paul wrote that "to depart and be with Christ" was "far
better" (Philippians 1:23) than staying here. How can we think
about being with God and our hearts not be set on fire with joy?
Even now, "our salvation is nearer than when we first believed"
(Romans 13:11), and at the end of this life it will be even nearer.

Whether we like to admit it or not, there are some things that
can only be enjoyed at the end of life. Yes, there are some joys that
are unique to youth, but lest we try to prolong our youth, let's not
forget the very special blessings of old age. With life as with many
other things, "the end of a thing is better than its beginning."

It is the great mystery of human life that old grief passes
gradually into quiet, tender joy. The mild serenity of age takes the
place of the riotous blood of youth. I bless the rising sun each day, and,
as before, my heart sings to meet it, but now I love even more its setting, its
long slanting rays and the soft, tender, gentle memories that come with
them, the dear images from the whole of my long, happy life — and
over all the divine truth, softening, reconciling, forgiving!

FEODOR DOSTOEVSKI

May 28
FORGETTING WHAT GOD HAS DONE

For this they willfully forget . . .
2 Peter 3:5

IT WAS JUST AS TRUE IN PETER'S DAY AS IT IS IN OUR OWN: MANY
QUESTIONED WHETHER THE DAY OF JUDGMENT PROMISED BY GOD
WOULD EVER COME TO PASS. They said, "Where is the promise of
His coming? For since the fathers fell asleep, all things continue
as they were from the beginning of creation." But to doubt that
God is going to destroy the world is to forget that He has already
destroyed the world once before, by water. And the promise to
us that God is coming in a judgment of fire is no less certain to be
fulfilled than His promise in Noah's day that the flood of water
was coming. When God says a thing is going to happen, it's going
to happen. Those who doubt it have simply forgotten their history.

But Peter said an interesting thing when he said, "This they
willfully forget." The doubters of his day were not just forgetting
the fulfillment of God's promises in the past; they were forgetting
willfully. That is, they were forgetting because they wanted to
forget. Evidences of the certainty of God's promises were inconvenient obstacles in the path they preferred to follow, so they simply
put this information out of their minds. But we don't do much
better today, do we? Eric Hoffer was right: "Far more crucial than
what we know or do not know is what we do not want to know."
We seal our own doom by what we don't want to know.

Yet the truth about God is independent of our attitude toward
that truth. What is true about God is true whether we care to know
it or not. What He has done, He has done whether we remember it
or not. And let this sink in: *what He will do, He will do whether we are
prepared for it or not.* God is the great reality that overarches and encompasses every other reality. Indeed, no other reality would exist
if He had not created it and made it real. It is greatly to our advantage, then, to think and act rightly in relation to the God who is
our Creator. Remembering — rather than forgetting — what God
has done in the past is the key to dealing reverently with God in
the present. And it's the key to clear thinking about His promises
in the future. If we're ever tempted to doubt or wonder *Will He do
it?*, what He's already done is all the answer we ever need.

The truth does not vary because men forget or ignore or traduce it.
IRWIN EDMAN

May 29
WHAT HUNGER HELPS US TO SEE

So He humbled you, allowed you to hunger, and fed you with manna
which you did not know nor did your fathers know, that He might make you
know that man shall not live by bread alone; but man lives by every word
that proceeds from the mouth of the LORD. *Deuteronomy 8:3*

A T THE PRESENT POINT IN HISTORY, INDEPENDENCE AND
SELF-SUFFICIENCY HAVE BECOME THE VIRTUES OF PRIME IMPOR-
TANCE. We cannot conceive of a worse problem than being depen-
dent on outside help. In our value system, "needy" is never good.

The truth, of course, is that none of us is ever really independent. We require the help of others — especially that of God — in
all kinds of ways. But material prosperity tends to *mask* our neediness, and financial affluence fosters the *illusion* that we're able to
take care of ourselves. Many of us nowadays go for long stretches
of time without having our independence bubble popped.

But it is to our advantage to have that bubble popped now
and again. Apart from the question of whether we need other people, we certainly need God. Indeed, the word "need" hardly does
justice to the utter dependency of our position in the presence of
God, to whom we owe our very existence. And if that's the truth
of the matter, then whatever it takes to remind us of it is good.

When we're counting our blessings we need to count those
times when we're *forced to face our need for God.* Any episode of
"hunger" that disrupts our sense of self-sufficiency and jerks us
back to reality is to be appreciated. Paul, for example, would not
have chosen to have his "thorn in the flesh," but it served as an attitude adjuster, and so he could say, "I take pleasure in infirmities,
in reproaches, in needs, in persecutions, in distresses, for Christ's
sake. For when I am weak, then I am strong" (2 Corinthians 12:10).

Jesus taught that the fortunate folks are not the self-sufficient
but the "poor in spirit" (Matthew 5:3). If that sounds absurd to
our ears, we need to hear it all the more. None of us needs God
any more than any other, but those who're painfully *aware* of their
need are farther down the road toward God than those who aren't.

The Greek picture of a great man is the picture of a man who is
conscious of nothing so much as of his own superiority, a man to whom a
confession of need would be a confession of failure. The blessings of the
Christian view are for the man conscious of his own poverty, the man
sad for his own sins, the man hungry for a goodness which
he is sadly conscious that he does not possess.

WILLIAM BARCLAY

May 30
LEARNING TO LONG FOR GOD

I remember the days of old;
I meditate on all Your works;
I muse on the work of Your hands.
I spread out my hands to You;
My soul longs for You like a thirsty land.
Psalm 143:5,6

IF WE DON'T LONG FOR GOD, THEN SOMETHING IS SERIOUSLY WRONG. We need Him, even more than the air we breathe, and if we've failed to pay attention to Him for so long that we're no longer conscious of any need or aware of any desire for Him, then we have become "insensitive" in the most tragic way imaginable.

When we fail to long for God, it's a great pity, for we miss one of the best joys available to us in this world. It may seem contradictory to say that joy can come from longing or wanting something we don't yet possess, but it's a fact. The feeling may be what we call "bittersweet," but with the proper mindset, bittersweet joys are often the ones that are most deeply felt. When we're conscious of the void in our hearts that was *meant* to be filled by God and that sense of emptiness moves us to yearn for the day when it *will* be filled, the longing that we feel is as good as it is great.

Longing for God, however, is more than a feeling; it is an inner disposition or attitude. As such, longing for God is a thing that can be *learned*. It is no coincidence that David, a man who surely longed for God, could say, "I remember the days of old; I meditate on all Your works; I muse on the work of Your hands." The way to have a deeper sensitivity to our need for God is to spend regular time thinking about Him. Thoughtfully appreciating His works in creation will cause us to long for Him, but even more than that, studying the biblical record of His acts in history will impress on us our need for His deliverance and redemption.

But it takes *time* to do the things that deepen our longing for God, and therein lies the rub. We are a busy people. We have little time to ponder God's works or study His words. But let's be honest: do we have so little longing for God because we're so busy, or are we so busy because we have so little longing for God? Once we answer that question with integrity, things will start looking up.

If you are never alone with God, it is not because
you are too busy; it is because you don't care for him,
don't like him. And you had better face the facts.

AL-GHAZZALI

May 31
WHEN HOPE MAKES US STRONG

*For we do not want you to be ignorant, brethren, of our trouble
which came to us in Asia: that we were burdened beyond measure, above
strength, so that we despaired even of life. Yes, we had the sentence of death
in ourselves, that we should not trust in ourselves but in God who raises the
dead, who delivered us from so great a death, and does deliver us; in whom
we trust that He will still deliver us. 2 Corinthians 1:8-10*

IN TODAY'S TEXT, PAUL SPOKE OF A "HOPELESS" SITUATION IN
WHICH HE HAD BEEN INVOLVED DURING HIS PREACHING IN THE
ROMAN PROVINCE OF ASIA. Burdened "beyond measure," he said
that he and his companions "despaired even of life." Whatever
it was, Paul could see no way of getting out of it alive. From a
human standpoint, not even the most optimistic assessment of the
situation would have suggested any way of escape.

Far from being a bad thing, this kind of hopelessness is actually good. If hope means that we can see some way in which the
problem is going to be solved to our satisfaction, then the less of
that hope we have, the better off we'll be. In those kinds of cases,
we tend to trust in human means and ends. It is only when all
hope is stripped from us and we have nothing but the "sentence of
death" written upon us that we learn to trust God. Looking back
on a situation in which there had been no hope, Paul learned one
more time that "we should not trust in ourselves but in God."

Do you have a problem? In order to have any peace of mind,
would you have to know how things are going to turn out? If so,
you are still at a relatively immature stage of spiritual growth.

In the real world, most of our deeds have to be done in the absence of any foreknowledge of their outcome. Genuine hope does
not mean confidence that things will work out according to our
wishes; it means confidence that God's purposes will be accomplished even though we have no idea what is going to happen.

If we only have hope when we can foresee the outcome, then
we do no more than the weak and the worldlyminded. If we never
hope except when things are hopeful, Jesus would probably say,
"What do you do more than others? Do not even the tax collectors
do so?" (Matthew 5:47). But the God of real hope is the God in
whom we trust . . . *whether He chooses to deliver us or not!*

As long as matters are really hopeful, hope is a mere flattery or platitude;
it is only when everything is hopeless that hope begins to be a strength. Like
all the Christian virtues, it is as unreasonable as it is indispensable.

G. K. CHESTERTON

June 1
EASE VS. EFFORT

Do your utmost to come before winter.
2 Timothy 4:21

REACHING FORWARD REQUIRES EFFORT. If it was important for Timothy to get to where Paul was before winter, it is all the more important for us to get to where God is before it is too late. On a higher level, God would surely say to us: "do your utmost."

The modern assumption, of course, is that difficulty and pain are to be avoided whenever possible. Ease and pleasure have come to be thought of as almost unqualified goods. But the modern assumption is questionable. Historically, as well as biblically, wise people have always understood that there are some things worth enduring difficulty and suffering pain for. The "easy chair" may be enjoyable at day's end, but the main part of life involves getting up and making a serious effort to accomplish worthy goals.

If the goal is heaven, we do need to be reminded that we can't get there by our own effort. If we are saved, it will be by the grace of a Father who was not willing to leave us in our lost condition. But neither will God's grace leave us sitting in our "easy chair." He will help us do whatever needs to be done (Philippians 4:13), but He won't force salvation upon any person who doesn't care enough about Him to seek Him diligently (Hebrews 11:6).

When Paul wrote about "reaching forward to those things which are ahead" (Philippians 3:13), he used some vivid language in Greek. The *Twentieth Century New Testament* brings out the strength of Paul's metaphor with this translation: "straining every nerve for that which lies in front." Going to heaven is not for the runner who casually strolls toward the finish line; it's for the one who *strives* forward — exerting significant, sober-minded *effort.*

The course of least resistance is the road to ruin, almost without exception. Mark it down: if we don't accept the pain of discipline, we will suffer the pain of regret. So let's not avoid the hard work that God gives us the privilege of doing. "Be diligent to present yourself approved to God," Paul said to Timothy, "a worker who does not need to be ashamed" (2 Timothy 2:15). If we go forward with anything less than diligence, we will not be pleased with the results. We will, to use Paul's word, be "ashamed."

Everything requires effort: the only thing
you can achieve without it is failure.

ANONYMOUS

June 2
IF WE PAY ATTENTION, WE'RE ENTICED

When I consider Your heavens, the work of Your fingers,
The moon and the stars, which You have ordained . . .
Psalm 8:3

THE WORKS THAT GOD HAS DONE CAN HAVE A GREAT IMPACT UPON US IF WE PAY ATTENTION TO THEM. Whether we consider God's works as those of *creation* (His world) or of *revelation* (His word), both can affect us powerfully, pulling us into a more reverent and grateful response to Him. Yet neither nature nor the Scriptures are powerful enough to impress us if we are unobservant. For the significance of what we see and hear to sink in and alter our character and conduct, we have to pay attention.

Senses. If all five of our physical senses are working normally, we should consider that a great gift. The ability to see, hear, taste, touch, and smell is a marvelous ability. Philosophers have long debated how much of our knowledge comes from sensory experience, but few would deny that our knowledge is linked to our senses in some important way. Our senses are our "connection" to the greater reality that surrounds us. But as wonderful an endowment as they are, our senses do us little good if we don't *use* them. Surely, most of us would profit from getting out of the artificial "cocoon" in which we live so much of our lives and getting our senses — all five of them — engaged with the world "out there." We need more, rather than less, contact with the sensory world that exists outside of our own minds and our own selves.

Minds. If our senses must be used, however, they must be used *thoughtfully,* and here is where our minds come into play. We need to think more *deliberately* about what we experience through our senses. Perhaps I may say it this way: we need to "savor" that which we experience rather than gulp it down mindlessly.

David spoke of good things that happened to his thinking when he "considered" the works of God. God has given His word and His world not only for us to *use* and to *enjoy* — but also for us to *meditate upon.* The fact is, *we need significant contact* with the works that God has wrought. When we disconnect either our senses or our minds from these great things, we deteriorate.

A day spent without the sight or sound of beauty, the contemplation
of mystery, or the search for truth or perfection is a poverty-stricken day;
and a succession of such days is fatal to human life.
LEWIS MUMFORD

June 3
TOO MUCH TRANQUILITY

Now the LORD had said to Abram: "Get out of your country, from your
family and from your father's house, to a land that I will show you."
Genesis 12:1

GOD'S COMMAND FOR ABRAM TO LEAVE THE FAMILIARITY OF HIS HOMELAND WAS "DISTURBING" IN THE VERY BEST SENSE OF THAT WORD. It is not a term that has very positive connotations, perhaps, but in regard to the more important side of life, events that are "disturbing" are often those that work to our greatest advantage.

Difficulty. No doubt it would have been easier for Abram to stay where he was than to make the long, dangerous trek to a strange country. From nearly any angle you look at it, it was a *hard* thing that God asked Abram to do. But Abram was not primarily concerned about ease, and years later, he was a better man for having endured the hardships that God brought into his life.

Disruption. We don't know what plans Abram may have had for his life, but if he had any, the Lord's call to leave home surely disrupted them. To disrupt is to "throw into confusion or disorder," and it's an unwelcome concept for those of us who thrive on order and predictability. But the Lord knows we need many other things more than we need to know what's going to happen next.

Disturbance. In my dictionary, "disturb" is only two pages over from "disrupt." It means to "break up or destroy the tranquility or settled state of." God's plans for Abram would have done that for him, to say the very least. Yet in the long run, Abram's great disturbance helped bring about his salvation — and ours. When God disturbed Abram's life, it was an act of sheer *grace.*

With too much tranquility in our own lives, we tend to forget God. Yes, we may continue to study our Bibles and attend worship services, but as long as our lives are pleasantly predictable, our need for God becomes a nice religious theory rather than a desperately felt desire. With no real *grief* or *fear* to keep us awake, we "doze off," spiritually speaking. For our own good, then, we need to get out of our ruts and go on some fearful adventures, the kind that require real *faith.* If we don't, God may have to disturb our comfort. He may have to say, "Get out of your country . . ."

You know no disturbing voice? God never points out for you a pathway
altogether different from the one you had planned? Then, my brother,
you are living still in the land of slavery, in the land of darkness.

G. CAMPBELL MORGAN

June 4
WE LEARN MORE FROM LOSING THINGS

Better to go to the house of mourning than to go to the house of feasting,
For that is the end of all men; and the living will take it to heart.
Ecclesiastes 7:2

TO LOSE IS TO LEARN. Rarely do we part with anything valuable without growing in wisdom. Yet the experience of loss is one we usually resist and resent. If it's a choice between gaining and losing, we'd much rather be gaining. As for any losing we might have to do, we hope to defer that as long as we can. Nevertheless it's true: we *learn* more from losing things than we do from gaining them. So Solomon said that it's better to go to the "house of mourning" than the "house of feasting." That will be our perspective during times of loss if our priorities are what they ought to be.

We humans are both "acquisitive" and "possessive" creatures, aren't we? We love to acquire — to get and to gain — and having acquired at least some of what we want in this world, we feel a sense of entitlement to it: *This is mine. I possess it. It would be wrong for this ever to be taken away from me.* We are loathe to part with anything we have acquired, whether our money, our possessions, our health, our pleasures, our privileges, or our relationships.

Yet in a "temporal" world, there is nothing that is not *temporary*. Do you understand what that means? It means that *there is nothing that is yours to keep*. Whatever you have, you are going to have to let go of it — except God. And I am not talking about what happens at death. If you live very long, you're going to part with most of what you enjoy *before* you die. And when the things you have cherished are taken away from you, one by one, you will grow in wisdom. You will learn more from losing things than you ever learned by gaining them. And what you will learn is that *God is all you have to have.* He is the only thing you can't do without.

If nothing ever changed and we were allowed to keep our situations and our relationships as long as we wanted, we'd soon forget about God. Our tendency is to try to "possess" the creation and pay little attention to the Creator. But knowing our nature, God lets us enjoy our boons and benefits *for a while* . . . and then takes them away from us. With every loss, He is teaching us to fix our hearts on Him. So let me ask you: looking at life like that, is losing what you love in this world good or bad? You be the judge.

Sometimes the best gain is to lose.
GEORGE HERBERT

June 5

CONFIDENCE IN GRACE

But may the God of all grace, who called us to His eternal glory by Christ
Jesus, after you have suffered a while, perfect, establish, strengthen, and
settle you. To Him be the glory and the dominion forever and ever. Amen.
1 Peter 5:10,11

A T SOME LEVEL OF OUR THINKING, WE KNOW THAT WE SHOULD
"TRUST" GOD. Whatever may happen, we understand that
God can be counted on to help us get through our difficulties. But
in practice, we find it hard not to worry. We become anxious about
what may happen in the future, and we fear that we may not
make it to heaven. The long haul often looks very long indeed.

Yet God *can* be counted on, and we ought not to let any discouragement cause us to doubt that fact. Never having failed us
before, God is the ultimately trustworthy source of help. "Let us
therefore come boldly to the throne of grace, that we may obtain
mercy and find grace to help in time of need" (Hebrews 4:16).

But here is something important to ponder: it is God's *grace*
that we should put our confidence in. The God whom Peter said
would "perfect, establish, strengthen, and settle" his brethren was
not just a powerful or a glorious God, but "the God of all grace."
One of the reasons we become fearful is that we know we don't
deserve God's help. But by definition, grace is *unmerited* favor, *undeserved* assistance, and that is what God's help always is. Granted,
God's grace won't help those who are actively and stubbornly
refusing what they know of His will, but for those who are willing
to take any step in His direction, they can be sure that He'll *help*
them take that step, whether they deserve to be helped or not.

We are rightfully thankful for God's grace in forgiving our
past sins, but grace looks forward as well as backward. The same
God who graciously gave us a fresh start when we obeyed the
gospel will help us in whatever way we need His help from that
point forward. Yes, the way seems long and the obstacles seem
fearful, but God will not begin a work in us and not finish what
He has started (Philippians 1:6). He will see us through! That is
precisely what grace means, and that ought to be the center and
support of our confidence. Our salvation is nearer than when we
first believed, and by His grace, we can make it the rest of the way.

Thru many dangers, toils, and snares I have already come;
'Twas grace that bro't me safe thus far, and grace will lead me home.
JOHN NEWTON

June 6
THE WRATH TO COME

You turned to God from idols to serve the living and true God,
and to wait for His Son from heaven, whom He raised from the dead,
even Jesus who delivers us from the wrath to come.
1 Thessalonians 1:9,10

TO TURN TO GOD AND OBEY THE GOSPEL OF HIS SON IS TO BE
"SAVED." But the word "saved" may have become so familiar to us that we miss the dramatic picture the word portrays.
In the text above, Paul said that the Thessalonians, like all other
Christians, were waiting for Christ to return from heaven, and
that when He returned, they would be delivered from "the wrath
to come." The world stands under the righteous judgment of God
for its rebellion against Him. Unremorseful and unrepentant, the
world is doomed to destruction. When Christ returns, that doom
will fall. The only ones who will not be touched by the universal
devastation will be those who are delivered . . . spared . . . saved.

The words "salvation" and "salvage" are almost twins. If a
thing is "salvaged" that means it's something "saved" for further
use out of a situation of general destruction. Perhaps only a small
part in comparison to what is destroyed, the part that is salvaged
is that which is "saved." Similarly, the Day of the Lord is going to
be, for the most part, a day of the punishment of evil. The saved
will be the *exceptions*, those who, in Christ, will be "saved from
wrath through Him" (Romans 5:9). To understand this concept,
consider the "salvaging" of Noah's family from the Flood, Lot's
family from Sodom and Gomorrah, the Israelites from the death of
Egypt's firstborn, Rahab's family from the devastation of Jericho,
and on and on. The Bible often tells of a remnant being "spared."

But can a God of love be a God of wrath? Certainly. Indeed,
to have no wrath, God would have to be neutral toward right and
wrong, neutral in the conflict of the world. And as Stephen Neill
put it, "To live in such a world would be a nightmare. It is only the
doctrine of the wrath of God, of his irreconcilable hostility to all
evil, which makes human life tolerable in such a world as ours."
Mark it well: the day of God's wrath will come. And the gospel of
Christ says, "Be saved from this perverse generation" (Acts 2:40).

I believe in a God of absolute and unbounded love, therefore I believe in a
loving anger of his which will and must devour and destroy all that is
decayed, monstrous, abortive in the universe.

CHARLES KINGSLEY

June 7
IF NOT HOPE, THEN DEFIANCE

Resist the devil . . .
James 4:7

THE DEVIL MAY DEPRESS OUR EMOTIONS BUT HE NEED NOT BREAK OUR WILL. We are not helpless victims of his, at the mercy of whatever he does. The devil can be *resisted*, and we surely need to do that more often, don't we? When we've been discouraged by the apparent hopelessness of our situation, we need to stiffen our resolve and do what is right, if not out of *hope* then out of *defiance*.

It would help us greatly if we could learn to operate with whatever the highest motives are that we have *at any given moment*. Perhaps we'd like to be motivated always by the highest motives in the world, but frankly, the higher motives sometimes elude us — sometimes we just don't *feel* like acting from those motives. But right conduct can't wait for perfect motives! We need to be willing to do what is right *for the highest reasons we can muster at that moment*. Conscience should always be our guide, of course, but once conscience has determined the right thing to do, it needs some sort of motivation — and it's willing to be motivated by a lesser motive until it can learn a higher one. So, for example, if we don't desire heaven as strongly as we should, then the fear of hell is an acceptable substitute, if that's the best we can do right then.

Now here is the application: if a pure love for the Lord is out of our reach in a moment of discouragement, then we may be saved by being *just too "stubborn" to let the devil have the last say!* When it comes down to it, we must want God with a passion that *simply will not be denied*. We must love Him with the kind of love that will not let go, period. He has loved us with that kind of love, and we owe Him a dedication that is no less persistent.

In the end, the victory will be won not by the noble "lords and ladies" but by the simple "peasants" who just refused to give up, those who simply kept going in the face of resistance. To do no more than keep going may seem like a small thing, but it is in fact one of the greatest deeds that any human being can do. So when we're made blind to *hope* by the tears in our eyes, let's summon enough stubbornness to *defy* the devil and put him on notice that we do not intend to quit. We intend to keep doing what is right.

We conquer by continuing.
GEORGE MATHESON

June 8
LETTING OURSELVES BE REMINDED

*And lest I should be exalted above measure by the abundance of the
revelations, a thorn in the flesh was given to me, a messenger of Satan to
buffet me, lest I be exalted above measure.*
2 Corinthians 12:7

PAUL'S THORN IN THE FLESH WAS TO SERVE A QUITE UTILITARIAN
PURPOSE. It was to be a simple *reminder*. Every time he thought
about the privileges he had been granted as an apostle, the pain of
his "thorn" was to remind him to remain humble. But Paul's thorn
in the flesh would not have served its purpose if he had not *let*
himself be reminded. When he felt the pain or difficulty, Paul had
to *think* about the purpose it was meant to serve. Otherwise, the
meaning — and *value* — of his thorn would have been lost on him.

A similar thing may be said of the manna given to Israel in
the wilderness. In Deuteronomy 8:3, Moses said, "So He humbled
you, allowed you to hunger, and fed you with manna which you
did not know nor did your fathers know, that He might make
you know that man shall not live by bread alone; but man lives
by every word that proceeds from the mouth of the LORD." The
manna was given to everybody, but the learning of its lesson was
not automatic. Only those "got it" who *thought* about it.

In the New Testament, we hear Jesus speaking of those who
have "eyes to see" and "ears to hear" (Matthew 13:10-17). The
point is not simply that some can see and hear while others cannot; it's that some are too *preoccupied with themselves* to see and
hear the truth about God. There is no such thing as a reminder so
powerful that it reminds those who aren't paying attention.

In truth, our lives are full of reminders every day. Both in our
personal circumstances and in the wider world around us, there
are numerous objects and events that should point us to greater
things. Even with regard to the world of nature, Paul said that
God "did not leave Himself without witness, in that He did good,
gave us rain from heaven and fruitful seasons, filling our hearts
with food and gladness" (Acts 14:17). But we have to *pay attention*
and *get the point*. And if we don't, we are the losers. If we fail to
make the connection between the "story" and the "moral" of the
story, then we will find it hard to keep in touch with God.

*Nothing happens that is not significant
if you can only see the significance.*

CHRISTOPHER ISHERWOOD

June 9
FLEXIBILITY IN REACHING THE GOAL

And see, now I go bound in the spirit to Jerusalem, not knowing
the things that will happen to me there, except that the Holy Spirit testifies
in every city, saying that chains and tribulations await me. But none of these
things move me; nor do I count my life dear to myself, so that I may finish
my race with joy, and the ministry which I received from the Lord Jesus,
to testify to the gospel of the grace of God.
Acts 20:22-24

AS CHRISTIANS, OUR GOAL IS TO GLORIFY GOD AND GO TO HEAVEN. We do not serve God in order to receive any particular blessing in this life; we serve Him because we want to go, when our journey is over, to the place that He has prepared for us (John 14:1-4) — *by any path through this world that may be necessary.*

As Paul traveled to Jerusalem following his third missionary journey, it appeared that trouble awaited him there, perhaps involving imprisonment or worse. But Paul said, "None of these things move me." Paul had *plans,* of course, but his only real *goal* was to serve God, and if that required imprisonment, then so be it.

Too often, we become rigid about what we want and what we plan to do. We develop "hardening of the categories," and we can't think outside of the narrowly defined set of circumstances that we've attached our minds to. We think we're pursuing a goal, when in reality we're only pursuing a particular path to that goal.

But with any worthwhile goal, especially that of glorifying God and going to heaven, the path may *change* — indeed, it probably *will* change, despite all our dreaming and planning. When it does, what then? Do we resent it? Do we become bitter? Do we give up the *goal* just because our preferred *path* has been denied?

One measure of how important a goal is to us is how flexible we are in reaching that goal. If our hearts are fixed on one scenario and we give up the goal if that situation doesn't materialize, then it was only the scenario that was important to us, and not the goal. But surely, glorifying God and going to heaven is a goal worth reaching by any path that may be required. The path may change dramatically (and even painfully, as it did for Paul), but that doesn't really matter. What matters is finishing the race. That's the goal, and reaching it is worth whatever flexibility is asked of us.

A windmill is eternally at work to accomplish one end,
although it shifts with every variation of the weathercock,
and assumes ten different positions in a day.
CHARLES CALEB COLTON

WHATEVER DRAWS US CLOSER TO GOD

Therefore I take pleasure in infirmities, in reproaches,
in needs, in persecutions, in distresses, for Christ's sake.
For when I am weak, then I am strong
2 Corinthians 12:10

W E OUGHT TO DEFINE AS GOOD ANYTHING THAT DRAWS US CLOSER TO GOD. Most things are good in some ways and bad in others, but if the overall result of a thing is that we are drawn closer to God, then we'd have to pronounce it good. We shouldn't complain about anything that enhances our hope of heaven!

It should be obvious, but we often overlook it, that whether we see something as "good" depends entirely upon our *value system.* If the here and now is our main concern, then values like "ease" and "pleasure" will be primary and anything inconsistent with those values will be seen as "bad." As Christians, however, we judge things by a different standard, and based on our values, we often welcome things that the world rejects, and vice versa.

If God is our main concern, then nothing will be more important than drawing closer to God. Spiritual growth will be our ultimate priority; it will be the value against which we measure everything else. In short, whatever is conducive to spiritual growth is good, and whatever hinders spiritual growth is bad.

Many of the things that are conducive to spiritual growth, however, are painful to experience! Are we prepared to give *thanks* for the experiences that make us grow? Well, we should. As Christians, we should find ourselves expressing gratitude for many things the world goes to great lengths to avoid. Turning worldly wisdom upside down, Paul said, "I take *pleasure* in infirmities, in reproaches, in needs, in persecutions, in distresses, for Christ's sake. For when I am weak, then I am strong." And James said, "Count it all *joy* when you fall into various trials, knowing that the testing of your faith produces patience" (James 1:2,3).

So we have a choice. We can back away from suffering or we can welcome it. But having made our choice, there will be consequences. If we make mere pleasantness our priority, then we won't grow in godliness. *That* result can only come from the *other* alternative: the patient endurance of hardship. We can't have the result without embracing the means that lead to that result.

It is the fire of suffering that brings forth the gold of godliness.
JEANNE MARIE DE LA MOTHE GUYON

June 11
WHATEVER CAUSES GOD'S PEOPLE TO GIVE THANKS

Yes, we had the sentence of death in ourselves, that we should not trust
in ourselves but in God who raises the dead, who delivered us from so great
a death, and does deliver us; in whom we trust that He will still deliver us,
you also helping together in prayer for us, that thanks may be given by
many persons on our behalf for the gift granted to us through many.
2 Corinthians 1:9-11

WE OUGHT TO DEFINE AS GOOD ANYTHING THAT CAUSES GOD'S PEOPLE TO GIVE THANKS. Whatever it may be that provides an occasion for God's people to rejoice and thank Him is a *good* thing — no matter what the sacrificial price of that benefit and no matter how painfully it may impinge upon us personally.

There may be times when something happens that makes us glad personally and also makes God's people glad. But there may be other times when something that makes God's people glad involves an element of sadness for us personally. For example, in just a few weeks I will have the honor of performing a wedding ceremony for a young man and woman who are known by very many of God's people. As husband and wife, they will do great good in the kingdom, and their wedding will be a day of happiness, not only for them but also for God's people far and wide. Yet there may be other women who would like to be marrying this man, and other men who would like to be marrying this woman. For them, there will be an element of sadness on this day. But shouldn't their sadness be caught up in the greater joy of an occasion that, in the larger sense, is a day of rejoicing for God's people?

One of the remarkable things about the apostle Paul is the extent to which he rejoiced in whatever God's people rejoiced about. If he had suffered some horrible ordeal and been delivered, such that thanksgivings to God were being made, then he was glad to have suffered the ordeal. Much more than how events were affecting him personally, Paul was concerned whether God's people were being given reason to rejoice. And so it must be with us. Whatever causes God's people to give thanks is a *good* thing!

In submission we are free to value other people. Their dreams
and plans become important to us. We have entered into a new, wonderful,
glorious freedom, the freedom to give up our own rights for the good of
others. . . . We can rejoice with their successes. . . . It is of little consequence
that our plans are frustrated if their plans succeed. We discover that it is far
better to serve our neighbor than to have our own way.

RICHARD FOSTER

June 12
EARTHLY SATISFACTIONS CAN BE MISLEADING

Because you say, "I am rich, have become wealthy,
and have need of nothing" — and do not know that you are wretched,
miserable, poor, blind, and naked . . .
Revelation 3:17

IT IS NOT WRONG TO WANT TO ENJOY LIFE IN THIS WORLD, BUT WE SHOULD BE AWARE OF THE DANGER OF THAT ENJOYMENT. The more we have what we *want* in this life, the more we're deluded into thinking we have all we *need*. The problem is not that earthly joys are *wrong*, but that if we're not careful, they can be *misleading*.

On the desk at which I write — within my reach at this very moment — is a handy dispenser of peanut M&M candies. I can't concentrate when I'm hungry, and what I've found is that a few mouthfuls of M&M's can always be counted on to make the hunger go away. Eating candy is very *satisfying*. But here is the catch: the very satisfaction that candy gives you is *misleading*. It makes you think you don't need anything else, when in reality, you do.

The Laodiceans were satisfied. They had what they wanted, and the very satisfaction of those needs blinded them to the fact that they were dangerously deficient in what they really needed. "You do not know that you are wretched, miserable, poor, blind, and naked," the Lord said to them. Would He be able to say anything different to those of us today who are enjoying life so well?

What should we do, then, in regard to this world's "candy"?

(1) *We should moderate our indulgence.* Like candy, the things that may be enjoyed in this life should not be overindulged, lest they "spoil our appetite" for the nourishment we truly need.

(2) *We should hold on to our priorities.* Even when our greater needs are not being felt, they are still there. We need to keep clear what is *important*, even when it doesn't feel particularly *urgent*.

(3) *We should discipline our thinking.* When we have what we want right now, our minds are drawn toward this world. But we can *choose* to "set [our] mind on things above" (Colossians 3:2).

It may sound contradictory, but there is a sense in which we need to *enjoy our earthly enjoyments a little less enjoyably!* Somehow, we must learn to be content without being complacent. We must learn to be thankful for what we already have while remembering that *we don't yet have what we need most of all.*

Show me a thoroughly satisfied man — and I will show you a failure.
THOMAS ALVA EDISON

June 13
MAN PROPOSES, BUT GOD DISPOSES

There are many plans in a man's heart,
Nevertheless the LORD'S counsel — that will stand.
Proverbs 19:21

IF WE THINK WE HAVE THE POWER TO ACCOMPLISH ALL OF OUR PLANS, WE ARE BEING NOT ONLY FOOLISH BUT ARROGANT. We may have our plans and purposes, and that is all well and good. But God also has purposes, and His are the only ones that are *certain* to be fulfilled. Our plans are always tentative; His, never.

There is nothing wrong with making plans, of course, and we surely ought to do so. Wisdom teaches us to look ahead, to whatever extent we can, and formulate both goals and strategies for reaching those goals. If we have no plans, then we're not the forward-looking, goal-striving beings that we were intended to be. It's hard to imagine how a person could "reach forward" without making a few plans for what he or she intended to do in life.

But there needs to be a healthy dose of *humility* mixed in with our plans. For one thing, the fulfillment of our plans depends on many factors that are, quite frankly, *beyond our control*. In many cases, our goals can't be reached if other people don't do certain things, and there is no way of knowing whether they will do them or not. But more important, the *Lord* may have plans that conflict with ours. He may have purposes the fulfillment of which require some adjustment in our intended path. It's good to have an "itinerary" in mind as we journey through this world, but we'd better not have an itinerary that can't be changed on short notice.

James said, "Come now, you who say, 'Today or tomorrow we will go to such and such a city, spend a year there, buy and sell, and make a profit'; whereas you do not know what will happen tomorrow. For what is your life? . . . Instead you ought to say, 'If the Lord wills, we shall live and do this or that'" (James 4:13-15). *If the Lord wills!* That must be our guiding thought constantly.

But obviously, the wonderful truth is that whenever God says *no* to some plan or purpose that we have made, it is always because He has something *better* in mind. It should be a *joy* to yield our plan to His purpose. So let's hold on to our plans, if need be, but let's hold them *loosely*. When we say, "Let's do *this*," and God says, "No, let's do *that*," then our love for Him will say, "*Yes!*"

Man makes plans; God changes them.

JEWISH PROVERB

June 14
PURSUING THE KNOWLEDGE OF GOD

Let us know,
Let us pursue the knowledge of the LORD.
Hosea 6:3

A S WE REACH FORWARD IN LIFE, ONE OF THE PRIMARY THINGS WE REACH FOR IS THE KNOWLEDGE OF GOD. Even in practical matters, there is nothing we need more than a knowledge of Him as He truly is, and the knowledge of God ought to be something that we pursue with a passion that is both diligent and persistent.

Gaining a "knowledge of God" requires more than the mere accumulation of facts about Him. Jesus, for example, rebuked the Jewish scholars of His day for their failure to know God, despite the fact that they had "search[ed] the Scriptures" (John 5:39). God is a personal Being, and we must desire to know *God Himself.*

Yet there is no knowing God in the personal sense without certain *factual information* about Him. We do not come to know God intuitively or with our feelings or by non-verbal meditation. If God exists, then He is a real entity, an objective reality. We can no more "know" Him in the absence of factual information than we could "know" any other reality without the facts about it.

But here is the point: if the knowledge of God is important and if that knowledge requires the learning of certain information, then the learning of that information ought to be a matter of *high priority* with us. Far above any other knowledge, the knowledge of God is one that we would want to *pursue.* But how diligently do any of us really do that? How high a priority is it with *you* to know more of the truth about God today than you knew yesterday? Honestly now, what would you *sacrifice* to gain an hour's worth of time to study the Scriptures? Anything of significant value?

We often wonder why our spiritual lives are so dry and static. But spiritual growth comes from an increasing knowledge of *God.* So I suggest not only that we need to study the Scriptures but that we do so with a more conscious intent *to know God.* That is our quest, and what a great one it is! If there is such a thing as a "high-leverage" activity, this would be the highest. You can't help yourself more greatly than by pursuing the knowledge of God.

> Nothing will so enlarge the intellect, nothing so magnify
> the whole soul of man, as a devout, earnest, continued
> investigation of the great subject of the Deity.
>
> CHARLES HADDON SPURGEON

June 15
WOULD YOU GO BACK?

Remember Lot's wife.
Luke 17:32

Do YOU EVER LOOK BACK LONGINGLY AT ANYTHING IN THE PAST? Do you ever wish you had back anything that you gave up for the Lord? If you could go back in time, would you go back?

Regret. Leaving Sodom was the right thing to do. It was a sacrifice made for the Lord. We don't know much about what Lot's thoughts were, but the fact that his wife "looked back" (Genesis 19:26) seems to suggest some regret on her part, regret that the Lord's requirement had cost her something she didn't want to give up. Regret in itself is not wrong, but if regret means that we "begrudge" not having what we once had, then that is not good.

Resentment. Worse than wrongful regret would be *resentment* that something we once had in the past has been "taken away" from us. When we think about the past, we may almost be filled with a bitterness or an anger that what was "ours" was unfairly removed from our possession. We are creatures who are prone to possessiveness and the protection of our "rights," and our memories often tempt us to believe that we have been "deprived."

Reconsideration. Worst of all, of course, we sometimes even *reconsider* whether we made the right choice when we left behind something that was hard to give up. The tempting thought may occur to us to try to go back to our previous situation and resume the life that we had back then. If it was Sodom that we left, we certainly ought not to go back, but even if it was something good that we gave up for the Lord, going back is rarely, if ever, the answer.

Memory is a two-edged sword, is it not? With it we may remember (helpfully) things that can energize us, but with it we may also remember (hurtfully) things that can hold us back. For fallen creatures such as we, there is no such thing as no regrets, but we need to be very careful. As someone has said, "The past is valuable as a guidepost, but dangerous if used as a hitching post." When we remember the past, as we certainly will, our effort must be to remember it with such an attitude that we are *helped* in the here and now. God intends for our lives to go *forward* — and when we're tempted to go *backward,* we need to remember Lot's wife.

There was — and O! how many sorrows crowd
Into these two brief words!
SIR WALTER SCOTT

June 16

ON HAVING HOPE

In this you greatly rejoice, though now for a little while,
if need be, you have been grieved by various trials.
1 Peter 1:6

WHEN PETER SAID THAT WE MAY BE "GRIEVED BY VARIOUS TRI-ALS," HE SPOKE A TRUTH THAT HAS BEEN BORNE OUT IN THE EXPERIENCE OF MOST OF US. This world is far from what it would have been had sin never entered the picture. It is a "vale of tears," a place where sorrow and suffering are the common lot of all.

But the suffering is only one side of the truth, at least as far as Christians are concerned. If we suffer, we also "greatly rejoice." Ironic though it may seem, we are able, because of our hope in Christ, to rejoice even while we suffer. When Paul spoke of the difficulties that might have to be encountered by the Christian, he said, "Yet in all these things we are more than conquerors through Him who loved us" (Romans 8:37). God does not eliminate the possibility of difficulty having to be endured; He gives us a hope that will see us through the difficulties. Indeed, it is *in* all these things — not *despite* them — that we are more than conquerors.

It is a pity if we ever ignore or underestimate the difference that hope makes in the life of the Christian. Yet we have a tendency to do that. If we've been Christians very long, we may not remember what it was like to try to deal with the sufferings of this life with no hope of anything better *than* this life. But one hour back in that situation would remind us how valuable our hope is.

We need not evade the truth: if Christ has not been raised from the dead, then we are still dead in our sins and there is no hope (1 Corinthians 15:14-19). Take away the eternal hope, and Christianity is not a "nice way to live"; it is a pathetic joke.

But the hope of the Christian *is* real, and we need to rejoice in the difference that it makes in the quality of our lives. We, like our brother Paul, "are hard pressed on every side, yet not crushed; we are perplexed, but not in despair; persecuted, but not forsaken; struck down, but not destroyed — always carrying about in the body the dying of the Lord Jesus, that the life of Jesus also may be manifested in our body" (2 Corinthians 4:8-10). If it weren't for Christ, there are days when the darkness would be too dark, and the pain too painful, to pretend that this life is worth living.

If it were not for hope the heart would break.

ENGLISH PROVERB

ON GIVING HOPE

We give thanks to God always for you all, making mention of you
in our prayers, remembering without ceasing your work of faith,
labor of love, and patience of hope . . .
1 Thessalonians 1:2,3

MOST OF US HAVE MORE INFLUENCE THAN WE THINK WE HAVE. Human beings have an amazing power to affect one another, and there is not a one of us (no matter how "little" we think we are) who shouldn't be concerned about *how* we are affecting others. *Are we giving others hope or are we taking their hope away?*

When I read the opening of Paul's first letter to the Thessalonian church, I am staggered by the thought that he would express appreciation to *them* for the patience of *their* hope. Can it really be that Paul, the great apostle, needed the encouragement that came from the steadfast hopefulness of his hard-pressed brethren in Thessalonica? I like to think that that was the case.

In regard to the "together" part of Christianity, one of our most important mutual responsibilities is that of helping to keep hope alive in the hearts of our brothers and sisters. That should be no small part of what we try to accomplish when we assemble. "Let us hold fast the confession of our hope without wavering, for He who promised is faithful. And let us consider one another in order to stir up love and good works" (Hebrews 10:23,24).

Long ago, an older man gave me some advice. He said, "Gary, folks have enough fears of their own. So don't share your fears — share your courage." He made a good point. Yes, there is a time to discuss our doubts and questions and fears, but the *main effect* of ourselves upon others needs to be that they have a greater *hope.*

By the time these pages are published I will have lived almost three score years in this world. The longer I live, the more I am conscious of the need to have a *hopeful* impact on those with whom I have influence. I believe in telling the truth, as you well know, and I would never want to give anyone *false* hope. But when the final tally is made, I hope that I won't have failed to encourage anyone who *needed* to be encouraged. It's a fine thing to *have* hope, but I believe it is an even finer thing to *give* hope. That, above all, is what I want to do. And I'm confident that you do too.

If I can put one thought of rosy sunset into the life of
any man or woman, I shall feel that I have worked with God.
GEORGE MACDONALD

June 18
SUBMISSION, SACRIFICE, AND STRONG JOY

I will very gladly spend and be spent for your souls.
2 Corinthians 12:15

THERE IS MORE THAN ONE KIND OF THING THAT MIGHT BE "SACRI-
FICED" OR "GIVEN UP" FOR THE LORD'S SAKE. Think, for example, of three situations in which we might let go of something:

(1) Repentance from sin. When we turn away from any sin, we
are "giving up" a practice that we know is displeasing to God.
Depending on the sin and how long we've been engaging in it, it
may be a hard thing to surrender, but the task is made somewhat
easier by the fact that the thing we are giving up is evil.

(2) Giving up something that is required by God's command. When
a parent makes a financial sacrifice for his or her child, it may well
be a sacrifice that involves difficulty, but it is hardly one that is optional. What is necessary will be done joyfully, of course, but even
so, God's command left very little choice about whether to do it.

*(3) Voluntarily relinquishing something exceedingly good in order
that someone else may have something they need.* Here we come to a
very different kind of sacrifice. When Jesus left heaven to come
and die for us, He gave up things the goodness of which we can
only imagine. But let us keep our thinking clear: the things the
Lord gave up were not sinful things that *needed* to be given up, nor
were they things He was under any *obligation* to give up. These
were sacrifices made voluntarily — in the sheer purity of love.

Too often, when we have an opportunity to learn something
of this kind of love in our own lives, we miss our chance by trying
to hold on to what we want. But when our needs were coming
down the road, Jesus' attitude led Him to step out of the way so
that our needs could pass by unhindered. And Paul says, "Let this
mind be in you which was also in Christ Jesus" (Philippians 2:5).

This type of sacrifice, in which we yield our wants to someone
else's needs, is part of the *submission* that the Lord asks us to learn.
"Let each of you look out not only for his own interests, but also
for the interests of others" (Philippians 2:4). I can tell you, there is
not a purer joy in the world than doing this, and I can also tell you,
there is no more freeing, liberating experience. Yielding to someone else's dreams will break many a chain the devil has made.

In submission we are free to value other people.
Their dreams and plans become important to us.
RICHARD FOSTER

COSTLY LOVE

But what things were gain to me,
these I have counted loss for Christ.
Philippians 3:7

W E STAND AMAZED AT WHAT PAUL WAS WILLING TO GIVE UP IN ORDER TO KNOW CHRIST. Valuable though these things were, he was willing to count them "loss" for the more excellent value of knowing Christ. And yet, what Paul did is no more than what *any* of us should be ready to do. If there is some gift that should be given for the Lord's sake, then we should be willing to give it.

The word "gift" covers a lot of ground, however. There are convenient gifts, and then there are *costly* gifts. The latter are those in which we part with something that is a part of our very selves and our very hearts. When we give these gifts, we give up a part of precious life. We can hardly see how we can survive the loss.

As I write these words, tears are splattering on the paper on which I am trying to write. An event is taking place tomorrow that will involve the final, irrevocable loss of the most precious temporal treasure that I was ever privileged to enjoy for a while. The loss of this treasure is the ultimate result of a vow that I took a number of years ago that requires me to forgo such joys as this one, for the Lord's sake. Some would say that if it now requires me to give up this, the greatest joy of my life, I should never have taken the vow.

But are we to give the Lord only that which costs us nothing? To say "If I'd known how much I was going to miss it, I wouldn't have given it to Him" is to say that truly costly gifts should never be given. Isn't it better, when the poverty created by a gift begins to hurt us, just to remember the *goal* for which we gave the gift?

Although my life is one of constant sorrow, what I realize is that the sorrow is simply the other side of heaven. I am glad to have a hope that is *worth* the price that I am now having to pay. A life without such a goal would be a life devoid of meaning or joy, and I wouldn't trade the life I have for such a life as that. On my darkest days of emptiness and longing, I try to bow my head and give thanks for the fullness that will one day be mine. To gain it will be worth the loss of all the loving treasure that my soul so desperately desires right now. It will be worth it. *It will be worth it.*

Everyone should have a goal for which
he is willing to exchange a piece of his life.
CARLYLE BOEHME

Many daughters have done well,
But you excel them all.
Proverbs 31:29

As a child, I remember hearing old men pray, "Lord, suit unto us such blessings as You see fit." Even then, I think I was struck by the joyful blend of humility and gratitude that would prompt such a prayer. Left to our own devices, we may think we want this or that, but what we really want is whatever the Lord wants for us. And we don't just "settle" for how the Lord wants to bless us — we receive it openly, receptively, and joyously.

This truth is in the story of Éowyn and Faramir in the legends of J. R. R. Tolkien. Éowyn, a princess of Rohan whose heroism on the Pelennor Fields had turned back the tide of evil, would have loved, and been loved by, Aragorn, heir to the throne of Gondor, but it was impossible for Aragorn to be Éowyn's husband. The prince Faramir, however, who would later rule the land of Ithilien, came to love Éowyn as they both recuperated from battle in the Houses of Healing. "Éowyn, do you not love me," he said after courting her, "or will you not?" There is not a greater moment in all of literature than when Éowyn decided that . . . yes, she would.

I am no Aragorn, the Lord knows. But once upon a time, my path ran alongside that of a true Éowyn, a shieldmaiden of the Lord, both valiant and virtuous. Many were the long nights when I prayed for her a Faramir — and when in the Lord's grace he appeared, her virtue was such that she opened her heart to receive his love. "Behold the maidservant of the Lord," her willing spirit said. "Let it be to me according to your word" (Luke 1:38). And now, we can only imagine how many lives will have been blessed by the love of Éowyn and Faramir by the time our Lord returns.

O Éowyn, Éowyn. "I thank my God upon every remembrance of you . . . being confident of this very thing, that He who has begun a good work in you will complete it until the day of Jesus Christ" (Philippians 1:3,6). I do not say fare *well* — for on this life's voyage there will surely be storms — but I pray you'll fare *forward.*

How many loved your moments of glad grace,
And loved your beauty with love false or true,
But one man loved the pilgrim soul in you,
And loved the sorrows of your changing face.

WILLIAM BUTLER YEATS

June 21

THERE IS NO LOVE WITHOUT SORROW

. . . yes, a sword will pierce through your own soul also.
Luke 2:35

NEVER HAVING BEEN A WOMAN OR A MOTHER, I CANNOT IMAG-
INE THE BITTERSWEET JOY AND SORROW OF MARY, THE MOTHER
OF JESUS. To be the mother of the Christ, the Savior, must have
been a joy beyond what even other mothers could comprehend.
And yet . . . when the most special Child ever born was still a baby,
she was told, "A sword will pierce through your own soul also."
Having loved this Son as no other human being could, imagine
her torment as she stood at the foot of the cross. There is no love
without sorrow — and the greater the love, the greater the sorrow.

*To love is to know the sorrow of not being loved by someone whose
love you long for.* Love, at least between human beings, is risky
business. When you love someone, there is no guarantee that they
will feel the same way about you. As we all learned in elementary
school, "When you like someone and they don't like you back, it
hurts." No one has ever found any good way around that pain.

To love is to know the sorrow of losing the love of someone you love.
This is a more serious sorrow than the first. To have loved someone and been loved by them, and then to experience the ending of
that love, either by death or some other circumstance, is a sorrow
that mere words cannot describe. Yet we must sooner or later say
goodbye to all of our loves in this world — even the best of them.

*To love is to know the sorrow of giving up joy so that the one you
love may have joy.* With this third sorrow, we come to the most
poignant sorrow in the world. This, of course, was the sorrow that
Jesus was doomed to suffer in His love for us. He could not have
had the joy of His love for us without the sorrow of giving up His
life. And so it often is among those of us who love one another.
Love will lead us to die, if it means that our beloved can live.

To love, then, is to open ourselves to the possibility of one or
the other — and sometimes all three — of these sorrows. Yet what
shall we say? Shall we not love? I know not what choice others
may make, but I shall continue to keep my heart open to love.
Even at the bitterest ending of love's sweetness, there is no grief
great enough to keep me from the clear, pure joy of having loved.

Those who have the courage to love
should have the courage to suffer.

ANTHONY TROLLOPE

June 22
FINDING OUR JOY IN THAT WHICH IS RIGHT

You have put gladness in my heart,
More than in the season that their grain and wine increased.
I will both lie down in peace, and sleep;
For You alone, O LORD, make me dwell in safety.
Psalm 4:7,8

THERE ARE MANY DIFFERENT KINDS OF JOY, AND EACH OF THEM SHOULD HAVE A SPECIAL PLACE IN OUR HEARTS. There is a sense, however, in which the best joy is the joy of knowing that *we have done the right thing*. In every situation, we must ask what is the best thing that can be done, and having done what we knew was best, we must learn to be gratified by the knowledge that we've done the honorable thing. Integrity should be a source of joy to us.

Happiness and joy are very different things. Happiness is what we feel when what is "happening" is pleasant. But in regard to what happens, our thought should be: "Let not that happen which I wish, but that which is right" (Menander). There will be times when the right thing happens and it will involve great pain on our part. But if our joy comes from the happening of what is right, then we'll be willing to sacrifice happiness for joy!

There may be times when little other joy will be available to us and we must content ourselves with knowing that we've done the right thing. At such desperate times, our tears may have momentarily blinded us to many other blessings that we have, but if it ever came down to it that the joy of having done what was right was all the joy we had, then that joy should be enough to live on.

When we do what's right, we do so in the faith that somehow everything's going to work out all right in the end. "Faith is . . . doing the right thing regardless of the consequences, knowing God will turn the ultimate effect to good" (Pamela Reeve). So we go ahead and do what's right, even when it's difficult or painful, and our joy comes from our confidence in the ultimate outcome.

If we fail to find joy in the doing of what is right, then not only do we miss the highest joy we can have, but we degrade and demean ourselves. God gave us our conscience, and when we obey it, we thrive as beings made in God's image — but when we fail to act with honor and integrity, life is no longer worth living.

When faith is lost,
When honor dies,
The man is dead!

JOHN GREENLEAF WHITTIER

June 23
ALL THE SWEETER

A woman, when she is in labor, has sorrow because her hour has come; but as soon as she has given birth to the child, she no longer remembers the anguish, for joy that a human being has been born into the world. Therefore you now have sorrow; but I will see you again and your heart will rejoice, and your joy no one will take from you. John 16:21,22

I HAVE BOTH HEARD THE CRIES OF AGONY IN THE DELIVERY ROOM AND SEEN THE TEARS OF ECSTASY IN THE RECOVERY ROOM. I don't know which moves me more deeply, the agony or the ecstasy, but I know that in all the more important areas of life, you can't have the latter without the former. Jesus knew that too. And so He told His disciples, "You now have sorrow; but I will see you again and your heart will rejoice, and your joy no one will take from you."

Difficulty and hardship. Some people back away from these things, as if they were to be avoided at all costs. Other people, more wise, understand that the bigger the challenge, the deeper the satisfaction in overcoming it, and the more unpleasant the work, the better they feel at the end of the day. It's tired people who enjoy rest, and it's difficulty that makes us appreciate ease.

Suffering and sacrifice. There aren't many people who aren't hurting in some way, and while on a superficial level I wish it could be otherwise, on a deeper level, I know what suffering and sacrifice have done in my life. Having hurt as I do, the relief that will be in heaven is going to mean a lot more. And having struggled against pain, the pleasure of heaven is going to be much sweeter. So if it takes suffering to do these good things, so be it.

In this body, we *groan* (2 Corinthians 5:2). It's no fun, but anything that adds to our groaning right now simply means that heaven will be all the sweeter when it comes. How foolish we are to desire heaven as a place of rest and relief . . . *without suffering anything in this life that we would want rest or relief from!*

To the extent that our minds are fixed on heaven, this world will appear as little more than preparation for the one to come. Whatever ease and pleasure may be ours here, that should only whet our appetites for the real joys to come. And whatever difficulty or pain we may have to deal with while "on the job," that should only increase our capacity to enjoy "quittin' time."

The early Christians were so much in that other world that nothing which happened to them in this one seemed very important.

HANNAH HURNARD

WE ALL LIVE IN THE SAME WORLD

That which has been is what will be,
That which is done is what will be done,
And there is nothing new under the sun.
Ecclesiastes 1:9

THE MORE THINGS CHANGE, THE MORE THEY STAY THE SAME. You may call it a "cycle" or a "pattern" or a "rhythm," but there is a definite repetitiveness to this world. What has been done in the days gone by is what will be done in the days to come. There is, when you really think about it, nothing new under the sun.

Things that seem to be new in the world are usually just variations on a theme, and the theme has been around for a long time. Sometimes variations on a theme can be extremely important and quite innovative, but they are still just improvements on something that was already in the world. We are not, and cannot be, creators in the true sense. We can only be what J. R. R. Tolkien called "sub-creators," rearrangers of preexisting materials.

Unfortunately, most of the "new" things that people make such a to-do about are nothing more than fads and fashions, trends that come and go, and are labeled "old" as soon as the next "new" one comes along. On this kind of newness, Robert M. Pirsig commented: "'What's new?' is an interesting and broadening eternal question, but one which, if pursued exclusively, results only in an endless parade of trivia and fashion, the silt of tomorrow."

We may as well face it, in all the most important ways, the world remains the same generation after generation. But that statement is not meant to be depressing or demeaning to the dignity of human beings. It is simply to say that we all live in the same world. There is a certain "context" common to all men and women, no matter when and where they have lived. We experience the same joys, we suffer the same sorrows, and we encounter the same challenges. When we back up and look at life from the broadest perspective, none of us can say that our lives are unique.

That insight should do two things for us. First, we should have a greater *respect* for the experience of those who've gone before. And second, we should have a greater *humility* as to the importance and "newness" of our own contributions to the world. What we do may well be important, but it's all been done before.

Everything that has been is eternal: the sea will wash it up again.
FRIEDRICH NIETZSCHE

June 25
HOW MUCH DOES HEAVEN MEAN TO US?

*Though now you do not see Him, yet believing,
you rejoice with joy inexpressible and full of glory . . .
1 Peter 1:8*

HEAVEN OUGHT TO BE OUR MOST JOYOUS THOUGHT. We do not see our Lord right now, but we believe that, some sweet day, we shall see Him and remain in His perfect presence forever. In that hope, we "rejoice with joy inexpressible and full of glory."

But in practical, everyday terms, does heaven really mean as much to us as we say that it does? We are, after all, very busy with the details of living in the here and now, and since we've long since grown accustomed to the idea of going to heaven, many of us may be guilty of taking it for granted. If we're honest, we may have to admit that the concept of heaven has grown stale and the joy of thinking about it has disappeared. But how can we do that? How can we possibly have a "casual" attitude about heaven?

The first thing that should be said is that we need to make sure we're even *going* to heaven. Paul wrote, "Examine yourselves as to whether you are in the faith" (2 Corinthians 13:5), and we need to make a practice of doing that on a fairly regular basis.

But second, we need to acquire the habit of *thinking* about heaven more often. One way to do that is to engage in the old-fashioned discipline of "counting our blessings," consciously and deliberately enumerating to ourselves the things that we have to be thankful for. When we "count our blessings," heaven will always be at the top of the list. And with that list in hand, we are then ready to *meditate* on this great blessing, to *think* about it, and, yes, even *daydream* about it! If we don't find ourselves daydreaming about heaven, at least now and then, it really should cause us to question whether it means as much to us as we say it does.

But not only should we cherish the thought of heaven, I believe that we should *show* that we cherish it. It should "come out" in our conversation, our demeanor, our tone of voice, and even our countenance. There is no denying that, as we grow older, our faces come to be a mirror of the contents of our hearts. So what do those who see your face every day know about your enthusiasms, the things that mean more to you than anything else in the world?

> When you speak of heaven, let your face light up. When you
> speak of hell — well, then your everyday face will do.
>
> CHARLES HADDON SPURGEON

June 26
EACH HIS OWN BURDEN, HIS OWN GRIEF

When there is famine in the land, pestilence or blight or mildew, locusts
or grasshoppers; when their enemies besiege them in the land of their cities;
whatever plague or whatever sickness there is; whatever prayer, whatever
supplication is made by anyone, or by all Your people Israel, when each one
knows his own burden and his own grief, and spreads out his hands to this
temple: then hear from heaven Your dwelling place, and forgive, and give
to everyone according to all his ways, whose heart You know . . .
2 Chronicles 6:28-30

IN HIS PRAYER AT THE DEDICATION OF THE TEMPLE, SOLOMON
PRAYED THAT GOD WOULD HEAR THE PRAYERS OF EACH INDI-
VIDUAL WHO WAS IN NEED. "When each one knows his own burden
and his own grief, and spreads out his hands to this temple: then
hear from heaven Your dwelling place, and forgive."

It is certainly true that each person "knows his own burden
and his own grief." To live in this world is to know the pain of
struggle and sorrow — there is no way around it. So we can take it
for granted that every person we encounter is struggling. We may
not know the particulars, but it's a safe bet that every person we
meet is hurting. Each of us has his own burden, his own grief.

And our burdens and griefs really are unique. Unlike happiness, which is often very similar from person to person, sorrow
tends to be a more individual thing. Yes, we know that others
have suffered in similar ways (many have suffered more than we),
but there is still a distinct and undeniable *loneliness* that comes
with our burdens and our griefs. Since our circumstances vary
so greatly, there is rarely another human being who understands
exactly what we feel. And the longer we live, the more we realize
that the unique burden we have to bear is *intended* for us. No one
else should have to bear it. It is ours. And while we must avoid the
self-pity and the self-righteousness of the "martyr-spirit," it can't
be denied that our suffering is a burden that we alone must bear.
As Sir Thomas Fuller put it, "Every heart has its own ache."

Yet if each of us has his own burden and his own grief, it is
also true that our tears are those that God is able to wipe away.
He understands our experience completely, and that knowledge
ought to be both humbling and comforting: we are humbled to
know that He has suffered far more than we, and we are comforted to know that by His suffering He has defeated our enemy.

Earth has no sorrow that heaven cannot heal.

THOMAS MOORE

June 27
WAITING ON THE LORD

But those who wait on the LORD
Shall renew their strength;
They shall mount up with wings like eagles,
They shall run and not be weary,
They shall walk and not faint.
Isaiah 40:31

VERY FEW CONCEPTS ARE MORE IMPORTANT IN OUR SPIRITUAL GROWTH THAN THAT OF "WAITING ON THE LORD." But what does it mean to "wait on the Lord"? If it involves any real "waiting," most of us would find that a difficult thing to do, given our insistence on immediate gratification in all our endeavors. Whatever it may involve, "waiting" doesn't sound good to us.

In truth, "waiting on the Lord" does mean more than merely waiting ("remaining in a state of expectation"). We can speak of a servant "waiting" on his master, and that aspect of waiting is certainly included in our relationship to God. We are at His beck and call, at His service. Our job is to wait until He needs us, and then spring into action at His command. Young Samuel had the right idea: "Speak, LORD, for your servant hears" (1 Samuel 3:9,10).

But although waiting on the Lord involves more than mere waiting, it does not involve less. Reverence often requires us to wait patiently until He deems that the time is right for certain things to happen. Since He sees matters from a more complete perspective than we, and since He must take many more things into account than we, it is often the case that His timetable is different than ours. He may not act as quickly as we wish, and at such times we must be content to *wait* on the Lord, knowing that He will make all things beautiful . . . *in His time!* We would do well to take Guerric of Igny's advice: "Have courage and give God time."

But if it is *difficult* for us to wait, there is also a sense in which it can be *joyous*. You may not see anything good about yearning for what you desperately need but do not presently have, but I suggest that the idea of *joyful yearning* is one that can pay great dividends in life. Indeed, anticipation is a big part of the wholesome enjoyment of anything. So whenever it is necessary to wait on the Lord, can we not do so with joy and love and thanksgiving?

Let me discover the pleasure of anticipation. Give me what it takes to wait without complaining. Show me that there is more faith in waiting for what is unseen than in believing what is in front of my eyes.

BERNARD BANGLEY

June 28
DOES HEAVEN "FRUSTRATE" YOU?

For in this we groan, earnestly desiring to be clothed
with our habitation which is from heaven.
2 Corinthians 5:2

FOR SOME, THE VISION OF HEAVEN'S PERFECTION IS WONDERFULLY ENTICING, WHILE TO OTHERS IT IS MERELY FRUSTRATING. Perhaps a better word would be "tantalizing." In Greek mythology, Tantalus was a king condemned in Hades to stand in water that receded when he tried to drink and under fruit that receded when he reached for it. If we could *never* have heaven, the thought of it would certainly be tantalizing, but some people think of it that way just because it's *out of reach* and they can't have it *right now*.

Consequently, some people settle for what they *can* have right now. Deep down, they may know that in this world human beings are just "strangers in a strange land," but since the end of their sojourn is not immediately in sight, they feel that they might as well make themselves at home. They see this as being "realistic."

Other people simply reinterpret the gospel. Theologies such as the social gospel of the early twentieth century and the preterism of the late twentieth century are examples of efforts to remove the tension in the New Testament between the "already" and the "not yet." They do this by diminishing the "not yet," alleging that the gospel is primarily about what we can have in God right now.

Yet historically, Christians have *accepted* the "frustration" of tension between the already and the not yet. I agree with Harry Emerson Fosdick, who said, "This was the strength of the first Christians, that they lived not in one world only, but in two, and found in consequence not tension alone, but power, the vision of a world unshaken and unshakable." I also agree with C. S. Lewis, who said, "It is since Christians have largely ceased to think of the other world that they have become so ineffective in this."

Despite the joys of the "already," Paul said that in this life "we *groan*, earnestly desiring to be clothed with our habitation which is from heaven." Whether we look at "groaning" as a good thing or a bad thing is one measure of whether we understand what the gospel is about. So listen to me carefully: the gospel is not about *removing* the groaning from our lives — it's about *putting* it there.

Ah, but a man's reach should exceed his grasp,
Or what's a heaven for?
ROBERT BROWNING

June 29
MOVEMENT IS THE MAIN THING

What fruit did you have then in the things of which you are
now ashamed? For the end of those things is death. But now having
been set free from sin, and having become slaves of God, you have your
fruit to holiness, and the end, everlasting life. *Romans 6:21,22*

WE ARE TAUGHT IN THE SCRIPTURES THAT EVERY COURSE OF ACTION HAS A RESULT OR AN OUTCOME. The "end" of sinful conduct is death, while the "end" of godliness is everlasting life. With every decision that we make and every deed that we do, we are moving toward one outcome or the other. None of us is standing still. As Christians, we understand ourselves to be moving toward eternal life with God. But while that is an exciting prospect, our movement can be so slow sometimes that we become discouraged.

(1) *Where we've been may be shameful.* Like Paul, we may have some painful memories, memories of deeds that we wish could be undone. But while it is good to be humbled by our memories, what we have done in the past is not the most important thing about us. The more important consideration is in what direction we are *moving.* If we are moving toward God in the present, then our future stands a very good chance of being better than our past.

(2) *Where we are right now may be discouraging.* Even when our progress is toward God, the *pace* of our progress may be disheartening. Yet if our movement is in the right *direction,* that is what we need to concentrate on. It sometimes takes an honest person to see whether a certain step leads toward God or away from Him, but if we are sure that the action that lies before will move us in God's direction, then we need to be encouraged by that. It's not the *amount* of progress that matters; it's the fact that God is our goal.

So if we are moving in God's direction, that is the main thing, whether the movement seems to be significant to us or not. We ought always to be encouraged by the fact of positive movement.

The wonderful thing is that, as long as life lasts, it's always *possible* to move toward God. With every decision we face, the positive choice is always available. We will never come to a fork in the road where one fork will not be better than the other. And whenever we take the fork we know God would want us to take, we can do that knowing that we're going toward a good "end."

*The great thing in the world is not so much where
we stand, as in what direction we are moving.*

OLIVER WENDELL HOLMES

THE MOST DANGEROUS PLACE IS IN BETWEEN

He who is not with Me is against Me,
and he who does not gather with Me scatters abroad.
Matthew 12:30

JESUS CHRIST WAS A RADICAL RELIGIOUS TEACHER, TO SAY THE VERY LEAST. He claimed nothing less than to be God incarnate, born into the world to atone for our sins and provide eternal salvation. To such a figure as Jesus Christ, there is no "safe" response.

It is dangerous to be against Jesus Christ. Any person who makes of Jesus Christ an enemy has a dreadful enemy. John tells us, "His eyes were like a flame of fire . . . And the armies in heaven, clothed in fine linen, white and clean, followed Him on white horses. Now out of His mouth goes a sharp sword, that with it He should strike the nations. And He Himself will rule them with a rod of iron. He Himself treads the winepress of the fierceness and wrath of Almighty God" (Revelation 19:12-15). As the "Lion of Judah," Jesus has a fierceness that is extremely perilous to underestimate.

It is dangerous to be for Jesus Christ. Those who follow Jesus are in for trouble, at least as long as they live in this world. There is simply no convenient or carefree way to be a Christian. Jesus' enemies hated Him, and they will hate anyone who follows Him. His invitation is not to come to a seminar or a symposium but to an execution. "For whoever desires to save his life will lose it, but whoever loses his life for My sake will find it" (Matthew 16:25).

But it is most dangerous of all to be in between. When it comes to Jesus Christ, words like *hatred* and *hostility* are fearful words, to be sure. But let me give you some words that are far more fearful: *indifference, apathy, lukewarmness, nonchalance, unconcern, disinterest, detachment, uninvolvement, disregard.* The strongest language in the Scriptures, by far, is directed against those who simply *don't care* (Malachi 1:6-14; Matthew 23:23-28; Revelation 3:16; etc.).

There is a need, then, for us to make a clear-cut decision for or against Jesus Christ. There is no greater insult that we can offer to the Man of Galilee than to try to take both sides at once. If we don't love Him enough to stand with Him but don't despise Him enough to oppose Him, then we're living in the worst of all possible worlds. It's time to ask: *Does Christianity matter or does it not?*

Christianity, if false, is of no importance, and, if true, of infinite importance.
The one thing it cannot be is moderately important.
C. S. LEWIS

July 1

FOCUSING ON THE FINISH

. . . looking unto Jesus, the author and finisher of our faith,
who for the joy that was set before Him endured the cross, despising the
shame, and has sat down at the right hand of the throne of God.
Hebrews 12:2

BETWEEN NOW AND THE TIME WHEN WE REACH OUR HEAVENLY GOAL, WE NEED TO KEEP OUR MINDS FOCUSED ON THE FINISH. I am not so sure but what this is the major challenge of the Christian life. Most of our problems would shrink to manageable size if we would just do what Peter says: "Gird up the loins of your mind, be sober, and *rest your hope fully* upon the grace that is to be brought to you at the revelation of Jesus Christ" (1 Peter 1:13). After all, it was focusing on the finish that got Jesus through His suffering.

Sinful temptations. The devil is going to tempt us to leave the path we're on. A master at deception, he will try to convince us that where the Lord wants us to go is not where we would be the happiest going. He knows the truth, of course, but he will tempt us to sin with him and die, rather than walk with God and live.

Difficulties. In addition to temptations to sin, there are also difficulties that have to be dealt with, situations that don't necessarily involve sin but which are simply hard to handle. If anybody knows about difficulty, it is certainly our Lord, and He held up under the load that He carried only by thinking of the joy ahead.

Distractions. The third thing that we need help with is the multitude of distractions that have the effect of pulling our attention away from God. Even the things that God has *made* can do this if we're not careful. It is only by keeping heaven clearly in mind that we can keep the temporal world in proper perspective.

But do you think you can make a one-time decision to "focus on the finish" and then life will automatically unfold as it should? Well, I'm afraid it's not that simple. Keeping a right focus on heaven requires *refocusing our minds daily*, and maybe even *many times daily*. As often as we see that we're not setting our minds "on things above" (Colossians 3:2), we have to bring our minds back to their proper focus. It's a habit that we have to get ourselves into, but if we will do that, the sinful temptations, difficulties, and distractions that come our way will be much less of a problem.

Obstacles are those frightful things you see
when you take your eyes off the goal.

HANNAH MORE

July 2
WOULD YOU PRAY FOR MORE YEARS TO LIVE?

In those days Hezekiah was sick and near death. And Isaiah the prophet,
the son of Amoz, went to him and said to him, "Thus says the LORD:
'Set your house in order, for you shall die, and not live.'"
2 Kings 20:1

HOW LONG DO YOU WANT TO LIVE? If the Lord told you, as He did Hezekiah, that you only had a certain number of years left, would you pray for more? Most people, without batting an eye, would say that they want to live in this world *as long as possible*. And we are willing to employ any extreme medical method or scientific procedure to eke out even a few more minutes.

But let's try to look at this from a different angle. For a moment, think of an analogy. If you had a good bit of *money* lying around unused, or if you hadn't used your money very wisely, you probably wouldn't have the nerve to ask the Lord for more. You'd already know what He would say: "Look, you aren't using the money you already have. Why do you want more?"

Now come back to the subject of how long we want to live. Our lives are to be used not merely for our personal enjoyment but for the Lord's glory, to accomplish His purposes in this world. It's only a guess (but I think it's a safe guess) that the Lord is willing to give a person as many years as it takes to get done *what the Lord wants that person to do*. I agree with Henry Martyn, who said, "If God has work for me to do, I cannot die." As long as we're doing work the Lord wants finished, *the devil couldn't kill us if he tried*.

Now before life is over, our problem may be that of wanting to go home *before* our work is done, in which case we would need to start thinking about that as Paul did (Philippians 1:21-26). But as soon as our part in the Lord's work is done, why would we want to stay in this world one second longer? (And please don't define your work in the Lord as nothing more than enjoying your kids and grandkids. The Lord might have other plans. Your kids might profit from dealing with the hardship of losing you, and other people might have as good an influence on them as you have had.)

So am I going to pray for more years to live? Well, I may. But if I do, I'd better be sure that I've used the years I've already had, and that the reason I want more years is to do the Lord's work.

Millions long for immortality who do not know
what to do with themselves on a rainy Sunday afternoon.
SUSAN ERTZ

July 3
WINDOW OF OPPORTUNITY

See then that you walk circumspectly, not as fools but as wise,
redeeming the time, because the days are evil.
Ephesians 5:15,16

THERE NEEDS TO BE A HEALTHY SENSE OF URGENCY IN OUR LIVES. With regard to that which the Lord wants us to do in His work individually, there is not an unlimited amount of time in which to do that work. Each of us has a "window of opportunity," and after that is gone, we will give account for our stewardship of the time given us. We urgently need to "redeem the time," as Paul put it.

Granted, there is such a thing as an *unhealthy* urgency. Most of us are familiar with what that's like. It's the driven, compulsive, frantic mentality of competitors in the "rat race." But that is not the way to redeem the time. In fact, nothing is more unproductive.

Jesus showed that it is possible to be very busy and not fall into the "driven" way of thinking. At our busiest, few of us will match the Lord's activity, yet in the act of being busy, Jesus always had a calm, deliberate way about Him. He knew how to "hasten leisurely," to work steadily, and even urgently, without losing the peace that was at the center of His being. Jesus knew that He had a "schedule" to meet, and He met it. At the end, He could say, "It is finished" (John 19:30). As His disciples, we need to redeem the time and be able, one day, to say that we have finished our work.

A few days ago, I received an email from Ken Craig, a great friend who does full-time secular work but also manages to do as much work in the Lord as anybody I know. In an earlier email to him, I had mentioned being busy (forgetting to whom I was talking), and he wrote back, "I am in Shanghai, China right now on business, with meetings all day and three-hour Chinese dinners every evening. I had a glorious trip to India in April and had just recovered from that . . . I should be back on Sunday . . . Keep on keeping on. We will rest on the other side." Ken is not about to miss the window of opportunity that the Lord has given him.

As Gerry Sandusky, another great friend, says, "Heaven is pictured as a place of rest, and I intend to be tired when I get there." Like Ken, Gerry understands that now is the time for work, a time to spend and be spent. There'll be time enough for rest later.

We have all eternity to celebrate our victories,
but only one short hour before sunset in which to win them.
ROBERT MOFFAT

July 4
GLAD TO BE UNSATISFIED

He has made everything beautiful in its time.
Also He has put eternity in their hearts . . .
Ecclesiastes 3:11

THERE ARE SOME YEARNINGS THAT IT IS GOOD TO HAVE EVEN IF THE EMPTINESS OF THEIR UNFULFILLMENT IS HARD TO BEAR. Even if we use the word "pain" to describe the feeling of not having something that we need and desire, it is still a fact that pain can play a useful role in our spiritual lives. Young Samuel's mother, Hannah, would have had many long years to yearn for her son after she devoted him to the Lord's service at the tabernacle, but still she could say, "My heart rejoices in the Lord" (1 Samuel 2:1).

The fact is, no one gets to have everything they desire in this world. And even if a person were to do so (Solomon probably came close), they would still have to confess to an aching emptiness that never completely goes away. The reason for that is simply that God has placed "eternity in [our] hearts." He has given us needs that, to be quite honest, have no satisfaction in this world.

With regard to our unmet needs, the first mistake we make is to try to do the impossible and "have it all" in this world. It seems unnatural to us, if not unfair, for a person to have any need not met, and so we spend our lives trying to find something to stuff into every hole in our hearts. But that is a vain effort. God will see to it that we suffer some deprivation somewhere in our lives.

The second mistake we make is resisting, and maybe even resenting, the fact that some of our needs can't be satisfied right now. Rather than making us better, as it should, our emptiness can make us bitter if we don't discipline our thinking about it.

But someone says, "Oh, but God is all we need." Well, yes and no. He may give us some things that compensate for what we don't have, and He will certainly be all we need in *eternity*. But for now, there's no way around the pain of the needs that are not met.

Now here is the point: *we ought to be content to be unsatisfied in this world!* I know that sounds contradictory, but it isn't. We can be glad we *don't* have all we need, because if we did, we'd soon forget about God. Unmet needs are powerful attention-getters, and with them God is trying to get our attention focused on eternity.

I thank thee, O Lord, that thou hast so set eternity within my heart
that no earthly thing can ever satisfy me wholly.
JOHN BAILLIE

July 5

ETERNITY

Now behold, one came and said to Him, "Good Teacher,
what good thing shall I do that I may have eternal life?"
Matthew 19:16

THERE IS SOMETHING ABOUT THE IDEA OF ETERNITY THAT HAS A POWERFUL PULL ON US. Some would say that our fascination with a state of timeless being is mere curiosity, but I think that more is involved. We are *attracted* to eternity. We *long* for an existence without the limitations of time. We *yearn* for immortality.

Somehow, we understand that we are creatures who were meant to *live* — and we understand that what we have right now is not real life. Paul used a telling phrase in 1 Timothy 6:19, when he told Timothy to remind the rich to be generous and ready to share, "storing up for themselves the treasure of a good foundation for the future, so that they may take hold of *that which is life indeed*" (NASV). That's what we want, isn't it? Life *indeed*.

And that is precisely what the gospel of Christ is about. Yes, it makes for a better "life" in this world, relatively speaking, but that is not what the gospel is primarily about. It's about eternity. It's about immortality, as Paul said in 1 Corinthians 15:53,54: "For this corruptible must put on incorruption, and this mortal must put on immortality. So when this corruptible has put on incorruption, and this mortal has put on immortality, then shall be brought to pass the saying that is written: 'Death is swallowed up in victory.'"

The opening lines of Wolfgang Petersen's film *Troy* have always moved me: "Men are haunted by the vastness of eternity. And so we ask ourselves: will our actions echo across the centuries? Will strangers hear our names long after we are gone, and wonder who we were, how bravely we fought, how fiercely we loved?" Yet the "eternity" that haunts us is more than the vastness of historical time. The "immortality" that Achilles sought to gain at Troy is nothing compared to the thing that we really long for.

May we let ourselves be attracted to eternal *life* with all its fearful glory. Yes, there is warm affection when we think of life with our Father, but who can think of *eternity* — with *God* — without tremors and chills of awe and wonder and reverence? It may not be "logical," but here it is: *the thing that we are the most attracted to is also the most terrifying.* Such is always the nature of real joy.

Eternity! thou pleasing, dreadful thought!
JOSEPH ADDISON

July 6
EVERGREEN

Then He who sat on the throne said, "Behold, I make all things new."
Revelation 21:5

ALL OF US KNOW THE EXCITEMENT THAT COMES FROM STARTING OVER. Perhaps that's why we enjoy springtime so much. It's a fresh beginning. Old growth is gone, and everything is green again. But imagine a land where everything is always as if it had just been refreshed and rejuvenated. That would be heaven.

If we've obeyed the gospel and are living faithfully to Christ, then there is a sense in which all things have become new for us already (2 Corinthians 5:17). And when the apostle John heard God say, "Behold, I make all things new," there is a sense in which we can say that God has already done that for His people.

But the richest experience of newness that even the most faithful Christian can have right now will pale in comparison to the newness that will be ours in heaven. If you are a Christian and you think there is a big difference between your life right now and the one you used to have, just wait till you see the difference between what you have right now and what you'll have with God in eternity. What is now is but the merest foretaste of what is to come.

I predict that one of the things that we'll find most striking about heaven is the absence of anything resembling decay or decline. Right now, even our highest and purest joys are attacked by age and decrepitude. No sooner have we begun to enjoy something than it is taken away from us, and we've only started to appreciate its beauty when it withers away. But in eternity, neither the beauty or value of anything will be diminished by the aging process. Not only will everything be new, but it will *stay* new!

I make the prediction in the preceding paragraph because I believe everything in heaven will partake of God's nature, in which there is no loss due to age. "Of old You laid the foundation of the earth, and the heavens are the work of Your hands. They will perish, but You will endure; yes, they will all grow old like a garment; like a cloak You will change them, and they will be changed. But You are the same, and Your years will have no end" (Psalm 102:25-27). Given the nature of God, I'm looking for heaven to be a place where the word "new" has a whole "new" meaning.

In eternity everything is just beginning.
ELIAS CANETTI

July 7
THE CHALLENGE OF ABUNDANCE

I have learned both to be full and to be hungry,
both to abound and to suffer need.
Philippians 4:12

WOULD YOU RATHER LIVE IN A LAND OF ABUNDANCE OR ONE OF SCARCITY? Would you rather have most of what you want in life or little of what you want? To a worldly person, the question would be simply ridiculous, but think twice before you answer, and try to be honest about what your priorities really are.

Maybe we could start by totaling up the *disadvantages* on both sides. The disadvantages of having *little* are obvious — perhaps painfully so — but the disadvantages of having *much* are just as real, even if they aren't so obvious. Having all, or even most, of what we want can destroy us spiritually if we don't face frankly the principal problem that goes along with satisfied circumstances: *the fact that it is much harder to keep God in the right place in our hearts.*

Most people assume that being poor is hard and being rich is easy, but Paul said that he had to learn how "both to be full and to be hungry, both to abound and to suffer need." Probably more people have been hurt by satisfaction than by dissatisfaction, but neither scenario is easy or automatic — both take *learning* and *discipline* before we can handle them and not be harmed spiritually.

Now you may say that if you had to choose between the problems of being full and those of being empty, there would be no contest: you'd choose the challenge of abundance. And truthfully, most of us would. That's why we have so little patience with successful people who complain about the disadvantages of their success, such as celebrities who whine about not having any privacy. We just want to say, "As problems go, that one compares pretty favorably to some others. Why don't you just grow up and get used to the difficulties of having gotten what you wanted?"

But what about us? If God would let us have the kind of life that *we* want, all of our problems would be over, wouldn't they? No, they wouldn't. If we ever got what we wanted in this life, we would soon find ourselves faced with challenges that we never even knew existed before. In this broken world, having what we want is not easy. So if you find yourself "abounding," watch out.

The problems of victory are more agreeable than those
of defeat, but they are no less difficult.
WINSTON CHURCHILL

July 8

YOU'LL HAVE TO LET GO

Whoever of you does not forsake all that he has cannot be My disciple.
Luke 14:33

To FOLLOW JESUS IN THIS LIFE, WE MAY HAVE TO FORSAKE SOME THINGS, BUT TO FOLLOW HIM ALL THE WAY TO HEAVEN, WE'LL HAVE TO FORSAKE EVERYTHING. Nothing is ours to keep. There is nothing — *nothing* — that we won't have to let go of, except God.

Most people would say that the rich, wonderful love that can exist between a husband and a wife is the highest of the temporal blessings available to us. In the midst of enjoying a good marriage, most people would say, "It doesn't get any better than this." But without denigrating the joys of marriage, it must be said that marriage is earthly. It won't be in heaven. It must be let go of.

I want to share with you one of the starkest statements that I have ever come across, considering who made it. This is James Dobson talking, the man who, for many folks, is the foremost *family* authority in America: "Nothing is really important in [this] life, not even the relationships that blossom in a healthy home. In time, we must release our grip on everything we hold dear." I suggest that if James Dobson, a man who has devoted his life to the importance of the home, sees that marriage and family life are not "really important," the rest of us had better sit up and take notice.

Most of us, I suppose, would *say* that we love the Lord more than anything else and that heaven is going to be better than anything we have here. But do you really believe that? Do you love God more than you love your spouse? Would you give up marriage for the Lord? Is the spiritual life better than sex? If the Lord gave you a choice between going to heaven right now and staying in the world with your grandchildren for ten more years, which would you choose? Now certainly, we may enjoy these things right now and then have the Lord in heaven later on. But even now, the Lord had better be more important to us than these things. And the main measure of whether we have a proper attitude toward temporal joys is *how ready we are to let go of them.* And I don't mean "someday" — I mean *today*, if the need should arise.

What it comes down to is this: *Anything we can't let go of is an idol that will destroy our souls, however good that thing may be.*

Learn to hold loosely all that is not eternal.
AGNES MAUDE ROYDEN

July 9
WE DON'T CHANGE UNTIL WE HAVE TO

And the LORD will scatter you among the peoples, and you will be left
few in number among the nations where the LORD will drive you. And there
you will serve gods, the work of men's hands, wood and stone, which
neither see nor hear nor eat nor smell. But from there you will seek the LORD
your God, and you will find Him if you seek Him with all your heart
and with all your soul. *Deuteronomy 4:27-29*

HAVE YOU NOTICED IN YOURSELF A PATTERN OF HAVING TO BE PRODDED INTO ACTION? I've certainly seen it in my own life, and frankly, I am ashamed. There have been too many times when I didn't do something that I should have done until something outside of me "put a gun to my head" and *made* me do it.

Just look at how we live. We don't get out of bed until we have to. We don't go to the dentist until we have a toothache. We don't repair our houses until we have to sell them. And we don't do our taxes until the night before. But far worse, we don't dig deeper wells of faith until some crisis invades our lives and we are absolutely dying of thirst. Not everybody does this, to be sure. There are a few wise ones. But most of us have to be prodded by external circumstances before we do what we should toward God.

Thankfully, God is a Father who is willing to provide a "prod" when He sees that His people need one. In the text in Deuteronomy above, God predicted that Israel would not seek Him until He had scattered them among the nations and driven them into the misery of captivity in Babylon. If they had not sought Him before, they would certainly seek Him then. When they got sick and tired of being sick and tired, they would change.

There has to be a kind of "critical mass" before most of us act. As long as the ease and pleasure of the status quo is greater than the discomfort of changing, we don't change. It's only when the present has become less pleasurable, or the possible consequences of *not* acting have become scary enough, that we finally act.

It is a shame, really, that so many of us are so much like old King Nebuchadnezzar: we are unwilling to give the Lord His due until we are driven from civilized company and made to eat grass like the oxen until seven times have passed over us (Daniel 4:25). It's a shame, I say. But for most of us, that's the way it is.

We accept the verdict of the past until the need for change cries
out loudly enough to force upon us a choice between the comforts
of further inertia and the irksomeness of action.

LEARNED HAND

July 10
A WRONG KIND OF DETERMINATION

Yes, we had the sentence of death in ourselves, that we should
not trust in ourselves but in God who raises the dead . . .
2 Corinthians 1:9

ORDINARILY, DETERMINATION IS A GOOD THING, BUT FOR THOSE
WHO ARE CHRISTIANS, IT CAN SOMETIMES BE A BAD THING. For
example, if determination to overcome our problems leads us to a
wrong way of thinking about *ourselves,* then it will hurt us.

There is much to be said for having a "positive mental attitude," but unfortunately, many of those who motivate us in that
area impart to us an attitude that is dangerous for a human being
to have, at least from a spiritual standpoint. The critical issue is
how we view our own powers and abilities. Determination is fine,
but we dare not get to thinking that we ourselves are invincible.

Listen to a couple of fairly typical admonitions on this subject, both of which could be helpful or unhelpful depending on
how you look at them: "If it's going to be, it's up to me" (Robert
Schuller), and "The difference between the impossible and the
possible lies in a man's determination" (Tommy Lasorda). While
these sayings are helpfully empowering in one way, in another
way they seem to imply that a human being who is determined
enough can do anything he sets his mind to. But that is not true.
What is "going to be" involves a wide range of factors that are *not*
"up to me," and there is a good deal *more* that separates the possible from the impossible than my own personal determination.

Lest I be accused of being picky, let me hasten to say that I
appreciate, and have been helped by, these kinds of motivations.
They urge me to take responsibility for what I can do and not wait
for somebody else to accomplish my goals for me. But half-truths
can hurt us if we're not careful. We need to watch our thinking.

Paul would hardly have escaped from his ordeal in Asia
without being determined. He had to refuse to give up in the face
of difficulty. But what he learned from that experience was to have
less faith in the powers of his own determination and more faith in
God. In short, he learned "that we should not trust in ourselves."
That's not good "motivational speaking," but it's good theology.

Earnestness is not by any means everything;
it is very often a subtle form of pious self-idolatry because it is
obsessed with the method and not with the Master.

OSWALD CHAMBERS

July 11

UNDER THE TREE

For the love of Christ compels us, because we judge thus: that if One
died for all, then all died; and He died for all, that those who live should live
no longer for themselves, but for Him who died for them and rose again.
2 Corinthians 5:14,15

ONE OF LIFE'S MARVELS IS THE REDEMPTIVE POWER OF LOVE. There probably aren't many of us who haven't experienced the difference that it makes to know that somebody loves us. We can be discouraged and about to give up, but when we remind ourselves that there are those who love us, we find new hope.

Paul the apostle is a fascinating figure from many viewpoints, but one of the most interesting things about him is his motivation. We don't have to wonder what caused him work as hard and suffer as courageously as he did. He tells us. It was, he said, "the love of Christ" that compelled, or constrained, him. The love of Christ governed his thinking and pulled his actions in the right direction.

But was Paul talking about Christ's love for him or his love for Christ? I think he was talking about both, because it's not really possible to separate the two. Christ's love for us moved Him to die for our sins, and in response to that love, we love Him and live our lives for His sake. Christ died "that those who live should live no longer for themselves, but for Him who died for them." That was the key to Paul's motivation. Every move he made was an effort to show *gratitude* for the One who loved Him enough to die for him. And friend, if that motivation doesn't move you, you can't be moved. Motivation doesn't get any stronger than that.

As long as we live in this world, we are going to have days of discouragement. We can't fight on the front lines and not get wounded. But what a difference it makes to remember that Christ died for us! The thought that Somebody loved us like that can turn us around no matter what ditch the devil has dragged us into.

But there is a catch: we have to *think* about what Christ did for us. The redemptive, refreshing, strengthening power of that thought is not automatic. We have to *think* it. And not only do we have to think it, we have to let it have its proper effect on us. We have to go to the cross and get the point of what happened there.

If at any time you feel disposed again to say, "It is enough," and that
you can bear the burden of life no longer, do as Elijah did: flee into the
silence of solitude, and sit under — not the juniper tree — but under that
tree whereon the incarnate Son of God was made a curse for you.

FRIEDRICH WILHELM KRUMMACHER

July 12
THE WORST TIME TO DECIDE

And Samuel said, "What have you done?" And Saul said, "When I saw
that the people were scattered from me, and that you did not come within
the days appointed, and that the Philistines gathered together at Michmash,
then I said, 'The Philistines will now come down on me at Gilgal, and I have
not made supplication to the LORD.' Therefore I felt compelled,
and offered a burnt offering." *1 Samuel 13:11,12*

WHEN A MAJOR DECISION IS ASKING TO BE MADE, THERE IS A TIME
TO DECIDE AND A TIME NOT TO DECIDE. The more important
the decision is, the more we need to be in our best frame of mind
when we make it. So the very worst time to decide a major question is when we are fearful or discouraged or sorrowful.

Saul had not long been king when the Philistines attacked.
He gathered his army to defend the land, but when the prophet
Samuel did not come quickly, Saul went ahead and offered a sacrifice, begging the Lord for help. The problem was that Saul was not
authorized to make such a sacrifice. He knew it was wrong, but
when questioned about it, he explained the urgency of his need
and said, "I felt compelled, and offered a burnt offering." Under
the power of a fearful emotion, he decided to do a sinful thing.

The devil is not our friend. We are told that he is a shrewd,
malevolent enemy "seeking whom he may devour" (1 Peter 5:8).
In his ongoing effort to destroy us, he likes nothing better than
to frighten us, strip us of hope, and then pressure us into making
major decisions while we're in a desperate state of mind.

Emotions like fear, sorrow, and shame must be handled with
special care. They make a very poor "environment" or "context" in
which to make decisions. So when we're being pressured by these
emotions and a decision must be made that involves the possibility of committing sin, *we must postpone the decision until the painful
emotion has passed.* The worst time to decide is when we're hurting.

Of all the painful emotions, perhaps the worst is despair —
the loss of hope. We all have desperate *days*, of course. That's to be
expected. But desperate *decisions* are dangerous, and so desperate
days are the worst time to decide whether we're going to yield to a
temptation or say no to it. As an emotion, despair is not inherently
sinful; in fact, it can do some useful things for us. But one thing it
can't do for us is tell us what course of action we ought to take.

Despair is an evil counselor.
SIR WALTER SCOTT

TURNING FROM, TURNING TO

But we are not of those who draw back to perdition,
but of those who believe to the saving of the soul.
Hebrews 10:39

A S THOSE WHO HAVE OBEYED THE GOSPEL OF CHRIST, WE HAVE BOTH AN OLD LIFE AND A NEW. We can think not only of what we turned away *from* but also of what we turned *to*.

Our "turning from" needs to be decisive. When Paul wrote to the Galatians, some of whom were going back to their old lives, he said, "After you have known God, or rather are known by God, how is it that you turn again to the weak and beggarly elements, to which you desire again to be in bondage?" (Galatians 4:9). We need to burn our bridges behind us. For us, there is no going back.

Our "turning to" needs to be passionate. Nature abhors a vacuum, as the saying goes, and no matter how decisively we have rejected our sinful past, if that void is not filled with a passionate pursuit of something new and better, we're in trouble. The old will come back all too quickly if we don't lovingly and joyously throw ourselves into the quest for God and our eternal home with Him.

Depending on our personality and our past history, the things we want to move away from may furnish a more powerful motivation than the things we want to move toward. Most people are motivated by a combination of fear and hope, with one or the other predominating at various times. But all things considered, shouldn't Christians think more of what's ahead than of what's behind? "Forgetting those things which are behind and reaching forward to those things which are ahead," Paul said, "I press toward the goal for the prize of the upward call of God in Christ Jesus" (Philippians 3:13,14). Our hope is in what we've turned *toward*.

As long as our lives in this world last, there is always the possibility of apostasy. But we need to be a people of genuine *hope*, eager to believe the best in others and in ourselves. As the Hebrew writer said, we are not "of those who draw back to perdition, but of those who believe to the saving of the soul." So having turned from futility and death to salvation and life, let us be as passionate in what we pursue as we are decisive in what we reject.

A turn involves two things: it involves a *terminus a quo*
and a *terminus ad quem*. It involves a turning from
something and a turning to something.

WILLIAM BARCLAY

July 14
DISQUALIFYING OURSELVES BY DEFAULT

Therefore let it be known to you that the salvation of God
has been sent to the Gentiles, and they will hear it!
Acts 28:28

THREE DAYS AFTER PAUL ARRIVED AS A PRISONER IN ROME, HE CALLED TOGETHER THE LEADERS OF THE JEWISH COMMUNITY THERE. He told them that he was in prison for preaching to the Gentiles — and he warned them that he intended to keep preaching to the Gentiles. If you won't hear the gospel, he said, they will.

It certainly gave Paul no pleasure to think that most of his fellow Jews and former colleagues were rejecting the gospel (Romans 9:1-5). But Paul understood that their rejection didn't mean that the gospel wouldn't go forward. There would be others who *would* receive it, and the Jews were hurting no one but themselves by refusing to accept the salvation that was being offered to them.

But what does that have to do with us? For one thing, it ought to have a *sobering* effect on our thinking. The gospel has to be *accepted*. While a few of the Jews persecuted the gospel, most of them simply did *nothing*, and if we do about the gospel what they did, then we will get the same results. In our present condition, we are under condemnation for our sins, and so the "default position" is condemnation. Taking the course of least resistance always leads downhill, and doing nothing will get us nothing but hell.

But the situation of the Jews in the first century also ought to have a *humbling* effect on us. If we reject the gospel, we will be left, as they were, standing on the outside looking in while others enjoy salvation. God will have a people who accept Him, and it will be a great, numerous people — with or without us. Although it will grieve Him terribly, our Father will have to say to us, "Despite My efforts to save you, you have refused My offer. But know this: the same offer will be made to others, and they *will* accept it."

Thankfully, the kingdom of God does not depend on any of us. It will stand no matter what we do, and God's eternal purposes will be accomplished even if God has to find a way to work around our lack of cooperation. But oh, what a *tragedy* if we are not present when the celebration of His triumph begins! What are we *thinking* if we default on our duties right now and disqualify ourselves from the heaven that so many others will enjoy?

The day will happen whether or not you get up.
JOHN CIARDI

July 15
WE PROMISED WE'D REACH FORWARD

I have kept the faith.
2 Timothy 4:7

SAVING FAITH INVOLVES NOT ONLY CREDENCE IN THE TRUTH AND CONFIDENCE IN GOD, BUT ALSO CONSTANCY IN OUR COMMITMENT. We must finish what we started when we confessed our faith and were baptized into Christ, and we will be lost if we can't say what Paul said at the end of his life: *I have kept the faith.*

"Reaching forward" is an important idea, and most people would say that it's a good thing to do. But I hear some folks talking about it as if it were optional. It is, however, anything but optional. When we obeyed the gospel, we *committed* ourselves to reaching forward. We made what amounted to a public promise to strive for heaven the rest of our lives. And if we ever quit doing that, we've broken the most important promise we ever made.

But the promise to keep the faith and to keep reaching forward is like other promises in that it often ends up being harder to keep than we thought it would be at the time we made it. Even if we carefully "count the cost," we can't know all of what the future may entail. So our commitment to keep the faith is the signing of an open-ended contract: we must keep the faith *no matter what.*

In the Scriptures, there is a steady emphasis on what we would call "following through." Hear Paul, for example, urging the Corinthians to do as they said they would about the contribution for the needy saints in Jerusalem: "You also must complete the doing of it; that as there was a readiness to desire it, so there also may be a completion out of what you have" (2 Corinthians 8:11).

If we take God seriously, keeping our commitment to Him is going to involve some surprises. Some of these will be pleasant, but others will be very difficult. (Imagine Abraham's surprise the morning he got up and heard the Lord say, "I want you to sacrifice your son.") But if the only promises we keep are the easy ones, what kind of character is that? When David asked, "LORD, who may abide in Your tabernacle?" (Psalm 15:1), one of the answers was: "He who swears to his own hurt and does not change" (v.4). If you don't know what that means, then try this translation: "He who stands by his pledge at any cost" (Jerusalem Bible).

Dependability: fulfilling what I agreed to do
even though it requires unexpected sacrifices.

BILL GOTHARD

HERE BE DRAGONS

And they commanded the people, saying, "When you see the ark
of the covenant of the LORD your God, and the priests, the Levites, bearing
it, then you shall set out from your place and go after it. Yet there shall be a
space between you and it, about two thousand cubits by measure. Do not
come near it, that you may know the way by which you must go,
for you have not passed this way before."
Joshua 3:3,4

I LOVE MAPS, AND THE OLDER THEY ARE, THE MORE THEY FASCINATE
ME. Especially intriguing to me are maps of the "world" made
in ancient times by cartographers who knew little of the world
beyond their own immediate area. These mapmakers would draw
the territory that was known at the time, and beyond that, they
would just leave blank space and write, "Here be dragons." It was
assumed that if territory lay beyond the bounds of current knowledge, then dragons must surely dwell there, and any explorers
who ventured into that mysterious zone should be on their guard.

Metaphorically speaking, there is a good deal of unknown
"territory" in the lives of all of us. For example, the future lies
off the edge of the map. Nobody has been there yet, and no one
knows what that territory will be like. For all we know, "dragons"
may dwell there. But even in the present, there are activities, endeavors, and experiences that lie beyond our present knowledge,
and that which is unfamiliar often seems scary. Here be dragons!

If we are Christians, of course, God is our guide, so we don't
need to know what the territory is like through which we will
pass. We only need to trust that He will see us through, possible
"dragons" notwithstanding. No doubt He would say to us, as He
said to Israel when they were about to cross the Jordan, that we
should follow His lead, *"for you have not passed this way before."*

But to my way of thinking, the thrill of the unknown is a great
part of the *joy* of being a Christian. Yes, prudence counsels *caution* when we face the unknown, but faith counsels *courage*. Here
be dragons, you say? Fine. I am eager to see them and, if need be,
fight them. Whatever else it may be, life in Christ is never dull. Of
all the adventures in this world, it is truly the Great Adventure.

Oh, the depths of the fathomless deep,
Oh, the riddle and secret of things,
And the voice through the darkness heard,
And the rush of winnowing wings!

SIR LEWIS MORRIS

July 17
EXPECT THE UNEXPECTED

So passing by Mysia, they came down to Troas. And a vision appeared to
Paul in the night. A man of Macedonia stood and pleaded with him, saying,
"Come over to Macedonia and help us." Now after he had seen the vision,
immediately we sought to go to Macedonia, concluding that the Lord
had called us to preach the gospel to them.
Acts 16:8-10

LIFE WOULD BE A DREARY BUSINESS IF THERE WERE NO SURPRISES.
Getting our way all of the time and seeing things always turn
out exactly as we planned would not be delightful; it would, in
the end, be extremely tiresome. So it is really a blessing when God
tears up our itineraries and requires a change of course. Paul had
not planned to go to Macedonia, but he would be the first to say
that going there was one of the best things he ever had to do.

We should expect the unexpected. When it turns out that God has
something different for us than we expected, we shouldn't behave
as if some strange thing were happening to us. Unexpected turn-
ings in the pathway of life are the norm, not the exception, and it
helps to live with the possibility of change always in our minds.

We should adjust to the unexpected. If we've ever sung the song
Trust and Obey, we ought to be familiar with the concept of *yielding*
to the Lord's will. When God's will and our own plans are trying
to occupy the same space at the same time, something has to give.
Faith means that we yield to Him, adjusting ourselves as needed.

We should give thanks for the unexpected. Yielding to changes
that the Lord requires doesn't have to be a matter of grudging
acceptance. We can, if we choose, *embrace* the better path that the
Lord has indicated, with gratitude for the change rather than resentment. After all, growth does come from change, doesn't it?

What it comes down to is that we are the *servants* of God, and
servants who can't handle surprises don't make very good servants. As long as God is our master, we need not doubt that His
next order is going to be *good.* It may be disruptive and inconvenient, but it is going to be *good* nonetheless. So while we busy
ourselves with our present "assignment," may we eagerly await
the next one that the Master will give us. It may be very different
than what we had in mind — and it may come at any minute!

The only way a servant can remain true to God is to be ready
for the Lord's surprise visits. . . . This sense of expectation will give
our life the attitude of childlike wonder He wants it to have.

OSWALD CHAMBERS

July 18
THE NEXT STEP CAN ALWAYS BE TAKEN

For if there is first a willing mind, it is accepted according
to what one has, and not according to what he does not have.
2 Corinthians 8:12

BACK IN JANUARY, WE CONSIDERED THAT "THE NEXT STEP IS AL-
WAYS OUR MOST IMPORTANT." If our previous steps have been
bad, then the *next* one is very critical: it will either stop the damage
and start us in a better direction, or it will make matters worse.

Today, let's look at this same idea from a somewhat different angle: not only is our next step *important*, but whatever is the
next step we should take, it is always possible to *take* that step.
We need to grasp this second point as clearly as we do the first. If
I understood that my next step was critically important, but I believed that it required more of me than I could handle, I would be
discouraged rather than encouraged. So I need to understand that,
whatever step I *should* take, it will always be one that I *can* take.

God does not expect the impossible. As Paul wrote to the
Corinthians, God's expectations are "according to what one has,
and not according to what he does not have." The thing that we
will be held accountable for is the choice that we make among the
alternatives that are *available* — not those that are unavailable.

If the next step that we should take *seems* impossible to us, we
are probably looking at something bigger than the next step. We
need to break that step down into smaller and smaller ones until
we find something we are capable of doing. I can tell you, there
are days when "writing the next page" in this book is more of a
step than I can take. Even "outlining an idea for the next page" is
more than I can handle. Sometimes I can do no more than get out a
blank piece of paper and place it in front of me on the desk. But if
that's the biggest step that I can take, then I need to go ahead and
take it. Indeed, nothing else can happen until I do the *first* thing!

So no matter how overwhelming the work to be done may
seem, let us always be willing to *begin*. We don't know what lies
ahead, but for all practical purposes right now, we don't *need* to
know. Some things are worth beginning, even if we can't see how
they may be finished. So what we need is not more knowledge or
ability but the courage to take the step that *can* be taken, the one
that lies right in front of us. We need the courage to *get started*.

The journey of a thousand miles begins with one step.

LAO-TSE

July 19
WHY A GOOD NAME MATTERS SO MUCH

A good name is to be chosen rather than great riches,
Loving favor rather than silver and gold.
Proverbs 22:1

PEOPLE WHO HAVE ACQUIRED WISDOM UNDERSTAND THAT IT'S IM-PORTANT TO BUILD A GOOD NAME. If we could have riches or a good name, but not both, a good name would be the better choice.

At the very least, having a good name requires honesty, fairness, and complete integrity. And we aren't talking about "image" here. A good name means *having* these qualities, not *pretending* to have them. As Edward R. Murrow, the great World War II broadcaster, said, "To be persuasive, we must be believable. To be believable, we must be credible. To be credible, we must be truthful."

But having a good name also requires taking precautions against the appearance of wrongdoing. There is an old Chinese proverb that says, "Avoid suspicion. When you're walking through your neighbor's melon patch, don't tie your shoe." It takes not only a wise person to see the sense in that, it takes a person who cares more about his name than about his rights.

But speaking of rights, having a good name also means yielding our rights for the sake of things like love and mercy, and even courtesy and neighborliness. The person who insists on "doing his own thing," regardless of how it impinges on others, is not going to have much credibility, even if what he's doing is "right" from a technical standpoint. Paul wrote, "Do not let what is right for you become a matter of reproach" (Romans 14:16 TCNT).

But why does a good name matter so much? The answer is simple. If we are Christians, we bear the name of our Lord. In the eyes of the world, His reputation stands or falls with our own. To quote Paul once more, we are to "adorn the doctrine of God our Savior in all things" (Titus 2:10). So the issue here is *evangelism*, and the question is whether our reputation is helping or hurting the gospel. "What other people think of me is becoming less and less important; what they think of Jesus because of me is critical" (Cliff Richards). *So Jesus Christ is why a good name matters so much.*

That said, it's also true that a reputation for integrity is a valuable thing for us to have personally. In fact, it's worth a good deal more than the trinkets most people spend their time acquiring.

A good name keeps its brightness even in dark days.
LATIN PROVERB

July 20

THE DAY OF OUR DEATH IS COMING

So teach us to number our days,
That we may gain a heart of wisdom.
Psalm 90:12

NOT MANY THINGS IN THIS WORLD ARE CERTAIN, BUT DEATH IS ONE THAT IS. For every one of us who is living today, the day of our death is coming. We may delay it, but we can't avoid it.

There is one exception, of course, and that would be the possibility that the Lord might come back before we die. If we happen to be living at that time, we will enter upon our eternal destiny without having died physically (1 Thessalonians 4:13-18).

But if the Lord tarries, we will die. And since that is true, I believe it's important for us to decide *how we're going to think about* that reality. Like every other subject, our own death can be looked at from a variety of perspectives, some more comprehensive than others, and some more helpful than others. For example, all things considered, is the fact that we must die a curse or a blessing?

Surely, the answer to that question has much to do with whether or not we die in a right relationship with our Creator. But even among those who, through Christ, expect to live with God in eternity, there might be a difference of opinion about our mortality.

If mankind still lived in the sinlessness of Eden, physical immortality would be a delightful, joyous prospect. But we don't live in Eden, and in the world as it presently is, how many of us would really want to live much longer than the current human lifespan? If only a few of us could die and the rest had to live here forever, wouldn't we see those who could die as the fortunate few?

From the vantage point of the faithful Christian, the day of one's death is not such a bad day after all. In Christ, life in this world can be viewed as good (because it involves service in the noblest of causes), but death looks like an even better prospect. As Paul said, "To live is Christ, and to die is gain" (Philippians 1:21).

But to look at death in this way, we must be ready to die. And to be ready to die, we must reckon realistically with the fact that *the day of our death is coming.* If you are like me, that is a very hard thing to reckon. We know it, but it just doesn't seem real to us. "So teach us to number our days," Moses prayed, "that we may gain a heart of wisdom." May our own death be real to us . . . *right now!*

Everyone knows he will die, but no one wants to believe it.
JEWISH PROVERB

THE WEALTH OF GOD'S WISDOM

Oh, the depth of the riches both of the wisdom and knowledge of God!
How unsearchable are His judgments and His ways past finding out!
Romans 11:33

GOD'S WISDOM IS AN INEXHAUSTIBLE STOREHOUSE OF RICHES. The wealth of what God knows is simply incalculable. It is *marvelous* in the literal sense of the word: it causes us to marvel.

Think about the sea for a moment. Imagine a sea where the water was crystal clear. You could look into it, but you couldn't see the bottom. You could look as far as the horizon, but you couldn't see across it. The sea is vast beyond our imagination — and so is God. As John Ruskin said, "The infinity of God is not mysterious, it is only unfathomable — not concealed, but incomprehensible. It is a clear infinity — the darkness of the pure, unsearchable sea."

But does this make any practical difference as far as we are concerned? I believe it should. Anything that produces *awe* and *wonder* in us is important. A greater *love* for God is engendered by meditating on the riches of His wisdom, as are *praise* and *worship*. *Humility* comes from seeing the great gap between His knowledge and our own. And *trust* is the product of seeing that God knows all that needs to be known, even when our knowledge falls short.

Is there not a sense in which our minds should be "attracted" to the wealth of God's wisdom? We should be fascinated by it, drawn to it, pulled in by its power and majesty. What right-thinking person could get a glimpse of God's wisdom and not be moved to meditate upon it and contemplate it? If "reaching forward" is something that we want to do, then here is something truly worth *reaching* for. Learning and growing and knowing more of the mind of God is the great goal before us. We can never learn it all, but the more we learn, the more we will want to learn!

It is in Jesus Christ, of course, that we have our greatest opportunity to learn of God. I say *opportunity* because that's all it is. But let's *avail* ourselves of the opportunity to learn of the Father through His Son. If not, we shall hear the Son say, "Have I been with you so long, and yet you have not known Me?" (John 14:9).

Every passage in the history of our Lord and Savior is of
unfathomable depth and affords inexhaustible matter for contemplation.
All that concerns him is infinite, and what we first discern is but
the surface of that which begins and ends in eternity.

JOHN HENRY NEWMAN

July 22
ON BEING BATTLE-READY

For the weapons of our warfare are not carnal but mighty in God
for pulling down strongholds, casting down arguments and every high
thing that exalts itself against the knowledge of God, bringing every thought
into captivity to the obedience of Christ . . . *2 Corinthians 10:4,5*

LIFE IN CHRIST CAN BE DESCRIBED AND DISCUSSED IN MANY WAYS.
Many different metaphors are used in the Scriptures to illustrate the Christian's experience, and one of the most vivid of these is "warfare." While the Christian's life is one of *peace*, it is also one of *conflict*, and it is extremely important to understand this.

Being naive about the conflictual side of Christianity is nothing short of dangerous. We have a powerful adversary who is intent on destroying us, and we need to have our eyes wide open to the reality of what we're up against. Hence the Scriptures speak of our need to be sober-minded, alert, and vigilant (1 Thessalonians 5:8; 1 Peter 5:8). This world is being fought over, and living in it is a high-stakes affair. There is much to be gained by those who are paying attention — and much to be lost by those who aren't.

We also need to be filled with knowledge and wisdom. The warfare in which we are engaged is an *ideological* struggle between truth and untruth. There is no winning this war — indeed there is no *surviving* it — without mental preparedness. So we need to know God's word and understand the truth by which we may be saved. Granted, some of us enjoy reading and studying and thinking more than others, but even if we're not inclined in that direction, there is a certain amount of truth that we must master. If we don't, we'll be casualties in the warfare in which we're engaged.

But in addition to knowledge, we also need courage. Fighting on the Lord's side is not for the fainthearted but for the daring. And we must understand one important fact: courage does not mean not being afraid; it means that we go ahead and do whatever needs to be done, despite our fear. In the face of fear, God would say to us, "Be courageous, be strong" (1 Corinthians 16:13 RSV).

Day to day, we need to be "braced for action." The clash between God and His foes is going to impact our lives, so let us not be surprised. Let us expect that some fighting will have to be done.

Recognizing that our cause is, and will be, combated by mighty, determined
and relentless forces, we will, trusting in him who is the Prince of Peace,
meet argument with argument, misjudgment with patience, denunciations
with kindness, and all our difficulties and dangers with prayer.

FRANCES ELIZABETH CAROLINE WILLARD

July 23
JEREMIAH

I would comfort myself in sorrow;
My heart is faint in me.
Jeremiah 8:18

JEREMIAH, THE GREAT PROPHET, OUGHT TO BE AN ENCOURAGE-
MENT TO THOSE WHO SUFFER AND THOSE WHO SORROW. He was
the "brokenhearted" prophet, the man who drew the assignment
of delivering God's message of doom to Jerusalem in its last days.
Jeremiah loved God, but he also loved God's people, sinful though
they were. Having a sensitive heart, he could not have done his
duty without weeping at the tragedy of sin. By his faithfulness to
what was right, and also by his sympathy for his peers, he shows
us that there is a higher calling than the call to happiness.

Modern people tend to think that if they're not happy, there
must be something wrong with them. We pursue the happy, "well-
adjusted" personality as the *summum bonum*, the ultimate good.
But mere happiness is a questionable priority even in secular matters, and it is certainly not the primary object of religion.

Listen to this penetrating comment by Malcolm Muggeridge
on the pursuit of happiness: "Of all the different purposes set
before mankind, the most disastrous is surely 'the pursuit of happiness,' slipped into the American Declaration of Independence
along with 'life and liberty' as an unalienable right . . . Happiness
is like a young deer, fleet and beautiful. Hunt him, and he becomes
a poor frantic quarry; after the kill, a piece of stinking flesh."

Things like happiness, ease, and pleasure are fine, but it is not
always possible to have them while we're "on the job." Now is
the time for work. Now is the time for struggle against sin. As we
faithfully enter into the various assignments the Lord has for us,
we should expect to be assailed with sorrows and uncertainties. It
is perfectly natural to respond to the difficulties of our duty like
Jeremiah: with a broken heart. So let us have a higher goal than
being "well-adjusted." Let us have the goal of *truth* — at all costs.

Jeremiah refutes the popular, modern notion that the end of religion is an
integrated personality, freed of its fears, its doubts, and its frustrations.
Certainly Jeremiah was no integrated personality. It is doubtful if to the end
of his tortured existence he ever knew the meaning of the word *peace*. . . . The
summons of faith is neither to an integrated personality nor to the laying by
of all questions, but to the dedication of the personality — with all its fears
and questions — to its duty and destiny under God.

JOHN BRIGHT

July 24

INDEPENDENT FAITH

At my first defense no one stood with me, but all forsook me.
2 Timothy 4:16

PAUL MAY HAVE BEEN DISAPPOINTED AT TIMES WHEN NO ONE STOOD WITH HIM, BUT HE STOOD STRONG ANYWAY. He wasn't arrogant or egotistical, and like any of us, he needed the support of friends, but his faith was an independent faith. He knew in whom he believed (2 Timothy 1:12), and he knew how to stand alone.

The content of our faith. These days, many of us are guilty of drifting with the prevailing winds. We get our beliefs, if not from the majority, at least from that segment of society that we personally see as being "cool" or "sophisticated" or "broad-minded" or whatever. Despite our talk of independence, very few of us would be willing to believe something different than what is believed by those who matter to us, however many or few they may be.

The strength of our faith. On rare occasions, we may part with our peers, but we don't do so very strongly or vocally. Not wishing to be thought odd or eccentric, we keep our divergent beliefs to ourselves, avoiding at all costs the charge of being "dogmatic." Unlike Paul, who would speak up boldly for whatever the truth was, whether anyone spoke up with him or not, we often test which way the wind is blowing before we take a strong position.

The steadfastness of our faith. Sometimes life calls upon us to make a hard choice: when others are falling by the wayside, do we keep going or do we join the crowd and give up? In any test of endurance, the hardest thing to endure is the sight of those around us not enduring. And so our faith often fails us simply because the faith of others is failing them. Yet there is a better way. We can believe what we believe, with a strength born of our own convictions, and run the race to the finish, even if we run alone.

True faith can be a lonely experience. At any given moment, we may or may not have the support of those whose approval and help are important to us. When we don't have that support, we must be prepared to stand anyway. Following our conscience, we may be led into some very lonely territory. But listen to me: there are far worse things in this world than mere loneliness.

Believe to the end, even if all men go astray and
you are left the only one faithful; bring your offering
even then and praise God in your loneliness.

FEODOR DOSTOEVSKY

July 25
MUCH MORE THAN MERE SAFETY

Have I not commanded you? Be strong and of good courage;
do not be afraid, nor be dismayed, for the LORD your God
is with you wherever you go.
Joshua 1:9

DOES THE TERM "CONSERVATIVE" HAVE A POSITIVE OR A NEGATIVE CONNOTATION TO YOU? The word means "tending to conserve" and indicates a wish to preserve or protect that which is presently being held. A conservative approach to something is an approach that wishes to maximize safety and minimize risk. And whether conservatism is good or bad depends totally on the nature and relative value of *what* a person is trying to conserve.

Conservatism is a good thing when it prompts us to protect valuable things that should not be thrown away. But there is a danger: conservatism often causes us to make safety our main priority in situations where other values should be given higher rank.

Imagine a baseball player who has reached first base and is considering whether to "steal" second base on the next pitch. Will he take the risk or will he play it safe and stay on first base? He shouldn't take the risk foolishly, of course, but the worst thing he could possibly do is *try to have it both ways at once*. No player in the world can reach second base with one foot still safely on first!

In our lives as Christians, there is more to think about than mere safety. There will be times when we need to put ourselves at risk, moving at the Lord's bidding into territory that is "dangerous." At such times, we can leave safety behind in the confidence that the Lord will be with us every step of the way and help us with whatever difficulties may arise. God never commands anything that He doesn't make it possible for us to do, so He would say to us as He said to Joshua, "Be strong and of good courage."

We need to have a greater and grander vision of our lives in the Lord. We need to aspire to more than coziness and comfort in this world. The really good things almost always lie outside our comfort zones, and yes, they do involve risk. But a life without any risk is a life without any accomplishment, so let's quit putting such a premium on safety. In the Lord, much more is possible than our safety-conscious thoughts have ever dared to imagine.

Vision encompasses vast vistas outside the realm
of the predictable, the safe, the expected.
CHARLES R. SWINDOLL

July 26
NO DAY EVER COMES BACK

I must work the works of Him who sent Me while it is day;
the night is coming when no one can work.
John 9:4

IT IS INTERESTING THAT, IN TAKING HUMAN FORM, THE LORD OF HEAVEN AND EARTH SUBMITTED HIMSELF TO THE CONFINES OF SPACE AND TIME. The infinite God allowed Himself to be limited by time-bound considerations. The work that Jesus came to do had to be done during the "day," because "night is coming when no one can work." Not even the Son of God had an unlimited number of days in which to do His work; each day had to be used wisely.

It is a serious thing to "waste time." Time isn't a physical commodity, of course, and so we speak of "spending" or "wasting" time only metaphorically. But the metaphor is powerful. Time is the "stuff" of life, and to waste the *present* day is to throw away the only life that is really ours. "He who neglects the present moment throws away all he has" (Johann Friedrich von Schiller).

With regard to the preciousness of the present moment, you have probably observed that people go to two opposite extremes. Obsessed with not wasting any instant, some people rush through life with a frantic urgency bordering on panic. Others have the exact opposite problem: they slouch through life as if time were an unlimited resource and there was no need to get in a hurry about anything. Both extremes are harmful and counterproductive.

What is needed is an attitude that sees time as a resource over which we've been made *stewards*. This treasure has been committed to us with the understanding that we are to use it to the best possible advantage, and that we will eventually have to give account for our stewardship. Neither frantic urgency nor lazy procrastination will produce good results. It is a wholesome blend of *wisdom* and *self-discipline* that uses today as it should be used.

If we fail to use well today's opportunities, there may be some other ones tomorrow that we can use — but they will be *different* opportunities. Once lost, *today's* possibilities can never be regained. And whatever is lost, by just that much we will have failed to glorify God as fully as we could have. We don't have so many days coming to us that we can afford to be wasteful. And not only that, each day is unique. Today — *this* day — won't ever be back.

Consider that this day ne'er dawns again.
DANTE ALIGHIERI

July 27
AS THE DAYS GO BY

The glory of young men is their strength,
And the splendor of old men is their gray head.
Proverbs 20:29

EACH DAY THAT PASSES LEAVES US ONE DAY OLDER. Life happens to move in one direction only: from younger to older. But is that good or bad? Contrary to the assumptions of our youth-centered culture, I believe that advancing age should not be thought of in totally negative or unwelcome terms. While the glory of young men is their strength, the splendor of old men is their gray head. Does not the word "splendor" suggest something positive?

Most people probably look at old age as an unfortunate "leaving behind" of youth. But why can't we change the metaphor? Rather than a "leaving behind," why can't we see it as a "building on"? If we see the strength, beauty, and joy of youth as a "foundation," we can look at age as building an "edifice" that is far more valuable and impressive than the foundation would be by itself.

Last week, I had the privilege of spending the better part of two days with James Finney in Colorado Springs, Colorado. At ninety-two years of age, James is a wonder. He drove me around the countryside, talked with me about spiritual priorities, suggested books that I was not familiar with, shared insights into the Scriptures that had not occurred to me, and even took me to the gym where he works out every morning! I have known and loved him for many years, but I *really* love him now, having seen him up close and in action. Truly, here is a man who is *reaching forward* — not only to heaven but also to his utmost usefulness in this world.

From several important perspectives, the last stage of our sojourn should be considered the "prime" of life. Yes, the physical and mental disabilities that often arise can alter the level of our activity and take much of the happiness out of life. As we near the end, there are some unique challenges and difficulties to be dealt with. But be that as it may, the years of our greatest maturity should be the *culmination* of what we have learned and done. Autumn is not the downside of spring — it is the *fruition* of spring.

Time converts knowledge into wisdom, energies spent into
experience gained. Time leaves us richer for what we have had.
And time thoughtfully permits us to use the fire of youth to drive
the energies of age. We can be young and old at the same time.

SIDNEY GREENBERG

July 28
FAITH, HOPE, AND PATIENCE

These all died in faith, not having received the promises, but having
seen them afar off were assured of them, embraced them and confessed
that they were strangers and pilgrims on the earth. . . . But now they desire
a better, that is, a heavenly country. Therefore God is not ashamed to be
called their God, for He has prepared a city for them. *Hebrews 11:13,16*

PROMISES ARE INTERESTING THINGS, AND THE PROMISES OF GOD
ARE THE MOST INTERESTING OF ALL. Promises always have to do
with the future. They create an expectancy, a forward-looking attitude toward some event that is not yet a reality but only an idea.
Consider how the three great virtues — *faith, hope,* and *patience* —
work together to determine our response to God's promises.

Faith. The virtue of faith determines our "intellectual" response. It means that we believe that God's promises will be kept,
that whatever God has predicted will come to pass just as He has
said. It involves more than a merely intellectual processing of information, of course, but even so, it is an act of the intellect. When
God says, "This is going to happen," we must trust His prediction.

Hope. Based on the faith that God's promises can be counted
on, hope makes an "emotional" response to those promises. It
fervently *longs* for those promises to be fulfilled. In the confidence
that whatever God brings to pass, or even allows to come to pass,
will be better than any other possible scenario, we eagerly anticipate the fulfillment of His promises. We don't merely *accept* the
realities that God brings about — *we embrace them joyfully.*

Patience. With this virtue, we come to a "volitional" response
to God's promises. Volition has to do with our *will,* and so patience
means that we exercise the power of our will to obey God faithfully *while we are waiting for His promises to come to pass.* This is not
easy to do, especially since we are looking forward to them with
such eagerness and since the conditions in which we have to wait
are so painful. When our hearts cry out "How long, O Lord?" and
God says "Not yet," we must make the choice to be patient.

Faith and hope are important, obviously, but without patience
all is lost. Since the beginning of time, many have put their faith in
God, and some even their hope. But few have had the patience to
wait until He is ready to make all things beautiful . . . *in His time.*

God makes a promise; faith believes it, hope
anticipates it, patience quietly awaits it.

ANONYMOUS

THE INDISPENSABLE FACT

And if Christ is not risen, then our preaching is empty
and your faith is also empty.
1 Corinthians 15:14

FUNDAMENTALS ARE . . . WELL, FUNDAMENTALLY IMPORTANT. And the most fundamental truth of Christianity is the resurrection of Jesus Christ. As John S. Whale expressed it, "The Gospels do not explain the Resurrection; the Resurrection explains the Gospels. Belief in the Resurrection is not an appendage to the Christian faith; it is the Christian faith." The resurrection is the indispensable fact of the gospel. Without it, the gospel is not good news. It is not even helpful religious philosophy. It is simply nonsense.

So we must come to grips with the question of whether the resurrection actually took place or not. The New Testament documents allege it to have happened, and we must decide whether we find the allegation credible. But how shall we decide? Is it merely a matter of personal preference? No, we are jurors listening to evidence in the most important trial that has ever taken place — and the evidence is the testimony of the New Testament itself. *The primary witness is on the stand!* Our job is to listen to the witness carefully, desiring only one thing: *to reach the right conclusion.*

Of course, we must listen not only to the witness but to the cross-examination. But having heard the claims of the witness and the critics of those claims, our job is to render a verdict. Do we believe the primary witness or not? Is the truth being told?

It may be hard work to make up our minds whether to believe the testimony of the New Testament to the resurrection, but the one thing we must not do is say that "what really happened" is not important. This is a question with the highest possible stakes: it is nothing less than a matter of our own life and death. So let us work our way through the transcript of this most important trial and take the time we need to deliberate about our verdict. But having thought about it, let us take a firm position one way or the other. The witness is either telling the truth or lying. Which is it?

If you are irrevocably committed to the proposition that it would
have been impossible for Christ to triumph over death, you may as well
quit fiddling around the fringes of Christianity, because, as Paul bluntly
said, the whole thing stands or falls on the fact of the Resurrection. Either
it happened, or it didn't, and if it didn't, Christianity is a gigantic fraud,
and the sooner we are quit of it, the better.

LOUIS CASSELS

July 30
THE VERY WORST KIND OF WEARINESS

Therefore, to him who knows to do good
and does not do it, to him it is sin.
James 4:17

WHAT IS THE ACTIVITY THAT MAKES YOU THE TIREDEST? I would like to suggest that most of us are made the tiredest not by activity but by the *avoidance* of activity. We are worn out by the constant pressure of what we *don't* do. After all, procrastination is a very hard road to travel — its emotional toll is exceedingly high.

It's a serious sin to do something that God has said "thou shalt not" do, but it's also a serious sin to run away from a "thou shalt." And unfortunately, many of us spend a good part of our lives doing that. We aren't necessarily rebellious; we're just a bit lazy. We just don't "get around to" obeying God very quickly.

Procrastination is a common failing, and we often joke about it. But if what we're procrastinating is something we know *God* expects us to do, then that is no laughing matter. We have no guarantee of tomorrow, and the opportunity to complete our obedience may run out sooner than we expect. But in any case, we insult God by postponing His requirements as if they were unimportant.

The simple statement of James is one of the most challenging in the New Testament: "Therefore, to him who knows to do good and does not do it, to him it is sin." When we see there is something God would want us to do, we come under an obligation to do it, and to fail to do it is a sin. I would go even further: to *delay* to do it is a sin. Yes, it's a sin that we all commit at times, but that doesn't make it any less serious. It's not a thing to giggle about.

Don't you remember how *good* you felt the last time you finally did something you'd been putting off for a long time? That wonderful feeling of *relief* came from the lifting of a heavy burden that you had been carrying for who knows how long. And you probably didn't realize how tired the avoidance of your duty had been making you until you finally did what was needed and the burden was removed. So think of the duties you've been avoiding: they're a big bag of rocks you've been dragging around all this time. Wouldn't it be nice to *do* what you should do and not have to drag that burden around any longer? You know it would.

Nothing is so fatiguing as the eternal
hanging on of an incompleted task.
WILLIAM JAMES

TAKING TIME TO THINK

Meditate on these things; give yourself entirely to them,
that your progress may be evident to all.
1 Timothy 4:15

SPIRITUAL GROWTH REQUIRES TAKING TIME TO *THINK* ABOUT THE
THINGS OF GREATER IMPORTANCE. We are doers, most of us, but
we can't always be doing, doing, doing — there comes a time
when we have to *think* about our doing. Socrates said it at his trial
a very long time ago, but it is still true, even if he wasn't talking
about spiritual things: the unexamined life is not worth living.

Here are three things we need to take the time to think about:

What is happening. Events can rush by us so rapidly that we
hardly take conscious note of them. But there is a great value in
training ourselves to *notice* what is happening with minds that are
wide awake. Especially with the good things that happen, we need
to *relish* them. We need to enjoy the fact that we are enjoying them!

The significance of what is happening. Nothing happens that
does not have some meaning. Granted, some things have a larger
significance than others, but we will hardly be able to tell the difference without doing some thinking. If we're not paying attention, we'll miss the meaning of even the biggest occurrences.

*The connection of what is happening to the unchanging principles of
God's truth.* All of us "see" what is happening through some kind
of "lens" or "filter." To the extent that we've learned God's word,
that will become the lens through which we look at everything
that takes place. And the longer we live, the more we'll be able to
make the connection God wants us to make between the timeless
principles of His word and the time-bound events around us.

It goes without saying that it is *hard* to take time to think. In
this age of the world, life unfolds at an increasingly hectic pace,
and so many duties press upon us that we can't attend to them all,
let alone sit down and think. But there is an irony here. The less
time we have to think, the more we *need* to think! So I recommend
to you my discovery: *I've found that I need an hour each day just to
think — except on extremely busy days, when I've found I need two.*

Remind me each day that the race is not always to the swift and that
there is more to life than increasing its speed. . . . Slow me down, Lord,
and inspire me to send my roots deep into the soil of life's enduring
values, that I may grow toward the stars of my greater destiny.

O. L. CRAIN

August 1
DON'T BE IMPEDED BY THE IMPOSSIBLE

Then he who had received the one talent came and said, "Lord, I knew you to be a hard man, reaping where you have not sown, and gathering where you have not scattered seed. And I was afraid, and went and hid your talent in the ground. Look, there you have what is yours."
Matthew 25:24,25

FEAR AND PRIDE ARE MORE OFTEN FACTORS IN OUR DECISIONS THAN WE LIKE TO ADMIT. Some of our duties seem overwhelming. Some of our tasks seem impossible. And so we do nothing. Fearing failure, we fail to act at all. But like the unfaithful servant who was rebuked for having done nothing with his master's money, we may hear our Lord's rebuke for what we didn't do.

When it comes to our work in the Lord, there is a parallel to the point that Paul makes in 1 Corinthians 10:13 concerning temptation. There, the apostle says that there will always be a "way of escape." Similarly, when we face any responsibility, there will always be something that we can do that will be worth doing.

Sometimes in life, it can be helpful to step back and look at the "big picture." But there are other times when that would be a discouraging and unhelpful thing to do. It may look comprehensive, but the big picture can also look intimidating, and when the totality of what has to be done seems so huge as to be impossible, we need to dismiss the impossibilities from our minds and just concentrate on the small, doable tasks that lie right before us.

Any time we have to make a decision about what to do, we need to remember that we are *accountable*. In the end, we will be *judged*. But it's not for the things we could *not* have done that we will answer; it's for those that we *could*. We will be examined as to the choices we made *between the alternatives that were open to us*.

There is a bit of the perfectionist in all of us, I think. At times, we won't stoop to doing a job at all if we think we can't do it at an extremely high level of excellence. But look at the good that doesn't get done in the Lord's work with that kind of attitude. It really is true that *the enemy of the good is often the best*. If our effort is going to fall somewhere along the "good-better-best" continuum, let's not allow the impossibility of the "best" to keep us from going ahead and doing a deed that would be "good." If we will do the good that we *can* do, the best will usually take care of itself.

Do not let what you cannot do interfere with what you can do.
JOHN WOODEN

August 2

ON HAPPINESS: BIG AND LITTLE

The lines have fallen to me in pleasant places;
Yes, I have a good inheritance.
Psalm 16:6

DO YOU THINK DAVID EXPERIENCED MUCH OF WHAT WE MODERN PEOPLE CALL "HAPPINESS"? In many respects his life was a hard one, filled with terrible uncertainty and great sorrow. And yet, he could say, "The lines have fallen to me in pleasant places." Now certainly, any person who has a right relationship with the Lord can say this, regardless of their outward circumstances. But I have a hunch that David knew a good deal about the happiness of life "under the sun" as well as the joy of life "beyond the sun."

Many of us think we can't be happy at all if the "big" things in life aren't all lined up just exactly right: health, wealth, marriage, children, friends, and so forth. If any of these "major" departments of life are giving us trouble, we suppose that all hope of happiness must be given up. We don't want any of it if we can't have it all!

But David strikes me as a man who would have found happiness in many of the "little" things in life, even when there was hardship in his "big" circumstances. David would have known the pleasure of sunrises, sunsets, clouds, and the cool breeze on his face. He would have known the banter of comrades around a campfire. He would have known the whistle of old men at their work. He would have known the laughter of children at their play.

Think of happiness the same way you think of growth. For organic beings, growth is something that takes place in increments so tiny that you can't see them. If I asked you whether you were growing, you might not see yourself growing by leaps and bounds. But in reality, you might be growing more than you think you are, based on the many little changes that you haven't been paying much attention to. Similarly, many of us may be happier than we think we are, based on the abundance in our lives of the "little" things that happiness is really made out of.

No doubt we'd all like to have as much as we can of *both* kinds of happiness, the big *and* the little. But let's not despise the little sources of happiness. Let's not miss what is *available* to us.

The happiness of life is made up of minute fractions — the little soon
forgotten charities of a kiss or smile, a kind look, a heartfelt compliment, and
the countless infinitesimals of pleasurable and genial feelings.

SAMUEL TAYLOR COLERIDGE

August 3
WHICH SHALL WE CHOOSE?

Therefore we do not lose heart. Even though our outward
man is perishing, yet the inward man is being renewed day by day.
2 Corinthians 4:16

THERE IS NO QUESTION WHETHER SUFFERING WILL CHANGE US OR NOT; THE ONLY QUESTION IS *HOW* IT WILL CHANGE US. What the change will be depends on our *response* — and in the final analysis, there are only three basic ways that people respond to suffering.

Passivity. Some people see themselves as little more than the passive victims of whatever happens to them. Unwilling to acknowledge any responsibility for their own actions or any freedom to choose their response, these individuals are at the mercy of their surroundings and their circumstances. They don't really live their lives. Their lives are "being lived" for them by outside forces.

Bitterness. Unfortunately, the passive mentality of the victim often degenerates into something even worse: a resentment that life should be so unkind and so unfair. In such cases, pain and suffering come to be the source of bitterness and anger. The fortunate few who are happy are resented, and God Himself may even be complained against for His cruel mismanagement of the universe.

Transformation. This response is radically different from either passivity or bitterness. It is the response which says, "I will do the best I can to do whatever is right, and I will respond to suffering with the dignity of a person made in God's image." When our chosen response is to trust God and obey Him, pain changes us for the better. Even while "perishing," we are "renewed day by day."

When we look at the kind of people we are now as opposed to the kind of people we used to be, we all see a difference, a contrast between "before" and "after." *We've either grown upward or downward.* And the difference between those who've grown upward and those who've grown downward is not that some have suffered and others have not. In one way or another, all have suffered. But those who have grown toward God are those who, when faced with suffering, have chosen the upward path rather than the downward. Transformation to greater glory is always a *choice.*

Pain and suffering produce a fork in the road. It is not possible
to remain unchanged. To let others or circumstances dictate your future
is to have chosen. To allow pain to corrode your spirit is to have chosen.
And to be transformed into the image of Christ by these difficult
and trying circumstances is to have chosen.

TIM HANSEL

August 4
SLOWLY BUT SURELY

Therefore do not cast away your confidence, which has great reward.
For you have need of endurance, so that after you have done the
will of God, you may receive the promise . . .
Hebrews 10:35,36

WHAT THE HEBREW WRITER SAID IS CERTAINLY TRUE OF ALL OF US: WE HAVE NEED OF ENDURANCE. Some days in this world we may enjoy, but others we must simply endure. And even the enjoyable days must be "endured" while we wait for the best day of all: the day of our Lord's final appearing (Hebrews 9:28).

Patience is a wonderful quality in general, but I think we sometimes need to be more patient with *ourselves*. In regard to our spiritual growth, we expect too much too soon, and we find ourselves developing a crabby, ill-tempered disposition. *"After all the effort I've put into it, why aren't things getting any better?"* But we should understand that as long as our earthly pilgrimage lasts, we will never be anything more than "on the way" to our destination. Or to change the illustration, we will never be anything more than "works in progress." We see the need for patience with other people — why can't we be more patient with ourselves?

It helps to be reminded that growth, whether physical or spiritual, is an "incremental" process. An increment is a small change in something, so small as to be barely perceptible. And that's how growth usually occurs: by small changes. So what we must do is patiently make regular investments in our growth, trusting that the result will be seen later, even if we can't see it right now.

"My brethren, count it all joy when you fall into various trials, knowing that the testing of your faith produces patience. But let patience have its perfect work, that you may be perfect and complete, lacking nothing" (James 1:2-4). Isn't it interesting that James says we must *let* patience have its perfect work? We can go through all the growth-producing events in the world and not be profited by them if we give up before the process is complete.

But finally, we must not let patience with the process of growth turn into *complacency*. We must accept the fact that growth doesn't take place very *quickly* right now, but we must never tolerate the fact of *no* growth — for not to be growing is to be dying.

Be not afraid of growing slowly,
be afraid only of standing still.

CHINESE PROVERB

August 5

GOD WRITES THE STORY

When they asked him to stay a longer time with them, he did not
consent, but took leave of them, saying, "I must by all means keep
this coming feast in Jerusalem; but I will return again to you,
God willing." And he sailed from Ephesus.
Acts 18:20,21

PAUL HAD WISHES AND MADE PLANS, AS WE ALL DO, BUT HIS
PLANS WERE ALWAYS TENTATIVE. What he wanted to happen
was always contingent on what God's will turned out to be. "I will
return again to you," he said to the people in Ephesus, "God willing." Paul had turned everything about his life and work over to
God, and having done that, he really believed that whatever happened to him *was* God's will. So he had ideas now and then . . . but
he would wait to see how God would write the actual story.

In these latter days, God does not speak personally and
directly to us; He speaks to us through His written word. So we
would not expect audible messages directly from God explaining
to us what His will is for our personal lives. Yet we do not *need* to
receive such messages. If we have committed ourselves to Him,
we can trust that whatever comes our way is coming from Him.

And bear in mind that this includes the *obstacles* as well as
the *opportunities*. When we turn everything over to God and ask
Him to set the agenda for us completely, some of the agenda that
He sets will involve pain and suffering. He knows we need some
difficulty, and He loves us too much to "protect" us from what we
need. So we may face some situations and ask, *"How could this have
come from God?"* But more good than we realize may come from
the "useless" and "unpromising" situations that He puts us into.

In all cases, we must trust that the story of our lives is being
written by God — and we should be content with the story as He
writes it. There will be unexpected turns in the plot. There will be
unwelcome events, at least from our perspective. The true story
may turn out to be very different from the scenario of our dreams.

But my friends, let us resist the temptation to take the pen out
of God's hand and write the story ourselves. Let us rather wait
and see how it all comes out. "It is good that one should hope and
wait quietly for the salvation of the LORD" (Lamentations 3:26).

God engineers our circumstances as he did those of his Son; all we
have to do is to follow where he places us. The majority of us are busy
trying to place ourselves. God alters things while we wait for him.
OSWALD CHAMBERS

August 6
RESTING IN GOD'S SOVEREIGNTY

Who has directed the Spirit of the LORD,
Or as His counselor has taught Him?
Isaiah 40:13

TO SAY THAT GOD IS "SOVEREIGN" IS TO SAY THAT HE EXERCISES SUPREME, PERMANENT AUTHORITY. We might say that God is in "control" of His creation, but that would be putting it mildly. God is the *Creator* of all else that exists. Nothing can happen that He does not cause to happen or permit to happen. And this thought of God's sovereignty ought to be a consoling, reassuring thought.

One of the most important concepts in the Scriptures is that of "committing" ourselves to God. Paul spoke of that which he had "committed" to God (2 Timothy 1:12). When suffering, Jesus "committed" Himself to God (1 Peter 2:23). And when we suffer, we are to "commit" our souls to God, "as to a faithful Creator" (1 Peter 4:19). The idea is that of entrusting everything to God, holding nothing back. And the assumption is that God will take what we have committed to Him and manage it all to His glory.

When we do that — commit everything to Him — look at how many things we no longer have to worry about. *What is going to happen?* We don't have to know. *Will what happens work out for the best?* We can assume that it will. *How can I control what happens to make sure it is good?* Control is no longer an issue. In all these ways, committing ourselves to God is a freeing, liberating experience!

But sometimes we forget. Sometimes we lapse back into our old "managerial" role, inquiring into the secrets of God's working and offering helpful suggestions as to the betterment of life on planet earth. At such times, we need to remember Deuteronomy 29:29: "The secret things belong to the LORD our God, but those things which are revealed belong to us and to our children forever, that we may do all the words of this law." The fact that certain things are none of our business is not meant to insult us; it's meant to free us from concerns that are unnecessary for us to have.

The role of the Creator is radically different from the role of the creature. As creatures, our role is to "trust and obey," and that is quite enough to keep us busy. As for God, we can always rest in His sovereignty, knowing that He will do His work very well.

Keep your heart with all diligence and
God will look after the universe.

A. W. TOZER

August 7

FULLY EMBRACING GOD'S WILL

Whatever your hand finds to do, do it with your might . . .
Ecclesiastes 9:10

A S EACH NEW DAY REVEALS TO US WHAT GOD'S WILL IS, WE NEED TO THROW OURSELVES WHOLEHEARTEDLY INTO WHATEVER WORK THE LORD SETS BEFORE US. If we are Christians, then the adage "Whatever your hand finds to do, do it with your might" applies to us in a unique way. If we've submitted ourselves totally to the Lord, then what our "hand finds to do" will never be anything but what He wills for us to do (Colossians 3:17). Consequently, we can give our best to every single task the Lord puts on our "desk."

When we commit ourselves unreservedly to the Lord, what we are asking Him to do, in effect, is to show us the path He wants us to follow, on the understanding that we will follow wherever He leads and do whatever He wills. But He doesn't reveal what He wants us to do in advance; He does it one day at a time. So if you've prayed for the Lord to open the doors that He wants you to go through, *then the doors that are open to you today are the ones He wants you to go through!* (You did believe that the Lord would answer that prayer, didn't you?) The work He wants you to do is the work that is right in front of you. *Today's work has been sent by Him,* and if you refuse to do it with all your might, then you need to reconsider whether you are actually willing to do the Lord's will.

And don't forget: we can consider the difficult things no less than the easy ones to have been sent by the Lord. There is just no way around having to deal with some difficulty. But in reality, if it's the *right* road we're on (and the Christian will always make sure that it is), then it doesn't *matter* whether it's an easy road or not. So the advice of Confucius turns out to be especially good advice for Christians: "Wherever you go, go with your whole heart."

If we have committed ourselves to God and prayed for Him to set our agenda and send our way what He wants us to do, then there need be no doubt in our minds that that prayer will be answered. That being true, we can embrace everything that comes our way with a whole new confidence. Believing that it is His will, whether easy or hard, we can dive into it and give it all we've got. *There need be no holding back for those who live within His will.*

Wherever you are, be all there. Live to the hilt
every situation you believe to be the will of God.

JIM ELLIOT

August 8

THE ENCOURAGER IS ENCOURAGED

For I long to see you, that I may impart to you some spiritual gift,
so that you may be established — that is, that I may be encouraged
together with you by the mutual faith both of you and me.
Romans 1:11,12

THE PROCESS OF "ENCOURAGEMENT" IS RARELY A ONE-WAY STREET. Almost without exception, the encourager is encouraged in the very act of trying to encourage someone else. And the reverse is also true. By neglecting to encourage others, we deprive ourselves of much-needed encouragement that we might otherwise receive.

Paul's relationship with the Christians in Rome is interesting. He expected, when he got to Rome, to encourage their faith, but he also expected to be encouraged by them as well. Great apostle though he was, he needed the mutual strengthening that would come from their association. He need their strength hardly any less than they needed his. But his encouragement would come from helping them — not by saying, "What can you do for me?"

Perhaps the mutual nature of encouragement is one reason that so many of us spend so much time in the dark valleys of discouragement. We spend so little time trying to encourage anyone *else*, it's little surprise that we find ourselves so downhearted. Epidemics of discouragement should be expected in societies that are as self-centered as ours. One of the most disheartening things in the world is to be focused on whether others are lifting us up and brightening our spirits as they "ought" to be doing.

But even when we're encouraging others, we won't be encouraged if we don't *listen* to ourselves. When we're figuring out what the other person needs to hear, we usually discover things that *we* need to hear, but those lessons will be lost on us if we don't listen to our own instruction. And really, why should our friends take our advice if we're not willing to take it ourselves? "Physician," our friends might say, "heal yourself!" (Luke 4:23).

But teaching — whether by instruction, exhortation, or encouragement — can be a wonderfully beneficial exercise. It can help both parties, the giver no less than the recipient. So look for somebody to encourage. Find out what truth *they* need to hear, and then listen to that truth *yourself*. You'll be encouraged.

We cannot hold a torch to light another's path
without brightening our own.

BEN SWEETLAND

August 9

ANTICIPATION

For God is my witness, how greatly I long
for you all with the affection of Jesus Christ.
Philippians 1:8

A NTICIPATION IS NO SMALL PART OF THE ENJOYMENT OF ANY GOOD THING. Thanksgiving is my favorite meal of the year, both to cook and to eat. But as much as I enjoy the satisfaction of it, I almost enjoy the anticipation of it more. There is nothing quite like the aroma of good cornbread dressing baking in the oven!

If you haven't learned it by now, you need to learn that *longing is not inconsistent with joy.* When Paul said that he "greatly longed" for his brothers and sisters in Philippi, we do not hear that as the complaint of a sad, miserable man. No, we hear it as the exuberant expression of a man who knew how to enjoy the goodness of the things he longed for, *even while he was longing for them!*

It is often said that we live in an age of "instant gratification," and I suppose that is true to a large extent. But imagine a world where there was *nothing but* instant gratification, a world where you could have anything you wanted . . . and have it instantly. Would you want to live in such a world? I don't think I would. Of the many things that would be lost in such a world, one of the most tragic would be the joy of *anticipation.* Imagine never knowing the childhood joy of *looking forward* to Christmas morning!

On a much more serious note, however, it is *heaven* that is our greatest anticipation. That is what we look forward to more than anything else; we deeply long to see our Father's face. But might it not be true that our Father is preparing us for that joy by sending us through a time of anticipation in this world, a time when our primary joy comes from relishing the thought of what will one day be ours? I think that is not unlikely. And if the joys of this world are meant to be "appetizers," let us enjoy them exactly as such. Let us appreciate that they make us more eager for the main course.

But even with the lesser joys of *this* world, may we let ourselves enjoy the blessings of anticipation. Not every day on the calendar can be a day of fulfillment; some must be days when we're looking forward to a fulfillment — and those days of anticipation can be days of great joy if we let them be. It is, after all, the space between the holidays that makes those days such happy occasions.

Every day cannot be a feast of lanterns.
CHINESE PROVERB

ARE WE HAPPY? YES, BUT ARE WE HELPFUL?

I have shown you in every way, by laboring like this, that you
must support the weak. And remember the words of the Lord Jesus, that
He said, "It is more blessed to give than to receive."
Acts 20:35

HAPPINESS IS SOMETHING MOST OF US WOULD LIKE TO ENJOY AS MUCH OF AS POSSIBLE. Given a choice, most of us would prefer what "happens" to us to be pleasant rather than unpleasant. And in fact, God has graciously blessed most of us with a good deal of happiness — much more than most of us ever give thanks for.

But the Lord laid down the principle that "it is more blessed to give than to receive." And this principle applies to happiness as much as anything else that may be given: more "blessedness" comes from giving it than from getting it. No matter how absurd that sounds to many people, it always proves to be true in the long run. It is simply one of the many instances where true, deep wisdom runs counter to the wisdom of self-centeredness.

One helpful way to think of happiness is to see it as a re-source, or perhaps as a raw material. It is not given to us for our private enjoyment alone; it's to be used for the good of others. And like the other resources that have been entrusted to us, happiness is something that we'll one day be held accountable for. When the Lord asks what we have done with our happiness and we say, "Well, we *enjoyed* it," He may press the issue. "Is that *all* you did with it? Did no one *else* get anything out of My gift to you?"

Unfortunately, we have a tendency to enjoy our blessings without regard to anyone else. We wouldn't put it so bluntly, but we sometimes appear to believe that, when it comes to happiness, it's every man for himself: "If I've got what I want, that's all that matters." But under the "more blessed to give than receive" rule, the "independently" happy person will not end up very happy.

To sum up, then, what should we say about happiness? That the desire for happiness is wrong? No, but if we *are* happy, the question is what we're doing *with* our happiness. Happiness makes a wonderful "foundation" for a life of service to those around us. But if the foundation exists and nothing is built upon it, people may rightly ask, "What good is the foundation by itself?"

Many people are extremely happy, but are
absolutely worthless to society

CHARLES GOW

August 11
WHEN WILLINGNESS BECOMES WORK

Be ready in season and out of season.
2 Timothy 4:2

MANY OF US MAY HAVE BEEN PRETTY NAIVE WHEN WE PROMISED THE LORD WE WOULD ALWAYS BE FAITHFUL. We might have "counted the cost" and understood that there would be difficulty, but we probably thought that the parts of Christianity that weren't pleasant would at least be exciting, adventurous, and interesting.

Over the long haul, however, many of us find that there is an unexpected difficulty that must be met. What started out as an exciting adventure comes to look like *drudgery*. There comes a day when we have to admit that we are *procrastinating* the very things that we were so enthusiastic about at first. When we promised the Lord we would do His work, we never knew how *tiresome* it would become. We never expected it to become *uninteresting*.

As a writer, I can tell you that something like this happens during the writing of a book. The project starts with great excitement, and the blank page is an exciting challenge. But before it is over, that blank page will have become a most unpleasant sight. The exhilaration of being a "writer" will have vanished, and the whole thing will have come to look like ordinary, tedious *work*.

But what do we do when our willingness to serve confronts us with the mundane reality of hard work? Reconsider our commitment? Renege on our promise? No, that is simply not an option. Paul warned Timothy that he must be prepared to fulfill his responsibilities "in season and out of season." That means whether it is easy or not, whether it is exciting or tedious, whether it makes you happy or unhappy. And frankly, what we do about that says much about our character. *Do we have what it takes to keep going?*

Lifelong faithfulness to the Lord is like most other worthy endeavors: the battle is won or lost by how we deal with the *ordinary* things. It is not the mountaintops of exaltation that save us or the valleys of despair that defeat us. Instead, our destiny is usually determined by how we respond on the days when there was nothing very positive or negative to deal with, just a lot of *work* to be done. In the end, being "dedicated" enough to go to heaven comes down to rolling up our sleeves and putting our hand to the plow.

Faithfulness is consecration in overalls.
EVELYN UNDERHILL

NO LITTLE JOBS, ONLY LITTLE PEOPLE

He who is faithful in what is least is faithful also in much;
and he who is unjust in what is least is unjust also in much.
Luke 16:10

EVERY HONORABLE JOB IN THIS WORLD DESERVES TO BE DONE WELL. When we're asked to do a thing, especially in the Lord's work, it really doesn't matter whether the thing is "important" or not. The saying is true that there are no little jobs, only little people — people of too little character to see the value of work well done.

Our real attitude toward service is probably not measured by our performance in the big, glorious situations but rather by our steadfastness in the small, inglorious ones. *"He who is faithful in what is least is faithful also in much; and he who is unjust in what is least is unjust also in much."* As has been said, a person can't be trusted with a big job who won't give his best to a little one.

Whatever we do in the Lord, we can do it knowing that it will accomplish something worthwhile. That's true because it is the Lord, not we ourselves, who will take it and turn it into something good. It doesn't depend on us or the "importance" of what we've done. So Paul said, "Be steadfast, immovable, always abounding in the work of the Lord, knowing that your labor is not in vain in the Lord" (1 Corinthians 15:58). *Our labor is not in vain in the Lord!* It doesn't matter *what* the job is, it's not in vain if it's in the Lord.

"When you are invited by anyone to a wedding feast," Jesus said, "do not sit down in the best place, lest one more honorable than you be invited by him; and he who invited you and him come and say to you, 'Give place to this man,' and then you begin with shame to take the lowest place. But when you are invited, go and sit down in the lowest place, so that when he who invited you comes he may say to you, 'Friend, go up higher.' Then you will have glory in the presence of those who sit at the table with you. For whoever exalts himself will be humbled, and he who humbles himself will be exalted" (Luke 14:8-11). So in heaven, there may be some surprises. The most exalted places of honor may be filled by simple souls whose work in this world was hardly ever noticed.

If a man is called to be a streetsweeper, he should sweep streets even as Michelangelo painted, or Beethoven composed music, or Shakespeare wrote poetry. He should sweep streets so well that all the hosts of heaven and earth will pause to say: "Here lived a great streetsweeper who did his job well."

MARTIN LUTHER KING, JR.

August 13

THE PAIN IS A PART OF THE HAPPINESS

Those who sow in tears
Shall reap in joy.
Psalm 126:5

A TIME WILL COME WHEN OUR TEARS ARE WIPED AWAY. But that time is not yet, and we are left to ponder the tears that we shed right now. If we want to think rightly, how should we think, for instance, about the pain of losing a love? "Those who sow in tears shall reap in joy" is part of the truth, but think about this . . . Our tears aren't just *followed* by joy. They are a *part* of the joy.

In *Shadowlands,* Richard Attenborough's film about the tragic, blissful love between C. S. Lewis and Joy Davidman, who died of cancer only a few years after they were married, there is an absolutely marvelous scene. "Jack" and Joy, whose cancer was in brief remission, have driven to Herefordshire for a romantic getaway, and they have taken shelter under a shed while a rainshower passes by. Jack has expressed how immeasurably happy he is to be with this woman whom he has come to love. And Joy says . . .

"It's not going to last, Jack."

"We shouldn't think about that now," Jack replies quietly. "Let's not spoil the time we have together."

"It doesn't spoil it," Joy says, "it makes it real. . . . Let me just say it before this rain stops and we go back."

"What is there to say?"

"That I'm going to die, Jack . . . and I want to be with you then too."

"I'll manage somehow," Jack says. "Don't worry about me."

"No, it can be better that that," Joy replies. "I think it can be better than just 'managing' . . . What I'm trying to say is, the pain is a part of the happiness. That's the deal."

In my own life, I've come to see that this is true. Pain is not inconsistent with happiness. It's not even a thing that must be endured *until* we can be happy. The pain is a *part* of the happiness. That's the deal.

Things which come to us easily have no significance.
Satisfaction comes when we do something which is difficult;
when there is sacrifice involved.
BARRY MORRIS GOLDWATER

August 14

ALONE WITH GOD

And when He had sent the multitudes away,
He went up on the mountain by Himself to pray.
Now when evening came, He was alone there.
Matthew 14:23

IT WOULD NOT HAVE BEEN EASY TO DO, BUT JESUS MADE THE SACRIFICES NECESSARY TO SPEND TIME IN SOLITUDE, ALONE WITH HIS FATHER. We can hardly comprehend the demands that others made on His time, nor can we imagine how tired He must have been some of those nights when He stayed up to pray. But apparently there was great value for Him in solitude. Even He, the very Son of God, needed significant time alone with the Father.

But think of it in the other direction. Even in terms of human relationships, we understand that we confer honor on those with whom we are willing to spend private time, and we withhold honor from those that we're only willing to be with in a group. What would you think if you were in a group with someone you had always wanted to talk to privately, and the group left the room? There you are, finally face to face, and after greeting you with a rather formalistic hello, that person says, "Well, I'd better be going now." How would you feel? How do you think God feels?

We need to hear again the words of W. D. Longstaff's familiar old hymn, *Take Time to Be Holy:* "Take time to be holy, the world rushes on; spend much time in secret with Jesus alone." In His teaching on prayer, Jesus emphasized the need for private, solitary prayer (Matthew 6:6). Yes, it's true that public prayer is permitted, and we have plenty of examples of Christians praying together in Acts. But let us not fail to heed Jesus' *emphasis* on private prayer. That is where our greatest growth comes from.

It is especially in times of pain and sorrow that we need to spend time alone with the Lord. We may also need counsel and companionship, it's true, but why are we so afraid for someone who is suffering to be alone? Are we afraid they might actually *think* about what is happening, see its significance, and open their hearts to God more fully? I may be wrong, but I think it's in solitude that suffering has its greatest opportunity to bless us.

In time of trouble go not out of yourself to seek for aid;
for the whole benefit of trial consists in silence, patience, rest,
and resignation. In this condition divine strength is found for
the hard warfare because God himself fights for the soul.

MIGUEL DE MOLINOS

August 15
ABOVE AND BEYOND

Now to Him who is able to do exceedingly abundantly above all that we
ask or think, according to the power that works in us, to Him be glory in the
church by Christ Jesus to all generations, forever and ever. Amen.
Ephesians 3:20,21

WHEN WE PRAY, WE BELIEVE WE ARE PRAYING TO A GOD POWER-
FUL ENOUGH TO DO EVEN MORE THAN WE ASK HIM TO DO.
It is extremely comforting to know that God can take our feeble,
shortsighted prayers and answer them in ways that give us more
than the pitifully little things we thought to ask for. He is "able to
do exceedingly abundantly above all that we ask or think."

What we need to understand, however, is that whenever there
is any discrepancy between what we asked for and what God provided, what God provided is *always* better. Theoretically, we know
that God *can* bless us with more than we asked, but sometimes we
look at God's answer to our prayers and say, "This is *less* than I
asked for." What I am saying to you is, *that is never true.*

Admittedly, it can be *hard* to see how what God provides is
better than what we wanted, but the problem here has to do with
our vision and not with God's gift. For one thing, it takes faith,
trust, and confidence to believe that, whether we can understand
it or not, God's way is always better. We must choose to believe
that He knows what He is doing. But second, seeing the goodness
of what God provides requires looking at more than the present
moment. We may not be able to see it right now, but later on, hind-
sight will surely show us that God's gift was, in fact, better.

Paul's prayer for God to remove his "thorn in the flesh" is a
good example. God's answer was, in effect, "No, Paul, it will be
better for you to continue to deal with it." And to his credit, Paul
not only *accepted* that answer, but he *embraced* it. "Therefore most
gladly I will rather boast in my infirmities" (2 Corinthians 12:9).

Our Father is benevolently inclined toward us, a "rewarder of
those who diligently seek Him" (Hebrews 11:6). The only time we
ever need to worry about God harming us is when we're in rebellion against Him. But if we humbly respond to Him in the obedience of faith, we can rest assured that the answer to our prayers
will never be anything less than good. And very often, the answer
will go beyond the *good* to the *better* . . . and even to the *best!*

God will either give you what you ask, or something far better.
ROBERT MURRAY MCCHEYNE

LEARNING TO TRUST THE GOD WE BELIEVE IN

Oh, taste and see that the LORD is good;
Blessed is the man who trusts in Him!
Psalm 34:8

THERE IS A DIFFERENCE BETWEEN BELIEF AND TRUST. It's one thing to give intellectual acceptance to a truth, but trust has to do with how much *risk* we'll take. Would we stake our *lives* on what we believe? To use the old illustration, belief is accepting that someone could walk across Niagara Falls on a tightrope pushing a wheelbarrow; trust would be getting into the wheelbarrow.

In regard to our faith in God, the main element that distinguishes belief from trust is the *personal* element. At some point, we have to pass beyond the mere acceptance of God as an "idea" and start putting our confidence in Him as a personal being. When Paul said, "I know *whom* I have believed and am persuaded that He is able to keep what I have *committed* to Him" (2 Timothy 1:12), he was speaking of far more than an academic or philosophical acceptance of God's existence. Paul dealt with God as a *personal* being — and he *trusted* the personal God that he believed in.

But Paul was an old man when he wrote those words, and while his faith would have always been real and genuine, there can be no doubt that Paul trusted God more deeply and personally as a result of his years of experience. Passing from mere belief to real trust takes time. It doesn't happen instantly or overnight. So we all need to be asking the Lord to do the same thing His disciples requested on one occasion: "Increase our faith" (Luke 17:5).

But our faith will not be increased by mere wishful thinking. A greater faith comes from *experiencing* that He is trustworthy in the actual living of our lives. David, for example, issued this invitation to those lacking in trust: "Oh, taste and see that the LORD is good." If we had a rebellious attitude, it would be wrong to "test" God, but He has always invited the humble seeker to make an honest, fair trial of Him and see that He can be counted on.

So learning to trust God is a *process.* We find ourselves having a deeper confidence in Him as we gradually take bigger — and riskier — steps. The more steps we take, the more we can see, looking back, that He has never led us astray. And as the weeks and months turn into years, we find that our trust has matured.

Confidence is a plant of slow growth.
ENGLISH PROVERB

August 17
WHEN WE THINK ALL IS LOST

Then Omri and all Israel with him went up from Gibbethon,
and they besieged Tirzah. And it happened, when Zimri saw that the city
was taken, that he went into the citadel of the king's house and burned
the king's house down upon himself with fire, and died.
1 Kings 16:17,18

DESPAIR COMES FROM THINKING THAT ONE'S "CAUSE" IS HOPE-
LESSLY LOST. It is the feeling that, though the battle may not be
over yet, the outcome is assured: the other side has won and there
is nothing that can now be done to avert disaster. When Zimri saw
that "the city was taken," he went inside and burned his house
down upon himself. In more modern times, we would think of
Hitler's final act in his bunker as Berlin was being taken.

At the *practical* level, what would it mean to have "no hope"
and be "without God in the world" (Ephesians 2:12)? In addition
to unbelievers who are alienated from God, there are probably
many believers who find themselves in situations that are, at least
from their perspective, hopeless. Whatever persons or problems
may be their "adversary," they see their battle as having been lost
to that adversary, and they give up hope. The prediction of defeat
may be premature, and may even turn out to be wrong, but the
prediction is made anyway, and despair is the sad result.

The problem of hopelessness is a problem of *perspective*. It
comes from not seeing the larger reality that always surrounds
the small set of circumstances in which we may lose something.
There is always a larger battle going on that may be won, even
if our individual battle is lost, and if we choose to think *rightly*
about our loss, we can still participate in the larger victory. Take,
for example, a soldier hitting the beaches of Normandy on D-Day.
Under withering machine-gun fire, he may know he is going to
die. But is his situation "hopeless"? It depends on his perspective.
Maintaining hope and conducting himself with honor are possible
if he looks beyond himself to the needs of his comrades-in-arms.

As the Lord's people, we are much too quick to describe ourselves as being "defeated." We may be bound by "chains" at times,
but "the word of God is not chained" (2 Timothy 2:9). So let's trust
that God's cause will be victorious — and in our personal lives,
let's quit paying defeat's bills before they even come due.

Hopelessness is anticipated defeat.
KARL THEODOR JASPERS

August 18
TRUTH FOR THE TIME TO COME

But you, beloved, remember the words which were spoken
before by the apostles of our Lord Jesus Christ.
Jude 17

THE CENTRAL TENET OF CHRISTIANITY IS THE RESURRECTION OF JESUS CHRIST, AND THAT IS A TRUTH THAT DOES NOT CHANGE. The resurrection is an unchangeable historical fact. So the gospel of Christ is not only true; it is true for all time to come. Having happened, the resurrection can never become "un-happened."

But sometimes we forget. There are some things (like tears, for example) that can hinder our "vision," and we may find ourselves unable to "see" the truth very clearly. Or to change the metaphor, having left the courtroom and gone back home, we may forget some of the testimony that we heard while we were sitting on the jury. The facts didn't change, and the testimony is still on the record. But we may forget what we heard in the courtroom.

Spiritual strength requires a vivid *remembrance* — and that means most of us have a problem, because our "rememberers" don't work very well. But God understands, and that's why we have such an emphasis in the Scriptures on *reminders*. Jude said, "Remember the words which were spoken before by the apostles of our Lord Jesus Christ." And Paul said, "Remember that Jesus Christ . . . was raised from the dead" (2 Timothy 2:8). Whatever it takes, we must make ourselves to go back and *remember.*

We can't say we haven't been forewarned. "Do not fear any of those things which you are about to suffer. Indeed, the devil is about to throw some of you into prison, that you may be tested, and you will have tribulation ten days. Be faithful until death, and I will give you the crown of life" (Revelation 2:10). Our Lord has told us ahead of time that there are going to be circumstances that will cloud our vision, so the admonition is to *remember* and *hold on.*

Under the pressure of pain and suffering (or bewilderment or anything else), we must not give up the truths that we saw so clearly in calmer moments. Those truths are still true. The fluctuation in our feelings has not changed the reality of our faith's foundation. So when it's dark, we must believe that daylight will come again. When it does, we will see that truth's great mountain is still there, right where it was yesterday . . . before the sun went down.

Never doubt in the dark what God told you in the light.
VICTOR RAYMOND EDMAN

August 19
YESTERDAY AND TODAY

Forgetting those things which are behind . . .
Philippians 3:13

A FAMOUS MOTIVATIONAL SPEAKER USED TO SAY THAT WE SHOULD LIVE IN "DAY-TIGHT COMPARTMENTS." He wasn't speaking in a religious context, but I believe what he said is true for religious people. Having learned from the past, we need to forget it . . . and seize the fresh opportunity that each *new* day brings to us.

One of my personal daily disciplines is to review each day at the end of the day. I don't always have a lot of time to do it, but I try to review each day at least briefly before going to bed. I try to learn as much as I can from the day, even from the mistakes that were made. But once that review is done, I commit that day to the Lord and go to bed looking forward to the next morning. When I arise, my morning routine has nothing to do with the day before — it has everything to do with the new day that has arrived.

I've never "put my hand" to any kind of literal plow, but even a boy raised "in town" can see that it would be hard to plow a straight furrow if one kept looking backward (at least in the days before GPS-guided tractors). And Jesus did say something about that, didn't He? "No one, having put his hand to the plow, and looking back, is fit for the kingdom of God" (Luke 9:62).

The past can be a valuable resource, certainly. We should be *encouraged* by it, and also *humbled* by it. Above all, we should be *instructed* by the past. But the past is gone. So whatever we *were,* what we are *now* matters more. We need to think about our past as Paul thought about his. What he had been was regrettable. "But by the grace of God," he said, "I am what I am" (1 Corinthians 15:10).

Many people nowadays keep a daily journal. Imagine a person writing in so much detail each day that he or she needed to begin a new journal book each morning. In a sense, that's what we are called upon to do at the start of each new day. But as we expectantly open that fresh, never-before-used book and start "writing," we need to have decisively *closed* the previous day's book.

Finish every day and be done with it. You have done what you could. Some blunders and absurdities no doubt crept in; forget them as soon as you can. Tomorrow is a new day; begin it well and serenely and with too high a spirit to be cumbered with your old nonsense. This day is all that is good and fair. It is too dear, with its hopes and invitations, to waste a moment on the yesterdays.

RALPH WALDO EMERSON

TODAY AND TOMORROW

I made haste, and did not delay
To keep Your commandments.
Psalm 119:60

WHATEVER TASKS THE LORD SENDS OUR WAY TODAY, WE NEED TO TAKE CARE OF THOSE THINGS TODAY. The Psalmist's remark about not *delaying* to obey God should make us think soberly. Strictly speaking, there is no such thing as *tomorrow's* obedience.

This book is about "reaching forward," and its main point is that we need to be future-oriented. But as we look to the future, we must understand that our *doing* has to be done *today.* You can *think* about the future and you can *plan* for it (and you're a fool if you don't), but you can't actually *do* anything *in* the future. Every bit of our doing is in the present. So there is a sense in which the future that we will have is the one we "buy" with our actions today. "The future is purchased by the present" (Samuel Johnson).

Problems. It's usually a safe bet that when tomorrow comes we are going to have to deal with a few *difficulties.* And very often, tomorrow's problems will be those that we created today by actions that we either took or didn't take. In fact, it may not be any exaggeration to say that most of our future problems will arise because we postponed "maintenance" work that should have been done — on our possessions and, more importantly, on our relationships.

Opportunities. Today's actions will also affect what *doors are open* to us tomorrow. And the strange thing is, some of the best doors that will open tomorrow will result from actions that, as we do them today, don't seem very significant. I once was offered a wonderful job in the credit department of a store where I had been doing some very menial janitorial work; the manager noticed the way I scrubbed the floors and offered me a better job. So taking *today's job* seriously is often the key to *tomorrow's promotion.*

Isn't it clear that we need to do everything we can to give tomorrow as much of an *advantage* as possible? Why would we put off doing anything today if doing it would put us "ahead of schedule" tomorrow? And if it's in our power today to make tomorrow easier, why would we do anything to make it more difficult?

The future is an opportunity yet unmet, a path yet untraveled, a life yet unlived. But how the future will be lived, what opportunities will be met, what paths traveled, depends on the priorities and purposes of life today.

C. NEIL STRAIT

August 21
THOUGHTS ON BEING "NEXT"

One generation passes away, and another generation comes . . .
Ecclesiastes 1:4

YOU MAY HAVE NOTICED THAT NOBODY'S GENERATION LASTS
FOREVER. Your grandparents' generation is gone. Your parents'
generation is going. And your generation will go sooner or later.
One generation passes away, and another generation comes . . .

My mother, Charlene Roberts Henry, passed away some years
ago, but my father, Leroy Parker Henry, died only recently. Since
Dad passed away, my brother, Phil, and I have talked about what
a different feeling it is to have both parents gone. As long as even
one parent is alive, there can still be some sense in which you view
yourself as the "younger" generation, but when both parents are
gone, the truth is unavoidable: you are "next" on the brink.

It is good to be reminded of our mortality. None of us has an
unlimited amount of time to do our work in this world, and whatever makes us better stewards of our time is a good thing.

But also, it is helpful to be reminded that there is a "chain" of
generations going on in the world. Here we are right now, living
in our own generation, but we are linked to all the generations that
have ever been and to all the generations that will ever be. While
we live, we are the connection that keeps the past and the future
from being severed. We are called upon to be just one link, but in
a chain, every link is critically important. The question we need
to ask ourselves is this: what kind of link are we, a strong one or
a weak one? Will we pass on the best of what has gone before and
thereby help make the future better than it would be otherwise?

But let's return to the idea of being "next." If your parents are
gone and you are "next," is that a dreadful thought to you? I must
say that to me it is exciting. I can only compare it to being on one
of those "log flume" rides that you see at some amusement parks.
On the way to the top, other "logs" are in front of you, but then
you get to the top. No one is in front. You are next. There is nothing between you and . . . a breathtaking plunge! For the faithful
Christian, what an exciting prospect to be next in line for eternity.
The unknown part of it just makes it more exciting. I can't wait!

When our parents are living, we feel
that they stand between us and death; when they go,
we move to the edge of the unknown.

R. I. FITZHENRY

REAL LIFE IS WAITING

For I know that my Redeemer lives, and He shall stand at last on
the earth; and after my skin is destroyed, this I know, that in my flesh
I shall see God, whom I shall see for myself, and my eyes shall behold,
and not another. How my heart yearns within me! *Job 19:25-27*

IF ANYONE EVER HAD REASON TO DESPAIR, IT WAS JOB. But he did
not despair. In the midnight blackness and horror of his ordeal
he hung on to the confidence that he had a Redeemer, a Vindicator.
"This I know," he said, "that in my flesh I shall see God, whom
I shall see for myself, and my eyes shall behold." This hope was
more than a bare fact to him; it was a truth he passionately embraced. Just thinking of the life that awaited him in God stirred
him with love and longing. "How my heart yearns within me!"

Job's hope was also David's, who prayed, "As for me, I will
see Your face in righteousness; I shall be satisfied when I awake in
Your likeness" (Psalm 17:15). Neither Job nor David believed that
death would interrupt or end the communion with God which
they had begun in this life. And notice that the life Job and David
looked forward to was not a mere merging of their personal identity into some vast, impersonal oneness of cosmic "being." It was
a real *life* — an actual life in the presence of a personal God who
could be known and enjoyed as only personal beings can be.

Even now, we recognize that life is at its best when we share
it deeply with *personal* beings, beings who correspond to our
"likeness." So imagine life with the God in whose image we were
made! That would be *real* life. And that is what is meant by "eternal life" (Titus 1:2; etc.). We can enjoy a foretaste of it, or a down
payment on it, right now if we obey the gospel and live faithfully
in Christ, but the full experience of it is waiting for us in heaven.

In our hearts, we know that death won't be the end of us. We
know that a greater life awaits us if we die in a right relationship
with God, and we know also that a lesser life — a living *death* —
awaits us if we die outside of the gospel. So let us resolve to spend
our days seeking Him and His forgiveness, on whatever terms He
stipulates, so that when this life slips away from us, as it surely
will, the thing that will be waiting for us is *real* life — life *indeed*.

Is this the end? I know it cannot be,
Our ships shall sail upon another sea;
New islands yet shall break upon our sight,
New continents of love and truth and might.

JOHN WHITE CHADWICK

August 23
ENJOYMENT AND RELINQUISHMENT

For the form of this world is passing away.
1 Corinthians 7:31

EVERYTHING ABOUT THE "TEMPORAL" WORLD IS "TEMPORARY," AND WE SEE EVIDENCE OF THAT EVERY DAY. Time is filled with "swift transition," as the song says. Nothing stays put; everything changes. Much may be enjoyed, but it is transitory. It goes away.

Since everything in this world is temporary, it behooves us to hold what is "ours" rather loosely. The good things that God made in this world are to be enjoyed — and then relinquished. That is the nature of the arrangement, and we all know it. So why is it the "end of the world" when we have to let go of these things?

We've all heard fiery sermons on the foolishness of the wicked who put their trust in "worldly" things. But "worldly" things are not only the *evil* things of this world; they also include the *good* things. "Worldly" things are simply the things of *this* world — time-bound things, whether good or bad. So what about us "godly" people? When we hang on to things like our homes and families as if they were ours to keep, is our security any more stable than that of the person who puts his trust in his bank account? We're not going to keep our earthly "treasure" any longer than he's going to keep his. At our funerals, both he and we will have left behind exactly the same thing: *everything we had in this world.*

The message of Ecclesiastes is one that we desperately need in these days of obsession with satisfaction and security. That great book makes the point that "life under the sun" was meant to be enjoyed, but always with the recognition that it is "vain," i.e. transitory. It is a "consumable" commodity, meant to be used rather than kept. The more we try to keep it, the less we get the intended enjoyment of using it. It makes a great servant but a poor master.

The bottom line is that there is nothing in this world that is ours to keep — we're going to have to let go of all of it. The only thing we'll never have to give up is God — and truth to tell, He is all we *have* to have even now. So may we allow the One Thing that was *meant* to be our security *be* our security. To lean on anything else, however good it may be, is to lean upon a broken reed.

If your security is based on something
that can be taken away from you — you will
constantly be on a false edge of security.

TIM HANSEL

August 24

IS THERE NOT A GREATER VICTORY TO BE WON?

Assuredly, I say to you, they have their reward.
Matthew 6:5

IN TEACHING ON PRAYER, JESUS SAID THAT WE MUST DO BETTER THAN THOSE WHO PRAY TO BE "SEEN BY MEN." Those who have no higher goal than reputation had better enjoy the reputation they get, because that's *all* they'll get. "They have their reward," Jesus said. But of course, even though they got what they wanted, the time would come when they would want more than what they had gotten. But by then it would be too late. Generally speaking, God gives every person whatever that person wants most of all — and not one bit more. Whatever our highest aspiration is, we can't complain when God withholds from us anything higher than that.

Now think with me. What is the only thing you could want and never be dissatisfied with it once you got it? That would be God Himself, wouldn't it? Anything else would be less than what it takes to fully satisfy the human heart. But most people are content to seek lesser things, and although they will later wish they had sought higher things, having gotten what they sought, God will say, "You have your reward. You had better enjoy it, because you are not going to get anything more than what you sought."

So as for me, I hope that I'll never seek anything so small that it *could* be received in this world. Short of heaven, I don't want to *ever* hear the Lord say, "You have your reward." I don't want anything in this world — or all of it put together. What I want can't be had in this world, and that's a perfect relationship with my *God*. If you ever hear that I've settled for less, I will have lost my soul.

A public figure died recently who "had it all" from a worldly standpoint, and his wife was quoted as saying, "He was one of the fortunate few. He got everything he wanted in life." I hope that such a thing will never be said about me. Until I am at home with God, I hope no one will ever accuse me of having been satisfied.

But I'm prone to the same temptations that you are. We win our little battles, and God says, "You have your reward." Thinking the struggle is over, we live like old soldiers: always looking back.

We ought to ponder soberly the fact that
many Christians already have their future behind them.
Their glory is behind them. . . . They are always lingering around
the cold ashes of yesterday's burned-out campfire.

A. W. TOZER

EARTHLY ADVANTAGES WILL DISAPPEAR

> But God said to him, "Fool! This night your soul
> will be required of you; then whose will those things
> be which you have provided?"
> *Luke 12:20*

THERE IS NOTHING THAT PERTAINS TO "LIFE UNDER THE SUN" THAT IS NOT "VAIN." This is the clear message of Ecclesiastes. Unlike the life to come, this life is fleeting, transitory, and ephemeral. Whatever we may accomplish and whatever we may accumulate of an earthly nature, all of it will be left behind when we die.

As a description of earthly life, the word "vain" does not refer to that which is evil but to that which is *temporary*, whether good or evil. When Solomon said, "I have seen all the works that are done under the sun; and indeed, all is vanity and grasping for the wind" (Ecclesiastes 1:14), he did not mean that there is nothing good that may be done; he meant that there is nothing about this world that is permanent. There are things to be done and things to be enjoyed here, but we must be ready to leave them all behind.

Many people work hard to get the kind of life they want in this world — and many end up getting it. Some acquire wealth or celebrity status. Others achieve historical greatness. Others are content to pursue the simpler forms of satisfaction and happiness. Whatever anyone might want to pursue, the advantages of that pursuit are available. As far as "life under the sun" goes, most of it is there for the taking, whether a person acknowledges God or not.

But when we die, every one of *those* advantages is wiped out. In their lifetimes, you might have preferred Winston Churchill's circumstances to those of his chimney sweep, but in death, the bones of one would have looked very similar to those of the other. As Julia C. R. Dorr put it, "Grass grows at last above all graves."

So while life *under* the sun lasts, we had better be giving some thought to life *beyond* the sun. Death is coming, and we need to ask whether we're doing anything that won't be erased by that event. Only one such thing is available to us, of course, and that is *godliness*. Paul said that "godliness is profitable for all things, having promise of the life that now is and of that which is to come" (1 Timothy 4:8). The only "profitable" thing that matters, then, is godliness. Every other kind of benefit will disappear at death.

> Death is the grand leveller.
> SIR THOMAS FULLER

August 26
ONLY ONE THING ABOUT YOU WILL LAST

For no other foundation can anyone lay than that which is laid,
which is Jesus Christ. Now if anyone builds on this foundation with
gold, silver, precious stones, wood, hay, straw, each one's work will become
clear; for the Day will declare it, because it will be revealed by fire; and the
fire will test each one's work, of what sort it is. If anyone's work which
he has built on it endures, he will receive a reward.
1 Corinthians 3:11-14

WASTED TIME AND WASTED EFFORT ARE THINGS MOST PEOPLE
LIKE TO AVOID. When some activity in which we engage
turns out to be a meaningless waste, we are disheartened, but if it
ever became apparent that our whole *lives* had been wasted, "disheartened" would hardly be the word. A wasted life would be the
ultimate human tragedy. Yet the only way to ensure that we're not
wasting our lives is to build our actions on *truth*. Nothing else will
stand the test of time. In the end, nothing else will matter.

Actions that aren't based on true *principles* will come to nothing, perhaps not immediately but eventually. Reality happens
to be very strong; it's an anvil that will break our hammer long
before our hammer breaks it. To see the point, consider a principle
like "honesty." A person who deviates from honesty in order to
achieve some short-term goal is going to find, in the long run, that
the tactic did not work. The effort will have come to nothing.

Even now, there is a "testing" that is going on. Our actions
are always being tested by the truth, and those that don't meet its
standards will falter and fail at some point. Those that are based
on truth, however, will stand. "Time will tell," as we say. Or as
Jesus put it, "Wisdom is justified by her children" (Matthew 11:19).

But a much greater testing is ahead: a day of judgment before
the God of all truth. Paul said that "each one's work will become
clear," whether it is built upon the foundation of Jesus Christ or
not. "For the Day will declare it, because it will be revealed by fire;
and the fire will test each one's work, of what sort it is."

Knowing that truth is what we'll be tested by is both comforting and sobering. It is comforting to know that our work "in the
Lord" will endure and not be "in vain" (1 Corinthians 15:58). But
it is sobering to realize that death will strip us of every advantage
we've ever gained by sidestepping the truth. So, my friend, is
there anything about you that is going to last? Time will surely tell.

Death cancels everything but truth.
ANONYMOUS

OPPORTUNITY AND OPPOSITION

But I will tarry in Ephesus until Pentecost. For a great and effective
door has opened to me, and there are many adversaries.
1 Corinthians 16:8,9

L IFE IN THIS WORLD IS A MIXTURE OF EASY THINGS AND HARD
THINGS. All of us have to deal with both kinds of situations, the
easy ones and the hard ones. But not only that, all of us have to
deal with some situations that are easy and hard at the same time!

In my life, I have found it helpful to give these two things,
"ease" and "difficulty," different names. I call them "opportunity"
and "opposition." And frankly, most of the circumstances that
we face in the real world are a mixture of both elements together.
There are hardly any opportunities that don't involve some difficulty, and there are hardly any difficulties that don't involve some
opportunity. When Paul wrote to the Corinthians, he said that he
was going to remain in Ephesus for a while: "for a great and effective door has opened to me, and there are many adversaries."
While most of us naively wish for opportunities that involve no
opposition, Paul was realistic enough to know that "open doors"
and "adversaries" go hand in hand. The same conditions that are
favorable to the Lord's work are those that the devil can use too.

So if we're serious about "reaching forward," we ought not
to back away from difficulty and opposition. There is nothing that
God wants us to do that He won't help us to do, and we ought to
have the courage to fight "the good fight" (2 Timothy 4:7).

But neither should we miss the *opportunities* that are presented
by our problems. It's good to have the courage to face our difficulties, but we can do better than just be courageous. We can see in
our difficulties the *productive possibilities* that they offer to us.

The question is simply where we're going to put the primary
emphasis. In a situation combining both opportunity and opposition, which one of these are we going to *concentrate* on? We can be
people who see the silver lining in every cloud — or people who,
when they see a silver lining, say, "There must be a cloud around
here somewhere." Optimism doesn't mean we ignore potential
difficulties or shut our ears to the warnings of the wise. It means
we ask what good thing *can* be done . . . and then get busy *doing* it.

The pessimist sees the difficulty in every opportunity;
the optimist sees the opportunity in every difficulty.
LAWRENCE PEARSALL JACKS

August 28

WHAT WOULD BE ON YOUR READING LIST?

For where your treasure is,
there your heart will be also.
Matthew 6:21

IF YOU ARE LIKE ME, YOU LIKE TO READ MANY DIFFERENT THINGS, SOME MORE IMPORTANT THAN OTHERS. But what if you knew that you only had a short time left to live? What would be on your reading list? You'd probably dispense with the trivia and use your remaining time reading (and rereading) what was most important.

It seems to me that life is like a reading list. Whereas a reading list contains books to read, life contains things to do. And the question is: what do we do first? And with a *limited* time, a second question arises: what should be done and what left undone?

Jesus said, "For where your treasure is, there your heart will be also." And He also said, "A good tree cannot bear bad fruit, nor can a bad tree bear good fruit" (Matthew 7:18). Our *outward* lives are the natural product of our *inward* lives. Whatever is most important to us, that is what we will think about. And whatever we think about, that is what will govern our outward activities.

So if our *activities* are concentrating too much on this life and too little on the life to come, it's because our *hearts* are set on this life. There is no use denying the truth: it's our *passion* that sets our agenda. Even with limited time, we always find the time to work on whatever our hearts are set on. The only lasting way to change our activities, then, is to change our hearts. When we've learned to *love* higher things, *working* on them won't be a problem.

There is an old adage that says, "Nothing concentrates a preacher's mind like the going down of the sun on Saturday evening." If a preacher has been toying with several ideas for his Sunday morning sermon, the realization that the pulpit is only a few hours away tends to clarify his mind. And similarly, when we see life's sun setting and we know our time is running out, we tend to see what's important more clearly. But in truth, we don't have to wait until old age or a dire doctor's report. We can concentrate on what's most important right now. We can, to use Paul's expression in Colossians 3:2, set our minds "on things above."

I have lost a world of time! Had I one year more,
it should be spent in perusing David's Psalms and Paul's Epistles.
Mind the world less and God more.

CLAUDIUS SALMASIUS

August 29

READY AND WAITING

And the Lord said, "Who then is that faithful and wise steward,
whom his master will make ruler over his household, to give them their
portion of food in due season? Blessed is that servant whom
his master will find so doing when he comes."
Luke 12:42,43

WE SHOULD LIVE IN FERVENT EXPECTATION OF THE LORD'S RE-
TURN, BUT IN OUR EXPECTATION, WE SHOULD ALSO BE BUSY. On
more than one occasion, Jesus compared His followers to servants
or stewards entrusted with work that was to be done while their
master was away. At some time in the future, the master would
return, and when that time came, it was to be hoped that the servants would not have neglected their master's work. "Blessed is
that servant whom his master will find so doing when he comes."

The point, of course, is that Jesus will one day return, and we
are to be ready and waiting for Him. He has not told us exactly
when that day will arrive, and it is a good thing that He has not. If
we knew precisely how much time we had left, most of us would
procrastinate doing the Lord's work until the very last moment.

We need to live and work *as if* we knew that our Lord would
return today. There is a real possibility that He might actually do
so, but even if He does not, it won't hurt us to have lived with that
expectation. We are more likely to work and to serve as we should
if we expect the end to come today rather than ten years from now.

But how could a person love the Lord and not hope that it
would be today? There are surely some good things about this
world that we enjoy and give thanks for. And in one sense, we
would like to enjoy these as long as we can. But the Lord has far
better things waiting for us, and we should have our hearts so lovingly set on *those* things that we would give up our temporal joys
instantly if the Lord said we could have heaven right now.

As we wait for the Lord's return, we can do so with confidence in His wisdom. His first appearing occurred "when the
fullness of the time had come" (Galatians 4:4), and we can rest assured that His final appearing will be timed with perfect wisdom.
Meanwhile, we can wait in faith and hope and love. We can be
faithful in His work, ready and waiting to see His face.

The only way to wait for the Second Coming is to watch that you do
what you should do, so that when he comes is a matter of indifference.
It is the attitude of a child, certain that God knows what he is doing.

OSWALD CHAMBERS

AWAKE!

For the Lord Himself will descend from heaven with a shout,
with the voice of an archangel, and with the trumpet of God. . . .
1 Thessalonians 4:16

WHEN THE MOMENT ARRIVES AND THE LORD RETURNS, THERE WILL BE NO DOUBT AS TO WHAT IS HAPPENING. As Paul described it, the Lord will descend from heaven with a shout. There will be the voice of an archangel. There will be the trumpet of God. Our attention will be "arrested" by this event, to say the very least.

That day will be one of great *change* for those who are faithful to the Lord. Paul wrote, "We shall not all sleep, but we shall all be changed — in a moment, in the twinkling of an eye, at the last trumpet. For the trumpet will sound, and the dead will be raised incorruptible, and we shall be changed" (1 Corinthians 15:51,52).

We don't sing "When the Roll Is Called Up Yonder" by J. M. Black much anymore, but it's a great song: "When the trumpet of the Lord shall sound and time shall be no more, and the morning breaks eternal, bright and fair; when the saved of earth shall gather over on the other shore, and the roll is called up yonder, I'll be there." When the trumpet sounds and "the morning breaks eternal, bright and fair," what a joyfully glorious day that will be!

Obviously, that day will be one of stark terror for those who have not accepted God's pardon on His terms. To borrow the language of Hosea, who spoke of the Lord's coming judgment upon Israel, "They shall say to the mountains, 'Cover us!' and to the hills, 'Fall on us!'" (Hosea 10:8). But it doesn't have to be that way. We can obey the gospel and look forward to seeing the Lord's face.

We sometimes think and act as if heaven were not as "real" as the world we live in now. But if anything, it will be *more* real. The trumpet-blast of the Lord's return will arouse us to a life that will be life indeed. If we are found in Christ on that great day, the thunderous voice of the archangel will open our eyes to the real life we were created to enjoy, and we will enjoy it forever. That day is coming. He has said so. What is happening right now is nothing more than preparation for the moment when He says, "Awake!"

Think of yourself just as a seed patiently wintering in the earth;
waiting to come up a flower in the Gardener's good time, up into the real
world, the real waking. I suppose that our whole present life, looked back on
from there, will seem only a drowsy half-waking. We are here in the
land of dreams. But cock-crow is coming.

C. S. LEWIS

August 31
PERFECTION?

Therefore, having these promises, beloved, let us
cleanse ourselves from all filthiness of the flesh and spirit,
perfecting holiness in the fear of God.
2 Corinthians 7:1

WHEN PAUL TALKED ABOUT "PERFECTING HOLINESS IN THE FEAR OF GOD," HE SET BEFORE US THE MAIN GOAL OF THE CHRISTIAN'S LIFE IN THIS WORLD. Having been created in God's image, we have marred and broken that image with our sinful rebellion against Him, but in the gospel of Christ, we are offered forgiveness and the perfect restoration of God's glory within us. "Therefore you shall be perfect," Jesus said, "just as your Father in heaven is perfect" (Matthew 5:48). Nothing less than that will do.

To most people nowadays, "perfectionism" is a word with a very bad connotation. But is being a "perfectionist" a bad thing or a good thing? Well, it all depends. Certainly a person who can't accept the goodness of anything less than perfect *right now* is doomed to a very sad life. But we don't have to go to that extreme to be perfectionists in the good sense. We need to be people who understand the loftiness of God's plan and *never lower our aim.*

As long as we live in this world, we will never be anything more than "works in progress." If we've obeyed the gospel, then we've entered a *process,* and we should certainly be grateful for God's grace "along the way." But the process that we've entered is one that will eventually be *completed,* and we dare not cease *yearning* for the time when that completion will be fully ours.

Whatever happens "along the way," we can't afford to take our eyes off the goal. As we make progress toward perfect holiness, there will be intermediate satisfactions that will be quite gratifying. But if we settle down in a country that we're only meant to be passing through, then we're lost. We're doomed if we ever say, "Others may want more, but I'm no perfectionist; I'm content with what I've already got." The question is not at what point *we* are satisfied, but at what point *God* is satisfied. And He will not be satisfied until we have been returned to the perfectly glorious image of holiness that He had in mind when He created us.

Aim at perfection in everything, though in most things it is unattainable;
however, they who aim at it, and persevere, will come much nearer to it than
those whose laziness and despondency make them give it up as unattainable.

LORD CHESTERFIELD

WHAT THE TEMPEST CAN TEACH US

And a great windstorm arose, and the waves beat into the boat,
so that it was already filling. But He was in the stern, asleep on a
pillow. And they awoke Him and said to Him, "Teacher,
do You not care that we are perishing?" Mark 4:37,38

MOST OF US ARE TOO QUICK TO CHARGE GOD WITH "DOING NOTHING." When He doesn't do what we wish or what we expect, we jump to some fairly irreverent conclusions: "God doesn't care that I'm suffering" or "God has let me down" or "God has rewarded me poorly for all the years that I've served Him." But surely we can think on a higher level than these thoughts.

At times, God does not help us until our *need* has grown greater. In the story of Jesus' calming of the storm on the Sea of Galilee, the disciples were too quick to assume that Jesus didn't "care" that they were "perishing." But they weren't perishing, at least not yet. Jesus would have taken action when the time was right; meanwhile the disciples should have hung on. So we need to learn the lesson of the tempest: we should let God decide when the situation has grown dangerous enough to warrant His action.

At other times, we can't *recognize* God's help until our need has grown greater. We're often hindered by pride and self-suffi-ciency from *seeing* God's help, and so we may have to "hit bot-tom" before we open our eyes to what has been there all along.

Elijah is a wonderful study in the dynamics of discourage-ment. Fleeing the murderous intent of Queen Jezebel, he fled to the desert, fearing that he was all alone in the world. If God had "cared" about Elijah, wouldn't He have relieved Elijah's depres-sion? No, it was only when Elijah's depression had *worsened* that he was prepared to hear the "still small voice" of God's help.

So has God been helping you with *your* problems? Be care-ful what you say. If it seems that He has not, He may be waiting until a bit more is in danger of being lost than what you think is at stake right now. He may be saying, "Trust me. I will act when the time is right." But even now, God may be helping you more than you realize. Are you receiving His "manna" every morning, but it doesn't seem very appetizing or nourishing? Well, you won't ap-preciate it until you've grown hungrier than you are right now.

God does not leave us comfortless, but we have to be
in dire need of comfort to know the truth of his promise.
PETER MARSHALL

September 2
GOD WILL HELP, BUT . . .

The time of my departure is at hand.
2 Timothy 4:6

IF WE DIE IN CHRIST, IT IS ENCOURAGING TO KNOW THAT GOD WILL BE THERE WITH US WHEN WE DIE. We should certainly have the confidence that David had: "Yea, though I walk through the valley of the shadow of death, I will fear no evil; for You are with me; Your rod and Your staff, they comfort me" (Psalm 23:4). But although He will help us, it is still we who will have to die.

Some people die well, and some people die poorly. Some die courageously while others die like cowards. Some die in faith and humility and gratitude, but others die in stubborn, defiant rebellion against the God who made them. There are all kinds of ways to die, and some of us might wish that we could turn over the task of our dying to someone who would "do a better job of it."

But such is impossible, of course. In this sense, each of us must die alone, each assuming responsibility for the manner in which he or she faces death. It will be up to each of us to think and act rightly about our death as we approach that great moment.

Christ's death on the cross can save us from the "second death" (Revelation 21:8), but nothing (except a preemptive return by Christ) can save us from the first death, the death of our physical bodies. A noble person might now and then wish that he could have died in the place of somebody else, just as David wished he could have died in the place of his son Absalom (2 Samuel 18:33), but this is never really possible. We are, as the song says, going down the valley "one by one." Even if two people jump hand-in-hand from a burning building and fall to their deaths on the street below, they have still not died "together." Each has died as a solitary being, thinking thoughts that no one knows but God, their Maker. Dying is the most individual thing any of us will ever do.

Jackson Browne's song "For a Dancer" makes this point well. I don't agree with his bleak assessment of the meaning of death, but Browne is absolutely correct when his song says, "No matter how close to yours another's steps have grown, in the end there is one dance you'll do alone." So I would ask you, as I ask myself: *what will you do when you have to do this thing that no one can do for you?*

Every man must do two things alone:
he must do his own believing and his own dying.
MARTIN LUTHER

September 3
LOST

For what profit is it to a man if he gains
the whole world, and is himself destroyed or lost?
Luke 9:25

IN THESE DAYS OF "PROGRESSIVE" PREACHING, WE DON'T HEAR MUCH ABOUT THE PROSPECT OF BEING LOST. But Jesus came "to seek and to save that which was lost" (Luke 19:10). We can hardly talk about the gospel and not discuss the consequences of *refusing* the gospel. Jesus did not go to the cross to keep us from losing our happiness in this world; He went to the cross to keep His Father from losing the entire human race forever. How can we love God and not contemplate what it would mean for us to continue in our sin? If any soul refuses His reconciliation, look at what will be lost:

What we will lose. To say no to God's offer of pardon would mean throwing away everything we were created to enjoy. It would mean losing everything "life" was ever meant to be. And far worse than every other loss, it would mean losing our Creator Himself. Eternity would be the unending learning of our losses.

What heaven will lose. If the angels rejoice when any lost soul is reclaimed (Luke 15:7), it must surely be that the angels weep when any soul refuses to be reclaimed. Every creature of God is precious to the inhabitants of heaven. The loss of even one is a tragedy that will not be taken dispassionately by those around God's throne.

What God will lose. God has far more at stake in our salvation than we do. He has more invested in us than we have invested in Him. And so if we are lost, He will lose far more than we. *What did He create us to be?* That will be lost. *What could we have been?* That will be lost. *What did Christ die to make possible?* That will be lost. God waits before bringing to pass the Day of Judgment, hoping that more might be rescued and fewer lost (2 Peter 3:9), but the time will come when judgment cannot be delayed any longer, and on that Day, God will lose many of His sons and His daughters.

No greater tragedy is thinkable. "For what profit is it to a man if he gains the whole world, and is himself destroyed or lost?"

The man who dies out of Christ is said to be lost, and hardly a word
in the English language expresses his condition with greater accuracy.
He has squandered a rare fortune and at the last he stands for a fleeting
moment and looks around, a moral fool, a wastrel who has lost in one
overwhelming and irrevocable loss, his soul, his life, his peace, his
total, mysterious personality, his dear and everlasting all.

A. W. TOZER

September 4
BETTER OFF NOT KNOWING

You do not know what will happen tomorrow.
James 4:14

W E ARE BETTER OFF NOT KNOWING WHAT IS GOING TO HAPPEN IN THE FUTURE OF THIS WORLD. It may be fun to imagine having magical powers of foresight, but in our more serious moments we realize that such predictive powers would be our undoing.

If we knew the *happy* things that were going to happen, and those things were certain and inevitable, what do you think would be the result? Well, if we knew those benefits would come our way no matter what we did in the meantime, we would probably grow lax in our behavior. We would soon take all the pleasant parts of life for granted, and eventually we would be tempted to pride.

But what if we knew the *unhappy* things that were going to happen? Can there be any question that our lives would be filled with fear? There is a sense, of course, in which we can deal with anything we have to deal with as long as we know what it is. Uncertainty is a horrible kind of suffering. But if, all at once, we knew *every* difficulty that life was going to throw at us, that would be a burden whose fearful weight would simply crush us.

Sir Henry Bulwer said, "The veil that covers the face of futurity is woven by the hand of mercy." It is not any miserliness or mean-spiritedness on God's part that moves Him to hide the future from us; it is His *grace*. If we knew the future, we could not handle it. That knowledge would overwhelm us, and so God is being benevolent and kind when He shields us from that burden.

But what is the practical point in this discussion? There are two points, actually. One is that our "reaching forward" is not to any particular thing that is going to happen in *this* life. What we are reaching forward to is *heaven*, and it simply doesn't matter what tomorrow may bring in this world. The other point is that although we have a future *goal*, our "doing" must be done *today*. The future, both earthly and heavenly, will come eventually, but today is the day when we must prepare for it. So let's spend less time predicting and prognosticating and more time doing good works.

God will not permit man to have a knowledge of things to come;
for if man had a foresight of his prosperity, he would become arrogant
and careless; and if he had an understanding of his adversity,
he would become listless and despairing.

AUGUSTINE OF HIPPO

WHEN MOONLIGHT FALLS ACROSS THE FLOOR

When I remember You on my bed,
I meditate on You in the night watches.
Psalm 63:6

NOW AND THEN, ALL OF US HAVE AWAKENED IN THE WEE HOURS AND NOT BEEN ABLE TO GO BACK TO SLEEP. Usually we see that as an undesirable event, but I want to suggest that being awake while the world is asleep is not necessarily bad. The handful of times when I have had the deepest communion with God and the clearest insight into reality have been in the watches of the night.

The quiet, dark hours can be a dangerous time, spiritually speaking. If grief or loneliness is what we're experiencing, we are more easily tempted in the night watches to certain sinful thoughts. So when we find ourselves awake and alone, we need God's protection and strength, as well as His help and comfort.

But if we discipline our thinking, we can use our time awake to gain greater spiritual depth. David often spoke of meditating on the Lord at night: "When I remember You on my bed, I meditate on You in the night watches." There is no better time for prayer and godly meditation than while everyone else is asleep. Indeed, it's worth it to get up deliberately during the small hours for the *purpose* of thinking about God. "My eyes are awake through the night watches, that I may meditate on Your word" (Psalm 119:148).

I once had a job as a nightwatchman for a college that I was attending. It still sends shivers up my spine to remember entering an old, creaking lecture hall at two-thirty in the morning, walking to the podium, and just standing there, listening to the quiet and imagining all the great teachers who had been there and the words they had spoken. I believe that we do have moments of numinous joy — moments (maybe only a few in a lifetime) when the supernatural breaks into our hearts with such a piercing joy that we know we were made for more than we can ever experience in this world. Those moments of sharp and joyous longing for God are unpredictable. They might happen in the daytime also. But in my life, they have usually come when moonlight falls across the floor.

When the house doth sigh and weep,
And the world is drowned in sleep,
Yet mine eyes the watch do keep,
Sweet Spirit comfort me!
ROBERT HERRICK

RESPONDING RIGHTLY TO THE PAST

> Now I rejoice, not that you were made sorry, but that your
> sorrow led to repentance. For you were made sorry in a godly
> manner, that you might suffer loss from us in nothing. For godly
> sorrow produces repentance leading to salvation, not to be
> regretted; but the sorrow of the world produces death.
> *2 Corinthians 7:9,10*

IF YOU'VE READ FIRST CORINTHIANS, YOU CAN IMAGINE PAUL'S AGONY AS HE WAITED TO HEAR HOW IT WAS RECEIVED. He had called upon the Corinthians to repent of their sins, but how would they *think* about these things? Would they be defensive? resentful? angry? In Second Corinthians we find him overjoyed: they had responded with a "godly sorrow" that had resulted in repentance.

We are no different than the Corinthians in that we have things in our past that should never have taken place. Looking back, we see many things we'd like to change. Even after we've repented and received the Lord's forgiveness, we still feel a regret that is extremely unpleasant and embarrassing. Oh, how we wish we could once again be people who had never done such things! But we can't change the past. The bell can never be unrung.

Sorrow is a natural response to our misdeeds, but we need to make sure that it is *godly* sorrow. That is always the right response to sinful aspects of our past; it moves us back in God's direction. And what makes godly sorrow different from worldly sorrow is that it is focused on God rather than ourselves. It grieves what our sins have cost Him and His people, and not what they've cost us.

Although we can't change the past, there is a sense in which our memories are always changing us. But are they changing us for the better? Are they making us more *humble* and *penitent?* Are we becoming more *reverent* and *grateful?* As we reflect on what has happened in our lives, are those reflections turning us into more *obedient* people? The answer to all of these questions can be yes, but only if we choose to think about the past with a godly attitude.

Our thinking is one thing we are always capable of changing. No matter what has happened, the alternative of better thinking is never closed, and it's a pity that we don't avail ourselves of this opportunity more often. When we've erred, why would we miss the benefit of thinking about that fact more constructively?

The past cannot be changed, but our response to it can be.
ERWIN W. LUTZER

September 7
AFTER THE DRAMA: AN INTERVIEW

And as it is appointed for men to die once, but after this the judgment, so
Christ was offered once to bear the sins of many. To those who eagerly wait
for Him He will appear a second time, apart from sin, for salvation.
Hebrews 9:27,28

THE HISTORY OF THE WORLD MAY BE COMPARED TO A GREAT PLAY,
A DRAMA. Every event is a part of the plot, and every person
ever born will have had a role. God, the Author, is writing the
story, and He is weaving all of its many elements together so as to
produce the ending that He has designed in His eternal purpose.
As we play our individual roles, we each become a part of the
drama. Each of us will also be present at the ending of the story.

Although God is moving the story toward a conclusion that
He desires, He preserves the freedom of our will as we each make
decisions about our own actions. When we make decisions consistent with His purposes, our actions are woven into the story. And
when our decisions are against His purposes, He still weaves them
into the story. Whether our actions are, on the surface, "helpful" or
"unhelpful" to His cause, God is able to make use of whatever we
do. There is nothing that we can do that He cannot work with, or
at least work around, to accomplish His ultimate, overall purpose.

But we will surely have to *answer* for how we participated in
the story God was writing. God created each of us with a unique
part in the drama, a part that no one else could play, and sin is
when we deviate from God's intention or will for us in our role. If
we die in sin, unreconciled to God's purposes, we will be banished
from Him forever and barred from entrance into His eternal kingdom. This is what "judgment" means (2 Corinthians 5:10).

At judgment some will hear the words "Well done" (Matthew
25:21), while others will hear "Depart from Me" (Matthew 7:23).
But remember one thing well: the inquiry will be about the role
that was actually *ours* — not the role that was somebody else's.

Many of us might like to know how long the play will go on.
But that doesn't matter. Nor does it matter how well others play
their roles. Judgment will be about faithfulness to one thing: what
we knew God wanted of us when we were making our choices.

The curtain may be rung down at any moment. . . . We do not know
the play. . . . When it is over, we may be told. We are led to believe that the
Author will have something to say to each of us on the part that each of us
has played. The playing it well is what matters infinitely.

C. S. L E W I S

September 8
THE BLESSED ARE THOSE WHO ENDURE

Indeed we count them blessed who endure. You have heard
of the perseverance of Job and seen the end intended by the Lord
— that the Lord is very compassionate and merciful.
James 5:11

MANY MAY AGREE TO LIVE THE CHRISTIAN LIFE WHEN IT'S EASY, BUT THERE AREN'T MANY WHO WILL LIVE IT WHEN IT'S HARD. Difficulty has often been the deterrent of those started out to follow the Lord. So James says, "We count them blessed who *endure.*"

One of Jesus' most familiar parables is the Parable of the Sower, the story of the seed scattered on different kinds of soil. In interpreting the parable, Jesus said that the "stony ground" represented the person "who hears the word and immediately receives it with joy; yet he has no root in himself, but endures only for a while. *For when tribulation or persecution arises because of the word, immediately he stumbles*" (Matthew 13:20,21). It's a sad fact that some will renounce the gospel when serious difficulty arises.

No doubt, there are times when all of us are tempted to say, "But Lord, this is *hard.*" At such times, He would probably say, "I told you that it would be hard. What were you expecting?" Paul said that we "must through many tribulations enter the kingdom of God" (Acts 14:22), and he often warned his hearers that being a Christian would involve hardship (1 Thessalonians 3:3,4).

It is not as if God doesn't *know* the difficulties we face. We can never say, "God, You have no idea what You have asked of us or how hard it is." He *does* know how hard it is, and He is not unaware of our efforts on His behalf (Hebrews 6:10). Besides, nothing we can do for God will ever be as hard as what Jesus did for us.

In secular matters, the honorable people are those who tackle difficulty with a do-or-die attitude. The quitters are soon forgotten; they are irrelevant to the real work that goes on in the world. In spiritual matters, it is no different. Those who complain, "Lord, I would have done my duty, but it was just so *hard,*" won't ever make much of a contribution to the kingdom — because "hard" is exactly what the work of the kingdom is. So we need to take heed how we deal with difficulty. The Lord has always been patient with those who are willing to keep trying. But those who *quit* trying shouldn't expect the Lord's praise or anybody else's.

Difficulty is the excuse history never accepts.
SAMUEL GRAFTON

September 9

BEARING BURDENS FOR A LONG TIME

Rejoicing in hope, patient in tribulation, continuing steadfastly in prayer.
Romans 12:12

MANY MAY AGREE TO BEAR A BURDEN FOR A WHILE, BUT THERE AREN'T MANY WHO WILL BEAR IT INDEFINITELY. Some hardships are short-term, but others last much longer. In the case of these long-lasting difficulties, we must not only accept tribulation, but be *"patient* in tribulation." It may be a long time (at least from our perspective) before rest and relief are able to be enjoyed.

Job would be a good example here, wouldn't he? The things he suffered would have been terrible even if only for a short time. But at the worst of his ordeal, he had no idea how long it would go on. It might have lasted the rest of his life! As we read Job's story, we know that his burden was eventually lifted, but he did not know that while he was suffering. His steadfastness in the midst of suffering is all the more amazing in that, for all he knew, it could have been indefinite. He was willing to endure whatever was necessary *for however long it took to see God's face* (Job 19:25-27).

I fear that our dealings with God sometimes involve a bit of "bargaining." We say to Him, "Lord, I will deal with this difficulty if You will remove it within a reasonable time." And, of course, it is we who define what is reasonable. When that time passes and the difficulty is still there, we grow resentful, as if God had somehow fallen down on His end of the bargain. But He never agreed to the bargain. He never said how long the difficulty would last.

I find myself reading Hebrews more often these days. Its message is that we need to accept whatever problems have to be dealt with *for however long it takes to get to heaven!* "Therefore do not cast away your confidence, which has great reward," the writer said. "For you have need of endurance, so that after you have done the will of God, you may receive the promise" (Hebrews 10:35,36). The promise will surely come, but it may not come very soon.

So let us not dictate to God the terms of our service to Him, as if we were only obligated to do what we define as reasonable. He asks of us an *unconditional* commitment to serve under *any* circumstances. When our service involves difficulty, as it often will, let us endure. Even when we can't see the end, let us *still* endure.

Patience: accepting a difficult situation
without giving God a deadline to remove it.

BILL GOTHARD

September 10
PAUL, THE AGED

Yet for love's sake I rather appeal to you — being such
a one as Paul, the aged, and now also a prisoner of Jesus Christ.
Philemon 9

WHEN HE WROTE HIS SHORT LETTER TO PHILEMON, PAUL WAS AN OLD MAN. We don't know exactly how old he was, but he was no longer young. He could call himself "Paul, the aged."

We live in a day when being "aged" is nothing to brag about. It is no longer viewed as being desirable in any significant way. Today, hardly anything can be imagined that would be worse than being old. Everybody wants to *grow* old, but nobody wants to *be* old. Most younger people flatter themselves that they'll live a long time, but having done so, they won't look old, dress old, or act old. Old age itself is despised, and it is assumed by our culture that agedness should be camouflaged in every way possible, as if the reality of being old were something to be embarrassed about.

I wish we could see that it's not old age that is undesirable, but only the *disabilities* that often come with it. What repels us is the thought that when we have reached that point in life where we have the most to offer, our bodies (including our brains) have often become so dilapidated that our ability to function is seriously hindered. It is the *decrepitude* of old age that is unwanted, the ravages wrought by time on the bodies in which our souls dwell.

Because of the decline of our physical "tabernacle," old age in this world can be a trying experience. In the Scriptures, we are warned to enjoy the years of our lives before our bodies begin to wear out. "Remember now your Creator in the days of your youth, before the difficult days come . . ." (Ecclesiastes 12:1).

But even so, there is a sense in which we ought to look forward to being like "Paul, the aged." Our last years can be our very best. And more than that, we ought to look forward to *heaven* and the state of being that we'll enjoy then. In our resurrected and glorified bodies, we'll enjoy an eternal *maturity* and *wisdom* that are *unhindered* by the disabilities that affect our joy and usefulness in this world. We will be perfectly "aged." We'll enjoy all the advantages of having "grown up" without any of the disadvantages!

Eternity has no gray hairs! The flowers fade, the heart withers,
man grows old and dies, the world lies down in the sepulchre of ages,
but time writes no wrinkles on the brow of eternity.

REGINALD HEBER

September 11

A BETTER COUNTRY

For those who say such things declare plainly that they seek a
homeland. And truly if they had called to mind that country from which
they had come out, they would have had opportunity to return. But now
they desire a better, that is, a heavenly country. Therefore God is not
ashamed to be called their God, for He has prepared a city for them.
Hebrews 11:14-16

GOD HAS PREPARED A CITY FOR HIS FAITHFUL PEOPLE, AN ETER-
NAL ABODE IN HIS PRESENCE. To say the least, such a prospect
ought to be something we *desire*. Going to heaven ought to be
something we want with all of our hearts. In comparison to the
"country" of our sojourn here below, that one is far superior. Think
with me, though, about the future in terms of *good, better,* and *best*.

Good. Despite whatever difficulties we may have experienced,
most of us can say *the past has been good*. Mercifully, the painful
memories recede as time goes by, and what we remember are the
acts of love and the moments of joy. Surely, these have been good.

Better. However good the past has been, we ought to be able
to say that *the present is better*. If we've been making choices that
are conducive to growth, then what we are today is something better than what we were yesterday. And even if not, we can always
make choices today that will make the present better than the past.

Best. By God's help we are what we are today, and that is better than what we were yesterday. But to be a Christian means that
we are *continuing* to grow. Never content with the progress we've
made so far, we are always reaching for higher goals tomorrow. So
we should not hesitate to say that *the future will be the best of all*.

But, of course, what will be better even than the best of this
world is the "better country" to which we are going when our
lives are completely done. That better country is a "heavenly
country," and that is what our hearts desire most of all. But here is
a wonderful truth: Our final destination is not only good, but the
whole *way* by which our Father is leading us there is good also.
So while we fervently long for heaven, let's also enjoy the *journey*.
Although difficult, it is still the "great adventure." In God, the
whole path — from start to finish — is full of grace and goodness.

A wonderful way is the King's Highway;
It runs through the nightland up to the day;
From the wonderful was, by the wonderful is,
To the more wonderful is to be.

JOHN MASEFIELD

A FORETASTE OF HELL

*But if you have bitter envy and self-seeking in your hearts,
do not boast and lie against the truth. This wisdom does not descend
from above, but is earthly, sensual, demonic. For where envy and
self-seeking exist, confusion and every evil thing are there.*
James 3:14-16

THE VERY ESSENCE OF SIN IS SELF-WILL. Whereas love is outwardly focused, sin is inwardly focused. It wants whatever it wants, regardless of the damage that anyone else may suffer. It is unconcerned with how it treats others; how it is *being* treated is its only concern. Sin is selfish. It is irritable. It is competitive.

In hell, there will be nothing *but* sin and the selfishness that drives it. On earth, even the most evil person lives in an environment where he gets the benefit of goodness in the lives of other people. But in hell, there will be no such moderating influence. There will be no goodness and no light at all. Everyone there will have become as selfish and sinful as it is possible to be. The corruption that started in this life will have reached its ultimate end.

It is horrifying to think of the souls in hell being utterly consumed with themselves, but we get a foretaste of what hell will be like every time we engage in acts of selfishness right now. Read again what James said and think about what you are reading: "But if you have *bitter envy* and *self-seeking* in your hearts, do not boast and lie against the truth. *This wisdom does not descend from above, but is earthly, sensual, demonic.* For where *envy* and *self-seeking* exist, confusion and every evil thing are there." Do you ever do any of these things? You are never nearer to hell than when you do.

Standing still is not possible. We are always moving toward God or away from Him. With every decision we make, we take a step toward the likeness of our Creator or a step away from Him. Eternity will simply be the final *end* of whichever path we are on, involving either complete glorification or total corruption.

How honest are you willing to be about your direction? No amount of "religious" activity will help you if you are self-willed and self-seeking. So be honest: *which way are you really headed?*

*We must picture hell as a state where everyone is perpetually
concerned about his own dignity and advancement, where everyone
has a grievance, and where everyone lives the deadly serious passions
of envy, self-importance, and resentment.*

C. S. LEWIS

LET US GO ON

Let us go on to perfection . . .
Hebrews 6:1

WHY IS IT THAT WE HAVE SUCH A HARD TIME REACHING FORWARD? Why do we insist on looking backward so often when the future is beckoning us to things that are so much better?

Laziness. The force called "inertia" often keeps us from doing what we ought to do. It takes extra effort to "press" toward a goal that is in the future, and many people are just not willing to make that effort. They are content to stay where they are and do nothing more than leaf through the scrapbook pages of their past. Whatever vision of the future they may have, it is not a powerful enough vision to move them forward. It's just too much work!

Grief at what we've lost. At other times, there is some loss that we have suffered, and our grief keeps us focused, at least temporarily, on what we had in the past but no longer have. Grief is not sinful, at least it need not be, and during times of grief we need to be patient both with ourselves and with others. But by its very nature, grief is past-oriented rather than future-oriented, and so we need to be careful not to let it become our *permanent* perspective.

Fear of the future. One way the past and the future are different is that the past is certain but the future is uncertain. While the past is already an accomplished "creation," the future is yet to be created, and there is no guarantee that we will not fail in some of our efforts to create it. We recognize that we depend upon God's help in all things, but He still requires us to do our part, and that can be frightening. So we just "play it safe" and avoid the risk of discouragement, secure within the comfort zone of past accomplishment.

Whatever the reasons for our fixation on the past may be, we need to work on overcoming them. The Hebrew writer said, "Let us *go on* to perfection." At times, we may need some *help* in seeing the importance of that effort. We may need to have our focus adjusted by pain or difficulty. Or we may need friends who will pull us out of the past. Indeed, we have no better friends than those who will turn us around and make us face in a forward direction. If you have such a future-oriented friend, you should be thankful.

I want to do away with everything behind man, so that
there is nothing to see when he looks back. I want to take him by
the scruff of the neck and turn his face toward the future!

LEONID NIKOLAYEVICH ANDREYEV

RATHER BE ABSENT FROM THE BODY?

*We are confident, yes, well pleased rather to be absent
from the body and to be present with the Lord.*
2 Corinthians 5:8

W E READ THE WORDS OF PAUL ABOVE AND WE DEEM THEM
NOBLE, BUT IF ANYONE SERIOUSLY SAID SUCH A THING TODAY,
WE WOULD CONSIDER HIM NEUROTIC RATHER THAN NOBLE. If the
truth be told, we are "well pleased" rather to be present in the
body and absent from the Lord. For us, going to be with the Lord
is all right, as long as it is *later.* But for now, we prefer living in
this body and this world. We wouldn't willingly give up this life if
there were one ounce of happiness left that we could get from it.

As for being "absent from the body and . . . present with the
Lord," we prefer that scenario only at the end of a long life of temporal satisfaction. I don't believe I'm exaggerating when I say that
the average Christian's true sentiment runs something like this:
"After I've drained all the happiness out of this world that I can
get and my body has fallen into ruin, then, yes, I would prefer to
leave this body and go to be with the Lord." But to say that such a
thing would be preferable *right now?* That is nonsense. We want to
go to heaven *only when we've exhausted every means of putting it off.*

Now, don't misunderstand me. I know that we don't have the
option of going to heaven until our *work* is done. But if *today* the
Lord were to say, "Your work is done," shouldn't we be *thrilled?*

So we have a dilemma, don't we? We want heaven but we
want this world too. And right now, we want this world *more* than
we want heaven. We are more in love with this world than we
like to admit. In theory we know that heavenly things are better than earthly things, but in practice we see heaven only as a
place the Christian "has" to go to when the doctors have run out
of alternatives. Only when we've glutted ourselves on happiness
below does heaven start to sound "interesting." We are not unlike children at an amusement park being asked by their parents,
"Wouldn't you like to go home now? Home is much better." *No,
we don't want to go home! Of course not! Not until we are sunburned
and sick of junk food and have absolutely, totally, and completely worn
ourselves out having fun! Then we might consider it . . . maybe.*

Everybody wants to go to heaven,
but nobody wants to die.

JOE LEWIS

PROMISES MADE IN DISTRESS

Then Pharaoh called for Moses and Aaron, and said, "Entreat
the LORD that He may take away the frogs from me and from my
people; and I will let the people go, that they may sacrifice to the LORD."
. . . But when Pharaoh saw that there was relief, he hardened his heart
and did not heed them, as the LORD had said.
Exodus 8:8,15

IT IS AN HONORABLE THING, AND OFTEN A VERY HELPFUL THING, TO BIND OURSELVES TO A COMMITMENT BY THE MAKING OF A PROMISE. Promises can have a steadying influence on our will. But often, we make promises under the influence of strong emotions, and we find that after the emotions have cooled, we are no longer willing to keep the promises we made. Surrounded by frogs, Pharaoh said, "I will let the people go." But later, "when Pharaoh saw that there was relief, he hardened his heart and did not heed them."

In general, we should probably avoid making promises while we are under the influence of strong emotions. I say "in general" because there are certainly times when deep feelings can lead us to make good and worthy commitments. Passion is not a bad thing.

But here is what we need to consider: whether they are made under strong emotion or not, *promises have to be kept.* We are not later released from the obligations we bound ourselves to simply because "on further review" we see that they are inconvenient.

Solomon had some very wise instruction on the keeping of commitments: "Do not be rash with your mouth, and let not your heart utter anything hastily before God. For God is in heaven, and you on earth; therefore let your words be few. For a dream comes through much activity, and a fool's voice is known by his many words. When you make a vow to God, do not delay to pay it; for He has no pleasure in fools. Pay what you have vowed. It is better not to vow than to vow and not pay" (Ecclesiastes 5:2-5).

Not long ago, I was on an airplane that flew through some of the worst turbulence I have ever experienced. The thought crossed my mind that we might actually crash, and I'm sure there were hasty promises being made to God all over the cabin: "Dear Lord, if you will just get me off of this airplane alive, I will _____ for the rest of my life." Most of those promises were probably forgotten by the time we got to baggage claim. But God has not forgotten.

Vows made in storms are forgotten in calms.
ANONYMOUS

FAITH AND HOPE

*Not only that, but we also who have the firstfruits of the Spirit, even
we ourselves groan within ourselves, eagerly waiting for the adoption, the
redemption of our body. For we were saved in this hope, but hope that is
seen is not hope; for why does one still hope for what he sees?*
Romans 8:23,24

ONE OF THE GREAT TRUTHS OF CHRISTIANITY IS THAT THE
CHRISTIAN LOOKS FORWARD TO RECEIVING AN "INHERITANCE."
There are many blessings the Christian can enjoy right now as a result of having obeyed the gospel, but heaven is what Christianity
is primarily about, and that is a "possession" that the Christian
doesn't yet "possess." It is an "inheritance" that he or she will one
day come into, but meanwhile, there is some waiting to be done.

Faith. One of the greatest of our human endowments is the
ability to exercise "faith." By faith, we can perceive many realities that are not "seen," i.e., not accessible to our physical senses.
Based on trustworthy evidence and testimony, we can apprehend
the truth of many facts that would otherwise be inaccessible to us,
and the fact of heaven is one of the most important of these.

Hope. Like faith, "hope" has to do with realities that our physical senses can't experience, but hope goes a step beyond faith.
Based on the truths arrived at by faith, hope eagerly takes "possession" of that which is still in the future. The faithful Christian not
only *believes* that heaven will one day be a reality, he or she passionately *desires it* and even *enjoys the possession of it in prospect.*

In a day when too many are reducing Christianity to a search
for the happy life in this world, we need to understand that the
object of the Christian's hope is, as Paul says, our "adoption, the
redemption of our body." Christianity is first and foremost about
eternity, and our "hopes" for this world ought to be quite minimal.

But true Christian hope is a potent force which produces powerful emotions. Paul said that we "groan within ourselves, eagerly
waiting" for the realization of our hope. Heaven ought to be a
thought that stirs us and moves us and makes us long to go there.

The difficulty, of course, is that because it is an *unseen* and a
future reality, heaven often seems unreal to us. So let's learn all we
can about *faith* and *hope.* Without these, we lose our inheritance!

Faith has to do with things that are not seen,
and hope with things that are not in hand.

THOMAS AQUINAS

HOPE AND PERSEVERANCE

But if we hope for what we do not see,
we eagerly wait for it with perseverance.
Romans 8:25

SINCE THE CHRISTIAN'S INHERITANCE IS TO BE RECEIVED IN THE FUTURE, THERE IS A "GAP" THAT HAS TO BE DEALT WITH. While we wait for the realization of our hope, there is the possibility that we may forsake the Lord and forfeit the inheritance that we would otherwise have received. Between now and the end of our earthly sojourn, we "have need of endurance, so that after you have done the will of God, you may receive the promise" (Hebrews 10:36).

Hope. Paul said that "if we hope for what we do not see, we eagerly wait for it." A great part of the power of hope comes from its *eagerness.* Appreciating how far the value of eternal life excels anything we possess right now, we passionately strain ourselves toward it. And the key to appreciating its value is the *vividness* with which we contemplate it. Just as those who accomplish great worldly goals are those who keep their goal clearly in mind, those who aspire to heaven need to concentrate on it with a keen focus.

Perseverance. Hope alone is not enough; it must be accompanied by perseverance. As we "eagerly wait" for the redemption of our body, we must wait for it "with perseverance." In the common vernacular, we would say that a person must not only keep on, but *keep on keeping on.* During the "gap" between now and the end, we will have many opportunities to give up and quit the faith. And we can be sure that our adversary the devil will tempt us to do exactly that. As powerful as our hope is, it will do us no good if we don't support it with a daily decision to persevere in the faith.

Even in Jesus' lifetime, we see that there were people who said they wanted to follow the Lord but were easily turned away (Luke 9:57-62). So I have often wondered if the Lord does not still use difficulties and discouragements to separate those who are determined to go to heaven from those who can be dissuaded.

Christ has loved us with a love that is stronger than any mood or momentary inconvenience. The question is: *with what kind of love do we love Him?* We wait to see His face, but do we "wait for it with perseverance"? Are our souls tied to the doorpost of heaven?

Perseverance is the rope that ties
the soul to the doorpost of heaven.
FRANCES J. ROBERTS

September 18
OUR PRESENT UNDERSTANDING IS LIMITED

And He said to them, "You are from beneath; I am
from above. You are of this world; I am not of this world."
John 8:23

WHAT WILL HEAVEN BE LIKE? That's the way we usually ask the question, and it's really the only way the question *can* be asked. Given our present inability to understand many spiritual realities, the best that can be done is for God to tell us a few things that heaven will be "like." We are given images, analogies, hints, and suggestions that describe our eternal relationship with God in terms of the most beautiful things that we know about right now.

God is not withholding information about eternity simply to tantalize us; it is doubtful that we *could* understand anything more than pictures and comparisons. Like a parent trying to explain an abstract concept to a child too young to engage in abstract thinking, God relates heaven to us in terms that we are familiar with.

So what should be our *attitude* toward what God has told us about heaven? To begin with, we should *relish* every syllable of every word that has to do with heaven. We should let our minds eagerly roam over the texts that talk about our resurrection. There ought to be nothing more enjoyable than reading what our Father has revealed about the inheritance that will one day be ours.

But as to the specifics, we ought to approach them with *reverence* and *reserve*. Rather than being dogmatic about the images of heaven given to us, we ought to have an open-minded willingness for the reality to turn out to be something quite different than what we had in mind when we visualized being with God.

After all, that is the main thing about heaven, is it not? *We will be with God!* Whatever the details turn out to be, we will be in a perfect, unmitigated relationship with our Creator forevermore.

Until the inheritance is actually ours, let us recognize the paucity of our present understanding and be prepared, when our Lord returns, to rejoice in *whatever* God has for us. Toward the end of his life, C. S. Lewis wrote descriptively about heaven and then concluded by saying, "Guesses, of course, only guesses. If they are not true, something better will be." I heartily agree. And one thing is absolutely certain: the reality will break the boundaries of everything we have ever dreamed of or ever *could* dream of right now.

The frog in the well knows nothing of the great ocean.
JAPANESE PROVERB

September 19

CAST YOUR BREAD UPON THE WATERS

Cast your bread upon the waters,
For you will find it after many days.
Ecclesiastes 11:1

TOMORROW IS UNCERTAIN, BUT THAT SHOULD NOT STOP US FROM DOING WHAT WE CAN DO TODAY. Our judgment of what we should do may not be the best sometimes, and even when our plans are well laid, unforeseen events may alter their outcome. Nevertheless, we must do the best that we know to do today.

Ecclesiastes 11:1 is one of those verses whose main point is fairly obvious in context, but interpreters differ as to the specific illustration or metaphor the writer had in mind. I personally think the image is that of a merchant sending his goods out on a ship, which in ancient times was a very risky thing to do. Risky or not, however, the merchant wouldn't make any money if he simply did nothing and kept his goods at home. The NEB translates it: "Send your grain across the seas, and in time you will get a return."

When we are contemplating what is the best course of action to follow, we should certainly exercise *prudence*. We should be careful and use the very best judgment of which we are capable.

But having been careful in our planning, we then need to exercise *energy* and *industry* in carrying out our plan. However hesitant we may have been in making our plan, once the plan is made we need to put our whole heart into its implementation. I well remember my youngest son's golf coach advising him on a very difficult hole where it was going to be hard to select the right club. Having helped him weigh the pros and cons, he then said, "It's your decision, Grant. But whichever club you choose, *commit* to it." In life, as in golf, we often "swing" hesitantly, as if we're not sure we selected the right "club." And when we swing hesitantly, not even the right club is going to help us do very much.

In the end, our confidence must be in God, and not in our own wisdom or ability. Having been as prudent as we know how to be and then acting as energetically as we can, we must trust that *God will take our actions today and bring about a good return tomorrow.*

Build a little fence of trust
Around today;
Fill the space with loving deeds,
And therein stay.

MARY FRANCES BUTTS

September 20
GOD, THE ETERNAL "I AM"

Then the Jews said to Him, "You are not yet fifty years old,
and have You seen Abraham?" Jesus said to them, "Most assuredly,
I say to you, before Abraham was, I AM."
John 8:57,58

THE "ETERNITY" OF GOD IS A DIFFICULT CONCEPT, BUT I BELIEVE
IT'S ALSO A VERY IMPORTANT ONE. God *has* always existed, and
He always *will* exist. He is "eternal," without either a beginning
or an end. And presumably, He is the *only* such being that exists.
Since He created everything else, everything else had a beginning.
But not having been created, God is self-existent. He is eternal.

In language, verbs can be in the past, present, or future tense.
God, we may say, is always in the "present tense." There was
never a "time" when He didn't exist, and there will never be a
"time" when He won't exist. When asked by Moses what His
name was, God said, "I AM WHO I AM" (Exodus 3:14). And Jesus,
who was God in fleshly form, said to the astonished Jews, "Before
Abraham was, I AM." He did not say, "I *was* before Abraham," but
"Before Abraham was, I AM." God is always in the present tense.

The eternity of God is one answer to the seeming contradic-
tion between God's foreknowledge and our freedom of will. God
can know what we are going to do without infringing on our freedom of will because He sees all that happens — past, present, and
future — as one present moment. It is only we finite, time-bound
creatures who see things in terms of what has happened, what will
happen, etc. Living in an eternal now, God simply sees what IS.

In a world broken by sin, time is our enemy in many ways.
We struggle with what has happened and what will happen. We
even struggle to have the right *attitude* toward past, present, and
future. So there is great comfort in knowing that God is above and
beyond time, that time is within His control and subject to His
sovereignty. Whatever problems the passage of time may present
for us, nothing that has to do with time is a problem for God.

There is an old song that says, "Many things about tomorrow
I don't seem to understand, but I know who holds tomorrow, and
I know who holds my hand." There is nothing about the past, the
present, or the future that He won't deal with in just the right way.

In God there is no was or will be, but a continuous and unbroken is.
In him history and prophecy are one and the same.
A. W. TOZER

DON'T MISS THIS MOMENT'S GRACE

Continue earnestly in prayer,
being vigilant in it with thanksgiving . . .
Colossians 4:2

IF GOD LIVES IN AN ETERNAL "NOW," THERE IS A SENSE IN WHICH WE SHOULD ALSO LIVE IN THE PRESENT MOMENT. The past is something we should learn from and the future is something we should plan for, but the present is the only chance we have to actually *do* anything. If we let the present moment go by unused, then we've wasted the very "stuff" of life. So we need to do three things:

(1) Pay more attention to the present moment. Many of us miss the value of the present moment because our minds are somewhere else. Whether we're "living in the past" or "daydreaming about the future" or we're just too busy with trivia to savor the moment, the end result is often the same: we find life getting away from us without our having *thought* about it as it went rushing by.

(2) Use the present moment. A normal human life is comprised of millions of "moments" — so many that there seems to be an endless supply of them, at least while we're young. It doesn't seem such a great tragedy to let some of them go by "unimproved." But truly, there is no "present moment" that should be despised or thrown away. To throw away any moment is to insult its Giver.

(3) Appreciate the present moment. I used to think that life was made up of many drab, ordinary moments and only a few that could be called wonderful or gracious. How wrong I was! And how sad I am now to see how much of life I missed while I was waiting for some "big" moment to come along. God's best gifts are often delivered to us in plain paper wrapping. *This* moment is almost always an extraordinary thing, if we have the eyes to see and the heart to appreciate it. Let us never underestimate the grace that may be in the present moment, whenever it may be.

In general, we need to be better stewards of all the "little" things that God's grace sends our way. Paul said that we need to be vigilant in prayer "with thanksgiving." And he also said, "In *everything* give thanks" (1 Thessalonians 5:18). There is not much that happens *at any moment of any day* that we shouldn't give thanks for — either because it is *enjoyable* or because it is *useful.*

The small moment is the carrier of God's most endearing gift.
It must not be permitted to slip away unsavored and unappreciated.
GERHARD E. FROST

PLEASURE, THE LEAST OF THE ENJOYMENTS

The kingdom of God is not eating and drinking,
but righteousness and peace and joy in the Holy Spirit.
Romans 14:17

THE WORD "ENJOYMENT" CAN REFER TO MANY DIFFERENT THINGS. In the world of God's creation, various things can be enjoyed, some more important than others — and some even more *enjoyable* than others. For example, eating and drinking are enjoyable, both sensually and socially. But for the Christian, things like righteousness and peace are *higher* enjoyments. And when any choice has to be made, the higher enjoyments ought to be given priority.

If we should try to categorize the enjoyments available to us, there would be at least three: *pleasure, happiness,* and *joy.* Pleasure is just what the word suggests: that which is pleasant, especially to the senses. Happiness is the state of well-being that comes when what is "happening" to us is just what we would prefer to happen. Joy, on the other hand, is a far greater thing. It is that poignant thrill that comes from the foretaste of eternal, otherworldly raptures, even when earthly pleasure and happiness are absent.

Pleasure is the lowest of the three enjoyments that God has given us, yet hedonism, the worship of pleasure, continues to grow in popularity. Making pleasure the ultimate good in life is surely a serious mistake, but it is also a *sad* mistake. Those who see nothing higher to enjoy than pleasure are missing out on real joy!

But let us be clear: pleasure is not to be despised. It is created by God and meant to be relished, as Ecclesiastes teaches us. Some people make the mistake of not drinking very deeply of pleasure and not being very grateful for it. That, too, is a sad mistake.

So all in all, what should we say? (1) We should accept pleasure as a gift from God. (2) We should never sacrifice higher priorities (such as purity, honesty, and justice) in order to get it. (3) We should control our appetite for it and not overindulge ourselves. (4) We should be willing to let go of it and do without it when the need arises. (5) And finally, we should set these words in stone: *Joy is the highest experience of the human heart.* Pleasure, as good as it may be in its proper place, is a poor, unsatisfying substitute for *joy.*

I doubt whether anyone who has tasted joy
would ever, if both were in his power, exchange it
for all the pleasure in the world.

C. S. LEWIS

September 23
STILLNESS AND JOY

Be still, and know that I am God.
Psalm 46:10

NOWADAYS, ONE REASON WE KNOW SO LITTLE ABOUT JOY IS THAT WE KNOW SO LITTLE ABOUT STILLNESS. In this age of the world, most of us are busy with a myriad of priorities and projects. And we *pride* ourselves on it. The person whose schedule is packed has more prestige than the fellow who "doesn't have much to do." But joy — real, spine-tingling *joy* — is in seriously short supply.

We'll try to define "stillness" in a moment, but just think, by way of contrast, how unlikely it would be for joy to surface in the kind of lives we lead. Our "busyness" produces so much clamor and clatter, the voice of joy is drowned out. It simply gets lost in the shuffle. Even if joy were to appear, it would go unnoticed.

But what does it mean to be "still" before the Lord? It doesn't mean being physically still, though stillness of the body is often involved. And it doesn't mean not saying anything, though that is often involved as well. "Stillness" before God means reverence, humility, openness, and forgetfulness of self. It means putting our minds into a thoughtful posture. It means having our activity stilled and our words hushed by a compelling sense of the power of God Almighty. Above all, it means having a servant's readiness to *obey:* "Speak, Lord, for your servant hears" (1 Samuel 3:9).

I suggest that it would be rare for a person to experience genuine joy if he or she were not mentally disposed in the manner we've just described. That is the only kind of environment in which real joy can make an appearance. Just as happiness eludes those who "pursue" it, joy is even harder to bring under our own power. It doesn't come "on command," but rather it is experienced, often quite unexpectedly, by those who are "still" before the Lord. Unstill people are simply not good candidates for joy.

So God's instruction to us is this: *Be still, and know that I am God.* We shouldn't obey that instruction selfishly, simply so we can have the joy we want. Nevertheless, we won't have any joy if we don't obey it. Without a reverent stillness at the center of our hearts, joy has no chance to break through the noise of earthly life. Of all the killjoys in the world, irreverent busyness is the worst.

The heart that is to be filled to the brim
with holy joy must be held still.
GEORGE SEATON BOWES

THE GREATEST JOY

The generous soul will be made rich,
And he who waters will also be watered himself.
Proverbs 11:25

IF IT'S JOY THAT WE DESIRE, WE OFTEN DEFEAT OURSELVES BY GOING AFTER IT IN THE WRONG WAY. We make it a self-centered pursuit having to do mainly with what we want to *get* — and we lose sight of the fact that the greatest joy is the joy of *giving*. The most joyful people in the world are those whose main intent is to foster joy in the lives of others as much as possible. They have great joy, but they're hardly conscious of having sought it for themselves at all.

Most of us underestimate how great a capacity we have to bring joy to others. We don't think we have anything to offer that would bring happiness, much less joy, to anybody else. But if we are Christians, we have great resources out of which we could give joy. There was probably nothing extraordinary about the Thessalonians, at least from a worldly standpoint, yet Paul was profuse in his praise for them. By their example of steadfastness in the face of hardship, they had greatly refreshed his heart and made it easier for him to endure his own afflictions. "For now we live," he said, "if you stand fast in the Lord" (1 Thessalonians 3:8).

Joy is one of those things that we get more of by paying less attention to it. When we obsess about it and seek it self-consciously, it slips out of our grasp. But when we forget about it, and focus on the needs of those around us, we find it coming our way.

Real joy, though, can be a bittersweet experience. If it comes from making possible the joy of others, that will often require letting go and losing some things that are exceedingly precious to us. Think of Jesus, for example. If joy comes from making possible the joy of others, then His joy must have been a great joy indeed! Yet He could not have known that joy without the grief that went with the sacrifice. And so it is for us too. True joy can be very costly.

In the long run, however, it is true, as Solomon observed, that the "generous soul will be made rich, and he who waters will also be watered himself." C. S. Lewis said it differently, but no less truly, "Nothing that you have not given away will ever truly be your own." Yes, that is a hard truth to accept. But it is still true.

The joy that you give to others
Is the joy that comes back to you.
JOHN GREENLEAF WHITTIER

ARE THE FAITHFUL NEVER IN DARKNESS?

Now David was greatly distressed, for the people spoke of stoning him,
because the soul of all the people was grieved, every man for his sons and
his daughters. But David strengthened himself in the LORD his God.
1 Samuel 30:6

IN A WAY, IT IS ENCOURAGING TO ME TO READ THAT "DAVID WAS
GREATLY DISTRESSED." If a man of his character could be distressed, then when I am frightened and discouraged, I shouldn't
assume that such feelings represent a failure of faith on my part.
Distress *may* mean a failure of faith, but then again, it may not.
David's faith didn't mean that he was never discouraged; it meant
that he responded to discouragement by *refusing to give up.*

As long as we live in this world, there are going to be some
dark days for us. Satan will see to that. Being a Christian does not
insulate us from hardship and heartache. And only a robot could
experience the sadness of this world without emotional distress.
So the mere presence of certain *feelings* shouldn't surprise us.

Faith doesn't mean always feeling confident. If I believe the gospel
of Christ is true, I believe it for the same reason that I believe my
next door neighbor is trustworthy: the evidence for it is stronger
than the evidence against it. But that doesn't mean that a doubt
may not arise now and then, either as to the gospel's truth or my
neighbor's trustworthiness. When a doubt arises, faith is not taken
aback. It simply asks, "Has anything about the evidence changed?"

Hope doesn't mean always feeling hopeful. Hope is based on faith,
and so, like faith, it can sometimes be buffeted by the distresses of
daily events. Even with the strongest possible reasons to believe
and to hope, we find that short-term happenings can make it seem
that our hopes are not going to be realized. In this respect, religious hope is no different than any other kind of hope. Those who
conquer, whether in spiritual or temporal affairs, are those who
hang on to their hopes with an "it ain't over till it's over" attitude.

I like to think of hope as *the active exercise of faith.* It doesn't
mean never being in darkness or doubt. It means that in darkness
or doubt we choose to look at the bigger picture, and based on the
bigger picture, we decide to keep going forward. And let me tell
you: *deciding to go forward when you're discouraged is as fine a thing as
you'll ever do.* "Hope is grief's best music" (Henry George Bohn).

Hope is faith holding out its hands in the dark.
GEORGE ILES

September 26
HAPPINESS IS NICE BUT UNNECESSARY

We are hard pressed on every side, yet not crushed;
we are perplexed, but not in despair.
2 Corinthians 4:8

PAUL HAD AN UNDERLYING JOY THAT COULD NOT BE TAKEN AWAY FROM HIM, BUT "HAPPINESS" COULD BE TAKEN AWAY, AND IT OFTEN WAS. Happiness is the enjoyment of pleasant *circumstances.* It is how we feel when what is "happening" is what we like, and that is an enjoyment that we should not fail to take advantage of whenever it's possible. But obviously, what is happening is not always pleasant. At such times, we need to be able to do *without happiness* and say what Paul said, "We are hard pressed on every side, yet not crushed; we are perplexed, but not in despair."

Happiness is nice. I don't want anything I say on this page to sound like "sour grapes." I value happiness as much as anyone else. When it is present in my life, I enjoy it greatly, and I hope that I'm as thankful for it as I should be. But whatever else you can say about happiness, one thing you can't say is that it is *essential.*

Happiness is unnecessary. We can do without happiness if we have to. It is not the *summum bonum* in life, the ultimate good. I don't think it rates anywhere near the top of the list of the most important things in this life. But even if someone disagreed and said it *was* the most important thing to have in this life, I would still stay it is unnecessary. There is simply nothing in *this* life that we can't do without. God is all we *have* to have. So things like happiness can be relinquished, if need be. We can survive their loss.

Obviously, it takes some *learning* to get to the point where we can live without things like happiness. Paul said that he knew how to be empty as well as full, but he said he had *learned* how to be empty: "I have *learned* in whatever state I am, to be content: I know how to be abased, and I know how to abound. Everywhere and in all things I have *learned* both to be full and to be hungry, both to abound and to suffer need" (Philippians 4:11,12).

But once we have learned to live without happiness, look at the strong position that puts us in! The devil's main power over most people is the threat of taking away their happiness. But the Christian can say, "Go ahead; take it away. I can live without it."

The greatest happiness you can have is knowing
that you do not necessarily require happiness.

WILLIAM SAROYAN

September 27

A HIGHER DEFINITION OF HAPPINESS

... the eyes of your understanding being enlightened; that you
may know what is the hope of His calling, what are the riches
of the glory of His inheritance in the saints.
Ephesians 1:18

IN OUR PREVIOUS READINGS, IF WE HAVE SEEMED TO DENIGRATE
HAPPINESS, WE HAVE NOT REALLY DONE SO; WE HAVE ONLY TRIED
TO *REDEFINE* IT. What needs to happen is for our minds to be reoriented with regard to things like happiness. We need to enlarge our perspective on what these things were truly meant to be.

It's perhaps risky to try to put ourselves in God's position, but don't you suppose that part of the "frustration" God experiences in working with us is that we are willing to settle for so little when He is trying to offer us so much? God knows that the pitifully little thing we call "happiness" is nothing compared to the thing that really deserves that name, and it must surely be "exasperating" to Him to see us hang on to our "happiness" so tightly and pay so little attention to treasures that are incomparably more precious.

Consider Paul's "thorn in the flesh" (2 Corinthians 12:7-10). When he prayed for its removal, he was saying, "I want to be happy. Please remove this hindrance to my happiness." But God said, "No, Paul. I have something for you better than what you call happiness, and this thorn will help you to get it." Later, in writing to the Ephesians, Paul prayed that the eyes of their understanding might be enlightened, "that you may know what is the hope of His calling, what are the riches of the glory of His inheritance in the saints." Paul understood that what would do us more good than anything else is *a clear vision of the greater things that God has for us.*

Growing in faith means learning to let God *define* things for us and then to be willing to receive these things *on His terms.* Take, for example, the concept of "salvation." Faith means that we let God define what salvation is and then that we have the humility to receive it on His terms. Now apply that to the "enjoyments" of human life. Wouldn't we be more mature spiritually if we let God tell us what these things really are and then let Him dispense these blessings to us on His terms and according to His wisdom?

I thought God's purpose was to make me full
of happiness and joy. It is, but it is happiness and joy
from God's perspective, not from mine.

OSWALD CHAMBERS

September 28
SUFFERING, JESUS CRIED LOUDLY

*Now from the sixth hour until the ninth hour there
was darkness over all the land. And about the ninth hour Jesus
cried out with a loud voice, saying, "Eli, Eli, lama sabachthani?"
that is, "My God, My God, why have You forsaken Me?"*
Matthew 27:45,46

OUR CONCEPT OF INNER "STRENGTH" IS SUCH THAT WE ARE SOME-
TIMES RELUCTANT TO REVEAL THAT WE ARE HURTING. We hide
our heartaches from everyone else, lest they think we are weak or
that we have "the wrong attitude." And sometimes even within
our own selves, we are reluctant to be honest about these things.

But if we think that strong people never experience anguish, that is a false notion of strength. Just as courage doesn't
mean the absence of fear, strength doesn't mean the absence of
pain. Strength is not inconsistent with anguish of spirit, nor does
strength mean that we have to try to keep our heartaches a secret.

Jesus' example is instructive here. By any spiritual or emotional measure, Jesus was the strongest person who ever lived.
Yet He was "a Man of sorrows and acquainted with grief" (Isaiah
53:3). Jesus' strength didn't keep Him from hurting, and it didn't
keep Him from *expressing* His hurts. We are told that He "offered
up prayers and supplications, with vehement cries and tears to
Him who was able to save Him from death" (Hebrews 5:7).

When we cry out in pain, however, the difficulty is to do it
with the same *humility* and *reverence* that Jesus did. Agony and
emptiness have a tendency to make us selfish and demanding. But
those are temptations we can resist, and when we resist them, our
cries of agony can be pure and sincere . . . and acceptable to God.

Anguish is simply an indication of unmet needs. When we
hurt emotionally, it means that there is something we deeply need
that we don't have, either because we never had it or because we
had it and lost it. In heaven there will be no unmet needs, but on
earth there are plenty of them. We were made for a different kind
of world than the broken one that now exists, and as long as we
live here, even as Christians, we will have needs that are achingly
unfulfilled. As long as we cry humbly and reverently, it is not
wrong to cry honestly and deeply, "How long, O Lord, how long?"

*If I ever wonder about the appropriate "spiritual" response
to pain and suffering, I can note how Jesus responded to his own
with fear and trembling, with loud cries and tears.*

PHILIP YANCEY

ZACCHAEUS

Now behold, there was a man named Zacchaeus who was
a chief tax collector, and he was rich. And he sought to see who Jesus
was, but could not because of the crowd, for he was of short stature.
So he ran ahead and climbed up into a sycamore tree to see Him,
for He was going to pass that way. *Luke 19:2-4*

IF WE'VE GOTTEN TOO OLD TO ENJOY THE STORY OF ZACCHAEUS, THEN WE'VE JUST GOTTEN TOO OLD FOR OUR OWN GOOD. Like most of the stories about the Lord, it makes a simple point that children can appreciate, but as adults we make a serious mistake when we suppose that the "simple" points are only for children.

"Reaching forward" requires energy. It takes effort. And the importance of those qualities is what we learn from Zacchaeus. Wanting to "see who Jesus was," he ran ahead and climbed a tree so that he could glimpse the Lord as He passed by. Compared to that display of interest, most of us should be ashamed of ourselves. We would be content *not* to see Jesus if He couldn't be seen on television from our recliner. And from all appearances, many of us would rather relax and go to hell than work to go to heaven.

Zacchaeus, of course, had a disability, a disadvantage in seeing the Lord: he was short of stature and could not see over the crowd. So he climbed a tree! How many of us would have thought of that? Judging from what I hear these days, many in Zacchaeus's position would have gone home complaining that they didn't get a "chance" to see Jesus because of the evils of "discrimination."

In the lives of most of us, there is probably going to be something that tests our resolve to see the Lord. The nature of the test may vary from one individual to another, but it is rarely, if ever, true that anyone gets to heaven easily. And I wouldn't be surprised to learn that the Lord set it up that way deliberately. In His providence, He may have built various "filters" into the world, to filter out those who don't really care whether they see Him or not.

The shortness of Zacchaeus's physical stature is symbolic of the situation that we all find ourselves in. He was trying to see the Lord; we are trying to get to heaven. He had a disadvantage; we have our own. He overcame his hindrance by the intensity of his interest; so can we. From this "wee little man," then, we should learn to reach forward to God with a passion that *will not be denied.*

Enthusiasm makes ordinary people extraordinary.
NORMAN VINCENT PEALE

September 30
WHAT CAN YOU SEE?

"Your father Abraham rejoiced to see My day, and he saw it and was glad."
John 8:56

ABRAHAM "SAW" THE DAY WHEN THE MESSIAH WOULD COME, A DAY THAT WAS, FOR HIM, IN THE FAR DISTANT FUTURE. He also saw heaven: "he waited for the city which has foundations, whose builder and maker is God" (Hebrews 11:10). So Abraham, like all people of faith and spiritual maturity, was a person of *vision*. He rejoiced to "see" many things that others close their "eyes" to.

What we ought to do. If all that a person can see is the status quo, he will never rise above it, and unfortunately, that is about all that most people can see (or at least all that they make the effort to see). What "is" can be seen by nearly anybody, but what "ought to be" takes extra vision. It is only by perceiving invisible *truths* and *principles* that we come to understand what our *obligations* are.

What we ought to hope for. The external appearances of present reality can be very discouraging, and those who can see only what is happening at the present moment are often prone to depression. We have to discipline ourselves and develop our vision to look outside of ourselves and our private discouragements. If we have the eyes to see, there are great and wonderful things to hope for.

What we ought to believe. The Jewish patriarchs were people who could see, by faith, the reality of some things that had not yet arrived. "These all died in faith, not having received the promises, but having seen them afar off were assured of them, embraced them and confessed that they were strangers and pilgrims on the earth" (Hebrews 11:13). The vision of *faith* is the best of all!

We don't think about our "vision" often enough, and when we do think about it, we often restrict it to things of a worldly nature. In business, we may have a vision of how much our company could grow. At home, we may visualize the dream house that we'd like to build. But what about matters of the heart and of the spirit? When you look at your own inner person, do you see what you *could* be as well as what you *are?* When you look at your relationship with God, do you see only *problems* or can you also see some *possibilities?* When you look at your private heart, *what can you see?*

> Vision looks inward and becomes a duty.
> Vision looks outward and becomes aspiration.
> Vision looks upward and becomes faith.
>
> STEPHEN SAMUEL WISE

DO WE EXPECT GOD'S HELP TOO SOON?

If anyone will not work, neither shall he eat.
2 Thessalonians 3:10

GOD GAVE US THE ABILITIES THAT WE HAVE, AND HE EXPECTS US TO EXERCISE OURSELVES IN USING THEM. "If anyone will not work," Paul wrote, "neither shall he eat." In a world obsessed with ease and convenience, the problem of laziness is more of a problem than many of us like to admit. If we're not careful, we may start taking it for granted that the easiest way is always the best way and start looking for ways to cut corners in our spiritual lives. In circumstances where we call upon God for help, we may expect God's help sooner than He is ready to give it.

In all of our needs, we should seek God's help — indeed, we should *rely* on it — but we should never think of dumping work on God simply because we don't want to do it ourselves. If you are a parent who has ever been asked for "help" with homework, you know how this works. There is a huge difference between "Can you help me with this?" and "Will you do this for me?"

"If anyone will not work, neither shall he eat" is the principle. God, our heavenly Father, will not do for us what He's given us the ability to do for ourselves. It may not be the most precise statement in the world theologically, but I believe the old saying is nevertheless true: God helps those who help themselves.

We already have a serious problem with ingratitude, but if God swooped in and rescued us at the first sign of any little difficulty, we'd be even less grateful than we are. (What kind of child is produced by a parent who takes full responsibility for the child's homework and does it all for him: a hardworking child who appreciates the help that he has been given? No, just the opposite.)

So let us expect God's help, but let us not expect it too soon. Sometimes God waits to help us until we have learned — the hard way — the insufficiency of our own efforts. Out of all the things we need His help with, we need His help in learning our dependence on Him. And the best way God can teach us that we need His help is by letting us do without it for a while. After that, we're in a much better position to be grateful for the help when it does come. And it surely *will* come . . . when God sees the time is right.

When you are at the end of your rope,
God is there to catch you — but not before.

ERWIN W. LUTZER

October 2
GIVING THE GREATER THANKS

Every good gift and every perfect gift is from above,
and comes down from the Father of lights . . .
James 1:17

GOD IS THE GIVER OF EVERY GOOD GIFT, AND LEARNING TO SEE
THE GOODNESS OF HIS GIFTS AND GIVE PROPER THANKS FOR
THEM IS ONE OF OUR GREATEST NEEDS IN LIFE. God blesses us in
many different ways, and some of these are more direct and obvious than others. It is at the times when God's gifts come to us
indirectly (through other people, for example) and in ambiguous
ways (they may seem more like difficulties than blessings) that the
appropriateness of giving thanks may be hard for us to grasp.

Without a doubt, we ought to give thanks to all the other
human beings around us who do so many wonderful things for
us. In our "interdependent" world, we all have to have the help of
others, and we need to be willing to acknowledge that help.

But the help that other people give us ultimately comes from
God, and we need to be even more thankful to Him than we are to
them. In very many cases, God acts in our lives by the instrumen-
tality of other people's doings, and so while we shouldn't fail to
thank the "instruments," it is God who should be given the greater
thanks. Let me share with you two compliments that came to me
by email a few years ago only two weeks apart, both of which
touched me deeply. One person wrote, "You have helped me to
grow spiritually more than anyone else I've ever read." The other
person wrote, "You are perhaps the one person that the Lord has
used the most to bring me closer to Him." Both of these thanks
were greatly appreciated by me. But the latter, bless that person's
soul, put the emphasis where it certainly needs to be — *on God!*

In truth, there is nothing for which we can't give this "greater
thanks." Everything God allows us to experience is, if not enjoyable, at least useful (James 1:2), and we should learn to thank Him
for all that happens. Joseph, for example, was thankful that his
brothers had sold him into Egyptian slavery (Genesis 45:5-8). Such
"useful" things are obviously harder to attribute to God and to
give Him thanks for. But Paul said, "In everything, give thanks"
(1 Thessalonians 5:18), and I believe he meant just what he said.

Take everything that comes into your life as
being from the hand of God, not from the hand of man.
JEANNE MARIE DE LA MOTHE GUYON

October 3
CHRISTIAN PESSIMISM

And the world is passing away, and the lust of it . . .
1 John 2:17

IS THE GOSPEL OF CHRIST OPTIMISTIC OR PESSIMISTIC? We normally think of it as optimistic (and in the long run it certainly is), but John's statement would not strike many modern people as being very upbeat: "the world is passing away, and the lust of it." A. W. Tozer wrote, "Strange as it may be, the holiest souls who have ever lived have earned the reputation for being pessimistic." Have you ever considered that spiritual growth might require you to start being more pessimistic about some things than you have been?

The mature Christian is pessimistic about the powers of the human mind. While the world grows more confident that, given enough time, the human mind can find a solution to every problem, the Christian understands the built-in limitations of human thought.

The mature Christian is pessimistic about the perfectibility of human character. The problems that beset individual human beings have roots that go far deeper than psychology or sociology can ever reach. Apart from God, the human psyche is incurably sick.

The mature Christian is pessimistic about the progress of human society. If Christianity is true, this world is not going to get significantly better. There may be occasional respites from the general degradation, but the long-term spiral is going down, down, down.

So there are some things that the mature, healthy Christian is pessimistic about, and unfortunately, the things the Christian is most doubtful of are *those that the world has its highest hopes set on.* When the Christian doubts the powers of the human mind, the perfectibility of human character, and the progress of human society, he calls into question the very foundation of modern activity: that "every day in every way, we are getting better and better" (and if we're not, "it's only a matter of time until we do"). But the bad news has to be accepted before the good news will sound good. If we're not stripped of our delusions about human power and progress, we'll never be humble enough to hear what God has in mind. So let's just go ahead and give up on the present world. As Christians, we should be too *optimistic about the new heavens and earth* to be anything other than *pessimistic about the present ones.*

The cross-carrying Christian . . . is both a confirmed pessimist and an optimist the like of which is to be found nowhere else on earth.

A. W. TOZER

BETWEEN PROMISE AND PERFORMANCE: A GAP?

> And in this I give advice: It is to your advantage not only to be doing
> what you began and were desiring to do a year ago; but now you also must
> complete the doing of it; that as there was a readiness to desire it, so there
> also may be a completion out of what you have.
> *2 Corinthians 8:10,11*

REACHING TOWARD HEAVEN REQUIRES SETTING SOME GOALS AND MAKING SOME COMMITMENTS. Without firm commitments, the hard things just aren't likely to get done. So there is great value in making plans and promises. In scriptural language, that means "purposing" what we will do (2 Corinthians 9:7). Then, having committed ourselves, there must not be a gap between our promise and our performance. As there was a "readiness to desire it," so there must also be a "completion" of it (2 Corinthians 8:11).

Even in terms of our short-term spiritual growth, we need to make more specific plans than we sometimes do. If all we have is a vague, unspecific desire to "make progress," we won't move ahead much. We have to commit ourselves to some specific goals.

The ultimate purpose of spiritual growth, of course, is reaching the long-term goal of seeing God's face in heaven. Having confessed our faith and obeyed the gospel, we have made what amounts to a commitment to go to heaven. But I believe it will help us to make that commitment explicit by *verbally promising those near and dear to us* that we are not going to give up. Folks need to have a pledge from us that we're going to do what's right.

Then, as we've said, we must *keep* our commitment, and that's not always easy. But let me tell you: it's a whole lot easier to keep the commitments you have made than the ones you haven't made.

The French writer La Rochefoucauld may have been a cynic, but on the gap between most people's promises and performance he was not wrong: "We promise according to our hopes and perform according to our fears." In other words, what we promise we'll do is often based on ideals and hopes that are lofty, but what we actually end up doing is just the least we can get by with, the bare minimum that will keep us out of trouble. But it doesn't have to be that way. If La Rochefoucauld described the norm, can we not, as people reaching toward heaven, be *exceptions* to the norm?

> We promise according to our hopes
> and perform according to our fears.
> FRANÇOIS DE LA ROCHEFOUCAULD

October 5

FIGHTING THE UNDERTOW

Peter answered and said to Him, "Even if all are made to stumble
because of You, I will never be made to stumble." Jesus said to him,
"Assuredly, I say to you that this night, before the rooster crows,
you will deny Me three times." *Matthew 26:33,34*

WE SET OUT TO "SWIM" TOWARD THE LORD, BUT SOMETIMES THE "UNDERTOW" GETS US. Peter's example shows how easy it is to profess love for the Lord in our words and then fall short in our deeds. As long as we live in this world, the devil will always make sure that we meet resistance in carrying out our good intentions.

When we're tempted to sin, there is always a "way of escape" (1 Corinthians 10:13). However strong the undertow may be, we never have to give in to it. The positive choice is always possible.

But though the way of escape will always be provided, it has to be *taken* before it will do us any good. The benefits of the Lord's protection and help are not automatic or involuntary — they have to be appropriated by a free-will choice to say "No!" to sin.

Without God's help, of course, we would be hopelessly lost. But even so, we have to exert ourselves to overcome our obstacles. We have to fight the undertow. And many are the scriptural exhortations to that end. "Put to death your members which are on the earth" (Colossians 3:5). "Put off . . . the old man" (Ephesians 4:22). "Do not let sin reign in your mortal body, that you should obey it in its lusts" (Romans 6:12). The point should be hard to miss.

But whatever sinful forces are out there, the face of the worst one can be seen in the mirror. As Walt Kelly said in *Pogo*, "We have met the enemy and he is us." The "old man" that Paul said must be put to death is not a nice person, and each of us needs to be very honest about the "me" that we would be without God. This person has to die. If not, the new person that Christ can create will never have a chance to live: "I have been crucified with Christ; it is no longer I who live, but Christ lives in me" (Galatians 2:20).

God harden me against myself,
This coward with pathetic voice
Who craves for ease, and rest, and joys.
Myself, arch-traitor to myself
My hollowest friend, my deadliest foe,
My clog whatever road I go.
Yet One there is can curb myself,
Can roll the strangling load from me,
Break off the yoke and set me free.

CHRISTINA GEORGINA ROSSETTI

October 6

WHY DO WE DREAD OUR GREATEST DAY?

For we who are in this tent groan, being burdened, not because we want
to be unclothed, but further clothed, that mortality may be swallowed up by
life. Now He who has prepared us for this very thing is God, who also has
given us the Spirit as a guarantee. *2 Corinthians 5:4,5*

IN OUR MORE HONEST MOMENTS, HOW MANY OF US CAN SAY THAT
WE LONG FOR OUR MORTALITY TO BE "SWALLOWED UP BY LIFE" AS
PAUL DID? The truth is, we're quite happy here, and we don't want
to die. We want to hang on to this life as long as we possibly can.

But why do we dread the day of our death, which from the
Christian perspective is the greatest day of all? What is there about
trading this "tent" for an eternal dwelling that is so unappealing?

Obviously, we may dread the *manner* of death. Certain *ways* of
dying are extremely painful, while others are completely humiliat-
ing. If we had our choice, I imagine most of us would like to pass
away quietly in our sleep when the time comes. But most of us
don't want that time to come until we have gotten everything we
want out of *this* life. We dread death *itself*. It is unwelcome.

Paul more than once compared the Christian life to a race
being run by an athlete, so let's think of it that way for a moment.
The right-thinking Christian doesn't dread death any more than a
runner dreads reaching the finish line. Can you imagine a runner
who, rounding the last turn and seeing the finish line ahead, says,
"Oh my! I don't want this race to be over! I think I'll slow down
and see if I can be the very last runner to reach the finish"?

Peter speaks of receiving the *end* or *goal* of our faith, the salvation of our souls (1 Peter 1:9). Unless the Lord comes back first, it
will be at our death that we reach this goal. So that day will be our
graduation, the culmination of all our training in godliness. Do
we want to be that "professional student" who dreads graduation
because it will be the end of a situation that he's loathe to give up?
Don't we *want* to graduate? And if, contrary to what we expect,
the Lord indicates that our training is finished sooner rather than
later, where is the problem in that . . . if we're reaching forward?

By all standards, death is the most dreaded event. Our society will pay
any price to prolong life. Just one more month, or even another day. Perhaps
our desire to postpone death reflects our dissatisfaction with God's ultimate
purpose. Remember, his work isn't finished until we are glorified. Most of
us would like to see God's work remain half finished. We're glad we are
called and justified, but we're not too excited about being glorified.

ERWIN W. LUTZER

October 7
WHEN TO CELEBRATE

A good name is better than precious ointment,
And the day of death than the day of one's birth.
Ecclesiastes 7:1

OUR CELEBRATIONS SAY A LOT ABOUT OUR VALUES AND PRIORITIES. For example, we send *congratulatory* cards to friends when they have a new baby, but if the same friends had a loved one who died and went to heaven, we'd send them a *sympathy* card. What are the values that cause us to celebrate a birth and not a death? Do we agree with the text in Ecclesiastes 7:1 or not?

"The day of death [is better] than the day of one's birth" is not a *universal* statement, of course. Death's not better in every way, just some ways. But the text implies that the ways in which death is better are *very important*. In other words, when all the pros and cons have been added up, death has more pluses than minuses.

But it's only for the person *saved from sin* that death has more pluses. To die in sin, having rejected God's conditions for grace and forgiveness, is to suffer the worst fate possible for a human being. Others may have benefited from his life, but as far as *that* person is concerned, it would be better if he'd never been born.

But at least for the faithful Christian, there should be a sense of relief as he or she nears the end of life. If most of the storms are behind and the harbor is in sight, shouldn't there be a joyful sense of completion and closure at journey's end? Is not "the end of a thing . . . better than its beginning" (Ecclesiastes 7:8)? As a writer, I can tell you that the joy of finishing a book far outweighs the excitement of beginning a new one. And with heaven on the last page, the "book" of our earthly life should be a joy to finish too.

In reality, a baby's birth into this world is a melancholy event, one of those experiences that the wise call "bittersweet." Naturally we rejoice, but we also know that pain and sorrow lie ahead for the child. The gate is narrow and the way is difficult that leads to life (Matthew 7:14). It is through many tribulations that we enter the kingdom of God (Acts 14:22). So isn't some kind of celebration in order when the fight has been fought and the race has been run? When we act as if it is better to have our temporal life in front of us, what are we thinking? Whose value system are we using when we pronounce birth totally "good" and death totally "bad"?

A man should be mourned at his birth, not at his death.
CHARLES DE SECONDAT MONTESQUIEU

QUESTIONS, QUESTIONS, QUESTIONS

Therefore let those who suffer according to the will of God
commit their souls to Him in doing good, as to a faithful Creator.
1 Peter 4:19

L IFE IN THIS WORLD PRESENTS US WITH SOME SERIOUS QUESTIONS. Many problems are hard to figure out, and much that happens is hard to explain. Our Father has revealed the answers to all of the questions we need to know (Deuteronomy 29:29), but He has left many other things unexplained. For now, He asks us to trust Him enough to obey His instructions and take it for granted that every question *has* a good answer, whether we know the answer or not.

Sometimes we make the mistake of thinking that we can't have any peace of mind if we don't know how everything works and what's going to happen. But God offers a different kind of security, one grounded not in our knowledge but rather in our trust. Paul's confidence, for example, came not from having every question answered but from knowing the person of God: "I know whom I have believed and am persuaded that He is able to keep what I have committed to Him until that Day" (2 Timothy 1:12).

Now the kind of faith that Paul had was not "blind" faith or mere credulity. He was a legal scholar, and it's doubtful that he would have come to trust God as he did without being shown *evidence* that God could be trusted. But having acknowledged the power of the evidence, Paul was willing to live his life (and it was a *difficult* life) on the assumption that God would take care of him.

When we reach the point where we believe the evidence for God's trustworthiness is compelling, then we are ready to do what Peter talked about in today's text: *commit* ourselves to Him. In the confidence that our God is a "faithful" Creator, we can make the calculated decision to trust Him — especially in situations where we have some questions that we don't know the answers to.

In all of this, the *future* must be factored into our thinking. As a thing that is "unseen," the future is one of the primary things that faith deals with. Faith does not ignore questions or minimize their importance, but it does exercise *patience*. Faith is willing to wait and see what happens. History is, after all, a story, and in a story, the conflicts don't usually get resolved until the end.

Faith makes the discords of the present
the harmonies of the future.
R OBERT C OLLYER

YOU HOPED FOR IT, BUT IT DIDN'T HAPPEN

At my first defense no one stood with me, but all forsook me.
2 Timothy 4:16

HOPE IS SIMPLY ONE OF THE FINEST THINGS IN LIFE. Ultimately, of course, our hope must be in heaven, but between now and the day of our death, there are many other good things to hope for. There is a big difference, however, between hoping for heaven and hoping for anything in this life: *despite our best efforts, our earthly hopes may not materialize.* God has not guaranteed that we'll get married, have children, and live as long as we'd like to. We may hope for blessings like these, but the reality is, we may not get some of them. What then should be our attitude when we hope for some good, honorable thing . . . and it just doesn't happen?

First, we should rise above bitterness, self-pity, and the like. When no one stood with Paul at his first defense, he must have been painfully disappointed, but he doesn't seem to have been bitter about it. Painful feelings don't have to produce sinful thoughts.

Second, we should accept that God sometimes has a different plan and learn to rejoice in that plan. If we ever seek something good from God and He says "No," it is always because He has a better gift in mind. In our disappointment, we can yield our will to His and then, over time, learn to be glad that His way truly was better.

Third, we should not quit hoping for things. It is better to have loved and lost than never to have loved at all. When we allow ourselves to long for something deeply and that longing ends up being disappointed, the very worst thing we can do is close up our hearts. That type of play-it-safe "conservatism" is deadly to the human spirit, and no one is pleased with it but our eternal enemy.

In summary, I would suggest what might seem like a strange thing: *disappointment is not necessarily an emotion to be avoided.* These days, many people assume that painful emotions are inherently evil and should be avoided at all costs. But that is a foolish philosophy, is it not? Vanilla is fine, but it would be a boring world if there were no flavor but vanilla. And we would soon grow tired of pleasantness if that were the only emotion available to us. Things like disappointment not only add variety to our lives, they add richness and texture to our character. Just ask the Man of Sorrows.

Disappointment is often the salt of life.
THEODORE PARKER

October 10

THE RESULT OF REFUSING GOD

And even as they did not like to retain God in their knowledge, God gave
them over to a debased mind, to do those things which are not fitting . . .
Romans 1:28

A LL OF OUR BLESSINGS HAVE RESPONSIBILITIES ATTACHED TO
THEM, AND THIS IS ESPECIALLY TRUE OF OUR FREE WILL. Right
now, we can use our freedom in any way we wish, but the blessing
of freedom has a responsibility attached to it: there is coming a day
of *reckoning*, and when it comes, we're going to have to answer for
the use of our freedom. So as we exercise the gift of our free will
day after day, tremendous *consequences* hang in the balance.

In this life, it is possible to refuse God and reject His rule over
us. Having given us a will that is free, God won't make our choice
for us. He loves us, but He won't force us to love Him back. And
insofar as eternal salvation is concerned, God won't compel us
to be saved. "Now then," Paul wrote, "we are ambassadors for
Christ, as though God were pleading through us: we implore you
on Christ's behalf, be reconciled to God" (2 Corinthians 5:20). Such
an appeal would be meaningless if we had no choice in the matter.

In Romans 1, Paul used some vivid language to describe those
in his day who had rejected God. They had "suppressed" the truth
about God (v.18). "Although they knew God, they did not glorify
Him as God" (v.21). They "exchanged the truth of God for the lie"
(v.25). And they "did not like to retain God in their knowledge"
(v.28). These expressions reflect not simply an ignorance of God
but a *willful* ignorance, a deliberate rejection of God's authority.

In view of this, God "gave them up to uncleanness" (v.24). He
"gave them up to vile passions" (v.26), and "gave them over to a
debased mind, to do those things which are not fitting" (v.28). In
effect, God *withdrew His restraining hand* and let them plunge to the
depths of their desired rebellion. God *abandoned them* to their sinful choice, and we can hardly imagine a more terrible thing.

Yet there *is* a more terrible thing: the *final* abandonment when
God withdraws Himself *forever* from those who have rejected Him.
At that time, God turns away, for eternity, from those who have
turned away from Him. And that will be the anguish of hell: being
abandoned by a God who would have loved us if we'd let Him.

> The gnashing of teeth . . . despair, when men
> see themselves abandoned by God
>
> MARTIN LUTHER

October 11

IMAGINE A FINAL, ULTIMATE LOSS OF HOPE

Now when neither sun nor stars appeared for many days, and no small
tempest beat on us, all hope that we would be saved was finally given up.
Acts 27:20

THE ONLY HOPE THAT WE REALLY HAVE IS THE HOPE OF GOD'S
GRACE AND FORGIVENESS. Whatever other hopes we may have
are little more than dust and ashes if we fail to find salvation and
eternal life in Him. "For what profit is it to a man if he gains the
whole world, and loses his own soul? Or what will a man give
in exchange for his soul?" (Matthew 16:26). Without the hope of
heaven, we are "lost" in every important sense of that word.

But what if we *had* no such hope? There is nothing more
frightful than the loss of hope. When Luke tells us that, on the
treacherous winter voyage to Rome, "all hope that we would be
saved was finally given up," we sense the sickening despair of the
mariners. But that kind of despair is not nearly the worst kind.

Imagine being without the hope of *heaven*. Many live without
this hope, of course, but few think about it very much. The need
for God is planted deep within us, having been put there by our
Creator, but we often deny that need and expend our energies so
frantically in the pursuit of other needs that we forget about our
need for God, at least for all *practical* purposes. Even so, it is still
there begging to be filled. But what if no such fulfillment existed?

We need to contemplate more seriously than we sometimes
do what it is, or would be, to be without "hope and without God
in the world" (Ephesians 2:12). We need to quit being naive and
face the ugly reality of life without God. To have had the hope of
eternal life and then lost it is to be in a most pitiable condition.

But imagine having lost the hope of life with God . . . *and there
be no chance of ever getting it back!* The horror of that hopelessness
is perhaps the main thing that will make hell, hell. "What do the
damned endure, but despair" (William Congreve). Yet if we persist
in our rebellion against God, despite His pleas for us to do otherwise, that is exactly what we are setting ourselves up for. In hell,
there will be no more chance of "reaching forward." There will be
no chance of ever being anything but lost, banished from God's
presence. In hell, there will be many things — turmoil, torment,
and terror — but one thing is certain: there will not be any *hope*.

All hope abandon, ye who enter here.
DANTE ALIGHIERI

October 12

THE KINGDOM OF SELF

"O Jerusalem, Jerusalem, the one who kills the prophets and stones
those who are sent to her! How often I wanted to gather your children
together, as a hen gathers her chicks under her wings, but you
were not willing! See! Your house is left to you desolate . . ."
Matthew 23:37,38

FREEDOM OF THE WILL MEANS THAT WE HAVE A CHOICE TO MAKE
CONCERNING GOD: SHALL WE SUBMIT TO HIS WILL OR NOT? As
our Creator, God is our Sovereign. We were created to live within
the protective boundaries of His authority, but we have rebelled
against our King and tried to set up our own kingdom. In this
"kingdom of self," the rule is "Not Thy will but *mine* be done."
Free to choose, we have often chosen our own will over God's.

We make a choice between God's will and our own every
time we decide between two courses of action, even in the "little"
choices that we make daily. With every decision, we either say
"Yes" to God or "No." We either submit to His will or refuse it.

But this is also true in a larger sense. The longer we live, and
the more our "little" choices begin to multiply, a pattern begins to
emerge. Over time, we develop a "character," a clear tendency to
obey God or disregard Him. As one decision gets added to another, we find ourselves moving either in God's direction or away
from Him. Our *lives* begin to be either a "Yes" or a "No" to God.

When we stand before God in judgment, God's verdict will
simply be an acknowledgement of the choice that *we* have made
— *either to submit to His rightful sovereignty over our lives or to reject
that sovereignty.* His pronouncement of eternal blessing or condemnation will not be arbitrary; it will be the only verdict that He can
render, given the choice that we have made while we lived.

When we were young most of us had some older person give
us this advice: *be careful what you want in life, because you are liable to
get it.* If this is true in life, it is even more true in eternity. At judgment, God will simply give us what we have said we wanted, as
evidenced by the choices that we made. The saved will be given
their hearts' true desire, God Himself, and to the condemned,
God will simply say, "All right, have it *your* way." As George
MacDonald said, "The one principle of hell is, 'I am my own.'"

If you insist on having your own way, you will get it.
Hell is the enjoyment of your own way forever.
DANTE ALIGHIERI

TOO LATE TO OBEY

. . . in flaming fire taking vengeance on those who do not know God,
and on those who do not obey the gospel of our Lord Jesus Christ.
2 Thessalonians 1:8

WHILE WE LIVE, WE MAY CHANGE OUR MINDS ABOUT GOD, BUT WHEN WE DIE, IT WILL BE TOO LATE TO CHANGE. At least, it will be too late to change the *consequences* of our choice. If we die in unbelief, we will certainly become believers when the awesome reality of God is no longer avoidable, but by that time it will be too late to do anything about it. It will be too late to obey God.

"For it is written: 'As I live, says the LORD, every knee shall bow to Me, and every tongue shall confess to God'" (Romans 14:11). When we meet our Maker, there will be no possibility of denying His existence. At that time, every person who has ever lived will acknowledge God's greatness, but for those who have never acknowledged Him before, this newfound "faith" will only be like that of the demons who "believe — and tremble!" (James 2:19).

If we live in rebellion against God, passing up every opportunity to repent and seek His forgiveness, and then die, the judgment day will find us falling at God's feet and begging for His mercy, not in love but in *fear*. We will cry to the mountains and the rocks, "Fall on us and hide us from the face of Him who sits on the throne and from the wrath of the Lamb! For the great day of His wrath has come, and who is able to stand?" (Revelation 6:16,17).

Paul used striking language to describe the coming of the Lord at the end of the world: He will be "revealed from heaven with His mighty angels, in flaming fire taking vengeance on those who do not know God, and on those who do not obey the gospel of our Lord Jesus Christ. These shall be punished with everlasting destruction from the presence of the Lord and from the glory of His power" (2 Thessalonians 1:7-9). If the lost are those who "do not obey the gospel," then *the time when the gospel may be obeyed* is a matter of great importance. That time is right now, but it won't continue indefinitely. At some point, it will simply be too late.

If we are among the lost, one of the worst aspects of hell will be the *helplessness* of the whole situation. Not having *wanted* to see the truth, we never did see it . . . until it was too late. And at that point, nothing can be done but to agonize over the truth. Forever.

Hell is truth seen too late.

TYRON EDWARDS

October 14

FORWARD!

"We remember the fish which we ate freely in Egypt, the cucumbers, the melons, the leeks, the onions, and the garlic; but now our whole being is dried up; there is nothing at all except this manna before our eyes!"
Numbers 11:5,6

SPIRITUALLY SPEAKING, WE CAN'T GO FORWARD WHILE WE'RE STILL IN REVERSE. A better tomorrow can only be ours if we're willing to let go of today, and if today has been pretty good, we may be reluctant to do that. That growth and progress always involve some *loss* is a hard truth to accept. But it's true: we can't grow without letting go. *Things can't change for the better without changing.*

So would you say that it's good for a person to be "nostalgic"? Well, nostalgia has a good side, obviously. Looking back and remembering past blessings can be a strengthening experience.

But it should be equally obvious that nostalgia can have a bad side. We may spend so much time thinking about the past that we don't do the work today that would move us forward. But even worse than that, we may look at the past from such a *crooked perspective* that it makes us want to go *backward rather than forward!* In the wilderness, the people of Israel found themselves remembering Egypt in such a way: "We remember the fish which we ate freely in Egypt, the cucumbers, the melons, the leeks, the onions, and the garlic; but now our whole being is dried up; there is nothing at all except this manna before our eyes!" The wilderness didn't seem like a good place to go forward into. They thought they would rather go back to the "good life" they had in Egypt.

Sometimes, going forward does move us into a more difficult set of circumstances, at least for a while. And if our main priority in life is ease or comfort, then progress won't be very appealing to us. But surely we can set our sights on some higher things, can't we? There are some destinations worth traveling to no matter how hard the road may be, and heaven is certainly one of them.

So it's not wrong to indulge in nostalgia, but we must be careful not to *over*-indulge. "Do not say, 'Why were the former days better than these?' For you do not inquire wisely concerning this" (Ecclesiastes 7:10). Life in Christ is about *progress*. It is for those who want to go *forward* — beyond even the best days of the past.

> It is of no use to pray for the old days; stand square where you are and make the present better than any past has been.
>
> OSWALD CHAMBERS

WHAT OUR CREATOR HAS IN MIND

And Jesus said to her, "Neither do I condemn you; go and sin no more."
John 8:11

IN THE STORY OF THE WOMAN TAKEN IN ADULTERY, JESUS DID NOT MINIMIZE THE SERIOUSNESS OF HER SIN, BUT HE SAW IN HER MORE THAN A WOMAN WHO HAD SINNED. Where others may have only seen problems, Jesus saw possibilities. He encouraged her not to reach backward to what she *had* been but to reach forward to what she *could* be. "Neither do I condemn you; go and sin no more."

In our dealings with others, most of us see the importance of doing what Jesus did: we know the value of helping people to see their own potential. When people know that we have positive expectations of them, they very often rise to meet those expectations.

Why is it, then, that we so rarely "believe the best" in ourselves? Why do we focus on our problems so exclusively that we lose sight of our possibilities? We defeat ourselves just as surely as we defeat others when we do this. How much better it would be if we saw ourselves as someone worth "salvaging," someone for whom the Lord was willing to die. No matter how serious our sin, would not Jesus say the same thing to us: "Go and sin no more"?

Painful memories can be helpful if they humble us and make us more compassionate toward others. But there is a difference between being humbled and being *humiliated*. If our memories drag us so far down into the black pit of despair that we quit reaching forward to heaven, then we've let our memories do something that God never intended. Even after forgiving us, God is still aware of our past, and we should remain aware of it too. But although our past is a part of the truth about us, it is not the *whole* truth. If we've been forgiven, that is also a part of the truth, not to mention the truth of what our *future* can be with God's help. *That* is the part of the situation that God is most interested in. So we need to adopt His perspective on our lives. We need to be concerned not only with where we've been but with where we can go.

So the crucial question is never "What have I done?" but "What does God have in mind for me in the future?" And more important, "Am I *cooperating* with what He has in mind for me?" That way of thinking about things can make all the difference.

In Christ we can move out of our past
into a meaningful present and a breathtaking future.

ERWIN W. LUTZER

THE IDEA OF "SPENDING"

*"Again, the kingdom of heaven is like a merchant seeking
beautiful pearls, who, when he had found one pearl of great price,
went and sold all that he had and bought it."*
Matthew 13:45,46

ONE MEASURE OF HOW VALUABLE SOMETHING IS TO US IS WHAT
WE WOULD GIVE UP IN ORDER TO HAVE IT. As for the kingdom
of heaven, Jesus said it is "like a merchant seeking beautiful pearls,
who, when he had found one pearl of great price, went and sold
all that he had and bought it." If we wouldn't do what this man
did, we probably don't know a precious "pearl" when we see one.

Most societies operate on the principle of "exchange." No one
can do everything that needs to be done or provide everything
that needs to be provided for himself. So we "exchange" things. If
you have something that I need, then I exchange something I have
for the thing that you have. This happens every time we spend
money, but it happens at other times too. In non-monetary transac-
tions, some resource other than money is "expended."

Now something like this principle operates in the spiritual
realm also. Paul, for example, said that the sacrifices he made for
his brethren amounted to an "expenditure" of himself: "I will very
gladly spend and be spent for your souls" (2 Corinthians 12:15).

Sometimes, however, we aren't as willing to spend as Paul
was. We hoard what we have and hold on to things that we should
let go of. But the truth is, everything we've been given right now
is "expendable" — it's all for the purpose of being *spent*. Getting to
heaven with a large "reserve" is not what life on earth is about!

We are often encouraged to "count our blessings," and that
is certainly something we should do. But as we count our *present*
blessings, let us also think about the *future* blessings that lie before
us. We can't have these greater things without "trading in" some
lesser things for them, and we should be willing to do that. As we
grow, we should have a clearer vision of what we would relinquish in order to gain what we don't yet have, and especially what
we would let go of to go to *heaven*. And frankly, if there is *anything*
in this life — even the best of the best — that we wouldn't exchange for heaven, then our values are not what they ought to be.

One half of knowing what you want is knowing
what you must give up before you get it.
SIDNEY COE HOWARD

October 17

DISAPPOINTMENT NEED NOT DEFEAT US

This punishment which was inflicted by the majority is sufficient
for such a man, so that, on the contrary, you ought rather to forgive and
comfort him, lest perhaps such a one be swallowed up with too much
sorrow. Therefore I urge you to reaffirm your love to him.
2 Corinthians 2:6-8

PAUL URGED THE CORINTHIANS TO FORGIVE AND COMFORT THE MAN WHO HAD BEEN DISCIPLINED, LEST HE BE OVERWHELMED BY SORROW AND GIVE IN TO DESPAIR. Apparently, he had repented of the sin for which Paul had commanded them to withdraw from him (1 Corinthians 5:1-13), and so the need was not for more discipline but for support and encouragement in his new path.

This event at Corinth illustrates an important point. When we have disappointed God, we should be disappointed in ourselves, and if others know about it, they also should be disappointed in us. But disappointment need not *defeat* us. If our sorrow is of a godly sort, it will lead us to repentance (2 Corinthians 7:8-10), and having repented, we can *hold a steady course in a new direction.*

Past failures can play a positive role in our lives. This is one of the hardest lessons in life to learn, but it is true. To see that it is, we need only look at the life of a man like Paul. In his past were horrible things, painful to remember. But having turned to God and received the forgiveness of those sins, the regret that Paul would have continued to feel was not a negative force in his life but a positive one. Remembering what he had done made him a humbler man. It also made him more compassionate toward others who were caught in the net of sin, and it made him work very hard in the Lord's service to show his gratitude for God's grace.

But past failures can be destructive if we let them be so. If we give in to self-pity, concerned only with what we have lost by our mistakes, then disappointment can eat us up. "The sorrow of the world," Paul wrote, "produces death" (2 Corinthians 7:10).

So we must make a choice. We must choose that our sorrow for past sins will be godly sorrow rather than the sorrow of the world. And more than that, a little *defiance of the devil* will help us. Our adversary wants us to be consumed and destroyed by our painful memories. We must make sure he does not get his way.

Out of every disappointment there is a treasure.
Satan whispers, "All is lost." God says, "Much can be gained."

FRANCES J. ROBERTS

October 18
GOD KNOWS WE NEED SOME STORMS

If you endure chastening, God deals with you as with sons;
for what son is there whom a father does not chasten?
Hebrews 12:7

STRANGE AS IT SEEMS, THE DIFFICULTIES IN OUR LIVES ARE EVI-
DENCE OF GOD'S LOVE. He knows that we need some storms in
our lives, and He loves us too much to give us only what we want
and never what we need. If we were coddled and protected from
ever having to deal with difficulty, the results would be disastrous,
as any parent knows who has seen what "spoiling" does to a child.

In a familiar text, James wrote, "My brethren, count it all joy
when you fall into various trials, knowing that the testing of your
faith produces patience" (James 1:2,3). Hardship is not pleasant,
and we shouldn't try to trick our minds into thinking that it is. The
point of this text is that the *result* of hardship is something we can
be thankful for. We can "count it all joy" that a particular hardship
draws us closer to God, although the pain itself is not joyful.

There is literally nothing that happens in this world that
can't be put to good use in some way. Even the things that Satan
confronts us with can strengthen us if we deal with them properly.
God does not tempt us, of course, but He does allow Satan to do
so. Within the limits imposed by God (1 Corinthians 10:13), our
adversary is allowed to make life difficult for us. Presumably, God
could keep this from happening, but He deems it better for us to
deal with the difficulty than to be isolated from it altogether.

So it is naive to *expect* that life will always be easy. When we
encounter serious obstacles on our way to heaven, we shouldn't
be surprised. This happens to be a hard world, and godly people
aren't going to get through it painlessly. Jesus certainly didn't.

But more than that, we shouldn't *want* life always to be easy.
Whatever hardship God sends, or allows to be sent, into our lives,
we should embrace the "problem" with *gratitude*. Paul's example
in dealing with his "thorn in the flesh" illustrates this principle.
It was a "messenger of Satan" (2 Corinthians 12:7) and not a gift
from God. But Paul was grateful for it anyway — *because of the*
result. "Therefore," Paul wrote, "I take pleasure in infirmities, in
reproaches, in needs, in persecutions, in distresses, for Christ's
sake. For when I am weak, then I am strong" (2 Corinthians 12:10).

All sunshine makes the desert.

ARABIAN PROVERB

October 19
WHAT DID YOU EXPECT?

Beloved, do not think it strange concerning
the fiery trial which is to try you, as though some
strange thing happened to you.
1 Peter 4:12

PETER ENCOURAGED HIS CHRISTIAN FRIENDS TO EXPECT HARD-SHIP, AND EVEN PERSECUTION, IN THIS WORLD. "Do not think it strange," he wrote, "concerning the fiery trial which is to try you, as though some strange thing happened to you." In counting the cost of discipleship, we shouldn't underestimate the amount of havoc the devil is capable of wreaking in our earthly lives.

In Eden, there was nothing that we would call a "hardship." (Yes, there was work to do, but prior to sin, that work seems to have been totally gratifying.) The truth outside of Eden, however, is that the world is no longer a pleasant place, at least not entirely. The presence of sin having caused God to withdraw His direct presence from the earth, the world has become a very hard place.

A certain "fellowship" with God has been made possible for us through Jesus Christ (1 John 1:3), but this is a far cry from what we were created to enjoy. Having been made in the image of God, we deeply need the kind of relationship with God that Adam and Eve had. We rejoice in what we do have and are grateful for it, but it still leaves us living in a world that is an alien environment.

What we truly need is simply not available to us in this world: *the total joy of perfect communion with our Creator.* That joy will be ours in eternity, if we are found in Christ at the resurrection, but for the time being, we remain as sojourners in this world. Israel encountered no small amount of hardship getting from Egypt to the Promised Land, and our "wilderness" won't be easy, either.

In this world, the only "easy" path is the "course of least resistance." This is the path always taken by a stream of water as it seeks lower and lower ground. It will never go over an obstacle, and even when it has to go around one, water will always find the easiest way around, the way that requires *as little work as possible.* This, you may have noticed, is what makes rivers crooked, and it makes men and women crooked too. The easy path never goes anywhere but downward, and spiritually, that is not the direction we want to go. Worthwhile destinations always take extra effort.

The course of true anything never does run smooth.
SAMUEL BUTLER

October 20

TO LIVE IS CHRIST, TO DIE IS GAIN

For to me, to live is Christ, and to die is gain.
Philippians 1:21

THIS WORLD IS NOT ALL THERE IS. In addition to the world that we can see, there is also an unseen realm of spiritual reality (2 Corinthians 4:16-18). This spiritual "world" is no less real than the one we live in; if anything, it is more real. The Christian expects that the end of his or her life in this world will be the beginning of life in that other one. Paul, for example, wrote of these two separate worlds, or lives, when he said, "For bodily exercise profits a little, but godliness is profitable for all things, having promise of the life that now is and of that which is to come" (1 Timothy 4:8).

The Scriptures describe the "life which is to come" in a number of different ways. It is "the world to come" (Hebrews 2:5), "the age to come" (Mark 10:30), the "everlasting kingdom" (2 Peter 1:11), etc. Often it is simply called "heaven" (Philippians 3:20).

That world exists even now, but we do not have direct contact with it. We live in this world for the time being, but at death, we will move from this one into that one. The death of our physical bodies, which is a consequence of sin having entered the world, will terminate our sojourn in this world, but it will not terminate our existence. Death will be a transition from one life to another.

Now here is the point: if we are faithful Christians, we ought not to be *reluctant* to move out of this life and into the next one. Yes, there are some very delightful things about life in this world, and these enjoyments will be hard to say goodbye to. But that which awaits us, in Christ, is so much greater in its joy that we would be fools not to look forward to it eagerly. Here, we have the good and the better. But at that time, we will have the very best.

For the Christian, then, to live is Christ, and to die is gain. In Christ, the conclusion of a faithful, joyous earthly life is not to be regretted, because it ushers us into the very presence of our Father. What this means is that the Christian has the best of both worlds. By keeping this world in proper perspective, he gets the most out of it that can be gotten. And when the goodness of this temporal world has been experienced and used to the Father's glory, the Father Himself waits for us in eternity with His arms open wide.

Death is but a sharp corner near the beginning
of life's procession down eternity.

JOHN AYSCOUGH

October 21
WHAT IS THE BIGGEST PROBLEM YOU HAVE?

While he was still speaking, another also came and said,
"Your sons and daughters were eating and drinking wine in their oldest
brother's house, and suddenly a great wind came from across the wilderness
and struck the four corners of the house, and it fell on the young people,
and they are dead; and I alone have escaped to tell you!"
Job 1:18,19

A T WHAT POINT WOULD YOU SAY THAT THE "WORST" HAS HAP-
PENED TO YOU? In the story of Job, he might have said the
worst had happened when all of his oxen and donkeys were stolen
by the Sabeans, but worse news was yet to come, and even worse
news after that, and worse and worse. He suffered not one tragedy
but a cascade of tragedies, each one making the ones that went
before seem small by comparison. By the time the worst truly had
come, he probably looked back at the initial loss of his oxen and
donkeys and was ashamed that he had called that a "problem."

In life, there are what we call "problems." A problem is a significant difficulty, something that hinders or hurts us in a major way.
And surely, there is no shortage of such things in the world as it
now is, broken and marred by the consequences of sin and strife.

But in life, there are also what we call "annoyances." These are difficulties of a lesser nature. They can be quite bothersome (think of
a tiny pebble in your shoe), but in the larger scheme of things, they
don't represent any serious threat to anyone's well-being.

Now the interesting thing is that a difficulty that one person
sees as a problem, another person thinks of as just an annoyance.
How do we account for the difference? The answer is simple. *Your
definition of a problem is relative to what you've had to deal with up to
now!* That ache in your leg won't seem like much of a problem if
there ever comes a day when you don't have any legs at all.

So what is the biggest problem you have? Whatever it is, be
aware that things could get worse, as they did in Job's life. But
don't let that scare you or depress you; just let it make you grateful for your present situation. (There are people who would jump
at the chance to have "problems" no worse than yours.) And let
it make you glad for this fact also: the problems you have today
have helped you to see that what you thought were your problems
yesterday weren't really problems — they were only annoyances.

Great pains cause us to forget the small ones.
GERMAN PROVERB

October 22
THE DEAD OF THE NIGHT

For we do not want you to be ignorant, brethren, of our trouble
which came to us in Asia: that we were burdened beyond measure,
above strength, so that we despaired even of life.
2 Corinthians 1:8

L IKE PAUL, WE OCCASIONALLY PASS THROUGH ORDEALS SO SERI-
OUS AND SEEMINGLY HOPELESS THAT WE "DESPAIR EVEN OF LIFE."
It is not that our faith has failed or that we've lost our hope of
heaven. It is just that, as far as the *immediate* crisis is concerned, it
does not look like it is going to be resolved without traumatic loss,
or even death, on our part. Maybe there is a way out, but we can't
see it right now. As in the case of Job's suffering, we may be called
upon to suffer without the aid of any explanation or assurance as
to the outcome, except that God will be the ultimate victor in the
end. Between now and then, we may find ourselves "in the dark."

The dead of the night is a hard time to endure. Things that may be
bearable when the sun is shining are much harder to bear in the
night hours. That is why those who suffer from depression dread
the closing hours of the day, when the daylight begins to vanish
and the darkness closes in. In the dark, pain and sorrow and discouragement are multiplied, especially in the wee hours that we
call the "dead" of the night. These are dangerous hours, when we
find ourselves much more vulnerable to the assaults of Satan.

But we can experience some "dark nights of the soul" even
when the sun is shining. Literal nights may be hard, but there is a
"darkness" that we often have to deal with that has nothing to do
with whether the physical sun is shining. Who among us has not
passed through something like Job's darkness, a time when God is
silent and not even one other person is willing to say anything but
a discouraging word? *The dead of the night is a hard time to endure.*

But what is especially hard is the *continuance* of such times.
We think it might help if we knew when the problem would be
resolved, one way or the other, but no such cut-off date is given to
us. The deadness and the darkness just go on and on and on.

Well, God has not guaranteed that we won't pass through
such murky waters in this world. What He has promised is that
He is our *Redeemer.* All will be well, *in the end.* And so, we endure.

In a really dark night of the soul it is always
three in the morning, day after day.

F. SCOTT FITZGERALD

October 23
ENDURE HARDSHIP

You therefore must endure hardship
as a good soldier of Jesus Christ.
2 Timothy 2:3

A S WE REACH FORWARD TO HEAVEN, THERE IS A CERTAIN AMOUNT OF HARDSHIP THAT WE HAVE TO ENDURE. Given the business that he is in, a soldier wouldn't expect anything other than hardship, and if he is a good soldier, he will simply endure it. And so it is on the spiritual battlefield. Hardship goes with the territory.

In the midst of hardship, our first instinct is to try to get rid of it. But that is not always a possibility. There may be honorable measures that can be taken to minimize the difficulty, but for the Christian, some hardships are unavoidable. Rather than running away from adversity, we'd do better to learn to deal with it.

From God's perspective, our learning to deal with difficulty is often much better than our having it removed. When Paul, for example, prayed that his "thorn in the flesh" be removed, God refused Paul's request and said, "My grace is sufficient for you, for My strength is made perfect in weakness" (2 Corinthians 12:9). In other words, "Paul, you will gain a greater good from continuing to cope with this pain than you would from having it removed. So I won't remove it. What I'll do is help you deal with it." That is not the answer to our prayers that we usually want, but it is the answer that is most conducive to our long term spiritual growth.

Many years ago, I was trying to back away from a problem that I had gotten myself into, and a wise friend told me, "The best way *out* of a problem is usually to go *through* it." When we pray to God for "deliverance," we may be wanting to get out of a difficulty, and we're disappointed to hear the Lord say, "No, let's go *through* it. I will help you." But that is the thrust of Paul's great statement in Philippians 4:13: "I can do all things through Christ who strengthens me." God will never leave us in the midst of any hardship and not supply the resources necessary to deal with it.

Paul urged Timothy to preach the word "in season and out of season" (2 Timothy 4:2). The same goes for discipleship in general. We need to be faithful when it's easy and when it's not. After all, if the Lord can count on us only when His work is easy, what kind of service is that? The worst slacker in the world can do as much.

Enjoy when you can and endure when you must.
JOHANN WOLFGANG VON GOETHE

SHEER DETERMINATION

> Do not fear any of those things which you are about to suffer.
> Indeed, the devil is about to throw some of you into prison, that you
> may be tested, and you will have tribulation ten days. Be faithful
> until death, and I will give you the crown of life.
> *Revelation 2:10*

WHEN THE LORD WARNED THE SAINTS IN SMYRNA THAT THEY WERE GOING TO BE PERSECUTED, HE URGED THEM TO HOLD ON AND REMAIN "FAITHFUL." They were going to be tested, and during their ordeal, the temptation to give up would have to be resisted.

The word "despair" basically means a loss of hope. To despair is to be overcome with a sense of futility and defeat. In that sense, despair is certainly a thing the Christian should stay away from, because there is always hope in Christ and to give up that hope would be an abandonment of faith. But there is a kind of despair that the Christian may feel from time to time, and that is the fear that *in the short term* the outcome of a particular crisis may not be good. The Christian never doubts the outcome of the overall *war* between good and evil, but he knows that Satan may be allowed to win an individual *battle* now and then. So without giving up his long-range hope, the Christian may suffer short-term despair.

In such situations, we need to hang on to our long-range hope and keep going, no matter how desperate the prospects seem to be in the short term. Just as there is a kind of "despair" that is not bad, there is a kind of "stubbornness" that we may engage in. While it is wrong to be perversely unyielding or close-minded, when it comes to hardship, we need to be stubborn enough not to give in to it. Stubbornness in the face of difficulty is a virtue.

Peter wrote, "Gird up the loins of your mind, be sober, and rest your hope fully upon the grace that is to be brought to you at the revelation of Jesus Christ" (1 Peter 1:13). The "girded-up" mind is a *determined* mind, braced for action. Peter is recommending that *we decide in advance that we're not going to give up!*

When they find themselves in despair, many people think they have no choice but to give up. But despair doesn't have to lead to that. If we choose, we can stay the course. Indeed, there is no finer courage than that of the soldier who sees no hope of getting off the battlefield alive but fights on because the *cause* is just.

> Never despair, but if you do, work on in despair.
> EDMUND BURKE

October 25

FAITH AND LOVE GIVE HOPE

. . . remembering without ceasing your work of faith,
labor of love, and patience of hope in our Lord Jesus Christ
in the sight of our God and Father.
1 Thessalonians 1:3

FAITH, HOPE, AND LOVE ARE CLOSELY RELATED IN THE GOSPEL OF CHRIST. Each virtue helps the others to grow, and on the other hand, a failure of any of the three will hinder the other two. In our meditations on "reaching forward," we have seen how very important hope is in the Christian's life. Hope is perhaps the principal thing that moves us toward God and toward heaven. So despair, the loss of hope, is a problem of eternal proportions. Today, let's see how faith and love can keep us from losing our hope.

The hopefulness of faith. Faith, when all is said and done, comes down to "trust." It means that, based on the mountain of evidence that God has kept His word in the past, we make the decision to leave the future in His hands. So faith makes possible a hope that is based on *trust* — trust in the Creator of heaven and earth.

The hopefulness of love. Love is the ultimate optimist. It is not naive, and if the evidence requires a negative assessment, love will go with the evidence. But love is a defender of *hope.* Rather than give up at the first sign of trouble, love *"bears* all things, *believes* all things, *hopes* all things, *endures* all things" (1 Corinthians 13:7).

So in the gospel, we have faith, hope, and love, these three. But Paul said the "greatest of these is love" (1 Corinthians 13:13). When all else fails and our hopes hang by a thread, it will always be love that keeps that thread from breaking. *How could we give up on the One who has never, not even in His darkest hour, given up on us?*

In our text for today, Paul spoke of three things in the Thessalonians' lives: their *work of faith,* their *labor of love,* and their *patience of hope.* When our work is based on our trust in God's faithfulness and our labor grows out of a love that is pure and strong, then the hope that is in Christ will produce a steadfastness that would hardly be possible any other way. As long as our hope is fed by *a hard-working faith* and *a long-laboring love,* the devil simply doesn't have what it takes to keep us from going toward God.

He who despairs wants love and faith, for faith, hope,
and love are three torches which blend their light together,
nor does the one shine without the other.
PIETRO METASTASIS

October 26
AFTER WE HAVE SUFFERED A WHILE

But may the God of all grace, who called us to His
eternal glory by Christ Jesus, after you have suffered a while,
perfect, establish, strengthen, and settle you.
1 Peter 5:10

IN CHRIST, IT IS CERTAIN THAT GOD WILL "PERFECT, ESTABLISH, STRENGTHEN, AND SETTLE" US. But that will come at the end of our earthly lives. God will do these things, Peter wrote, "after you have suffered a while." Right now, a character-building process is going on, and we should be patient while it is running its course.

Repentance. As hard as it can be at times, the continuation of this world allows us the time we need to repent of our sins. And it is not only the additional time that benefits us, but the hardness of our sojourn *encourages* us to repent. For most of us, repentance is not a one-time occurrence; it is a *process.* By a *sequence* of events, God is teaching us repentance, and the process can't be rushed.

Refining. God uses the illustration of a precious metal being refined by fire to help us see what needs to happen to our hearts. Peter wrote, "In this you greatly rejoice, though now for a little while, if need be, you have been grieved by various trials, that the genuineness of your faith, being much more precious than gold that perishes, though it is tested by fire, may be found to praise, honor, and glory at the revelation of Jesus Christ" (1 Peter 1:6,7).

Remediation. In many respects, life in the present world is like time spent in a "treatment center." The flaws in our character are being remediated, and the process (often very painful) takes time. Only when our inner characters have been prepared and made fit for the eternal enjoyment of God will they be given that privilege.

Among the many other benefits of our difficulties in this world, there is the fact that we will enjoy heaven all the more because we suffered while getting there. "No one truly knows happiness who has not suffered," as Henri Frédéric Amiel wrote. So we should not be surprised that our reward will come *later.* The Hebrew writer said, "For you have need of endurance, so that after you have done the will of God, you may receive the promise" (Hebrews 10:36). That word "after" is a little word, but oh, how important it is in this life. *After* we have done the will of God . . .

From the bitterness of disease
man learns the sweetness of health.
SPANISH PROVERB

October 27
COUNT IT ALL JOY

My brethren, count it all joy when you fall into various trials,
knowing that the testing of your faith produces patience. But let
patience have its perfect work, that you may be perfect
and complete, lacking nothing. *James 1:2-4*

WHEN WE SUFFER HARDSHIP, THE CHALLENGE IS NOT MERELY
TO ACCEPT IT WITH RESIGNATION BUT TO "COUNT IT ALL JOY."
Recognizing the *good* that can come from what we suffer, we must
learn to give thanks. Here are three thoughts that can help us:

(1) *If we are to share in Christ's glory, we must also be willing to
share in His sufferings.* Peter wrote, "Rejoice to the extent that you
partake of Christ's sufferings, that when His glory is revealed,
you may also be glad with exceeding joy" (1 Peter 4:13). They took
Jesus outside the city to crucify Him. "Therefore let us go forth to
Him, outside the camp, bearing His reproach" (Hebrews 13:13).

(2) *It is a privilege to suffer in Christ's name.* If it is honorable
to suffer for a *cause*, it is even more so to suffer for a *person*. And
when the person is none other than our Savior, no suffering is too
great to be anything less than a privilege. We can be thankful at
any time we're counted worthy of such an honor (Acts 5:41).

(3) *When we suffer for Christ, we are also suffering for the sake of
His body, the church.* Christ and the church are inseparable. Harm
to one is a harm to the other, and benefit to one is a benefit to the
other. So when we endure hardship, we need to do it, in part, for
our brothers and sisters. Paul said he was glad to suffer "for the
sake of [Christ's] body, which is the church" (Colossians 1:24).

The Christian's attitude toward hardship is one of many
things about the gospel that make no sense to the world. In the
world, unpleasantness is evil and hardship is to be avoided. But in
Christ, things are measured by a different set of values. Hardship
hurts the disciple of Christ no less than it hurts anyone else, but
the disciple's *attitude* is very different: "But what things were gain
to me, these I have counted loss for Christ . . . that I may know
Him and the power of His resurrection, and the fellowship of His
sufferings, being conformed to His death, if, by any means, I may
attain to the resurrection from the dead" (Philippians 3:7,10,11).

Be of good courage, all is before you, and time passed
in the difficult is never lost . . . What is required of us is that
we love the difficult and learn to deal with it.

RAINER MARIA RILKE

October 28

DIFFICULTY INCREASES THE SATISFACTION

I am filled with comfort. I am exceedingly
joyful in all our tribulation.
2 Corinthians 7:4

FOR THE CHRISTIAN, DIFFICULTY IS A FACT OF LIFE. In a world where horrendous war is being fought between good and evil, hardship is only to be expected. Paul said, "We must through many tribulations enter the kingdom of God" (Acts 14:22). And continuing the military metaphor, he urged Timothy to "endure hardship as a good soldier of Jesus Christ" (2 Timothy 2:3).

The hardship is not the whole story, however. For the Christian, no matter what hard things are happening, there is always a great *nevertheless*. Speaking of himself and his coworkers, Paul wrote, "We are hard pressed on every side, yet not crushed; we are perplexed, but not in despair; persecuted, but not forsaken; struck down, but not destroyed" (2 Corinthians 4:8,9).

Paul had the great ability to experience *joy in the midst of tribulation*. To the Corinthians, he wrote, "I am filled with comfort. I am exceedingly joyful in all our tribulation." The hardship was undeniable, and Paul wasn't one to underestimate it. But he had learned, in Christ, to see that the hardship was *worth* suffering.

For the people of God, there is coming a rest. "Then I heard a voice from heaven saying to me, 'Write: "Blessed are the dead who die in the Lord from now on."' 'Yes,' says the Spirit, 'that they may rest from their labors, and their works follow them'" (Revelation 14:13). But the rest is *not yet*; it will come "in due season" (Galatians 6:9). Meanwhile, we must derive our joy not from pleasant circumstances but from the hope of heaven — and the knowledge that, even now, many good things are happening that will eventually contribute to the Lord's triumph over all evil.

Difficulty and joy are not incompatible, as many people think. If a person wanted joy, even in *this* world, he wouldn't necessarily look for a completely wrinkle-free lifestyle. Difficulty *enhances* joy, and the Christian ought to have experienced the truth of that principle more than anyone else. Properly dealt with, difficulty increases the satisfaction we feel *when the hardship has been overcome*. So for those bound for heaven, the difficulty doesn't do anything but guarantee that their rest is going to be that much sweeter.

Difficulty and joy are mutual friends.
TIM HANSEL

October 29
LOVE SUFFERS LONG

Love suffers long and is kind . . .
1 Corinthians 13:4

IT IS NOTHING SHORT OF AMAZING HOW HEAVY A BURDEN LOVE CAN BEAR AND HOW LONG IT CAN BEAR IT. I once knew a woman who had never had any life as an adult except the life of taking care of her mother. Her mother was a quadriplegic with no one else to care for her, so the daughter had forgone marriage and any kind of independence just to take care of her mother. When I knew this dear woman, she had been doing this for over thirty years.

Love does not give up on people. Love doesn't do difficult work for a "respectable" period of time and then give it up. It hangs in there and endures, over an indefinite period if necessary. In the real world, people and their problems can be exhausting. So we try to help them for a while, but if they don't "shape up" pretty quickly, we have a tendency to write them off as losses. But love suffers long. It knows how to keep waiting when waiting is hard.

Love has a long fuse. Just as love does not "give up" easily, it does not "give in" easily to things like unkindness and ungentleness. It keeps acting kindly long after others would have started behaving unkindly. "Meekness" is sometimes defined as "strength under control," and I think that describes the idea very well. The kind person is not weak; his strength is simply being controlled more carefully than is the unkind person's. It is true, as Eric Hoffer said, that "rudeness is the weak person's imitation of strength."

I wish we could see the deadly seriousness of the "little" things we call irritability, grouchiness, touchiness, peevishness, and so forth. These are not little sins. If we do not repent of them and learn the laws of charity, they will carry us straight to hell.

If nothing else produces patience in our dealings with others, we at least ought to be moved by our Lord's patience with us. How long has the Lord waited and waited and waited for some of us to get rid of certain sins and weaknesses? How many times has He forgiven us of repeated offenses? "If You, LORD, should mark iniquities, O Lord, who could stand?" (Psalm 130:3). Why does He put up with us? It is only because He *loves* us. How is it then that we can claim to love others and be so short-tempered and unkind?

Patient endurance is the perfection of charity.

AMBROSE

October 30
WHAT WILL HAPPEN?

And see, now I go bound in the spirit to Jerusalem,
not knowing the things that will happen to me there . . .
Acts 20:22

IF YOUR PEACE OF MIND DEPENDS ON KNOWING WHAT IS GOING
TO HAPPEN, YOU PROBABLY AREN'T GOING TO ENJOY BEING A
CHRISTIAN. God does not supply us with any specific information
about what is ahead for us individually in this world. And the
reason for that, presumably, is that we don't *need* to know what is
going to happen. What we *do* need to know are these three facts:

God is in control. The extent to which God is involved in every
detail of what happens may be debatable, but surely we can agree
that, whatever happens, God is still on His throne. He is the sovereign Ruler of His creation, and we need to live our daily lives in
the confidence that nothing is going to happen that will take God
by surprise or cause Him to reconsider His eternal purposes. No
matter what happens, God's ultimate will is going to be done.

God will help us. When Paul said in Philippians 4:13, "I can do
all things through Christ who strengthens me," he stated a truth
of surpassing importance. As we yield ourselves to God's will, we
need never fear that anything impossible is going to be required
of us. Not knowing the future, we may wonder whether problems
will arise that we can't handle, but such a fear is quite unnecessary. Whatever needs to be handled, He will *help* us handle.

In the end, God will gain the victory. Although the decisive battle
against Satan was won on the morning of Jesus' resurrection, the
war against evil has not yet been brought to a conclusion. We
don't know how many more skirmishes will have to be fought,
nor do we know how many of those we ourselves will have to
fight in, but we do know that the *outcome* is a foregone conclusion:
God is going to vanquish His enemy. That's all we need to know.
What happens between now and then . . . well, time will tell.

So quit worrying and quit trying to figure out what is going
to happen. It doesn't matter. The Christian life does not consist
of predicting and planning. That's God's business. Our work is
just doing the simple daily duties that lie clearly before us, come
what may. And if the "uncertainty" of that kind of life makes you
uncomfortable, then you probably should just get used to it.

In the concert of life, no one receives a program.
DUTCH PROVERB

October 31
OUR PART IS TO TRY . . . AND TO TRUST

In the morning sow your seed,
And in the evening do not withhold your hand;
For you do not know which will prosper,
Either this or that,
Or whether both alike will be good.
Ecclesiastes 11:6

ONE OF LIFE'S GREAT DISCOURAGEMENTS IS THE THOUGHT THAT IT "WON'T DO ANY GOOD" TO DO WHAT WE ARE THINKING OF DOING. In some situations, we can't decide which of two actions would be the most effective. At other times, it looks as if nothing we might try to do would make any difference. So we do *nothing.*

But too often, our decision process is the reverse of what it should be. Rather than deciding up front what is *right* to do, based on timeless principles, we try to predict the *result* of an action, and then define what is "right" in terms of what we think will "work" the best. More often than we'd care to admit, we adopt the philosophy of "utilitarianism," the idea that the value of an action is determined by its utility or usefulness. If it looks like it "won't do any good," then we think nothing more needs to be said.

But in fact, there is a good deal more that needs to be said. What is right is right, whether we think it's "useful" or not. And not only that, it is often honorable to *begin* a work even when no hope has been vouchsafed to us that we'll be able to finish it.

The "crystal ball" is a notoriously unreliable device, and none of us has one that works very well. As creatures unable to see more than a few hours ahead, we are poor prognosticators. Even our best and most carefully considered predictions often turn out to be wrong. To be more specific, things that were *right* to do often turn out to do more good than we could have ever anticipated.

So we should just put away our forecasts and our predictions and go ahead and do whatever is the best thing we're capable of doing at any moment. We must be guided by *conscience* and the knowledge that it always "does good to do good" — whether we can see how it's going to happen or not. The advice of Ecclesiastes 11:1 is mighty good counsel: "Cast your bread upon the waters, for you will find it after many days." If we will keep busy doing the best we know to do, we need not doubt that good will come of it.

It is for us to make the effort.
The result is always in God's hands.
MAHATMA GANDHI

November 1
NOT ONLY A POSSIBILITY BUT A REALITY

Now faith is the substance of things hoped for,
the evidence of things not seen.
Hebrews 11:1

HOW STRONGLY WE REACH FORWARD TO HEAVEN IS DETERMINED BY HOW STRONGLY WE BELIEVE IT WILL ACTUALLY BE TRUE. If we're not sure whether heaven exists, or if we're just not concerned about it one way or the other, then we won't exert ourselves very strongly in the direction of heaven. But if the reality of heaven is a *conviction* with us, we'll reach forward to it fervently.

These days, many people define faith as "wishful thinking." In their opinion, religious people only believe in heaven because they *want* to believe in it. *But wanting something to be true makes it neither more nor less likely to be true.* The only question worth asking is which side the superior *evidence* is on: the side of belief or the side of disbelief? The weight of the evidence is all that matters.

Our text in Hebrews 11:1 describes faith as "the substance of things hoped for, the evidence of things not seen." Genuine faith is the assurance of certain hoped-for things, not merely because one hopes for them but because one sees that they have a solid "substance," that is, that they are "substantiated" in a sound way.

In 2 Corinthians 5:7, Paul says that Christians "walk by faith, not by sight." Christians are a *trusting* people. They live their daily lives on the principle of trust, willing, because of solid evidence, to stake everything on the reality of God and salvation and heaven.

I have sometimes heard people speak of belief in heaven as the "safe" course to follow. The argument runs something like this: if heaven turns out to be real, then the believer will have his hope, but if it turns out otherwise, the believer will be in no worse shape than anyone else. But I believe we can do much better than think of heaven as a safe bet. We can weigh the evidence and make our choice in favor of an idea that is so strong in its probability that we can be *confident* of it. For now, heaven (and hell too) may be, as the Hebrew writer says, "not seen," but unseen does not mean unreal. The immortality of our souls is a great possibility, to say the least. But faith sees that it is more than a possibility: it is the great *reality*.

As the essence of courage is to stake
one's life on a possibility, so the essence of faith
is to believe that the possibility exists.
WILLIAM SALTER

November 2

WHEN OUR LOVE FOR CHRIST GROWS WEAK

But He was wounded for our transgressions,
He was bruised for our iniquities;
The chastisement for our peace was upon Him,
And by His stripes we are healed.
Isaiah 53:5

REACHING FORWARD NORMALLY REQUIRES LOOKING AHEAD, BUT THERE IS A SENSE IN WHICH IT ALSO REQUIRES LOOKING BACK. We will not reach forward to God as lovingly as we should if we don't regularly remember the crucifixion of His Son for our sins. If, as I believe, gratitude for grace is the most powerful motivator in the world, then the cross of Christ, the greatest and, on our part, the most *undeserved* act of God, should move us the most.

Yet as powerful as the cross is to move us in the right direction, we tend to forget it. It fades from our minds. But that is the way it is with all things that are important to us. If their reality and their importance are not constantly *refreshed*, they fade. And so it's no surprise that God designed the Lord's Supper to remind us on the first day of every week that He gave His Son to die for us.

Anytime our passion for God begins to fade, the most important thing to do is *return to the cross*. The old, familiar hymn said it very well: "When my love to Christ grows weak, when for deeper faith I seek, then in thought I go to thee, Garden of Gethsemane. / When my love for man grows weak, when for stronger faith I seek, Hill of Calvary! I go to thy scenes of fear and woe. / Then to life I turn again, learning all the worth of pain, learning all the might that lies in a full self-sacrifice" (J. R. Wreford).

It is, of course, the *vicarious* nature of Christ's death that exerts such an emotional force upon us — He died in our place, for our sins. "He was wounded for our transgressions, He was bruised for our iniquities; the chastisement for our peace was upon Him . . ."

Going back to the cross is a painful thing to do. No sensitive human being could think of the agony that was involved in death by crucifixion and not be gut-wrenched, but to know that *our own sins* made it necessary for God's Son to endure such torment makes us want to turn away from the scene in shame and sorrow. But there is no other way for us to be healed of what hurts us.

For him to see me mended
I must see him torn.
LUCI SHAW

November 3
WHEN THE DREAM COMES TRUE

Hope deferred makes the heart sick,
But when the desire comes, it is a tree of life.
Proverbs 13:12

THERE WILL COME A TIME WHEN OUR DREAMS COME TRUE, IF WE ARE FOUND IN CHRIST AT HIS COMING. The God who created us put "eternity" in our hearts (Ecclesiastes 3:11). He planted in us a deep need for perfect fellowship with Him, something that can no longer be had in this world. So it's no coincidence that we dream of *another* world, the kind of world for which we were made. We dream of heaven. But although it's a dream, it's not *just* a dream.

With any dream, there can sometimes be a long gap between the dream and its fulfillment, and no one who has experienced the deep yearning and heartache that go with an unfulfilled dream would disagree with Solomon: "Hope deferred makes the heart sick." And with regard to heaven, Paul put it in vivid language: "In this [body] we groan, earnestly desiring to be clothed with our habitation which is from heaven" (2 Corinthians 5:2).

But the "overcomers" are those who keep hope alive during the delay. The agony and emptiness of waiting only intensify the joy of the dream once it is realized, and it's only a fool who says he doesn't want a thing at all if he can't have it right now.

So we ought to pursue our dreams *passionately*. Even in this broken old world, there are many worthy things that the Christian may dream of enjoying. These "life-under-the-sun" dreams may or may not come true, but whether they do or not, I hope you won't give up having dreams. To be without dreams is to be less than human. But far more precious than any earthly dream is the dream of heaven. It is surely the greatest dream of the human heart, and unlike earthly dreams that must be held somewhat tentatively, there need be nothing tentative about the way we hold the hope of heaven. We should hold that hope with a love that will not let go.

So whoever you are, please don't let go of heaven. Don't stop dreaming. Don't stop reaching forward. For the time being, unfulfilled desires are difficult to deal with, but the emptiness of our hearts right now will only make the dream sweeter when it comes true. *And one day, my dear friend, the dream is going to come true!*

Climb every mountain, ford every stream,
Follow every rainbow, 'til you find your dream.
OSCAR HAMMERSTEIN

November 4
WE CAN'T GROW IF WE CAN'T LET GO

Then they all wept freely, and fell on Paul's neck and kissed him,
sorrowing most of all for the words which he spoke, that they would
see his face no more. And they accompanied him to the ship.
Acts 20:37,38

GROWTH TOWARD GOD IS A POSITIVE EXPERIENCE, BUT IT'S ALSO A PAINFUL EXPERIENCE. We all want to make progress, but since grasping greater things always requires letting go of lesser things, it can be painful to go forward. Even when we're going someplace exceedingly wonderful, saying goodbye is never easy. So this thing we call *growth* is a bittersweet blessing if ever there was one.

Paul's painful farewell to his beloved Christian friends in Ephesus illustrates the agony that often attends progress. Paul was going to Jerusalem, for the last time as it turned out, and then to Rome, though he did not yet know the circumstances. Everything Paul had worked for as a Christian, as an evangelist, and as an apostle was coming to a climax, and if he had stayed in Ephesus just because he loved the people there, he would have not been reaching forward. But it would take a hard-hearted person not to be touched by his grief, and theirs, when goodbye had to be said.

In our language, there is an old adage that says, "You can't have your cake and eat it too." That's the way it is with growth. We can't change for the better without . . . changing. We can't get where we're going and still stay where we are. Progress, by its very definition, means moving beyond our present "location."

Sometimes progress means leaving behind things that we're only too glad to leave behind: things that are unhealthy, unpleasant, and even sinful. At other times, however, the choice is harder: we must choose between good, better, and best. The road forks, and some *good* things have to be given up — even some lovingly *cherished* things — in order to move toward the *ultimately good* thing for which we were created: *perfect, unending fellowship with God in His very presence, in a realm unbroken and unmarred by sin.*

If we are to have the future that God wants to give us, we must be willing to let go of our present. That is one of life's most important lessons. So let's keep a clear head, say our goodbyes with gratitude, and then "go on to perfection" (Hebrews 6:1).

Growth is demanding and may seem dangerous,
for there is loss as well as gain in growth.

MAY SARTON

November 5

WHAT IS THAT TO YOU?

Peter, seeing him, said to Jesus, "But Lord,
what about this man?" Jesus said to him, "If I will that he
remain till I come, what is that to you? You follow Me."
John 21:21,22

WHEN THE LORD INDICATED THAT PETER WOULD DIE A MARTYR'S DEATH, PETER TURNED TO JOHN AND SAID, "BUT LORD, WHAT ABOUT THIS MAN?" Jesus' answer may seem abrupt to us, but it made an important point: "If I will that he remain till I come, what is that to you? You follow Me." Peter needed to be reminded to keep his focus on his own obedience. Whatever the Lord's arrangements with others might turn out to be, the main thing we need to be concerned with is the quality of our own obedience.

Why does the Lord sometimes deal more generously with others than with us? On the surface, it appears that the blessings and benefits to be had in this world are not apportioned evenly. Some people seem to get more breaks than others. And especially when it comes to the Lord's grace, things don't always make sense. How can eleventh-hour penitents get the same grace as the rest of us?

Why am I called upon to do things that others don't have to do? If the blessings of life aren't spread out equally, the responsibilities don't seem to be fairly assigned either. The burdens that have to be borne seem to be piled quite high on the backs of some, while others aren't called upon to do nearly as much. "If I have to die a martyr's death," Peter would say, "why doesn't John have to?"

Why does the Lord require things that seem to do more harm than good? Here, perhaps, is the area of our most perplexing questions. When the Lord clearly commands something that, from our vantage point, seems to lack "common sense," we tend to dismiss the directive as unrealistic. "Lord, that will never work. What about this complication over here and that complication over there?"

But all of these questions, and a number of others that may distract us, are irrelevant to our own responsibility. At best they are secondary issues, and secondary issues shouldn't be allowed to determine our primary responsibility. If we know what the Lord would want us to do, then doing it is all that matters. Now is the time for obedience. There will be time enough for questions later.

I find doing the will of God leaves me
no time for disputing about his plans.

GEORGE MACDONALD

November 6
GODLY JOY

Yet I will rejoice in the LORD,
I will joy in the God of my salvation.
Habakkuk 3:18

WE OFTEN EMPHASIZE THE NEED FOR OUR SORROW TO BE GODLY SORROW, BUT IS IT ANY LESS IMPORTANT FOR OUR JOY TO BE GODLY JOY? If it is dangerous for worldly thinking to infect our sorrow, is it any less of a problem when it jeopardizes our joy?

To begin with, what is it about godly joy that makes it "godly"? The answer is not hard to find. Just as godly sorrow is focused on God rather than self (it grieves what our sins have cost Him and not us), godly joy is also focused on God. It rejoices in whatever God rejoices about: the accomplishment of His purposes, the triumph of His cause, the redemption of those who have accepted His salvation, and, yes, even the carrying out of His justice.

I believe one prominent feature of godly joy is that it rejoices in the life-path that God lays out before us. That is, it finds joy in following the path that God indicates rather than the one we might have chosen. It genuinely rejoices in the accomplishment of God's will, whatever that might mean for us personally. As Evelyn Underhill put it, "This is the secret of joy. We shall no longer strive for our own way, but commit ourselves, easily and simply, to God's way, acquiesce in his will, and in so doing find our peace."

Jesus is obviously the great example here. He experienced no greater joy than being a part of the fulfillment of His Father's purposes, even when the role required of Him was painful and difficult. On one occasion, He said, "My food is to do the will of Him who sent Me, and to finish His work" (John 4:34). He derived more joy from obedience than most people get from a great meal.

Without the focus that Jesus had on the Father's glory, joy tends to degenerate. It becomes the product of nothing more than the selfish indulgence of our desires, with little or no regard for whether that indulgence helps or hinders the outworking of God's purposes in the world. And in the end, that kind of "joy" (if it even can be called that) is a distinctly unsatisfying thing. It leaves a dry, dusty taste in our mouths. But *godly* joy, that is a different thing altogether! When our joy is the overflowing of *God's* joy, well, that is what Eden was about. And our Father has not given up on it.

Oh the joy of that life with God and in God and for God!
OSWALD CHAMBERS

November 7
IN THE HEART OF GOD, WE ARE INDIVIDUALS

Then those who feared the LORD spoke to one another, and the LORD
listened and heard them; so a book of remembrance was written before
Him for those who fear the LORD and who meditate on His name.
Malachi 3:16

A T ALL TIMES, GOD IS AWARE OF HIS WHOLE CREATION, BUT HE
IS ALSO AWARE OF EACH PART OF HIS CREATION. God did not
merely create "the human race," but He created each of us as individual persons. Surely God must have had a purpose in making
the creation as He did, with many various parts, all unique and
different from one another. Surely His Fatherly joy must come not
only from thinking of His work as a whole, but from thinking of
the uniqueness of each part. "Thou thinkest, Lord, of me . . ."

Do you ever envision the "mass of humanity" as a faceless,
nameless crowd? Do you lose sight of your personal identity as a
unique creature? There may be times when our thinking goes too
far in the direction of individuality, no doubt, but I believe there
are also times when we need to nourish our hearts with Jesus'
words in Matthew 10:29-31: "Are not two sparrows sold for a cop-
per coin? And not one of them falls to the ground apart from your
Father's will. But the very hairs of your head are all numbered. Do
not fear therefore; you are of more value than many sparrows."

Do you ever despise your own set of particulars: your circumstances, your characteristics, your life? Do you ever wish you had
someone else's situation? Do you ever doubt that what you can
do is going to matter in the larger scheme of things? If you do, my
prayer is that you will learn to appreciate (1) the greatness of the
creation of which you are a part, and (2) the uniqueness of the part
that God had in mind for you personally. In the grand oratorio of
creation, God wasted no effort on duplicate or unnecessary parts.
Without your voice, the music will be marred and diminished.

But finally, let us consider that if we've obeyed the gospel and
are walking faithfully with God, we each have a *relationship* with
Him that is absolutely unique. God would have sent His Son to
the cross if you were the only person who needed to be saved, and
having saved you, He loves the way *you* respond to His goodness.

Each of the redeemed shall forever know and praise some one aspect of the
divine beauty better than any other creature can. Why else were individuals
created, but that God, loving all infinitely, should love each differently?

C. S. LEWIS

IT DOES GOOD TO DO GOOD

... that you may become blameless and harmless, children of God
without fault in the midst of a crooked and perverse generation,
among whom you shine as lights in the world.
Philippians 2:15

IF GOD'S CREATION IS MADE UP OF "UNIQUE" PARTS, IT'S ALSO TRUE
THAT THE PARTS ARE "INTERCONNECTED." No part can act (or fail
to act) without having some impact on the other parts. God has
constructed the world in such a way that the "ripple effect" is one
of its characteristics. Even the least pebble thrown into the pond
sends out rings of influence that spread and spread and spread.

It does good to do good. When we face difficult circumstances,
one of the devil's worst lies is that the situation is hopeless: "There
is nothing you can do that will make a difference," he would say.
The truth is, however, it always does good to do good. We don't
need to see in advance how it's all going to work out; we just need
to act in the confidence that good deeds will have a good impact.

It does evil to do evil. The world being interconnected, of
course, it's also true that evil deeds have an impact. Whether we
can see it or not, doing evil always contributes to an evil outcome.

Perhaps the most amazing thing about all of this is that even
the *small* things and the *secret* things we do change the world in
some way. When I am sitting alone in my room and make a decision either to do or not do the thing I know God would want me
to do at that moment, by my decision I either add a little bit of
goodness to the world or take a little out. Whether we can see it
from our perspective or not, *every choice we make* impacts the world
to which we are connected, either for better or for worse.

Recognizing that our actions always have some impact on
others, we should resolve that our influence will *always be for good
and never for evil.* We don't have the luxury of considering only
ourselves. "Let each of you look out not only for his own interests,
but also for the interests of others" (Philippians 2:4). So let's take
responsibility for the effect we are having on the other parts and
members of God's creation. There is too much darkness already —
we dare not add to it. In every single thing we do, *let there be light!*

Keep in mind that each of you has your own vineyard. But every
one is joined to your neighbor's vineyards without any dividing lines.
They are so joined together, in fact, that you cannot do good or evil
for yourself without doing the same for your neighbors.

CATHERINE OF SIENNA

November 9
TAKING PLEASURE IN THE HAPPINESS OF OTHERS

Therefore, brethren, in all our affliction and distress
we were comforted concerning you by your faith.
For now we live, if you stand fast in the Lord.
1 Thessalonians 3:7,8

ONE MEASURE OF MATURITY IS WHETHER WE CAN TAKE PLEASURE
IN THE HAPPINESS OF OTHERS. In other words, a happiness
should not have to be *our own* in order for it to bring us pleasure.

In the New Testament, Paul's ability to enjoy the blessings of
others is one of the most admirable aspects of his character. After
embarking on his work as an apostle, he very often found himself
in difficult circumstances. To say the least, it was a hard life that
Paul led. If he never had any happiness except the kind that comes
from pleasant personal conditions, he would have had little happiness. But Paul was thrilled when any good thing came his brethren's way. What got him through his own travail was knowing
that his fellow Christians had what they needed and were thriving
spiritually. "For now we live, if you stand fast in the Lord."

What if we started thinking like that? Consider two examples:

(1) When the other person enjoys something that we don't have.
Steve Forbert, a super songwriter from my hometown of Meridian,
Mississippi, has a great line in one of his songs: "Driving a Jaguar
is impressive, but you can't watch it go by." The owner of a Jaguar
gets one kind of happiness, but he misses the other kind, the kind
that "watches it go by," happy for what somebody else has.

(2) When the other person's happiness has come at our expense. The
principle of sacrifice teaches us to spend and be spent that others
might have what they need. Love is eager to do without in order
to open doors of happiness for someone else. At such times of
sacrifice, where should we put the emphasis: on the price that has
been paid or the happiness of the other that has been procured?

The fact is, there is plenty to rejoice about in the world. Some
of it may have to do with our own blessings, but much of it has to
do with the good things that have come to others. As someone has
said, "It is a poor heart that never rejoices." We will never learn
contentment until we climb out of our own circumstances and see
that many good things are happening around us. Regardless of
how much of the "pie" is our own, the pie is really quite good!

Glad of other men's good, content with my harm.
WILLIAM SHAKESPEARE

November 10
LEARNING TO BE GLAD WHEN GOD IS GLAD

... as always, so now also Christ will be magnified
in my body, whether by life or by death.
Philippians 1:20

THERE WILL BE TIMES WHEN AN EVENT IS BOTH A GAIN FOR GOD'S KINGDOM AND A LOSS FOR US PERSONALLY, AT LEAST IN THE SHORT RUN. Progress never comes except at a price, and it must occasionally be true that we have to bear a part of the price personally. At such times, we should be glad that the event represents a gain for God's cause and His kingdom, in the larger perspective.

John the Baptist is a study in the attitude that we need to have. As Jesus' forerunner, John's role was only temporary. Once Jesus appeared, the progress of the kingdom would require John to leave the stage, so to speak. To his credit, John had the right attitude: "He must increase, but I must decrease" (John 3:30). If the kingdom was going forward, God would be glad, and so John would be glad too, no matter what the private implications were.

Our highest joy should always come from God's purposes and their fulfillment. We should define as "good" anything that forwards the Lord's cause, without regard to any gain or loss of a private nature. Yes, we will have our preferences, as Paul must have had when he wondered whether he would continue to live or be put to death. But deep down, Paul only wanted that "Christ will be magnified in my body, whether by life or by death." If a gain for God's kingdom required a loss for Paul, he was only too glad to accept the loss. On a much higher plane than Nathan Hale ever knew, Paul would regret that he had but one life to give.

Having this attitude does not mean that we don't grieve what we're called upon to give up. Jesus willingly — we could even say *gladly* — gave up His life to make possible some things that would bring His Father joy, but if you think His loss did not bring Him grief, you have never read the account of Gethsemane. A willing sacrifice and a broken heart very often go together, and if you haven't learned that lesson yet, you probably will before you die.

It all comes down to looking at things from the larger perspective. Things that make us sad in the "small picture" are very often those that, in the "big picture," should make us the gladdest of all.

Happiness is the spiritual experience of living
every minute with love, grace, and gratitude.
DENIS WAITLEY

November 11
ORDER OUT OF CHAOS

Then Peter took Him aside and began to rebuke Him, saying,
"Far be it from You, Lord; this shall not happen to You!" But He turned
and said to Peter, "Get behind Me, Satan! You are an offense to Me, for
you are not mindful of the things of God, but the things of men."
Matthew 16:22,23

IF IT WERE UP TO US, THE KINGDOM OF GOD WOULD PROGRESS IN A MORE "ORDERLY" FASHION. We would plan things more neatly. We would make them more predictable and businesslike. Intrusions, interruptions, and interferences would not be allowed.

But in reality, of course, the kingdom does not progress that way. With God in control, many things happen that seem haphazard, if not counterproductive and detrimental, as far as we can see.

When the Lord began to explain to His disciples that He was going to be crucified, Peter objected. Based on Peter's concept of what needed to happen for the kingdom to be established, the death of the King didn't seem like a very good idea. But rather than gently correct Peter's erroneous concept, the Lord strongly rebuked him: "Get behind Me, Satan! You are an offense to Me, for you are not mindful of the things of God, but the things of men."

Why such a strong rebuke? It is an indication, I believe, of how easy it is to deceive ourselves about God's purposes. Like Peter, we need to be careful. When we "plan" for things to happen in a certain way, is the driving force truly God's will? Might not the demand for "orderliness" really be coming from elsewhere?

In our personal lives, there is nothing wrong with dreaming, nor is there anything wrong with planning and preparing. But we should not hold on to our expectations with too tight a grip — God may have other plans, plans which seem messy and inconvenient compared to ours. The wonderful thing is that many of the greatest blessings in our lives come out of situations in which it seems that our own plans have been frustrated. This is true even when we first obey the gospel. As C. S. Lewis said, "Every story of conversion is the story of a blessed defeat." That being so, we should not be surprised that, after our conversion, God graciously vetoes our "legislation" from time to time. So, yes, we need to plan . . . but we also need to yield gladly when God has other plans.

God's order comes in the haphazard, and never
according to our scheming and planning. God takes
great delight in breaking up our programs.
OSWALD CHAMBERS

November 12

DISAPPOINTED?

Then Martha, as soon as she heard that Jesus was coming, went and
met Him, but Mary was sitting in the house. Then Martha said to Jesus,
"Lord, if You had been here, my brother would not have died."
John 11:20,21

WE CAN EASILY IMAGINE THE DISAPPOINTMENT OF MARY AND MARTHA WHEN JESUS DID NOT COME TO BETHANY IN TIME TO HEAL THEIR BROTHER LAZARUS AND KEEP HIM FROM DYING. They knew that Jesus had the power to prevent their brother's death, and they had made their request respectfully, as between close friends. But their initial hopes were dashed. Though He ended up doing a greater thing, Jesus did not do what they had first asked.

How do we deal with "unanswered" prayer, the kind in which God does not do the thing that we have asked Him to do? Is it right for us to be "disappointed"? Let me suggest that there are two different kinds of disappointment, one of which is right and acceptable to God while the other is wrong and insulting to God.

The sinful kind of disappointment is sinful because it's selfish and demanding. We resent that we didn't get our way. Or we're shocked that our plans didn't work out. Or we question God's goodness. Or we wonder whether there's any point in praying in the future. These kinds of thoughts betray a sinful lack of faith.

But there is another kind of disappointment, and this is nothing more than the sincere brokenness of heart that comes from a desire that God has left unfulfilled for the time being. In Gethsemane, was Jesus "disappointed" when God did not "hear" His plea to be spared from the cross? If you think He could have received His Father's answer without a broken heart, then you've not thought about the bitter agony in which He pleaded with God. But Jesus' broken heart would have been a pure and unselfish heart: willing, in true love, to yield to the higher and better way.

God never says no to any honorable request except to accomplish a greater good. The absence of the lesser good may leave us in pain for a while, and God will help us deal with that. But the key is truly wanting *the Lord's will to be done.* If *that's* what we desire, then we can be sure: *our desire will never be disappointed!*

God will inevitably appear to disappoint the man who is
attempting to use him as a convenience, a prop, or a comfort for
his own plans. God has never been known to disappoint the man
who is sincerely wanting to cooperate with his own purposes.

J. B. PHILLIPS

HUMILITY ABOUT TOMORROW

Do not boast about tomorrow,
For you do not know what a day may bring forth.
Proverbs 27:1

OUR ATTITUDE ABOUT "TOMORROW" IS ONE OF THE MAIN FACTORS THAT INFLUENCE OUR SPIRITUAL GROWTH. If we choose to think rightly about it, we will find that it helps us on our way to heaven. But if we think wrongly about it, we will be greatly hindered.

One of the problems that we have concerning the future is "boasting" about it, and our text in Proverbs warns us not to do that. When we say that there is a certain thing that we are going to do tomorrow, we must not attribute more power to ourselves than we actually have. When the time comes, we may not be *able* to bring to pass what we have proposed. So we must not be like the quack in a traveling "medicine show," making claims for our "elixir" that promise more than it has the power to deliver.

Few things in this world are as important as "reaching forward," but we need to understand what's involved in this concept from a scriptural standpoint. While there may be some value in being "forward-oriented" in general (that is, looking more to the future than to the past), the future that the Christian is always looking forward to is *heaven*. So when I speak of "reaching forward," I'm not talking about striving for any particular goal in *this* life; I'm talking about striving for *eternity in the presence of God*. We can be very definite about that goal, but with any goal between now and then, we must be somewhat tentative. We may want to do certain things tomorrow. We may even plan to do them. But we must not "boast" about them. In other words, we must not be too *sure* they will come to pass, since the Lord may have other plans.

With respect to tomorrow, I would recommend learning to be content with *whatever* it turns out to be. If tomorrow takes us places that weren't on our itinerary, well, that's what lends a sense of excitement and adventure to the life of faith. Come what may, there is one thing that is certain: *there won't come a tomorrow that God can't use for our good.* And that, really, is all we need to know.

Lord, give me faith to leave it all to thee!
The future is thy gift;
I would not lift
The veil thy love has hung 'twixt it and me.
JOHN OXENHAM

November 14
FUTURE PLANS

Come now, you who say, "Today or tomorrow we will go to such
and such a city, spend a year there, buy and sell, and make a profit";
whereas you do not know what will happen tomorrow. For what is your life?
It is even a vapor that appears for a little time and then vanishes away.
Instead you ought to say, "If the Lord wills, we shall live and do this or that."
But now you boast in your arrogance. All such boasting is evil.
James 4:13-16

JAMES REMINDS US THAT WHILE WE HAVE THE POWER TO MAKE FU-
TURE PLANS, WE DON'T ALWAYS HAVE THE POWER TO ACCOMPLISH
THEM. When it comes right down to it, life in this world is a very
uncertain business, as far as we are concerned. We don't really
know what is going to happen, and much that does happen is
beyond our power to control. So as Christians, we should have the
humility to say, *"If the Lord wills, we shall live and do this or that."*

Henry Ward Beecher once said, "We steal if we touch tomorrow. It is God's." To make future plans that don't take the Lord
into account, and even to inquire into the future too closely, is to
intrude into territory that does not really belong to us. Tomorrow
is the Lord's, and we should not try to seize it for ourselves.

In dealing with the future, we tend to go to extremes: either
we don't make any plans at all or we make plans and then adopt
an attitude about them that is too rigid and possessive. Surely
there must be a happy medium between these extremes, a balance
between the foolishness of no planning and the arrogance of leav
ing the Lord out of our planning. Can we not make plans that are
humble, plans which are important to us but which also bow reverently before the Lord's sovereignty? I believe we can. It doesn't
diminish the value of our planning to factor the Lord into our
thinking and say, *"If the Lord wills, we shall live and do this or that."*

So we should make plans, but we should keep in mind that
they may not materialize. That is not a bad thing, however. The
world would be a poorer place if all our plans materialized, for
God's plans are much better than ours and we can be glad that His
take precedence. It is in the brokenness of our expectations that
God often accomplishes His greatest works. "What we look for
does not come to pass; God finds a way for what none foresaw"
(Euripides). Thinking rightly, we wouldn't want it any other way.

There are no disappointments to those
whose wills are buried in the will of God.
FREDERICK WILLIAM FABER

November 15

THE WAY IS NOT EASY

We must through many tribulations enter the kingdom of God.
Acts 14:22

WHEN PAUL AND BARNABAS REVISITED THE CONGREGATIONS THAT HAD BEEN ESTABLISHED ON THEIR FIRST MISSIONARY JOURNEY, THEY WARNED THEM TO BE PREPARED TO SUFFER. Having obeyed the gospel, we are on our way to heaven, but it will only be through "many tribulations," they said, that we enter the kingdom of God. So when hardship comes, we shouldn't be surprised.

This echoes Jesus' warning in the Sermon on the Mount: "Enter by the narrow gate; for wide is the gate and broad is the way that leads to destruction, and there are many who go in by it. Because narrow is the gate and difficult is the way which leads to life, and there are few who find it" (Matthew 7:13,14). The easy, no-risk path has never led anywhere but downward . . . to death.

So we shouldn't *expect* life as a Christian — at least in *this* world, marred as it is by the intrusion of sin — to be anything other than difficult. That doesn't mean there won't be some pleasant days now and then, relatively free of pain and struggle. But it does mean that we should guard against unrealistic expectations. Peter wrote, "Beloved, do not think it strange concerning the fiery trial which is to try you, as though some strange thing happened to you; but rejoice to the extent that you partake of Christ's sufferings, that when His glory is revealed, you may also be glad with exceeding joy" (1 Peter 4:12,13). We should expect life to be hard.

When we defy difficulty and remain faithful to Christ, we place ourselves in a great company of saints. Many thousands of God's faithful people in days gone by have done the same thing. When we choose to endure, we do exactly what they did, and they are cheering us on, so to speak. "Therefore we also, since we are surrounded by so great a cloud of witnesses, let us lay aside every weight, and the sin which so easily ensnares us, and let us run with endurance the race that is set before us" (Hebrews 12:1). It is an honor to be among these people and a privilege to be their comrades. Let us determine that we will join them in heaven!

When compassed about on every side with tribulations, remember
that it is the way of the saints, through which they passed to the kingdom
of heaven. Learn to comfort thyself also, because that in this thou
are made like unto Christ Jesus, thy Lord.

THOMAS À KEMPIS

WHEN STRENGTH IS A DISADVANTAGE

And He said to me, "My grace is sufficient for you, for My strength
is made perfect in weakness." Therefore most gladly I will rather boast
in my infirmities, that the power of Christ may rest upon me. Therefore
I take pleasure in infirmities, in reproaches, in needs, in persecutions, in
distresses, for Christ's sake. For when I am weak, then I am strong.
2 Corinthians 12:9,10

NORMALLY, WE THINK OF OUR OWN ABILITY AS AN ADVANTAGE.
Whatever we think we need to do, we'd rather be able to
do it than not be able. We cringe at the thought of personal insufficiency, of coming up short. But in our relationship to God and
in our work in His kingdom, there is a sense in which our own
personal strength can be a disadvantage. "Natural strength is often
as great a handicap as natural weakness" (Hannah Hurnard).

Whenever there is something that we can do and we know
that we can do it, we are tempted to believe that our strength is
our own: this is *our* ability, *we* have learned how to do this thing,
and so forth. We begin to feel independent and self-sufficient, and
our need for God recedes into the background. It is strange but
true, the more we think of the things God has made us able to do,
the less we pay attention to the God who made us able to do them.

To Paul, God said, "My strength is made perfect in weakness."
Paul, like all of us, probably enjoyed days when he felt adequate
and sufficient to do what had to be done. But in truth, God could
do a good deal more with Paul on the other days — when Paul felt
weak rather than strong. So God gave Paul a "thorn in the flesh"
to multiply the number of days when he would feel weak. Those
would be the days when he was most conscious of his dependence
on God's help and therefore the days of his greatest usefulness.

When a "thorn in the flesh" makes its painful appearance in
our own lives, our natural response is to want it to go away as
quickly as possible. Yet if it is God's will for us to continue to deal
with it, our attitude needs to be the same as Paul's: "I take pleasure in infirmities . . . For when I am weak, then I am strong."

God uses chronic pain and weakness, along with other afflictions,
as his chisel for sculpting our lives. Felt weakness deepens our dependence
on Christ for strength each day. The weaker we feel, the harder we lean. And
the harder we lean, the stronger we grow spiritually, even while our bodies
waste away. To live with your "thorn" uncomplainingly — that is, sweet,
patient, and free in heart to love and help others, even though
every day you feel weak — is true sanctification.

J. I. PACKER

WHEN YOU'VE GOTTEN IT, CAN YOU ENJOY IT?

> There is an evil which I have seen under the sun, and it is common
> among men: A man to whom God has given riches and wealth and honor,
> so that he lacks nothing for himself of all he desires; yet God does
> not give him power to eat of it . . . *Ecclesiastes 6:1,2*

IN SETTING OUR GOALS AND MAKING OUR PLANS, WE OFTEN ATTRIBUTE TO OURSELVES MORE POWER THAN WE ACTUALLY HAVE. When we aspire to material wealth, for example, we've been taught by the motivational speakers to believe that we can have anything we want: it is only a matter of having enough drive and ingenuity. But there are two faulty assumptions hidden in this thinking. One is that we can acquire however much wealth we want to acquire, and the other is that we will be able to enjoy it once we get it.

But it is God who determines, first, whether we'll be allowed to accumulate wealth and, second, whether we'll be able to enjoy it. Any of us might be the "man to whom God has given riches and wealth and honor" and yet "God does not give him power to eat of it." The truth is, God can keep us from accumulating wealth if He wants to (despite our drive and ingenuity), and He can just as easily keep us from getting any lasting joy out of it. So write this down and never forget it: *if we wrongfully aspire to wealth, one of God's worst punishments is to let us have the thing we thought we wanted and then make us more miserable than we were before we got it.*

So when our "dream comes true," will it make us happy? Maybe it will, but then again, maybe it won't. Foolishly, we *assume* that getting the wealth we desire will provide the freedom to enjoy life and open the door to happiness. But that won't be the result if God doesn't grant the enjoyment of the things He permits us to acquire. God may see to it that our wealth gives us not freedom but slavery, and there is no worse bondage than bondage to wealth. As the saying goes, "Chains of gold are stronger than chains of iron."

At the end of the day, freedom has little to do with what we have or don't have. In fact, it doesn't have much to do with our external circumstances at all. Even in prison, Paul had more freedom than most of those walking the streets outside his prison. Freedom is freedom from the sinful desires that have bound us to the devil.

> Freedom does not mean I am able to do whatever I want to do.
> That's the worst kind of bondage. Freedom means I have been set
> free to become all that God wants me to be, to achieve all that God
> wants me to achieve, to enjoy all that God wants me to enjoy.
>
> WARREN W. WIERSBE

November 18
HUNGER IS THE BEST SAUCE

A satisfied soul loathes the honeycomb,
But to a hungry soul every bitter thing is sweet.
Proverbs 27:7

IN THIS AGE OF AFFLUENCE AND ABUNDANCE, MANY OF US HAVE BECOME JADED. Tragically, we've lost our childhood sense of wonder at the big, wide world around us. We've bought so many things and been so many places, it's impossible to impress us anymore. No matter what it is, we've been there and done that. Frankly, we are bored. The law of diminishing returns has set in.

There is an old adage that says, "Hunger is the best sauce." When we're not very hungry, we might add a little sauce to a dish to make it taste better. But the food doesn't need any sauce when we are ravenously hungry; we appreciate it without any "help." And this is exactly what Proverbs 27:7 is about: "A satisfied soul loathes the honeycomb, but to a hungry soul every bitter thing is sweet." When we're full, we tend to get picky. But when we're hungry, even bitter things become sweet. The principle here is that abundance presents a challenge for us. When we have not only what we need but more than we need, it is harder (most people naively think it is easier) to enjoy life. The poor man has the advantage of being hungry enough to enjoy every little thing.

As we mature, we learn that moderation really is a good practice after all. I love a What-a-Burger hamburger about as enthusiastically as a man could love any food on the face of the earth, but I find that I enjoy them more now that I don't live in Texas and can't get one any time I want it. I've gone down hard on this, but I'm gradually coming to see that, in *this* world, less is more.

You see, the feelings that we call "hunger" and "emptiness" (and we used physical food only as an illustration) are not to be avoided. They can be our best friends. I know that fact is hard to grasp now that we've lived so long in a world dominated by consumerism, but it's true. Unmet worldly needs remind us of our need for God, and therefore play a very important role in our lives. In an affluent world, it's possible to ruin our appetite for God with a worldly feast and delude ourselves into thinking we have what we need. But if that happens — if we are too full of temporal satisfactions to have any room left for God — then we're in big trouble.

Even God cannot fill what is full.
TERESA OF CALCUTTA

WHERE GOD'S GLORY DWELLS

LORD, I have loved the habitation of Your house,
And the place where Your glory dwells.
Psalm 26:8

IF WE DILIGENTLY SEEK GOD, OUR JOY WILL BE IN PROPORTION TO HOW NEAR WE ARE TO GOD. David's sentiment will be our own: "LORD, I have loved the habitation of Your house, and the place where Your glory dwells." In whatever sense we may speak of God's "habitation," what we want is to be as near as possible to the place where His glory dwells. For the seeker, nearer is better.

(1) *The Old Testament tabernacle.* When God entered into a special relationship with Israel (a temporary arrangement that was preparatory to the coming of the Messiah), He designated a physical place as the location of His dwelling in their midst. To come to the tabernacle, and later the temple, was to be as close to God's glory as it was possible to be anywhere in the world at that time.

(2) *The New Testament church.* Israel's physical temple anticipated the building of a *spiritual* temple, a people in whose *hearts* God would dwell, and those people are the ones who make up the Lord's church today (1 Peter 2:5). So it is possible to be nearer to God today than you could ever have been in Israel, even if you had gone into the Most Holy place in the heart of the tabernacle.

(3) *Heaven.* But just as Israel looked forward to a time when they could be nearer God's presence than they could be in the tabernacle, we look forward to a time when we can be nearer God's presence than we can be in the church. Just as they looked forward to the kingdom of the Messiah or Christ (1 Peter 1:10-12), we look forward to the heavenly completion and perfect fulfillment of that kingdom (2 Peter 1:10,11). Heaven will be the end of the progression, the great goal that everything else was leading up to. Heaven will be the saints of all ages in the actual, real presence of God!

My friends, we need to cherish the thought of that with all our hearts. Loving God as we do and desiring deeply to be as near Him as we can be, there won't be a single day when we aren't fired by the expectation of looking upon the face of our Father in heaven. That's what the gospel is all about. Death is not the end — it is the *beginning* of what Christ died to make possible for us.

The early Christians were looking not for a cleft in the ground
called a grave but for a cleavage in the sky called Glory.
ALEXANDER MACLAREN

November 20
FACES TURNED TO GOD GROW BRIGHTER

They looked to Him and were radiant,
And their faces were not ashamed.
Psalm 34:5

FOR THE CHRISTIAN, THE MAIN THING IS NOT WHERE WE ARE OR WHAT IS HAPPENING AROUND US AT THE MOMENT, BUT WHERE WE ARE GOING. Just as in a sports contest, where the thing that matters is not what the score is but which side has the *momentum*, the thing that matters for the Christian is that he is making *progress in the right direction*. Our progress may seem slow and there may be obstacles in our path, but what our hearts and minds are fully set on (or should be) is this: "the grace that is to be brought to you at the revelation of Jesus Christ" (1 Peter 1:13). Our faces are turned toward God — and since they are, they grow brighter every day.

Love. It's hard to imagine how a person could have any significant understanding of God's love and not love Him back. The Scriptures are replete with stories of the acts of God's love, but if there were only one story — the story of the cross — surely that would be enough to move us to love God with a grateful love.

Desire. To love God is to desire to be *with* Him, to be in His actual presence. In this world, no human being has had that joy since Adam and Eve were cast out of Eden. But in Christ, God is offering the hope of being in His presence once again. To desire that perfect joy is to desire the very thing for which we were created.

Expectation. The Christian does not merely wish that he might one day see God's face; he actually expects to do so. When Paul said, "I know whom I have believed and am persuaded that He is able to keep what I have committed to Him until that Day" (2 Timothy 1:12), we do not detect a trace of doubt in his conviction.

Now these three things — *love, desire,* and *expectation* — combine in the Christian's heart to produce *hope*. And, of course, hope is the thing that produces the Christian's *joy*. Volumes have been written over the centuries about the joy that is in Christ, but what I want to say about it here is simply this: *it can't be hidden*. If you not only desire to see your Father but actually expect to do so, it will show in your face. "They looked to Him and were radiant, and their faces were not ashamed." There are simply no brighter faces in the world than the faces of those who are turned toward God.

The joy of the heart colors the face.

ANONYMOUS

November 21
ALL THAT WE LONG FOR IS KNOWN TO GOD

Lord, all my desire is before You;
And my sighing is not hidden from You.
Psalm 38:9

DAVID WAS COMFORTED, RATHER THAN FRIGHTENED, BY THE KNOWLEDGE THAT GOD KNEW EVERYTHING ABOUT HIM. Can we go any place and God not be there? No. Can we do anything and God not know about it? No. Can we think any thought and God not be aware of it? No. But these facts are not fearful; they are encouraging. At least they *can* be and *should* be. "O LORD, You have searched me and known me. You know my sitting down and my rising up; You understand my thought afar off" (Psalm 139:1,2).

One of the heaviest burdens we ever have to bear in life is to have a deep, aching need within us and to have to bear it alone. Sometimes there is not even one other human being who could do anything about our need, even if they knew about it. What an unspeakable source of comfort, then, to know that God knows. "All my desire is before You . . . my sighing is not hidden from You."

So God knows what we need even before we ask Him for His help. Jesus said, "Your heavenly Father knows that you need all these things" (Matthew 6:32). But here is the amazing thing: *God knows what we need even before we are aware that we need it!* Having created us, He knows more about our needs than we do. And when our hearts are broken by the pain and emptiness of some need that must, for the time being, remain unfulfilled, our hearts do not hurt half as much as He hurts for us. He loves us more than we love ourselves, and we cannot hurt without His feeling it.

On top of all of that, there is the additional fact that God has taken upon Himself our fleshly form and lived among us, experiencing every ounce of what it is like to suffer human sorrow. "For we do not have a High Priest who cannot sympathize with our weaknesses" (Hebrews 4:15). God knows our needs not only theoretically; He knows them *experientially.* He has been one of us.

But although God knows our needs even before we ask Him for His help, He still wants us to *ask.* And when we do so, we can ask knowing that He understands and He cares. He is our *Father.*

There is no thought, feeling, yearning, or desire, however low, trifling,
or vulgar we may deem it, which, if it affects our real interest or happiness,
we may not lay before God and be sure of His sympathy.

HENRY WARD BEECHER

WHAT IS OUR HOPE? WHO IS OUR HOPE?

And now, Lord, what do I wait for?
My hope is in You.
Psalm 39:7

IF ANYONE EVER HAD CONFIDENCE IN GOD, DAVID SURELY DID. Many were the times when, in the midst of difficult circumstances, David prayed for God's help, and having done so, was able to lie down and go to sleep. Even before he knew what the outcome would be, David could rest in hope, since his hope was not set on any particular outcome of the crisis but on *God Himself*.

God's Power. The first thing that hope in God means is that we trust in His power and ability. As the Creator, God can do anything that needs to be done, so there is no such thing as a problem that has no solution. "Now to Him who is able to do exceedingly abundantly above all that we ask or think, according to the power that works in us, to Him be glory in the church by Christ Jesus to all generations, forever and ever. Amen" (Ephesians 3:20,21).

God's Wisdom. God's power is always governed by His wisdom. Out of all the things He is *able* to do, God can be counted on to select the one thing that is *best* to do. In this respect, of course, God is very different from us. Even when we *can* do something, we don't always know what *should* be done. But God is never perplexed or puzzled by such things. Taking every single factor into consideration, He unfailingly does what is the wisest and best.

God's Goodness. But God's power is also governed by His goodness. Benevolently inclined toward us, He hears our prayers with mercy and compassion. We tend to think of "wisdom" as an abstract quality, but God's wisdom is always a *loving* wisdom. He will never do anything unwise, but neither will He do anything that is not conducive to the highest, eternal good of His creatures.

The problem with resting our hope in God is that we tend to do it only when the situation looks fairly hopeful anyway. In other words, we only hope in God when it seems likely that things are going to turn out the way we want them to. But that kind of hope requires little faith. Real hope is the kind that rests in God's power, wisdom, and goodness even when, from our vantage point, we can see no desirable outcome of the problem. *Hope is not human optimism — it is trust in a God who has proven His trustworthiness.*

Hope means expectancy when things are otherwise hopeless.
G. K. CHESTERTON

A GREATER GOOD THAN LIFE

Because Your lovingkindness is better than life,
My lips shall praise You.
Psalm 63:3

GOD'S "LOVINGKINDNESS" IS HIS COVENANT FAITHFULNESS. Having promised, in effect, never to hurt us, His lovingkindness is the quality that keeps Him from breaking that promise.

In Genesis 31, there is the story of the covenant that Jacob and Laban entered into in the mountains of Gilead. After they had set up a memorial pillar and heap of stones, Laban said, "This heap is a witness, and this pillar is a witness, that I will not pass beyond this heap to you, and you will not pass beyond this heap and this pillar to me, for harm" (v.52). Among human beings, such covenants are of little value if those who enter into them don't keep their promises, but God can be counted on never to violate the covenant that He has entered into with His people. He has promised never to act in anything less than our best interests, and we can rest our hopes completely on His faithfulness to that promise.

David saw God's lovingkindness as being "better than life." More than any blessing that life might hold for him, indeed more than the goodness of life itself, was the promise of God's dependable love. With or without any "thorn in the flesh," God is always saying to us, "My grace is sufficient for you" (2 Corinthians 12:9).

It's unfortunate that we sometimes define God's goodness in terms of how consistently He grants our wishes. For example, a friend recently told me that, in answer to many prayers, a relative's cancer surgery had been completely "successful." He ended the conversation by saying, "God is so good!" Well, yes. God is good. But is He good only when things turn out as we want them to? No, God's lovingkindness is better than life, and Job had the right idea: "Though He slay me, yet will I trust Him" (Job 13:15).

God's lovingkindness should be a *compelling force*. How can we realize the faithfulness with which God has loved us and not love Him? "For the love of Christ compels us, because we judge thus: that if One died for all, then all died; and He died for all, that those who live should live no longer for themselves, but for Him who died for them and rose again" (2 Corinthians 5:14,15).

The love of God is no mere sentimental feeling;
it is redemptive power.
CHARLES CLAYTON MORRISON

UNTO THE HILLS!

> I will lift up my eyes to the hills —
> From whence comes my help?
> My help comes from the LORD,
> Who made heaven and earth.
> *Psalm 121:1,2*

WHEN WE'RE IN TROUBLE, WE HAVE A DANGEROUS TENDENCY TO LOOK FOR HELP IN ALL THE WRONG PLACES. Although human sources of help — those "real" kinds of security — have disappointed us time and time again, we still seem to prefer them when any serious problem comes up. But David's trust was different. "From whence comes my help? My help comes from the LORD, who made heaven and earth." It was not to the lowlands of human help that David looked. "I will lift up my eyes to the hills."

The thought is not that God lives in the mountains rather than the plains. It is simply that the mountains symbolize the steadfastness and immovability of God — in contrast to many things that are less permanent. We are speaking the same language when we use the expression "old as the hills." In this world, mountains are as permanent as anything can be. They are the "oldest" of all: many things have come and gone since the mountains were lifted up. And so we look to the "hills" for God's help. He will be there to help when all other helps have had their day and disappeared.

I believe there is a clue here as to why mountains have the effect on us that they do. It's a rare person who can go to the mountains and not have his perspective restored. In contrast to even the most "permanent" of man's makings (the Egyptian pyramids, for example), a mountain is durable. Given enough time, of course, even a mountain would erode away, but the mountains are solid enough that they seem to be unchanged even after many lives of men. The mountains are *constant*. And since they are, they remind us of the God who is *eternal*. "Change and decay in all around I see; O Thou who changest not, abide with me" (Henry F. Lyte).

Few are the human beings who do not crave security. We all want to be sure that we'll have what we need. But in truth, there is no security in this world. Only in the God who *made* the world is there any confidence that our needs will be provided. And if that is true of the here and now, it is even more true of the hereafter.

In God's faithfulness lies eternal security.
CORRIE TEN BOOM

THE WATCHMAN WAITS FOR THE MORNING

I wait for the LORD, my soul waits,
And in His word I do hope.
My soul waits for the Lord
More than those who watch for the morning —
Yes, more than those who watch for the morning.
Psalm 130:5,6

OUR LONGING FOR THE LORD OUGHT TO BE NO LESS FERVENT THAN THE EAGERNESS OF THE WATCHMAN FOR THE MORNING. Those whose job it is to stay up and guard or wait while others are asleep have a job that is not easy. Especially during the last few hours before dawn, time slows to an agonizing crawl, and the watchman longs for that first hint of light in the east, a sign that the sun is coming up. But it is not only the watchman who waits for the morning. There are others who wait through the long night hours, hoping for the relief which comes from the rising of the sun.

Sickness. There is nothing longer than a night of physical pain and fever. We toss miserably in our comfortless beds, and the hands of the clock do not seem to move at all. But when the rosy glow of dawn begins to brighten our sickroom, the suffering seems to ease up a bit. With the coming of the morning, there is hope.

Sorrow. When we've lost something or someone who was dear to us, our hearts are racked with the emotion that we call "grief." The sense of loss can be almost unendurable, and it is especially so at night. Darkness seems to intensify the sorrow, making the nighttime dreadful. In our grief, we wait for the morning to come.

Distress. Even if we don't "worry" in the worldly sense of that term, we certainly do suffer distress. Even the Lord did. Speaking of His crucifixion, He said, "But I have a baptism to be baptized with, and how distressed I am till it is accomplished!" (Luke 12:50). In distress, the night is long and the morning, welcome.

Even if we aren't suffering sickness, sorrow, or distress, however, we should still be able to say what the Psalmist said: "My soul waits for the Lord more than those who watch for the morning — yes, more than those who watch for the morning." There ought not to be a "night" of any kind in which we do not desperately yearn for the coming of the sun. Nay, the coming of the Son.

In life troubles will come which seem as if they will never pass
away. The night and storm look as if they would last forever;
but the calm and the morning cannot be stayed . . .

GEORGE MACDONALD

November 26
SEEKING AND LOSING

Whoever seeks to save his life will lose it,
and whoever loses his life will preserve it.
Luke 17:33

MANY PEOPLE REACH "FORWARD," BUT THEY REACH FOR THE WRONG THINGS — AND END UP LOSING THE BETTER THINGS THEY COULD HAVE REACHED FOR. And there is no sadder fate in life than to get what we wanted and discover that, in the very process of getting it, we have given up what we *should* have wanted.

Consider the word "life" for a moment. Most people have some concept of the kind of life they would like to have, and they pursue that concept more or less diligently. Some may think of real life as consisting of pleasure or wealth or power. Others may think of it as service or relationships or philanthropy. Very likely, most people have some *combination* of these targets in mind when they sit down to write their personal "mission statement."

Now the striking thing about Jesus' teaching is that He said you could put all of these things together and still not have "life." Not *anything* in this world — not even *everything* in it — is enough to give us what we really need. "For what is a man profited if he gains the whole world, and loses his own soul?" (Matthew 16:26).

But not only that, Jesus also taught that by seeking these things and holding on to them greedily, we *lose* them. We "get" them, in the highest sense, by giving them up! "Whoever seeks to save his life will lose it, and whoever loses his life will preserve it." What does this seemingly contradictory statement mean?

It means that we must put life at risk (and maybe even give it up completely) in order to gain that which is life indeed. Most of the things in this world that people suppose they have to have are little more than hints or pointers to real life. If we make these lesser things our main objective, neglecting the greater life they were meant to point us to, then we lose everything, both the lesser and the greater. So we need to be careful when we're writing our "mission statement" to make our goals those that we won't regret later on. It would be the ultimate tragedy if we set our hearts on having (and never letting go of) some of the "preliminary" things and lost out on all the permanent joys we could have had. Let's not lose the life to come hanging on to the one we have right now.

Beware lest you lose the substance by grasping at the shadow.
A E S O P

ALL IS VANITY

"Vanity of vanities," says the Preacher;
"Vanity of vanities, all is vanity."
Ecclesiastes 1:2

L IFE IN THIS WORLD IS "VAIN." That does not mean it is unimportant; it only means that it is *temporary*. Whatever we accomplish of a this-worldly nature, it will not last. Whatever work we do while we live, it will be forgotten after we're gone, if not before then. So our work is like sandcastles. It's not that we shouldn't build any; we just shouldn't be surprised when they wash away.

Sadly, we often try to attach more meaning and permanence to earthly things than they were ever meant to have. We lean more weight upon them than they can support. Take friendships, for example, or even marriage. When we expect from other people a joy that only God can provide, we impose an unfair burden on them and set ourselves up for disappointment. As Oswald Chambers said, "If we try to find lasting joy in any human relationship, it will end in vanity, something that passes like a morning cloud. The true joy of a man's life is in his relationship to God."

But we mention human relationships only as an example. The same principle holds true with regard to every other temporal treasure: these things were only meant to be enjoyed for a while, and even while we enjoy them, they were not meant to be our end-all and be-all. Unfortunately, many of us live as if that were the case. Succumbing to the powerful pull of what is "here" and what is "now," we put tremendous effort into goals that, even if we achieve them, will not turn out to be very tremendous. To borrow Shakespeare's phrase, we make "much ado about nothing."

What, then, is the point of this "vain" life? Solomon summed it up succinctly in Ecclesiastes 12:13: "Fear God and keep His commandments, for this is the whole duty of man" (New King James Version). "Respect and obey God! This is what life is all about" (Contemporary English Version). "Stand in awe of God, obey his orders: that is everything, for every man" (Moffatt). Any way you translate it, the point is basic: *only in reverence and obedience to God can we accomplish anything*. Without that priority, "all is vanity."

To become like Christ is the only thing in the world
worth caring for, the thing before which every ambition
of man is folly and all lower achievements vain.

JOHN DRUMMOND

November 28

WILL WHAT YOU'RE "REACHING FOR" LAST?

What profit has a man from all his labor
In which he toils under the sun?
Ecclesiastes 1:3

WHEN ALL IS SAID AND DONE, WHETHER WE THINK WE'VE AC-
COMPLISHED ANYTHING IN THIS LIFE DEPENDS ON WHAT WE
WERE *TRYING* TO ACCOMPLISH. The question "What profit has a
man from all his labor in which he toils under the sun?" can be
a depressing question to ask if the "profit" we are looking for is
something *permanent*. In this world, there is simply no such thing.

The world, however, can supply some other things, and these
are very enjoyable and fulfilling when they are kept in perspective.
Even though it is broken and marred by the sad consequences of
sin, this world is still our Father's world, and He has filled it with
many delights. It is wrong to fail to enjoy this world's blessings, to
be good stewards of them, or to be grateful to God for them.

But because they are *temporal* (think "temporary"), these
things will not last. The time will come when they must be laid
aside. Sin having entered the world, God's plan is not to remake
this world and take the pain out of it; His plan is to remake *us* —
and then bring us to live in the realm where He is (John 14:3). As
for this world, it will be destroyed completely (2 Peter 3:10-13).

So we need to be careful what we "reach" for while we're
here. There are many worthy goals that we could set for ourselves,
and even if it's just our future in this world that's under consideration, it's better to be forward-oriented than to be stuck in the past.
But there is no future that we can get to in *this* world — no goal
that we can achieve — that won't be erased by the passing of time.

Most of us simply focus *too much of our attention* on the passing pleasures and fleeting accomplishments of this world. When
we look at our schedule books, we see that we have devoted most
of our time to things that were only of transient importance. But
majoring in minors is always a losing proposition in the long run.
No one, not even those who are Christians, can reach for "profit"
in this world and not be disappointed at how unprofitable it is.

The empire of Caesar is gone; the legions of Rome are smouldering in the
dust; the avalanches that Napoleon hurled upon Europe have melted away;
the prince of the Pharaohs is fallen; the pyramids they raised to be their
tombs are sinking every day in the desert sands . . .

ALBERT BAIRD CUMMINS

November 29
WITH EVERY DECISION, YOU PICK YOUR PAIN

*Now no chastening seems to be joyful for the present, but painful;
nevertheless, afterward it yields the peaceable fruit of righteousness
to those who have been trained by it.*
Hebrews 12:11

DURING OUR SOJOURN IN THIS WORLD, THERE IS NO AVOIDING
PAIN AND DIFFICULTY. We may avoid certain kinds of hardship,
but we often find that the "easy" situation we've gotten ourselves
into has a set of difficulties all its own. When we make decisions
between one scenario and another, it's rarely a decision between
difficulty and no difficulty; it's usually a choice of which set of difficulties we prefer over another. With that in mind, think with me
about one of the most basic choices we ever make: whether we're
going to choose the pain of *discipline* or the pain of *regret*.

The pain of discipline. The person who thinks training is fun has
probably never tried it in any serious way. By definition, training
means forcing yourself, over and over again, to do things that are
hard. It simply can't be done while we're in our comfort zones.

The pain of regret. If we "wimp out" on the pain of discipline,
that choice sets us up for a worse kind of pain later. Think of the
older people you know. Those who never paid the price to master
their impulses, are they happy as senior citizens? No, they are not.

Jesus "learned obedience by the things which He suffered"
(Hebrews 5:8). He did hard things daily, training and disciplining
Himself to do His Father's will. And in the end, He reaped the
benefit of embracing the pain of hardship. He had no regrets.

But here is the tough truth for many of us: *there is no middle
way.* We can't live lives of constant self-indulgence and still get all
the good benefits of self-denial. Spiritual strength comes at a price,
and we either pay it or we don't get the benefits. There is no quick-
fix trick or technique you can figure out that will let you have an
easy life and still get the results of training and discipline.

Nobody wants the results of self-indulgence, but there is only
one way to avoid them: going through the pain of self-discipline (1
Corinthians 9:27). "But self-discipline is so hard," you say. "I don't
want to do it." Well, take your pick. There is no other way. Either
do what is hard now . . . or live your later years wishing you had.

We will either submit to the pain of discipline
or suffer the pain of regret.
ANONYMOUS

November 30

INCREASING IN STRENGTH

But Saul increased all the more in strength, . . .
Acts 9:22

THE PAUL WE KNOW IN HIS EPISTLES WAS A MAN OF ADMIRABLE STRENGTH. But Paul did not become strong easily or instantly. He began, like all of us, as a new Christian, and then "increased all the more in strength." It was a gradual process, involving no small amount of diligence on Paul's part. Let me suggest that increasing in strength requires that all of us do two things on a daily basis:

(1) *Inflame the spirit with love.* We have to do things every day that fuel the fires of our love for the Lord. Our "want to" has to be stirred up. That burning "Yes!" has to be made to burn ferociously.

(2) *Train the flesh with discipline.* Even when the spirit is filled with strong love, the flesh is often too weak to carry out the will of the spirit. It needs to be trained. So we have to build into our daily lives a training regimen that progressively makes the flesh our servant, rather than our master. The flesh has to be taught to follow our spirit's orders. "If there is no element of asceticism in our lives, if we give free reign to the desires of the flesh . . . we shall find it hard to train for the service of Christ" (Dietrich Bonhoeffer).

Deeply ingrained habits of spiritual weakness and fleshly indulgence are not broken easily. Just as a small child can be trained and disciplined more easily than a spoiled teenager who has never done anything except what he or she wants to do, the longer we've been without spiritual training, the harder it's going to be.

But it can be done, and it is worth it. I don't know of a passage that sums up this important line of thought any more clearly than Titus 2:11-14. So read this slowly and thoughtfully, lingering over every word: "For the grace of God that brings salvation has appeared to all men, teaching us that, denying ungodliness and worldly lusts, we should live soberly, righteously, and godly in the present age, looking for the blessed hope and glorious appearing of our great God and Savior Jesus Christ, who gave Himself for us, that He might redeem us from every lawless deed and purify for Himself His own special people, zealous for good works."

God does not supply us with character, he gives us the life of his Son,
and we can either ignore him and refuse to obey him, or we can so obey
him, so bring every thought and imagination into captivity, that the
life of Jesus is manifested in our mortal flesh.

OSWALD CHAMBERS

JESUS, THE EXEMPLAR

. . . looking unto Jesus, the author and finisher of our faith,
who for the joy that was set before Him endured the cross, despising the
shame, and has sat down at the right hand of the throne of God.
Hebrews 12:2

JESUS IS THE PREEMINENT EXAMPLE OF FAITH. In the history of the world, no one has shown as much confidence in the Father as He did. In Hebrews 11, for example, many people are listed who demonstrated great faith, but Jesus is before them all and after them all; the steadfastness of His trust in God simply has no equal. And so when dealing with difficulty in our own lives, Jesus is our perfect *exemplar* ("one that is worthy of imitation, a model").

There were a number of shameful things that Jesus had to endure in His life, the worst of which was the cross, of course. If we are to identify with Him as His people, we are going to have to share in His shame and in His cross before we share in His glory. In speaking of what he had sacrificed for Christ, Paul said that he had given those things up not only to know "the power of His resurrection" but also "the fellowship of His sufferings, being conformed to His death" (Philippians 3:10). And to the Colossians he wrote, "I now rejoice in my sufferings for you, and fill up in my flesh what is lacking in the afflictions of Christ" (Colossians 1:24).

But our text says that Jesus *endured* the cross. That means He put up with it! And so it must be with us. We may try to minimize the amount of trouble that comes to us in the world, but before our lives are over, there will have been things that simply had to be *endured*. "There is no detour to holiness," Leighton Ford said. "Jesus came to the resurrection through the cross, not around it."

But if Jesus is our example, we must emulate the *reason* for His endurance as well as the fact of the endurance itself. And why did He endure? It was "for the joy that was set before Him." The pure, priceless joy on the other side pulled Jesus through this world.

And now, having endured the cross, Jesus "has sat down at the right hand of the throne of God." By not giving up, He conquered the enemy — and so can we! "For if we died with Him, we shall also live with Him. If we endure, we shall also reign with Him" (2 Timothy 2:11,12). A crown awaits those who keep going.

Not in the achievement, but in the endurance of the human soul
does it show its divine grandeur and its alliance with the infinite God.
EDWIN HUBBEL CHAPIN

December 2
THE CROWN OF RIGHTEOUSNESS

*Finally, there is laid up for me the crown of righteousness,
which the Lord, the righteous Judge, will give to me on that Day,
and not to me only but also to all who have loved His appearing.*
2 Timothy 4:8

IF PAUL WAS CONFIDENT OF ANYTHING, HE WAS CONFIDENT OF
GOD'S RIGHTEOUSNESS. God is "the righteous Judge." He can be
counted on to do what is *right*. And part of God's righteousness
is the fact that He will reward those who have been faithful to
Him. Having kept the faith, Paul was confident that his earthly life
would be crowned with victory when he stood before the Lord.

When Paul spoke of the "crown" of righteousness to be given,
he used the Greek word *stephanos*. This was not a reference to the
royal crown of a king but rather the victory crown of an athlete.
Paul had "fought the good fight . . . finished the race . . . [and] kept
the faith" (v.7) — and he was in no doubt as to the result. His decision to keep on running, when he might have given up and quit,
would be recognized by God as a *victorious* decision. A righteous
God will not fail to reward those who have persevered.

The possibility of apostasy shouldn't diminish our hope of
receiving the crown of righteousness. Yes, we need to be humbled
and sobered and urged to be careful (1 Corinthians 10:12), but
we don't need to be doubtful about our salvation if we choose to
remain faithful as Paul did. Nor should our emphasis upon God's
grace mean that we don't look for Him to reward us. He is, after
all, "a rewarder of those who diligently seek Him" (Hebrews 11:6).

But notice that Paul speaks of the crown being given to those
"who have loved [the Lord's] appearing." Today, we can have
Paul's same confidence concerning the crown of righteousness, but
only if we have his same passion for the Lord's return. God forbid
that we should be so in love with this world that we wouldn't be
overjoyed to hear that it was all coming to an end *this very day*.
Paul's attitude was, "O Lord, come!" (1 Corinthians 16:22).

Our fondest hopes should be set on the "not yet" part of the
faith more than on the "already." Christianity is about receiving
the crown of righteousness — so we ought not to dread the day of
our death (or that of the Lord's coming) any more than a runner
dreads to cross the finish line. To get to the finish is why we run!

Life bears love's cross, death brings love's crown.
DINAH MARIA MULOCK CRAIK

December 3
WE LONG FOR WHAT WE NEED

For I long to see you . . .
Romans 1:11

PAUL'S CHARACTER WAS A STRONG ONE IN EVERY IMPORTANT WAY, BUT HE ALSO WAS CAPABLE OF VERY TENDER FEELINGS. Speaking of his fellow Christians in Rome, he said, "I long to see you." And in his other letters, he spoke of longing to see brethren elsewhere. Paul *needed* face-to-face contact with those whom he loved, and when he didn't have it, he longed for it. For Paul, yearning was an unavoidable part of living and serving the Lord in this world.

Unfulfilled wants, needs, desires, longings, yearnings, hungerings, and thirstings are a part of life in a damaged world. It is no longer possible, now that we all live "east of Eden," to have all of the desires filled that God planted within us. (We can have some of them filled some of the time, but not all of them all of the time.) God's remedy for this is not to bring this world back up to the level where our needs can be met, but to *destroy* this world and bring us into His perfect presence. Until that happens, there will be a time to rejoice now and then, but there will also be "a time to weep . . . a time to mourn" (Ecclesiastes 3:4). It's just that simple.

When we find ourselves longing or yearning, it's usually because there is something we need which we don't have at that moment. (To be sure, what we *think* we need is sometimes not what our yearnings are really about, but that's another issue.) To be a human being living in this world is to be *incomplete* — and the sooner we accept that, the better. *There is nothing wrong with longing.* Paul did it. The Lord did it. And so will we, if we're honest.

There may be some who feel their needs so obsessively that they experience unnecessary distress, but most of us have a different problem. Our distress comes not from *feeling* our yearnings, but from all the frustration of *avoiding* them. Perhaps we've accepted the philosophy of ancient Stoicism more than we think: the idea that the good life is the life of *apathy* ("no feeling"). It is, however, as foolish as it is frustrating to deny something that is so obviously a part of our created nature. Granted, we need to think and do what's *right* about our feelings, but we shouldn't avoid *feeling* them. When we try to do that, our spirits shrink and shrivel.

The wealth of a soul is measured by how much
it can feel; its poverty by how little.
WILLIAM ROUNSEVILLE ALGER

December 4
CONTRADICTORY CONCEPTS?

But the day of the Lord will come as a thief in the night, in which
the heavens will pass away with a great noise, and the elements will melt
with fervent heat; both the earth and the works that are in it will be burned
up. Therefore, since all these things will be dissolved, what manner of
persons ought you to be in holy conduct and godliness . . .
2 Peter 3:10,11

IN THE NEW TESTAMENT, AS IN LIFE, THERE ARE MANY PAIRS OF CONCEPTS OR IDEAS THAT SEEM CONTRADICTORY BUT ARE ACTU-ALLY COMPLEMENTARY. "Faith" and "works," for example, seem on the surface to cancel one another, but on closer examination we see that they strengthen one another. In order to get what the gospel of Christ offers us, we have to emphasize *both* concepts. Consider some other examples of complementary couplets:

Development of one's own spiritual life vs. evangelism/edification of others. Various individuals may lean in one of these directions more than the other, but neither can be totally ignored. And when we see ourselves overemphasizing one of these at the expense of the other, most of us try to supply some balance on the other side.

Contentment vs. the desire to better one's situation. Some may find it hard to get the balance just right, but it is possible to be both content and motivated to improve one's station in life. And what we see, in fact, is that our motivation enriches our contentment and vice versa. The two concepts are not enemies but friends.

Doing today's work vs. longing for the Lord's return. Theologians have long debated whether Christianity is about the "here and now" or about the "hereafter." And historians have argued whether Jesus was a social reformer or a preacher of the endtime. But in the New Testament, there is no conflict. Which truth needs to be emphasized at a given moment depends on who the audience is and what the needs of that audience may be at that time.

In 2 Peter 3:10,11, there is a striking reminder of the importance of the Lord's return. But in the same passage, we also see an emphasis on the Christian's responsibility right now: "what manner of persons ought you to be in holy conduct and godliness." If this is a "tension," it is a healthy one; being pulled both ways *helps* us. We *need* to be pulled in the direction of our present duty and in the direction of our future hope. The truth runs both ways.

Christianity is a system of balanced obligations.
MALCOLM MUGGERIDGE

BEYOND OUR ABILITY

*For I bear witness that according to their ability, yes, and beyond their ability,
they were freely willing, imploring us with much urgency that we would
receive the gift and the fellowship of the ministering to the saints.*
2 Corinthians 8:3,4

A S WE REACH FORWARD TO HEAVEN, THERE IS SOMETHING ELSE WE NEED TO REACH FOR IN THE MEANTIME, AND THAT IS GREATER ABILITY IN THE LORD'S WORK. Participation in the Lord's work is the greatest privilege that a human being can enjoy in this world, and we ought to want to contribute to that work in every way possible, including some ways that may be beyond us right now.

What we CAN do is important. It is a sin to undervalue our abilities and waste them. Recognizing that these abilities would not be ours if it weren't for the Lord's grace, we ought to have Paul's frame of mind: "I labored more abundantly than they all, yet not I, but the grace of God which was with me" (1 Corinthians 15:10).

What we COULD do is more important. If the Lord gets the glory for what we are, He should also get the glory for what we could become, if we would accept the help that He wants to give us. When we minimize what is possible for us, we call into question the bounty of the Lord's grace. But there is no limit (practically speaking) to what He would provide for our growth if we were only willing to stretch. "And God is able to make all grace abound toward you, that you, always having all sufficiency in all things, may have an abundance for every good work" (2 Corinthians 9:8).

The problem of the "plateau." When we first started out as Christians, most of us went through a growth spurt. In the early excitement of our faith, we eagerly availed ourselves of opportunities to grow in our knowledge and abilities. But after a certain amount of growth, most of us leveled off, and sadly, it has been a long time since many of us learned how to do any new thing.

I have long preached the truth of this equation: *ability + opportunity = responsibility*. If the Lord returns today, we'll be held accountable for our use of the abilities we've acquired up to this point. But what if He doesn't return today? Tomorrow, will we be content to have no more ability than we had today? Out of all that we can't do, isn't there something we could *learn* to do?

Unless you try to do something beyond what you
have already mastered, you will never grow.
RONALD E. OSBORN

110%

Whatever your hand finds to do, do it with your might . . .
Ecclesiastes 9:10

THE SIGNIFICANT FACTOR IN FAILURE IS VERY OFTEN A LACK OF ENTHUSIASM AND EFFORT. The problem is not that some human beings are capable and others are not (almost anybody can learn how to do anything he needs to do) — it is that some are fired up about what they want to do and others aren't. As Thomas Fuller said, "The difference between men is energy." And this is as true in the matter of going to heaven as it is in temporal matters. Heaven is for those willing to put their whole hearts into it, and getting there is worth giving no less than 110% of our very best effort.

If we've been giving less than our best effort, we need to ponder the point that Paul makes in Colossians 3:23: "And whatever you do, do it heartily, as to the Lord and not to men." It doesn't matter whether the activity is "religious" or "secular," the Christian will do his best because he's offering the deed as a gift to the Lord. The Christian employee, for example, will give his employer his best effort because he's doing it "as to the Lord" and not merely to the employer. If God is the recipient, who in his right mind would want the action to be anything less than his best?

But the Christian also has another motivation: he acts out of gratitude for having been forgiven. And this motive, gratitude for grace, is the most powerful force in the world. "He died for all, that those who live should live no longer for themselves, but for Him who died for them and rose again" (2 Corinthians 5:15).

While we live in this world, we are in a struggle, a conflict, and a warfare. Nowhere is intense effort any more important than on the battlefield. Marshal Ferdinand Foch said it bluntly: "The will to conquer is the first condition of victory." So in the war between good and evil, many will be defeated because they didn't have what it took: *the will to conquer.* This does not diminish our reliance upon God's help at all; it simply emphasizes the need for us to do our part *with all our might.* Paul wrote to Timothy, "For God has not given us a spirit of fear, but of power and of love and of a sound mind" (2 Timothy 1:7). So my friend, if you're a Christian, whatever you do needs to be given 110% of your effort.

What counts is not the size of the dog in the fight,
but the size of the fight in the dog.
DWIGHT D. EISENHOWER

December 7
EVERY TONGUE SHALL CONFESS

For we shall all stand before the judgment seat of Christ.
For it is written: "As I live, says the LORD, every knee shall bow
to Me, and every tongue shall confess to God."
Romans 14:10,11

ONE OF THE REQUIREMENTS OF THE GOSPEL IS THAT WE "CON-
FESS" THE TRUTH ABOUT JESUS CHRIST. This means that we
openly reveal to others the truth about our convictions: *we believe
that Jesus is the Son of God* (Matthew 10:32,33; Romans 10:9,10). At
the present time, of course, not everybody believes the truth of
that proposition, and of those who do believe it, not all would be
willing to admit it. But there is coming a day when all of that will
change. When the Creator brings this world to a conclusion, the
truth about Him will become undeniably and inescapably evident.

Paul wrote that "we shall all stand before the judgment seat of
Christ." Among the members of the human race, there is *universal accountability* to God. As many as have been created in God's
image, the same will be judged by Him. No one is exempt.

When the day of judgment comes, there will be nowhere to
hide. Not all will *want* to hide, of course, for there will be some
"who have loved His appearing" (2 Timothy 4:8). But those who
have denied the truth about God and His Son will cry to the
mountains and rocks, as have others during times of God's judgment, "Fall on us and hide us from the face of Him who sits on the
throne and from the wrath of the Lamb! For the great day of His
wrath has come, and who is able to stand?" (Revelation 6:16,17).

For the time being, the truth about God is not unequivocal.
It is possible to deny that He exists. But when the Father and His
Son openly declare themselves, the truth will be unavoidable.
Every knee shall bow and every tongue shall confess the truth.

Reality is a strong and a sturdy thing. We can't break it; we
can only break ourselves trying to break it. In the great courtroom
of cosmic history, after all the other witnesses have had their say,
the Great Witness will stand up at last and set the record straight.
Reality will assert itself. The truth will come out. And those who
have denied it will find their denials falling away. So let us not run
away from the truth right now, and later, when we are hopelessly
lost, have to admit that the truth was the truth all along.

Man cannot cover what God would reveal.
THOMAS CAMPBELL

EACH ONE SHALL GIVE ACCOUNT

So then each of us shall give account of himself to God.
Romans 14:12

GOD'S JUDGMENT OF EVERY HUMAN BEING IS BOTH A COMFORTING AND A SOBERING THOUGHT. On the one hand, the day of judgment will be a day of vindication for the downtrodden. Right will be done about every wrong that has ever been perpetrated, and justice will prevail over injustice. But on the other hand, it will be impossible to escape the consequences of our own actions. "Each of us," Paul wrote, "shall give account of himself to God."

Consider for a moment the concept of "accountability." The word *accountable* is similar to words like *responsible, answerable, liable,* and *amenable.* All of these words mean being obliged to answer for our actions to an authority with the power to penalize failure. Now surely, if God created us, then He has authority over us. Having given us our free wills, He can rightly ask us for an explanation (or "account") of why we used our freedom as we did.

But notice that Paul says each one must give account of *himself* to God. When we stand before God, we'll be expected to take responsibility for our own actions. Evasion of personal responsibility may be the major mentality of the modern age, but there will be no such evasion before God. What others have done won't matter. The only question will be: "What choices did *you* make?"

And finally, in 2 Corinthians 5:10, Paul wrote that we will answer for "things done in the body." That implies that we'll account for our actual *deeds* — not for what we knew to do or planned to do or had good intentions of doing as soon as we got around to it.

The judgment day will clarify many things. For example, it will clarify what was *important* (rather than trivial) and *permanent* (rather than temporary). If we would look with honesty and courage, we could see these realities right now. At least we could see them well enough to understand that we ought to obey the gospel of Christ and wait obediently for His coming. So let's try to see what's important and what's permanent. When the time comes for each of us to give account, we're going to wish that we'd been putting first things first. *Wouldn't today would be a good day to start?*

> When shall we awake to the sublime greatness,
> the perils, the accountableness, and the glorious
> destinies of the immortal soul?
>
> WILLIAM ELLERY CHANNING

TOIL AND TEARS: NOW IS THE TIME

Then I heard a voice from heaven saying to me, "Write:
'Blessed are the dead who die in the Lord from now on.'"
"Yes," says the Spirit, "that they may rest from their
labors and their works follow them."
Revelation 14:13

L IFE IN THE PRESENT WORLD IS A MIXTURE OF JOY AND SORROW, AND THAT IS A FACT THAT WE OFTEN RESENT. We wish that our joys didn't always have to be messed up by sorrow rearing its ugly head. And in fact, a day is coming, according to the gospel, when complete joy and rest *will* be given. But that time is not yet! For now, we need to accept the reality of both our toil and our tears.

Toil. Work was not a punishment for sin (for there was work to do in the Garden of Eden), but when sin entered the world, work became *onerous.* As a result, our lives in this world are character-ized by a wearisomeness that we were never meant to experience. What once would have been richly fulfilling is now a burden.

Tears. Just as sin perverted the natural cycle of work and rest, it also perverted the rhythm of human emotion. Gut-wrenching sorrow and grief at the loss of things that, in Eden, we would never have lost break our hearts to pieces. And the more we know of the ways of the world, the harder it is to be anything but sad.

Rest and Joy. Heaven is presented to us as a place where we'll be *refreshed* from our toil and *relieved* from our sorrow. "Blessed are the dead who die in the Lord . . . that they may *rest* from their labors." And oh, how that promise tugs at our hearts, even more than the "pearly gates" and the "streets of gold." This empty, weary world has worn us out, and we long for simple *rest* and *joy.*

But what should we do about the un-rest and the un-joy right now? Accept them! In *this* world, toil and tears are not the excep-tion but the norm. To see that, we need look no further than Jesus' life. He had times of rest, but basically He came here to work. And He went to a wedding feast now and then, but basically He was a Man of Sorrows. He understood that great joy was waiting for Him in heaven, but He also understood that there was work to be done in the meantime. So yes, we will have our toil and tears, but what of that? Now is the time for work. The rest will come later.

God washes the eyes by tears until they can behold
the invisible land where tears shall come no more.
HENRY WARD BEECHER

WHAT A SERVANT WANTS ABOVE ALL

Therefore we make it our aim, whether present
or absent, to be well pleasing to Him.
2 Corinthians 5:9

PASSIONATE DESIRE IS OF GREAT IMPORTANCE, BUT EVEN MORE
IMPORTANT THAN DESIRE IS THE *OBJECT* OF OUR DESIRE. Some
things are more worthy to be desired than others, and so we need
to be careful in our choice of what we desire. And when it comes
to our *ultimate* desire, we should be the most careful of all.

If we are Christians, what should be the one thing we want
more than anything else? Well, think of it this way: we are privileged to be the *servants* of God — and should a servant want anything more than to *please his master?* In terms of earthly servitude,
a servant might not be highly motivated to please his master, but if
God is the Master, shouldn't it give us great delight to please Him?
Isn't that the highest goal that we could ever reach forward to?

Too often, we give greater priority to pleasing other people,
and if we think of pleasing God at all it is only after we've pleased
everybody else. But we've been given some very plain warnings
about that kind of thing (Matthew 23:1-7; John 12:42,43; Galatians
1:10). When a choice has to be made, if we would rather please
other people than please God, then we're unfit to be His servants.

But another problem we have is thinking that "pleasing God"
constitutes some special group of actions. We divide life into
"religious" and "secular" departments and suppose that God is
only pleased when we are operating in the "religious" realm. But
William Tyndale made a good point when he said, "There is no
work better than another to please God; to pour water, to wash
dishes, to be a cobbler, or an apostle, all is one." Those who please
God are those who do so in *every* area of their lives; whatever they
do, they want to do it in a manner that would please Him.

Paul wrote, "And whatever you do in word or deed, do all
in the name of the Lord Jesus, giving thanks to God the Father
through Him" (Colossians 3:17). If we fail to see the importance of
doing that, it's probably a failure of perspective on our part. What
we "desire" is often governed by what's in front of us at the moment. What we need to do is back up and look at the bigger view.

If we fully comprehended the brevity of life, our greatest desire
would be to please God and to serve one another.
JAMES C. DOBSON

December 11

BIRTH PANGS

For we know that the whole creation groans
and labors with birth pangs together until now.
Romans 8:22

MEANING AND PURPOSE MAKE THE DIFFERENCE BETWEEN SUF-FERING THAT IS TOLERABLE AND SUFFERING THAT IS NOT. If when we suffer we know that the struggle is leading to something worthwhile, we can bear it. And "birth pangs" is perhaps the most powerful metaphor with which to make that point. In the physical realm, the agony of the birth process can be endured because of the joyous prospect of new life. And in the spiritual realm, a similar thing is true. If the "pangs" that we experience are those of a "birth," then we can tolerate what would otherwise be intolerable.

In Romans 8:22, Paul uses this analogy with reference to the corruption of the physical universe. The consequences of human sin have fouled even the habitat that God created for us, and Paul pictures the earth as longing to be released from the ravages of our rebellion against God: "the whole creation groans and labors with birth pangs together until now." The universe is in agony, but the "labor" is one that is striving toward a significant "birth."

But just as the creation "groans and labors," so do we. As we struggle through this world, we can only imagine what it must have been like to live in Eden, prior to the pain. We live in a broken world, but we yearn for one that isn't. To put it plainly: we *suffer.* But our suffering is not meaningless. A "birth" is coming.

The difficulty, of course, is to *keep in mind* what we know about the meaning and purpose of our sufferings. The birth may be coming, but the labor right now tends to dominate our thinking. So as hard as it may be, we need to make ourselves look *beyond* the birth pangs. "Gird up the loins of your mind," Peter wrote, "be sober, and rest your hope fully upon the grace that is to be brought to you at the revelation of Jesus Christ" (1 Peter 1:13).

Yet there is a sense in which the birth pangs themselves are useful. If that's what it takes to make us enjoy heaven when we get there, then we can be glad to have experienced them.

Even in evil, that dark cloud that hangs over creation,
we discern rays of light and hope and gradually come to see,
in suffering and temptation, proofs and instruments of the
sublimest purposes of wisdom and love.

WILLIAM ELLERY CHANNING

THE DAWN IS BREAKING

And do this, knowing the time, that now it is high time to awake out of
sleep; for now our salvation is nearer than when we first believed. The night
is far spent, the day is at hand. Therefore let us cast off the works of
darkness, and let us put on the armor of light. *Romans 13:11,12*

THE HUMAN RACE SUFFERED THROUGH THE HORRIBLE ENVIRON-
MENT CREATED BY SIN IN THE WORLD FOR A LONG, LONG TIME
BEFORE THE SAVIOR APPEARED, BUT NOW THAT HE HAS COME, THE
DARKNESS HAS BEGUN TO DISAPPEAR. The dawn is breaking.

The word "kingdom" is used in more than one way in the
New Testament. Sometimes it refers to the reign of God that began
on Pentecost shortly after Jesus went back to heaven. The Book of
Acts describes the inauguration and spread of that kingdom. It is
a present reality, and it is the fulfillment of many prophecies made
long before, such as the one recorded in Daniel 2:39-44.

But "kingdom" can also refer to a reign of God that is still *future*, one for which we are taught to *hope*. For example, when Paul
was faced with possible martyrdom, he expressed confidence that
even if he had to die, God would still be with him. There would
be a "kingdom" that no human court of law could keep him out
of. "The Lord will deliver me from every evil work," he said, "and
preserve me for His heavenly kingdom" (2 Timothy 4:18).

So what are we to make of this? Does the "kingdom of God"
exist right now or must we wait until we get to heaven to experience it? Both answers are correct, depending on how the word
"kingdom" is being used. The last of God's enemies will not be
subjugated until the end of the world (1 Corinthians 15:24-26), and
so in that sense, the fullness of God's kingdom is not yet a reality.
But on Pentecost, the rightful King began to reign. And that means
the darkness is no longer in total control. The dawn is breaking.

So the world is still in darkness, but the power of the darkness
has been broken. Its days are numbered. The church still sojourns
in a hard, painful place, but with every day that passes, the saints
are nearer home. And personally? I still hurt. I still weep. My heart
aches with an emptiness that nearly kills me. But this I know: the
rightful King is reigning, and one day every bit of this darkness
will be sent back to the hell from whence it came. Dark night once
had me in its grip, but it has me no more. The dawn is breaking.

Christ has turned all our sunsets into dawns.
CLEMENT OF ALEXANDRIA

December 13
REACHING FORWARD REQUIRES LETTING GO

Forgetting those things which are behind . . .
Philippians 3:13

REACHING FORWARD IS A HARD THING TO DO WHEN IT REQUIRES US TO LET GO OF THINGS THAT WE'RE NOT READY TO LET GO OF. We're willing to surrender certain things in order to move ahead, but other things may not be so easy to relinquish. Yet there is no other way. We can't stay in the same spot and move ahead too.

The blessings that God has given us in this "life under the sun" are meant to be enjoyed, but they're meant to be enjoyed *and then let go of*. In contrast to what we'll enjoy in life *beyond* the sun, all things here are temporal and transitory. None of these enjoyments — not even the best of them — are ours to keep permanently. Job spoke for all of us when he said, "Naked I came from my mother's womb, and naked shall I return there" (Job 1:21).

As with all "consumables," we should be willing to let go of these favors once they've served their purpose in God's will for our lives. We understand this to be true when we *die* — we will surely leave all earthly benefits behind at that point. But many of them will have to be relinquished *before* we die. So even while we have them to enjoy, we should hold them gently. God shouldn't have to pry our fingers off of them when the time comes.

If there is any "thing" that we can't let go of, that thing is an idol, and idols destroy souls. Jesus urged us to lay up for ourselves treasures in heaven, and He contrasted the permanence of those treasures to the perishability of all things earthly (Matthew 13:44). But we make a tragic mistake if we think Jesus had in mind only the wicked and their trust in things like money. A Christian who holds his family relationships as tightly as some people hold their money is being just as worldly. All *earthly* things, even the good ones that "we" prefer, are *temporary*. And we should be willing to part with them whenever reaching forward requires us to do so.

The sad thing is, our won't-let-go attitude often diminishes our enjoyment of what we have even while we have it. That's the message of Ecclesiastes, and it's a part of the gospel of Christ as well. Whatever God has given us in this world, we get more out of it, not less, when we loosen our grip and hold it more openly.

In the kingdom of God the surest way to lose something
is to try to protect it, and the best way to keep it is to let it go.

A. W. TOZER

JOY IS WORTH THE SORROW OF LOSS

For what thanks can we render to God for you, for all the joy
with which we rejoice for your sake before our God . . .
1 Thessalonians 3:9

THOSE WHO BECOME CYNICAL ABOUT LOVE ARE FOOLS. The fact that we're going to have to relinquish all of our loves in this world shouldn't mean that we don't enjoy them deeply. And having already lost some of our cherished relationships, if they were virtuous we should never say that we wish we'd never had them.

Consider, as a case study, Paul's relationship with the church in Thessalonica. When Paul first came to that city, he was only able to stay there a short time. After less than a month, it was felt best for him to leave the city due to the intense persecution that had arisen. But Paul was not ready to leave; it grieved him to depart from those whom he had so quickly come to love. And when he wrote back to Thessalonica, he spoke openly of his sorrow, his concern, and his longing for the saints there: "when we could no longer endure it, we thought it good to be left in Athens alone, and sent Timothy . . . to encourage you concerning your faith" (1 Thessalonians 3:1,2). Paul was in agony over the difficulties that these brethren faced. He longed desperately to see them and wasn't sure if he would ever have that joy again. All things considered, Paul's heart was broken, and that would never have happened if he'd never loved these people. But do you think Paul had any regrets? If you do, then you've seriously misjudged this man's heart: "For what thanks can we render to God for you, for all the joy with which we rejoice for your sake before our God." Paul understood that, in this world, love is a bittersweet blessing.

The grief of loss is a part of the *price* that must be paid for the privilege of earthly love. Anyone who has ever truly loved understands this aspect of love. "Ae fond kiss, and then we sever! / Ae farewell, alas, for ever! / Deep in heart-wrung tears I'll pledge thee, / Warring sighs and groans I'll wage thee!" (Robert Burns).

But love is worth it! Our great Father has placed within our earthly home many joys *worth* loving. When we love them, we are blessed. And what is more, when we love them deeply and truly, we are drawn to their Maker. That they must be given up, even sorrowfully, is a small price to pay for the glory that they lead to.

Better to have loved and lost than not to have loved at all.
LUCIUS ANNAEUS SENECA

December 15
GIVING THE LORD THAT WHICH COSTS US

Then the king said to Araunah, "No, but I will surely buy it from you
for a price; nor will I offer burnt offerings to the LORD my God with that
which costs me nothing." So David bought the threshing floor
and the oxen for fifty shekels of silver.
2 Samuel 24:24

A NY LOVE THAT WILL NOT MAKE A SACRIFICE FOR THE BELOVED IS NOT TRUE LOVE. By its very nature, love is giving, and the higher the quality of the love, the more costly a sacrifice the lover is willing to make as a gift. In the direst need, love would give all that one had to give, even to the extent of life itself (John 15:13).

When King David found himself needing to make a burnt offering to the Lord, beseeching His favor on behalf of the people of Jerusalem, Araunah offered to donate the offering necessary for the sacrifice. "No," said David, "but I will surely buy it from you for a price; nor will I offer burnt offerings to the LORD my God with that which cost me nothing." David apparently understood that a sacrifice is not a sacrifice unless it is a . . . sacrifice!

Today, we are often tempted to do what David refused to do: give the Lord that which cost us nothing (or very little). Many of us live in lands of abundance. When it comes to money, we can give sums of money to the Lord's work that seem large but which represent no real sacrifice on our part. We can give and still have plenty left over. But the giving of money is only the tip of this subject's iceberg. Whether it is time, energy, allegiance, or whatever, we often seem willing to give only that which is *easy* to give.

We need to learn the principle of *sacrifice* and acquaint ourselves with the value of giving things to the Lord *even when we can hardly see any way to survive without them.* And when the magnitude of what we've given begins to weigh heavily upon us, we need to remember the *love* that motivated our sacrifice, knowing that it is "a cheerful giver" (2 Corinthians 9:7) whom the Lord loves.

So if the value of what we've given up for the Lord is any indication, how much can we say we love the Him? We're not talking about works righteousness here; we're talking about love. And even among those whom we love in this world, how much love is indicated by the costliness of what we've given up for them?

The value of a thing sometimes lies not in what one
attains with it, but in what one pays for it — what it costs us.
FRIEDRICH WILHELM NIETZSCHE

December 16
THE HIGHEST DESIRE OF LOVE

For you know the grace of our Lord Jesus Christ,
that though He was rich, yet for your sakes He became poor,
that you through His poverty might become rich.
2 Corinthians 8:9

L OVE MEANS MANY THINGS TO MANY PEOPLE. It can mean a casual "crush." It can mean true romance. It can mean marital commitment. It can mean sexual ardor. All of these things, and many more, are involved in love. Love always involves a *desire*, but in its higher forms, the desire is to give something to the beloved. So what would be the *highest* thing that a lover could desire for his or her beloved? What is it that true love really wants?

Here it is: *love wants the highest good of the beloved.* I understand that "highest good" will be defined very differently from person to person, but true love will always want the *highest* needs of the beloved to be met, whatever those needs are thought to be. And not only that, true love will serve those needs *sacrificially*. That is, a lover will give up things of great goodness so that the beloved can obtain a good that would not be possible without the sacrifice.

Whatever might be true of those outside of Christ, Christians certainly ought to understand the importance of sacrificial love, for that's the very kind of love which Christ demonstrated. Paul said that "though He was rich, yet for your sakes He become poor, that you through His poverty might become rich." At the cross, Christ redefined love for all time to come. And if we are His followers, growing in likeness to His character, we cannot fail to emulate His quality of love in our dealings with those whom we love. "True spirituality manifests itself in . . . the desire to see others advance at one's expense" (A. W. Tozer). Love's highest desire is not only for the other person to have what he or she needs, but it says, "Here, let me pay for it. Let me make it possible for you to have it. Let me do without, so you can have what you need."

This definition of love obviously goes far beyond romantic love, as wonderful as that is. Romantic love is not wrong, but there is a finer love that we can have, even among human beings. From that love flows a true desire which says, "I want above all for you to have what you need, even if I can't have it along with you."

In real love you want the other person's good.
In romantic love you want the other person.
MARGARET ANDERSON

WHERE IS THE PROMISE OF HIS COMING?

. . . knowing this first: that scoffers will come in the last days, walking according to their own lusts, and saying, "Where is the promise of His coming? For since the fathers fell asleep, all things continue as they were from the beginning of creation." 2 Peter 3:3,4

FAITH MEANS BELIEVING THAT THE LORD IS TELLING THE TRUTH WHEN HE TALKS ABOUT THINGS THAT WE CANNOT VERIFY AT THE MOMENT. Faith is not "blind faith," for it is based on solid evidence of the Lord's proven trustworthiness, but nevertheless, faith is faith. It is trust. It is confidence. And one of the principal things the Lord asks us to have confidence in is His second coming.

Peter wrote that there would be "scoffers" who would deny that the Lord would come back or that the world would come to an end at His coming. To scoff is to "mock or treat with derision." The scoffers Peter spoke of would ridicule the very idea of such things happening as the Lord promised. They would laugh at it.

And this scorning of the Lord's promise would result from a "uniformitarian" view of history: the view that history always continues uniformly. They would say that if a thing hasn't happened after all these years, then it's not going to happen: "Where is the promise of His coming? For since the fathers fell asleep, all things continue as they were from the beginning of creation." But one-of-a-kind events do take place sometimes, and Peter points to one of the most dramatic: the flood in Noah's day. Those who scoff at the Lord's coming make the same mistake that Noah's neighbors made when they laughed at the improbability of the flood.

But mockery is hard to bear, so Peter prepared his readers for it. By the time 2 Peter was written, enough time had elapsed since the Lord's ascension that many, even among the faithful, would have been wondering what was happening. "He promised that He would come back. Where is He?" they might have said. Two thousand years later, we need to hear Peter's reassurance even more than they. *"Beloved, do not forget this one thing, that with the Lord one day is as a thousand years, and a thousand years as one day. The Lord is not slack concerning His promise, as some count slackness"* (2 Peter 3:8,9). To forget the faithfulness of God is exceedingly foolish.

God is the God of promise. He keeps His word,
even when that seems impossible; even when the
circumstances seem to point to the opposite.

COLIN URQUHART

December 18
THE END OF THE EARTH AND THE HEAVENS

But the day of the Lord will come as a thief in the night,
in which the heavens will pass away with a great noise, and
the elements will melt with fervent heat; both the earth and
the works that are in it will be burned up. *2 Peter 3:10*

WE NEED TO ENJOY THIS WORLD AND BE GRATEFUL FOR IT — BUT WE ALSO NEED TO UNDERSTAND THAT IT'S COMING TO AN END. Peter wrote of a coming day when the heavens "will pass away," the elements will "melt with fervent heat," and the earth "will be burned up." It's old-fashioned but it's still true: *the end is coming.*

The earth and the heavens will come to an end, according to Peter, on the "day of the Lord." This expression will be familiar to any Bible student. We hear it first in the Old Testament, where it originally referred to a day of judgment in which God would pour out His wrath on some city or nation. Then some of the prophets used this expression to describe the coming of the Messiah into the world, and specifically the inauguration of His kingdom and the outpouring of the Spirit. In the New Testament, we get further extensions of this terminology. The "day of the Lord" can refer to God's judgment upon Jerusalem, and later to His wrath against Rome. But surely, the day of the Lord spoken of in 2 Peter 3:10 will be the day of the Lord to end all days of the Lord. On this day will come the final, cataclysmic termination of this entire world.

Peter says that it will come suddenly, as a thief in the night, and that ought to be a warning to every one of us. As we pursue the frantic busyness of our worldly work and play, let us beware lest we be caught by sad surprise — unprepared for the end.

From the times of its earliest use, the "day of the Lord" was always thought of as a day of *judgment* and *destruction.* But unlike the destruction wrought by previous days of the Lord, the devastation of the final one will be complete and irrevocable. *"Both the earth and the works that are in it will be burned up."* There are no more decisive words of physical *termination* in all of the Scriptures.

My friends, I love the remnants of God's goodness in this world as much as anybody else, but the truth is: *this world is a temporary arrangement.* God existed before He created this world, and He will exist after it has been concluded. Broken by sin, this world is *doomed.* Our hopes must lie beyond the day of its destruction!

The created world is but a small parenthesis in eternity.
SIR THOMAS BROWNE

December 19
HASTENING THE COMING

Therefore, since all these things will be dissolved, what manner of persons
ought you to be in holy conduct and godliness, looking for and hastening the
coming of the day of God, because of which the heavens will be dissolved,
being on fire, and the elements will melt with fervent heat?
2 Peter 3:11,12

THE EARLIEST CHRISTIANS WERE KNOWN FOR THEIR FERVENT ANTICIPATION OF THE LORD'S RETURN. They saw themselves as those whose citizenship was not on earth but in heaven: "from which we also eagerly wait for the Savior" (Philippians 3:20). Not merely content to *accept* that the end was coming, they eagerly *longed* for it to come. And as the years wore on and the Lord had not come, the disciples encouraged one another to stay focused and keep their hopes fixed on what was still ahead (1 Peter 1:13).

Peter left no doubt about what was going to happen. "These things will be dissolved," he said. When the right time comes, God is going to annihilate the world that He once created, its history having finally run its course. "The heavens will pass away with a great noise, and the elements will melt with fervent heat; both the earth and the works that are in it will be burned up" (v.10).

Since that is going to happen, our lives ought to be those of radical reverence and obedient faith. Paul wrote that Christ's return will be "in flaming fire taking vengeance on those who do not know God, and on those who do not obey the gospel of our Lord Jesus Christ" (2 Thessalonians 1:8). On that day, many may have obeyed the gospel initially, but if they've not *continued* to obey it, they won't be spared the wrath that comes upon the ungodly. Peter put it pointedly: "Since all these things will be dissolved, *what manner of persons ought you to be in holy conduct and godliness?*"

But what Peter urges us to do is something we *can* do. We *can* choose holy conduct and godliness over the alternative, and when we do, we can be those "who have loved His appearing" (2 Timothy 4:8), eagerly "looking for and hastening" the day. As Christians, we need not *dread* the Lord's return, but neither should we fail to *desire* it. As the world gets painfully worse, we've got many reasons to wish that the Lord will come sooner rather than later. Pray tell, why wouldn't we want to look at it that way?

I hope that the day is near at hand when the advent
of the great God will appear, for all things everywhere are
boiling, burning, moving, falling, sinking, groaning.
MARTIN LUTHER

NOT ONLY NEW BUT DIFFERENT

Nevertheless we, according to His promise, look for
new heavens and a new earth in which righteousness dwells.
2 Peter 3:13

THE PROMISE OF THE GOSPEL IS THE PROMISE OF A NEW HEAVENS AND A NEW EARTH. Peter said that this new reality is something we "look for." Indeed we do! This new state of things, beyond the confines of this world, is the great, central hope of Christianity. Take it away, and what you have left is not the gospel of Jesus Christ. If there were no heaven, Christianity would be nothing but a pathetic hoax. As Paul wrote, "If in this life only we have hope in Christ, we are of all men the most pitiable" (1 Corinthians 15:19).

You probably have never read a writer more dogmatic than I about the reality of heaven — but you probably have never read a writer less dogmatic about the details. I take it that heaven, like our resurrected bodies, is something we could not presently understand even if God explained it to us. Concerning our bodies, John wrote, "Beloved, now we are children of God; and it has not yet been revealed what we shall be, but we know that when He is revealed, we shall be like Him, for we shall see Him as He is" (1 John 3:2). Something similar could probably be said of heaven. "It has not yet been revealed," so I'm open-minded about the details.

Nevertheless, I am going to make two guesses about heaven. One is that the "new heavens and earth" are going to be very different from anything that we know *right now*. And the second is that it's going to be very different from any of our *expectations*. But whatever differences there may be, they're going to be in the direction of being *better* than we expected, even in our loftiest dreams.

We look for heaven, Peter said, "according to His promise." And just think: the promise began before God even created the present world! Paul said that we are saved "in hope of eternal life which God, who cannot lie, *promised before time began*" (Titus 1:2).

But lastly, Peter said that after this world is gone, there'll be a place "in which righteousness dwells." That's why we long for it so, and I agree with Anatole France: "We thank God for having created this world, and praise him for having made another, quite different one, where the wrongs of this one are corrected." In that realm — praise God! — sin will have finally been left behind.

Heaven begins where sin ends.
THOMAS ADAMS

December 21
DON'T DEVALUE WHAT YOU PURCHASED

But recall the former days in which, after you were illuminated,
you endured a great struggle with sufferings . . . Therefore do not
cast away your confidence, which has great reward.
Hebrews 10:32-35

THE HEBREW WRITER SAID THAT AFTER HIS READERS HAD BECOME
CHRISTIANS THEY "ENDURED A GREAT STRUGGLE WITH SUFFER-
INGS." But he encouraged them not to give up the "great reward"
they were pursuing. "Do not cast away your confidence," he said.
The Hebrews needed to remember something we all need to remember: good things come at a price — and when the price begins
to hurt, we have to recall the value of what we have gained.

Life is full of what we call "tradeoffs." A tradeoff is the giving
up of one advantage for another advantage of greater benefit. It is
hard to imagine any significant gain in the real world where this
kind of exchange does not have to be made. We do it all of the
time, understanding that there are very few blessings that don't
have a downside, very few pluses that don't have some minuses.

The problem comes when the *present moment* begins to exert a
powerful pull on us. I may have moved further outside the city for
the benefit of my family, but when I'm caught in traffic during that
two-hour commute, the frustration of *that moment* is all I can think
of. It is easy to forget the plus for which I accepted that minus. "So
I'll just get a job in a small town," I say. But that too will have its
disadvantages. The fact is, everything has its price. The only question is: which advantages do you want the most, and what disadvantages are you willing to accept in order to obtain them?

As people who are reaching forward to heaven, let's not "cast
away [our] confidence, which has great reward." When we're in
the midst of "a great struggle with sufferings," we need to remember that there was a time when we counted the cost of discipleship
and decided that the advantages were worth the disadvantages.
Now that the disadvantages are pressing upon us heavily, the
thing to do is back up and remember *the goodness of the advantage
that we gained.* May we never devalue what we have purchased.
Being found in Christ at the resurrection is worth *whatever* tradeoff
has to be made. In fact, it is worth a good deal more than that.

Let us not be shocked by the suggestion that there are
disadvantages to the life in Christ. There most certainly are.

A. W. TOZER

THE WORK OF JUST ONE LINK

For David, after he had served his own generation by the will
of God, fell asleep, was buried with his fathers . . .
Acts 13:36

MOST OF US WANT TO MAKE SOME CONTRIBUTION TO THE WORLD WHILE WE LIVE HERE. Rather than just be takers, we would like to be givers. But some people want more than that: they want to make a mark that will be remembered long after they're gone. They're appalled by the thought of vanishing "without a trace," and even while they live, they fear being passed up and written off as a "has been." But is that how we should look at this life?

I must tell you frankly, there is a sense in which "John Doe" funerals are profoundly sad to me, those graveside services in which the person who died had no friends or family and nobody came to the funeral. Some people really do pass through this life and vanish without a trace, and if you're not a funeral director, you might be surprised to hear how often that happens.

But the John Does of the world have something to teach us, something that is desperately important to understand about "life under the sun." *Our work in this world is the work of just one link in the chain, no more.* The people we are to serve are those we are connected to *while we live.* And when the time comes for us to leave this world, that will be the time for us to be forgotten and somebody else to take our place. "One generation passes away, and another generation comes . . . There is no remembrance of former things, nor will there be any remembrance of things that are to come by those who will come after" (Ecclesiastes 1:4,11).

In this world, we are meant to be replaced! Even as great a man as David was, no greater thing could be said of him than this: "For David, after he had served *his own generation* by the will of God, fell asleep, was buried with his fathers, and saw corruption." *In the chain of generations, his work was that of just one link.*

But if our work is that of one link, we ought to want it to be the best link possible. Having done our part, we will be replaced (and forgotten by those who replace us), but mighty consequences hinge on whether we do our part well — while we still live.

> Life is not a "brief candle." It is a splendid torch
> that I want to make burn as brightly as possible
> before handing it on to future generations.
>
> BERNARD SHAW

December 23
ETERNITY IN OUR HEARTS

*He has made everything beautiful in its time. Also He has
put eternity in their hearts, except that no one can find out
the work that God does from beginning to end.*
Ecclesiastes 3:11

ONE THING THAT SETS HUMAN BEINGS APART IS THEIR YEARNINGS.
We have deep desires for things that we don't have, longings
for joys that we sometimes can't even identify or express. There is
something about us that is infinite — and that something finds it
very frustrating to live in a world that is not only finite but broken.

In Ecclesiastes 3:11, we hear not only that "eternity" is in our
hearts, but that God put it there. We have longings for things beyond this world because we are *made* that way. Given our created
nature, we can no more not need eternity than we can not need joy
or beauty or any other desire that is part of the human package.
Some yearnings just won't go away no matter how hard we try to
ignore them, and eternity is one of them. We can deny it, suppress
it, or try to fulfill it with lesser things, but the need is still there.
Plainly, we were made for a different world than the kind of world
this one has become, and until our hearts find the home in which
they were intended to rest, we will have an unfulfilled yearning.

It is important to face fully what it means that eternity is in
our hearts. It doesn't just mean that we need something that is
hard to find in the temporal world; it means we need something
that is *impossible* to find here. When sin broke the perfection of
Eden, God was forced to withdraw Himself from direct contact
with the human race. But we were *made* for communion with Him,
and so now, the thing we were *made* for, we can only *long* for!

We should give our yearnings for eternal life free reign. There
is nothing wrong with groaning (2 Corinthians 5:1-8), and we
should give ourselves permission to do it. Indeed, there is something seriously wrong with a person who could live in this world
(ruined as it is by rebellion against what is right) and not groan.
So we should *embrace* the eternity that is in our hearts, even at the
price of the emptiness that it makes us feel right now. To set our
hearts on eternity is not to slight our responsibilities in the here
and now. It enables us to fulfill those responsibilities in *hope*.

He who has no vision of eternity
will never get a true hold of time.
THOMAS CARLYLE

December 24
ALL IN GOOD TIME

Wait on the LORD;
Be of good courage,
And He shall strengthen your heart;
Wait, I say, on the LORD!
Psalm 27:14

IF ETERNITY IS IN OUR HEARTS, THAT MEANS WE HAVE A DESIRE THAT CAN'T BE FULFILLED RIGHT NOW. And if this desire is, as I believe, our *deepest* desire, then our lack of fulfillment may be grievously felt. Whatever our hearts most truly need, they need it now, and the very depth of our longing means that its unsatisfaction is painful. So the thought of *waiting* is, to many, an unwelcome thought.

Impatience is more of a problem than we like to admit. In its more trivial forms, it can be amusing, of course, but in more serious matters, impatience can be destructive to our spiritual lives. In a sense, impatience comes close to being the taproot of sin. It is a *demanding* attitude: it wants its own way and it wants it *now*. Impatience insists that everything be done on its own terms.

From that perspective, then, might it not be *good* for us to have to wait for some of the things we need — and maybe even the thing we need the most? Whatever bit of "demandingness" lingers in our hearts, any discipline that would help remove it would be to our advantage. It is not a coincidence that in Psalm 27 where David said, "Wait, I say, on the LORD!" (v.14), he also said, "*Teach me Your way, O LORD*" (v.11). It may be hard, but in waiting for the Lord's salvation, we are taught virtues like *trust* and *reverence*.

If we are honest, our hearts often cry out, "How much longer, Lord? How much longer?" And if He were to speak to us personally and directly, He would surely say, "Be patient. You will get your heart's desire. All in good time — yes, all in good time. But for now, I ask you to trust Me." He is a Father who can be counted on to make all things beautiful, but He does so . . . *in His time.*

So we can heed the advice that we get in the Psalms and "wait on the Lord." But our waiting is not just any waiting. If our faith is where it needs to be, our waiting can be a waiting of *hope*, and that makes all the difference in the world. "I *wait* for the LORD, my soul waits, and in His word I do *hope*" (Psalm 130:5). Confident that the end is going to be good, we can wait until the story is finished.

Patience is the art of hoping.
VAUVENARGUES

THE BEAUTY OF THE LORD

One thing I have desired of the LORD, that will I seek:
That I may dwell in the house of the LORD all the days of my life,
To behold the beauty of the LORD, and to inquire in His temple.
Psalm 27:4

IN DISCUSSING THE ATTRIBUTES OF GOD, NOT MUCH IS SAID ABOUT THE CONCEPT OF "BEAUTY." But David expressed a desire "to behold the beauty of the LORD." What does this mean? We can quickly dismiss any notion of *physical* beauty in speaking of God, but having done that, what *does* beauty mean in this context?

One way to think of beauty is to define it as "perceived goodness." Goodness itself is imperceptible, but when it reveals itself in some way that we can perceive, we call it "beauty." Visually, when goodness reveals itself to the eye, we call what we see beautiful. Aurally, when we hear a sound or a song that expresses goodness, we describe it as beautiful. And even when we observe someone doing a good deed, we say that it was a beautiful act. The English word "aesthetics," which denotes the branch of philosophy that deals with beauty, comes from the Greek word *aisthanesthai* ("to perceive"). So beauty is a reference to what we perceive when goodness shows itself in any way that is perceptible to us.

Most people would admit that human beings *need* beauty. Our nature is constituted such that we require doses of it on a regular basis. And if you doubt this, just imagine how quickly your sanity would leave you if you were confined to an environment that had been totally deprived of any kind of beauty, day after day after day. After a while, you would find yourself becoming subhuman.

But what about God? Well, He is the *perfection of beauty* because He is the *perfection of goodness*. Right now, we can get little more than hints or inklings of Him, but these entice us and attract us. They open the doors of our imaginations to a realm where total goodness, and therefore total beauty, exists. Somewhere deep within our hearts we know that if we could ever "behold" Him as He truly is, our entire being would be ravished with beauty.

And that is why we long for heaven as we do. In this world, there is not enough goodness left to satisfy our need for beauty. We are grateful for the beauty that is here, but it is not enough. We long — we *desperately* long — "to behold the beauty of the LORD."

God is beauty.

FRANCIS OF ASSISI

December 26
WHAT DID CHRIST WANT WITH ME?

I press on, that I may lay hold of that for which
Christ Jesus has also laid hold of me.
Philippians 3:12

THE FACT THAT WE NEED TO SEEK GOD SHOULD BE OBVIOUS, BUT THERE IS ALSO A SENSE IN WHICH GOD IS SEEKING US. And if either of these two "seekings" were to be given priority or preference, shouldn't it be God's seeking of us? Harry Emerson Fosdick was right when he said, "Finding God is really letting God find us; for our search for him is simply surrender to his search for us."

Throughout this book, we've been pondering Paul's statement in Philippians 3:13,14: "Brethren, I do not count myself to have apprehended; but one thing I do, forgetting those things which are behind and reaching forward to those things which are ahead, I press toward the goal for the prize of the upward call of God in Christ Jesus." But in v.12, Paul had said, "I press on, that I may lay hold of that for which *Christ Jesus has also laid hold of me*." All Paul ever wanted as a Christian was to participate in the working out of *Christ's* purposes. And whatever Christ wanted with Paul, that was exactly what Paul wanted. It was all that mattered to him.

Unfortunately, there are times when we turn this emphasis around. When we became Christians, for example, there were certain things that *we* had in mind. There was a certain set of outcomes that *we* wanted to be achieved. So now, when what Christ wants from us seems to conflict with what we want from Him, we act as if it were a major tragedy that *our* plans aren't working out.

But each individual needs to ask very personally: What did Christ want with *me*? When He sought me and found me, a sheep that had gone astray, what were *His* purposes? Why did He "lay hold" of me? What does He want me to do? And in the end, what does He intend to be the outcome of His relationship with me?

God has given us free wills: we can *refuse* His purposes. But why would we ever do so? Why would we not say "Yes" to His plan of salvation and then yield to everything we can learn of His will? *Why would we want anything other than what He wants for us?*

Spare not the stroke! Do with us as thou wilt!
Let there be naught unfinished, broken, marred;
Complete thy purpose, that we may become
Thy perfect image, O our God and Lord!

HORATIUS BONAR

December 27
READY

Therefore, beloved, looking forward to these things, be diligent
to be found by Him in peace, without spot and blameless . . .
2 Peter 3:14

HAVING PORTRAYED THE EVENTS OF THE DAY OF THE LORD VIV-IDLY, PETER URGED HIS READERS TO KEEP THEMSELVES READY FOR ITS COMING. The word "therefore" is followed by the command "be diligent," and Peter's point is hard to miss: knowing that Christ will bring this world to an end, we ought to prepare ourselves for that day with an effort that is *earnest* and *persistent*.

Notice first that Peter says his readers were "looking forward to these things." In the previous verses, he had spoken of the end of the world that now is and the beginning of a "new heavens and a new earth in which righteousness dwells." These tremendous events are not those that Christians can think about dispassionately. We *anticipate* them and *desire* them. We *look forward* to them.

Since that is so, we ought to "be diligent to be found by Him in peace, without spot and blameless." Being "found" emphasizes the unexpectedness of Christ's coming. When He comes, we will be found, or discovered, in the act of living some kind of life or another. For us, heaven depends on whether it's a *faithful* life the Lord finds us living. Similarly, Paul said it was "in Him" that he wanted to be found: "Yet indeed I also count all things loss for the excellence of the knowledge of Christ Jesus my Lord . . . that I may gain Christ and be found in Him" (Philippians 3:8,9). Our aim, then, is to be caught in the act of being faithful to the Lord.

It's a fine thing to be waiting for the Lord, and every Christian ought to have that mindset. But there is another word we often couple with "waiting," and that is the word "ready." *Ready and waiting*. It takes *both* of these words to capture the Christian's attitude toward the Lord's return. As Paul wrote, "But you, brethren, are not in darkness, so that this Day should overtake you as a thief" (1 Thessalonians 5:4). *Ready and waiting*. That is the key.

In other words, our attitude needs to include a healthy blend of two priorities. We need, on the one hand, to throw ourselves eagerly into today's work. And also, we need to look forward with eager excitement to the day when the Lord will say, "Well done."

One of the great lessons the fall of the leaf teaches is this:
Do your work well and then be ready to depart when God shall call.
TYRON EDWARDS

December 28

THE BEST IS YET TO BE

But now they desire a better, that is, a heavenly country. Therefore God
is not ashamed to be called their God, for He has prepared a city for them.
Hebrews 11:16

ALL OF THE FAITHFUL PEOPLE OF GOD IN THE SCRIPTURES WERE FORWARD-LOOKING PEOPLE. They looked for "a better, that is, a heavenly country." And such a dream was not merely a dream: they looked forward to something that is one day going to be an objective reality. God "has prepared a city for them," and not being physical hardly makes that city any less real. If anything, it will be more real than the "city" in which we live right now.

For those in a right relationship with God, it is always true to say that "the best is yet to be." History is moving toward a grand culmination. In God, there is meaning and significance to this life. There is a vision of great goodness ahead and progress toward the realization of that vision. In God, there is the hope of total joy!

To say that the best is yet to be is to say a lot, because the present can be very good indeed. And certainly, no one ought to enjoy the good things in this world more than God's people. But what is coming is so much better! With regard to the blessings that God has in store for those who are found "in Christ," we really do have a wonderful problem: trying to stretch our imaginations wide enough to take in just how good it's going to be. "God's best gifts put man's best dreams to shame" (Elizabeth Barrett Browning).

So our focus needs to be *forward*. After all, life only moves in one direction: from beginning to end. And since the end is the goal that everything else is reaching forward to, we can honestly say that the "end of a thing is better than its beginning" (Ecclesiastes 7:8). In his familiar poem, Robert Browning said the "last of life" is that "for which the first was made." May we accept that for the wonderful truth that it is. For those who are in God through Jesus Christ, the best is always yet to be. On even the best day we've ever enjoyed in this present world, the best is still yet to be.

Grow old along with me!
The best is yet to be,
The last of life, for which the first was made:
Our times are in his hand,
Who saith, "A whole I planned,
Youth shows but half; trust God:
See all, nor be afraid."

ROBERT BROWNING

THE WORLD THAT ONCE WAS . . . AND WILL BE

The LORD God planted a garden . . .
Genesis 2:8

IN ALL THE VARIOUS VERSIONS OF OUR LONGINGS, WE ARE BASI-CALLY LONGING FOR A LIFE LIKE THE ONE THAT EXISTED AT THE BEGINNING OF THE WORLD. In the Garden of Eden, every heart was whole, and whenever our hearts are broken today, we wistfully imagine what it must have been like to be Adam or Eve, before the unhappy times came. We wish we could have something like that.

It is an interesting fact that nearly every culture in the world has some story or legend of a lost paradise. As with similar stories of a worldwide flood, the easiest way to explain the prevalence of such stories in so many cultures is to suppose that the events actually happened. The Garden of Eden is not a myth! To this day, the human race carries within its memory echoes of a time when no sin had yet been committed and everything was in perfect balance.

But think of what Eden would have been like! To say that Adam and Eve were perfectly happy is just the beginning. Their happiness was the result of every aspect of God's creation being just what it was meant to be, not only in itself but also in its relationship to everything else. There were no imbalances and no gaps or deficiencies. An "unfulfilled need" had not yet been heard of.

Needless to say, the highest and best part of the goodness of Eden would have been the perfect relationship of everything to God. Augustine of Hippo once defined heaven as "the perfectly ordered and harmonious enjoyment of God and of one another in God." Wouldn't that have been what Eden was? Nothing fractured or marred or out of kilter, but everything filling its precisely intended role in the creation — and all rightly related to the Creator.

Now here is the hope of the gospel of Christ: God has made it possible for us to regain the paradise that was lost — and more. The emptiness of our hearts is only temporary. Ahead of us, in Christ, is the kind of world that we were *made* for. In heaven, our inner hearts and our outward habitation will fit together perfectly. Never again will a broken world leave us empty or deny us joy. Our Father will be there, and for the first time since Eden, the sons of Adam and the daughters of Eve will know what "home" means.

It is not darkness you are going to, for God is light. It is not lonely,
for Christ is with you. It is not unknown country, for Christ is there.
CHARLES KINGSLEY

December 30

TEARS

Therefore you now have sorrow; but I will see you
again and your heart will rejoice, and your joy
no one will take from you.
John 16:22

D O GOODBYES BRING TEARS TO YOUR EYES? They do mine. I'm afraid I know no moderation when it comes to love. The things and the people that I love, I love with all of my heart, and it is a sore trial to say goodbye to any of them, from my favorite homely objects to my favorite places to my favorite people. In this world of loving and losing what we love, tears are a fact of life.

I have often imagined what it must have been like to know and love Jesus personally during His earthly sojourn. There would have been no way to love Him and not have your heart ripped apart when He left you. So we're not surprised to hear Him saying to His disciples, "Therefore you now have sorrow; but I will see you again and your heart will rejoice, and your joy no one will take from you." There is a great truth in these words, a truth that we need to hear as much as His original disciples did: *in Christ, there are never any tears except those that look forward to a greater joy.* The tears are not to be avoided (we shouldn't even try), but they are to be seen as a part of something much greater than the grief itself. Peter wrote, "Though now you do not see Him, yet believing, you rejoice with joy inexpressible and full of glory" (1 Peter 1:8).

Imagine the scene at Jesus' ascension. Having had a final conversation with His disciples, He had to leave them. Luke says, "Now when He had spoken these things, while they watched, He was taken up, and a cloud received Him out of their sight. And while they looked steadfastly toward heaven as He went up, behold, two men stood by them in white apparel, who also said, 'Men of Galilee, why do you stand gazing up into heaven? This same Jesus, who was taken up from you into heaven, will so come in like manner as you saw Him go into heaven'" (Acts 1:9-11).

As Jesus left these dear friends and disappeared from their view, there would have been tears streaming down their upturned faces. But Jesus would not have spared them this sorrow or scolded their broken hearts. For some tears are the tears of love. And the tears of love are ever the tears of gratitude. And of hope.

I will not say do not weep — for not all tears are an evil.
J. R. R. TOLKIEN

December 31
SOMETHING MORE

Why do you spend your money for that which is not bread,
And your labor for that which does not satisfy?
Isaiah 55:2 RSV

THE GREAT TRAGEDY OF HUMAN LIFE IS THAT WE DO NOT SEE HOW MUCH MORE WE NEED. God has made us such that we have an inescapable need for perfect, unmitigated, consummate fellowship with Him. That need cannot be filled in this life, even in Christ, and our tragedy is that we do not see how much more we need.

Foolishly, we spend great amounts of time, money, and energy pursuing satisfactions that, while good in themselves, having been created by God, were never meant to satisfy our deepest longings perfectly. We drink deeply of the creation and suppose that our thirst for the Creator has been satisfied. But it hasn't.

If we're honest, we see that we have longings that are not only *not* being filled in this world, but *cannot* be, even in the fullness of fellowship with God, as sweet as that may be. And those longings are perhaps our greatest clue to the existence of something more. C. S. Lewis said it well: "If I find in myself a desire which no experience in this world can satisfy, the most probable explanation is that I was made for another world." That being true, "contentment" with what is ours right now is the absolute worst thing that could happen to us. We were made for nothing less than what Adam and Eve had in Eden, and we'd better never forget it.

So let there not be a day during our sojourn that we do not *reach forward*. Not even the blessed joys of home and family should be wholly satisfying to us. Not even the treasures of membership in the Lord's church should satisfy our hunger and thirst. This world is irreparably broken, and not even the Lord Himself could be anything other than a Man of Sorrows while He lived here. We were made for a joy that simply cannot be experienced in our present environment. So may we never delude ourselves into thinking that what we have right now, even in Christ, is all that our hearts need. God has for His people something much, much more. We dare not, we cannot, we simply *must* not forget that true fact.

Whatever you love,
Whatever you give,
Whatever you think you need to live,
There's something more than this.
JULIE FLANDERS & EMIL ADLER

A Prayer for Daily Meditation

O God, I am yet unsatisfied,
because I do not enjoy enough of you.

I would have my soul more closely united
to you by faith and love.
I would love you above all things.

You, who has made me,
knows my desires, my expectations.
My joys all center in you
and it is you yourself that I desire.

It is your favor, your acceptance,
the communications of your grace
that I earnestly wish for,
more than anything in the world.

— *Susanna Wesley*

INDEX OF DAILY SCRIPTURE TEXTS

ACKNOWLEDGMENTS

THANKS, FIRST, TO THE READERS OF *DILIGENTLY SEEKING GOD*. If you hadn't responded as you did, I might have quit writing.

The members at Westside in Indianapolis, and more recently the members at Broadmoor in Nashville, have been kind to me while I was writing this book. Mike Roy and Jeremy Sweets, with whom I am privileged to work at Broadmoor, deserve special thanks.

Thanks again to Becky Voyles, who has tried her best to be my editor. Over the past seven years, no other person has devoted more hours to my writing than she. *Reaching Forward* is a crisper, more cogent book for having been edited by her. Bless you, Becky. A very special thanks to Jordan "Sunshine" Farquhar, who edited the index and found some critical errors. I never had a daughter, but if I did, I would want her to be just exactly like Jordan.

Brock and Grant, my amazing sons, will never know how much it means to me that their copies of *Diligently Seeking God* are so well-worn and dog-eared. And Phil, my brother, is the closest thing to a kindred spirit that I have. I'm glad I live close enough that we can have lunch together at the Smokey Pig anytime the craving strikes.

Thanks to Kyle and Katie Fisher, to whom the book is dedicated. I don't know how a man my age could have two more remarkable young friends. Their invitation to do their wedding ceremony pulled me out of a seriously painful ditch that I had been in for over thirteen years. Among my friends, they have a niche that is theirs alone, and if you haven't met them, you have missed a treat.

And finally, thanks to the former Misty Fink, who is now happily married to Patrick Cawthon. While I was writing, Misty extended to me a difference-making friendship during a period when my life could easily have crashed and burned. *Reaching Forward* would not exist if she hadn't encouraged its continuation at such a critical point. In many ways, this work is hers. Thank you, Misty.

As I look back on all that has happened since *Diligently Seeking God* came out, I know I've been blessed beyond what I deserve. Given that "crazy" vow of celibacy that I took in 1999, I guess there aren't many people who would trade places with me, but I can honestly say that I love the life that I have. No man has ever had more pleasant work to do or more pleasant people to do it for. It seems wholly inadequate to "acknowledge" my debt to you. For what is my hope, or joy, or crown of rejoicing? Is it not even you?

ABOUT WORDPOINTS

WORDPOINTS was created to produce "down-to-earth books that reach toward God." It publishes a line of distinctive, God-centered daily devotionals written by Gary Henry.

> **Book 1** — *Diligently Seeking God: Daily Motivation to Take God More Seriously.* What difference does it make whether we seek God? ISBN-13: 978-0-9713710-0-2.

> **Book 2** — *Reaching Forward: Daily Motivation to Move Ahead More Steadily.* Is there anything about tomorrow worth reaching for? ISBN-13: 978-0-9713710-1-9.

> **Book 3** — *Obeying the Gospel: Daily Motivation to Act on Our Faith.* How do we make a real commitment to Christ? (Currently in preparation.)

> **Book 4** — *Walking with Christ: Daily Motivation to Grow in Our Commitment.* How do we lead lives of real discipleship? (Currently in preparation.)

The publishing philosophy of WordPoints is guided by three principles: (1) reverence, (2) careful thinking, and (3) a comfortable communication style.

Focusing on the need of every person to take God more seriously, each book from WordPoints challenges the reader with a unique blend of candor and courtesy.

HOW TO GET OUR BOOKS

BOOKS by Gary Henry can be purchased or ordered almost anywhere books are sold, but here are a few special sources:

Amazon.com. To order from Amazon, go *www.wordpoints.com* and click on the Amazon link. (We make a little extra if you order that way.)

Religious Supply Center, Inc. 4001 Preston Highway, Louisville, Kentucky. 1-800-626-5348.

Florida College Bookstore. 119 North Glen Arven Avenue, Temple Terrace, Florida. 1-800-423-1648.

Truth Bookstore. 420 Old Morgantown Road, Bowling Green, Kentucky. 1-800-428-0121.

If your local bookseller does not carry our books in their current inventory, they will be happy to place a special order for you.

WordPoints books are available at **bulk discount prices** for congregations and other non-profit groups. For information on bulk pricing, call 615-944-0694 or email us at *garyhenry@wordpoints.com*.

CPSIA information can be obtained at www.ICGtesting.com
Printed in the USA
LVOW132255080712

289246LV00009B/62/P